THE MYSTERIES OF IDENTITY

OTHER BOOKS BY ROBERT LANGBAUM

The Poetry of Experience:
The Dramatic Monologue in Modern Literary Tradition

Isak Dinesen's Art:
The Gayety of Vision

The Modern Spirit:
Essays on the Continuity of Nineteenth- and Twentieth-Century
Literature

AS EDITOR

Shakespeare's *The Tempest*

The Victorian Age:
Essays in History and in Social and Literary Criticism

THE MYSTERIES
OF IDENTITY

A Theme in Modern Literature

ROBERT LANGBAUM

New York   OXFORD UNIVERSITY PRESS   1977

Library of Congress Cataloging in Publication Data
Langbaum, Robert Woodrow, 1924–
   The mysteries of identity.

   Includes index.
   1. English literature—19th century—History and
criticism. 2. English literature—20th century—History
and criticism. 3. Identity (Psychology) in literature.
I. Title.
PR469.I33L3   820′.9′3   76-42657
ISBN 0-19-502189-4

182/31

Thanks are due to the following for permission to quote copyright material:

Harcourt Brace Jovanovich, with Faber and Faber, for permission to quote from *The Complete Poems and Plays of T. S. Eliot*, copyright 1936 by Harcourt Brace Jovanovich, Inc., copyright 1950,

To the Memory of
Stanley Loomis

ACKNOWLEDGMENTS

This book began as a paper delivered at the Center for Advanced Study in the Behavioral Sciences, Stanford, California, where I was a Fellow during 1961–62. Since then I have been encouraged to write the book by much generous financial support—a Guggenheim Fellowship in 1969–70, a Senior Fellowship from the National Endowment for the Humanities in 1972–73, a Grant-in-Aid from the American Council of Learned Societies in 1976. Through all these years the University of Virginia Research Committee helped defray clerical expenses. Thanks to all these donors.

Part of Chapter 1 on Wordsworth appeared in my *The Modern Spirit: Essays on the Continuity of Nineteenth- and Twentieth-Century Literature* (New York: Oxford University Press, 1970). Part of Chapter 3 on Eliot appeared in *Eliot in His Time*, ed. A. Walton Litz (Princeton: Princeton University Press, 1973). Chapter 4 on Beckett appeared in *The Georgia Review* (Winter 1976); part of Chapter 5 on Yeats appeared in *New Literary History* (Spring 1976); and part of Chapter 8 on

Lawrence appeared in *The American Scholar* (Winter 1975–76). Thanks to the publishers and editors for permission to reprint these sections.

I am grateful to the Wordsworth Library, Dove Cottage, Grasmere, and to the National Library of Ireland, which made available to me their priceless collections of Wordsworth and Yeats manuscripts, and to the University of Virginia's Alderman Library for unfailing cooperation. Thanks to Samuel Beckett who answered questions of fact about his work; the interpretations are entirely mine. Mrs. T. S. Eliot kindly let me examine Eliot's annotated copy of F. H. Bradley's *Appearance and Reality.*

Special thanks to D. W. Abse, M. D., Ralph Cohen, George H. Ford, Peter Heath, Park Honan, Vivian Mercier, Thomas Mc-Farland, Thomas Parkinson, Charles L. Ross and Walter Sokel, who took time out from busy lives to read parts of the book and make valuable suggestions. Special thanks also for the extraordinary care with which Bernard Madura and Myles Walsh helped in research, Edith Good typed the manuscript, and my wife Francesca prepared the Index. It is difficult to express publicly the debt I owe Francesca for her patience and encouragement during the years this book was in preparation.

R. L.

Charlottesville, Virginia
May 1977

CONTENTS

THE MYSTERIES OF IDENTITY

INTRODUCTION

Identity and the concepts it suggests have become by now cli-chés. How easily we slip into the identity language to express our spiritual discomfort, to bemoan the need to "find our-selves." A remarkable proportion of books and articles in various disciplines carry in their titles the word *self* or *ego* or *identity* even when they turn out to say little about this mysterious en-tity. Such words—and *identity*, for reasons I shall discuss, sounds the most innovative—have become badges of contempo-rary relevance. A popular paperback of the 1970s calls ours an "identity society," where there is enough economic security "so that personal fulfillment *seems* possible for almost everyone." The young, to the consternation of their parents, give a higher priority to realizing themselves as human beings than to making a success at careers. To the optimistic author, Dr. William Glasser, *identity* signifies everything humane and progressive.[1]

In a recent *New York Review* article, Christopher Lasch takes a dimmer view of the current rage for identity. He shows that it has, in the "consciousness movement" of the 1970s, become institutionalized. Some commentators hail the consciousness movement as a new religion. It is not a religion, writes Lasch, it is therapy. But how distinguish therapy from religion? Christ was a healer, the first priests were witch-doctors. Lasch objects to the self-indulgence of the searcher for identity, whose therapist hardly encourages him

> to subordinate his needs and interests to those of others, to someone or some cause or tradition outside himself. Love as self-sacrifice or self-abasement, "meaning" as submission to a higher loyalty—these sublimations strike the therapeutic sensibility as intolerably oppressive, offensive to common sense and injurious to personal health and well-being. To "liberate" humanity from such outmoded ideas of love and duty has become the mission of the post-Freudian therapies and particularly of their converts and popularizers, for whom mental health means the overthrow of "inhibitions" and the nonstop celebration of the self.[2]

Such insipid permissiveness distorts the teachings of Freud, for whom the process of repression and sublimation is the worthwhile price we pay for civilization. It also distorts the romantic belief in self-expression and self-realization. The insights of prophets are usually distorted by institutionalization and popularization; yet the insights remain valid. The insights of D. H. Lawrence have in the same way been distorted by the sexual revolution of the 1960s with its promotion of a dehumanizing promiscuity.

The most important revelation in Lasch's article is indicated by its title, "The Narcissist Society." Drawing on the books he is reviewing, particularly Dr. Otto Kernberg's *Borderline Conditions and Pathological Narcissism*, Lasch confirms what one had gathered from Erik Erikson and others—that clinicians are seeing less of the classical neuroses, which derive from sexual repression, and more identity or "character" disorders. "The patient of today," writes Erikson, whose psychoanalytic books are largely responsible for the current vogue of the word *identity*, "suffers most under the problem of what he should believe in and who he should—or, indeed, might—be or become; while the patient of early psychoanalysis suffered most under inhibitions which prevented him from being what and who he thought he knew he was." ³ The typical patient nowadays, Lasch reveals, is a narcissist. Often charming and successful, he is socially and sexually promiscuous as a way of avoiding "close involvements." He is "facile at managing the impressions he gives to others, ravenous for admiration but contemptuous of those he manipulates into providing it; unappeasably hungry for emotional experiences with which to fill an inner void; terrified of aging and death." The origin of such personal devastation is social, says Lasch in his most powerful passage: "One of the gravest indictments of our society is precisely that it has made deep and lasting friendships, love affairs, and marriages so difficult to achieve." Lasch lays the trouble to the competitiveness of a society in which even personal relations "take on the character of combat." ⁴

The indictment is justified. But we have to look deeper for the cause of the social dissolution that produces a competitiveness that grows more subtly psychological as government regulation restrains economic competition and competitiveness itself falls into disrepute. I refer to the decline of social imperatives and the system of deference that goes with them; no values or persons seem real or important enough to be worth the sacrifice or even postponement of one's own gratification. Personal relations become increasingly difficult as society loses the confidence to tell us what these relations ought to be. As a result we start from scratch. Each individual retreats into his own shell, and every relation becomes a power struggle modified only by our need to rub up against each other for mutual pleasure or advantage. Fascism, however, has demonstrated the worse alternative of trying to pretend that obsolete values are still valid. I doubt that personal relations are more peaceful in the communist countries, though the warfare may be conducted differently if the Russians and Chinese are less self-consciously individualist than we are.

For we discover behind the decline of social imperatives in the West a problem in epistemology, in the theory of knowing and perceiving, that takes us back to the romanticists. The epistemological counterpart to narcissism is solipsism, the "theory that the self is the only object of real knowledge or the only thing really existent" (OED). Solipsism was the condition dreaded by the romanticists—the danger incurred by the individualism and self-consciousness that was their special glory. As heirs to the great critical effort of the Enlightenment, the effort that dissolved the Christian system of God-created values corresponding to a God-created soul in man, the romanticists or post-Kantians found that the values they nevertheless perceived in the world were values they had projected, that the beautiful and meaningful world of their liveliest perceptions was a world they had organized imaginatively. Since imaginative perception had to be self-consciously individual, a way of knowing the external world through the self and the self through the external world, the self had become the Godlike creator of the world!

From the height of such presumption, the romanticist stared down at an abyss—at the yawning question whether things outside himself, including other people, were real and whether, if he were indeed the only living reality, he would not die of claustrophobic loneliness in his prisonhouse of self. It took great vitality to overcome the Enlightenment, to make the imaginative organization of self and experience that could recombine the worlds of subject and object, value and fact that the Enlightenment had split asunder. When vitality failed, the romanticist was unable to project, to make connection with the outside world; he was thus unable to receive back from the outside world the vitality necessary to feed his own life. He felt himself withering away in the prisonhouse not only of self but of the skull, where his only remaining life resided. This is the meaning of the ancient Mariner's thirst and isolation when, after gratuitously shooting the albatross, he finds himself alone among dead shipmates upon a lifeless ocean. Living death is his punishment for rupturing the tie with nature.

The solipsist-narcissist syndrome defines the main problem of identity treated by literature since the romanticists. On the one hand, there is the need for a strong individuality that can reject old values and create new ones, that can create its own organization of the world. On the other hand, there is the danger that such an individuality will make a world of itself. The solution, as formulated by Lawrence and Erik Erikson, is to maintain a strong ego open to connections.

In the first chapter of this book I shall show how, after the Enlightenment attack on a God-created identity, Wordsworth asserted a new romantic self that drew sufficient vitality from an organic connection with nature to project into nature, to find itself out there and nature within itself, and thus bridge the Enlightenment split between subject and object, value and fact. I shall then in the next three chapters trace the steady decline in the organizing and projective vitality of the romantic self through Arnold, early Eliot and Beckett. The declining vitality of the self in literature has accompanied a declining confidence in society, in the spiritual power of nature, and in the organic connection of the self with nature. It has accompanied a loss of confidence in the individual and individual effort due to mass production, mass markets, mass media, to increasing urbanization, industrialization, specialization, and to the increasing alienation of the self, according to Marx's analysis, from all its specialized functions.[5] Nietzsche calls such specialized men "inverse cripples"; worse off than ordinary cripples, whole men without a leg, these modern men "are nothing but a big eye or a big mouth or a big belly." "I find man in ruins. . . . fragments and limbs and dreadful accidents—but no human beings." [6]

The declining vitality of the self in literature reaches its low point in my model with Beckett, whose characters dwell so entirely within their skulls—are often crippled to indicate they are "inverse cripples"—that they are alienated not only from society and nature but from their own bodies. I shall in the concluding six chapters discuss the attempts of Yeats and Lawrence to reconstitute the self by drawing upon and helping to create two modern secular religions: Yeats draws upon the religion of art, Lawrence upon the religion of love. The fact that Beckett follows Yeats and Lawrence in time leaves it doubtful whether the latter are prophets of a new reconstructed ego open to connections or simply, as Yeats put it, "the last romantics."

A sign that the self in question for all these writers remains romantic is the fact that the Enlightenment's attack on the self's original unity remains the issue. Wordsworth's solution indicates the pattern of subsequent solutions; for Wordsworth saw the self as evolving its unity through the association of fragments, through building upon and returning in memory to childhood sensations from outside and from within the body. Partly the Wordsworthian self is transcendent. But partly it is a many-layered psychosomatic entity that looks toward Freud's revolutionary mode of characterization, his libidinal types of which the anal-erotic type is the best-known example. In Wordsworth our characters are determined by pleasurable childhood sensations; in Freud our characters are determined by the bodily zones that gave us the most erotic pleasure in infancy. Erikson, too, sees identity as a many-layered formation built upon "organ modes," upon infantile experiences of incorporation and elimination, of oral and anal stages.[7] Since unity is the issue, we see why the word *identity* has gained such currency. For more than words like *self* and *ego*, *identity* emphasizes the problematical nature of the self's unity and also the historically changing nature of its delineations—the fact that individualism is a passing phase of identity.

The crisis of individualism—caused partly by what Wylie

Sypher calls "a collectivism dominated by the law of large numbers" [8]—is certainly a major reason for the current preoccupation with identity. Other reasons, according to Erikson, are the liberation from tribal and national identities that widens the range of choices, and the need in industrial democracy for "self-made identities ready to grasp many chances." [9] Erikson became preoccupied with identity through his own need, as an immigrant in America, to remake his identity.

The emphasis on unity, on the ego as organizer, began in psychoanalysis with Freud's radical revision of his own geography of self in his late book, *The Ego and the Id* (1923), which gave rise to the ego psychology of Anna Freud, Heinz Hartmann, Erikson and others. Early psychoanalysis divided the self into an unconscious, which was repressed, and a conscious, which did the repressing: the conscious ego was, like the society it represented, a merely restraining force, the lid on the steaming kettle. In his later years, however, Freud came to realize that, as he wrote in *Beyond the Pleasure Principle* (1920), "much of the ego is itself unconscious." [10] In *The Ego and the Id*, he extends the ego into the unconscious id. He also separates off from the ego a superego or voice of ancestral moral imperatives which extends even deeper into the id than the ego. In making the superego largely unconscious, Freud confirms the romantic intuition that man's highest nature derives from his lowest, that religion and art are erotic and unconscious in origin.

Now the ego becomes an active, if partly unconscious, organizer of self, negotiating between the contrary demands of id and superego. Repression no longer defines the difference between conscious and unconscious; it is now only one of the ego's unconscious defenses—others are regression, projection, introjection or identification—for maintaining unity. Freud had to work out his theory of narcissism in order to name the elements that the ego organizes. We begin life as narcissists, but gradually direct our erotic interest outward to our mother and other love objects. When in growing up we lose these love objects, we take them into the psyche as identifications: the ego offers itself to the id as substitute love object. All these identifications have to be organized into unity (where unity fails or is unconsciously rejected, the result is multiple personality) if we are again to direct our erotic interest outward and fall in love maturely. Here and in Jung's studies of individuation, we find the origin of Erikson's central idea that "identity formation" is the achievement of the adolescent, who in "the identity crisis" accomplishes "the selective repudiation and mutual assimilation of childhood identifications and their absorption in a new configuration" [11] in order to organize the psychosocial identity that can engage in social action and adult love. In "On Narcissism: An Introduction" (1914), Freud says: "A strong egoism is a protection against falling ill, but in the last resort we must begin to love in order not to fall ill." [12] "The development of psychosocial intimacy is not possible," says Erikson, "without a firm sense of identity." [13] All the literary men I shall discuss will say the same thing.

In *The Ego and the Id*, Freud uses *ego* in two main senses— one denoting "a bodily ego" enclosed within the skin; the other denoting an organizing function whose psychic space includes elements outside as well as inside the body. Freud tells us that he conceived the id in order to account for George Groddeck's sense of an exterior self—Groddeck's sense that, while the ego behaves passively, "we are 'lived' by unknown and uncontrollable forces": forces Yeats called Daimons. The "body-ego," says Freud, is mainly conscious; while "what is lowest but also what is highest in the ego can be unconscious." What is highest, the superego, also opens the self to external forces; the superego makes us feel guilty for crimes we never committed, makes a boy who has never been so threatened fear the primordial punishment of castration. Because the superego is formed from the id, "it has the most abundant links with the phylogenetic acquisition of each individual—his archaic heritage." Freud here enunciates a theory of racial memory similar to Jung's; like Jung he opens identity out to include selves exterior to the body-ego:

> The experiences of the ego seem at first to be lost for inheritance; but, when they have been repeated often enough and with sufficient strength in many individuals in successive generations, they transform themselves, so to say, into experiences of the id, the impressions of which are preserved by heredity. Thus in the id, which is capable of being inherited, are harboured residues of the existences of countless egos; and, when the ego forms its super-ego out of the id, it may perhaps only be reviving shapes of former egos and be bringing them to resurrection. [14]

These resurrected former egos resemble Jung's archetypes.

Such statements are, however, atypical. Erikson is thinking of the more typical Freud when he criticizes the mechanistic model by which Freud conceives a fixed amount of energy as transferred and transformed within a closed system. The reciprocal relation between group identity and ego identity "puts a greater energy potential" than Freud conceives "at the disposal of both ego synthesis and social organization." Erikson opens identity out not through the phylogenetic but through the social dimension. Despite the mechanistic model, Freud is a romantic who sees man as "psychologically alone," "forever projecting his infantile family constellation on the 'outer world,' " with man in the mass as a destructive mob, threatening self-fulfillment. For Erikson, instead, "societies create the only condition under which human growth is possible." Identity for Erikson as for literary artists is a psychosocial achievement. In writing that he has not "the knowledge to approach in any systematic fashion the relationship between ego qualities, social institutions, and historical eras," [15] he inadvertently describes what Yeats tries to do in A Vision.

Erikson stands between Freud's mainly psychological view of identity and the totally sociological view of Erving Goffman, who carries to an extreme the study of role-playing that has been sociology's principal way of treating the question of identity. The sociologists like to remind us that *persona* is the Latin word for the actor's mask, that a person is a mask or role. "It is in these roles," writes Robert Ezra Park, "that we know each other; it is in these roles that we know ourselves." [16] In *The Presentation of Self in Everyday Life*, Goffman develops all the implications of the theatrical metaphor. Social life consists of playing roles; we cooperate in acting out socially prescribed scenes designed "to define the situation." Goffman speaks of "impression management," and divides our living space into backstage and onstage areas. "One of the most interesting times to observe impression management is the moment when a performer leaves the back region and enters the place where the audience is to be found, or when he returns therefrom, for at these moments one can detect a wonderful putting on and taking off of character." He cites as example Orwell's comic description of a fiery Italian waiter who, after cursing brutally in the kitchen, is magically transformed as he enters the dining-room: he "sailed across it dish in hand, graceful as a swan." All Goffman's examples are the stuff of comedy (though he offers his research as sober fact); for his characters have no psychological depth, no residue of a self that might feel falsified by such masks, that might through rebellion or neurosis foul up the scene's requirements. Goffman's analysis raises a question that will appear throughout this book, the question of sincerity. Goffman regards self-deception and insincerity as functional necessities of masks and role-playing:

> The individual automatically becomes insincere when he adheres to the obligation of maintaining a working consensus and participates in different routines or performs a given part before different audiences. Self-deception can be seen as something that results when two different roles, performer and audience, come to be compressed into the same individual.

There is apparently no true self to be betrayed.

Goffman, like everyone who tangles with the word, offers contradictory accounts of the mask. On the one hand, he refers to William James's statement that *"a man has as many social selves as there are individuals who recognize him* and carry an image of him in their mind." On the other hand, he quotes Durkheim and Santayana to the effect that the mask fixes the self we present to the world, thus solving the problem of discontinuous selves.[17] The question remains whether this socially fixed self is an ideal that helps us organize and find our true self, or whether it is a deception. The existentialists consider it a deception and a trap. "A grocer who dreams," writes Sartre, "is offensive to the buyer, because such a grocer is not wholly a grocer. Society demands that he limit himself to his function as a grocer. . . . There are indeed many precautions to imprison a man in what he is, as if we lived in perpetual fear that he might escape from it, that he might break away and suddenly elude his condition." [18]

The romanticists, the existentialists' predecessors, would agree. Their role-playing was empathic, a free-wheeling projection into nature and other people as a way of evolving a true self whose unity is dynamic.[19] Is role-playing inwardly motivated or socially conditioned? Alfred North Whitehead clarifies the dilemma in his remark to the effect that the radical inconsistency in modern thought is our firm belief in man as a self-determining (sincere) organism and our equally firm belief in the validity of deterministic laws.[20] Masks and roles have become important terms in literary and sociological discourse as a reaction to the unqualified exaltation of sincerity by the romantic side of nineteenth-century thought.

The alternative answers to the question about role-playing have since the early nineteenth century grown increasingly extreme. Yeats accepts both alternatives: for subjective types, role-playing is inwardly motivated; for objective types, socially conditioned. Yeats and Lawrence strike a midway position between the modern extremes—between the Marxists, structuralists, behaviorists, technocrats, who see man as conditioned, and those who, like Rilke, Wallace Stevens, the existentialists, take the cue from Nietzsche and surpass even the romanticists in proclaiming the self's potential freedom and sovereignty. "The individual," Nietzsche proclaimed, is the latest value, "the most recent creation." "The delight in the herd is more ancient than the delight in the ego; and as long as the good conscience is identified with the herd, only the bad conscience says: I." "The *you* is older than the *I*; the *you* has been pronounced holy, but not yet the *I*." [21] The *I* will be pronounced holy when man has transcended himself, has recognized that he is God, the creator of his own values.

At the other extreme, we have been told that man is a machine directed by a mind different in essence from his body. This is Descartes' dualist position. Beckett, who sees man turning inevitably into a machine, explores the last vestiges of man's freedom while admitting everything that can be said against it. Now, however, that computers have advanced to the point where they threaten to exceed our capacities, the comparison of man with machine has been reversed. At what point, we now wonder, will computers become persons? In two startling essays, the philosophers Arthur C. Danto and Hilary Putnam show that the identity problem, which has always involved a mind-body or mind-brain problem, has now become a mind-machine problem no easier to solve for machines than for men. Danto's "On Consciousness in Machines" begins this way:

> Suppose all the physical discrepancies between the human brain and the currently most highly developed servomechanisms were someday overcome, and that the machine turned out to be conscious. What then would happen with the old quarrel between dualists and anti-dualists regarding the mind-body problem? I venture to say that nothing would happen,

because the problem would still derive from our definitions of *conscious, person* and *machine*. We now define "machines" as "not conscious." Could we change that definition without changing the other two? "Descartes, that arch-doubter," Danto concludes, "would cheerfully have taken you and me to be automata, differential behavioral criteria notwithstanding." In

"Minds and Machines," Putnam argues that "just as there are two possible descriptions of the behavior of a Turing machine— the engineer's structural blueprint and the logician's 'machine table'—so there are two possible descriptions of human psychology: the 'behavioristic' approach. . . . [and] a more abstract description of human mental processes, in terms of 'mental states.' " [22] The difference is between structure and function, between two aspects of the same entity.

The machine model suggests a new monism which makes mind as mechanical as body and makes identity, or self-consciousness, an illusion. Literature since the romanticists has mainly proclaimed the opposite monism, summed up by Yeats's phrase "the thinking of the body," [23] which distributes consciousness and identity throughout the body. "Man has no Body distinct from his Soul," Blake wrote in 1793; "for that call'd Body is a portion of Soul discern'd by the five Senses." [24] A century later Nietzsche put the same proposition conversely: "body am I entirely, and nothing else; and soul is only a word for something about the body." [25] The machine model makes clear that in modern times the question of identity involves nothing less than the question of our humanity. Literature since the romanticists has been concerned to salvage our humanity against the modern conditions that would turn us into machines.

In *Notes from Underground* (1864), Dostoevsky makes the minimum case for our humanity by inventing the "anti-hero," by showing that modern identity is inevitably pathological, that "we're all cripples to some degree." His unnamed antihero has evolved a pathological identity as a way of protecting himself against two modern challenges to his humanity. The first challenge stems from the nineteenth-century scientific, humanitarian view that since man can be counted on to pursue his own interests, to seek pleasure and avoid pain, he can be conditioned to become progressively more benevolent. Aside from remarking that civilization only makes our cruelty more subtle, Dostoevsky's antihero exhibits a "chronic perversity" that causes him to act destructively against his own interests as a way of asserting his freedom. The second challenge stems from the need, if one is to indulge in satisfying action, to be "stupid" or unselfconscious enough to believe in the reasons for such action in an age when ideals are no longer objectively valid. Since Dostoevsky's highly self-conscious narrator is not "stupid" enough to be a hero, he becomes an antihero, "a mouse with a heightened consciousness" who sinks into "inertia," turning upon himself and only deviously upon others the hatred he cannot vent openly in action. Through self-torment he asserts his freedom: "man will never give up true suffering," for "suffering is the only cause of consciousness," and though "consciousness is man's greatest plague, I know that he likes it and won't exchange it for any advantage."

Since he is a petty bureaucrat, his role-playing ought to be predictable. But he is also a fifth-rate intellectual and romantic, a dreamer of self-aggrandizing dreams who cannot cooperate in social performances because he demands a leading role others are unwilling to grant him. Where he most wants to be admired—as at a dinner party to which he has invited himself—he acts most obnoxiously, arranging the scenario of his own humiliation. He spends that night with a prostitute to whom he describes the degraded lovelessness of her life and the satisfactions of genuine love. When Liza arrives at his apartment the next day, offering him the love he described, his only thought is how to get rid of her though she offers him the fulfillment of his own ideal. "I wanted to be left alone in my mousehole. The whiff of real life had overwhelmed me, and I couldn't breathe." The mousehole is his own mind and enclosed ego, they are the same. He is—like all people with enclosed egos as Lawrence will show—sadomasochistic: "I couldn't fall in love because, for me, loving means bullying and dominating. . . . I never visualized love as anything but a struggle, starting with hatred and ending in the subjection of the loved object." [26]

The man is contemptible; therein lies his humanity. He has salvaged his humanity through what Erikson calls "negative identity"—the outsider role played by those who cannot realize their humanity through acceptable roles, who "would rather be nobody or somebody totally bad . . . than be not-quite-somebody." [27] Were he to play his social role consistently, he would be an ordinary mouse, a nonentity (the novel's Russian title is literally "Notes from a Hole in the Floor"). But since he has not the courage to break through to reality by loving Liza, he achieves through perversity a minimum of being denied his fellow clerks who are not self-critical and do not suffer. At least, as he says in his final address to the reader, his behavior has not conformed to an idea:

> All I did was carry to the limit what you haven't dared to push even halfway—taking your cowardice for reasonableness, thus making yourselves feel better. So I may still turn out to be more *alive* than you in the end. . . . Why, today we don't even know where real life is. . . . We even find it painful to be men—real men of flesh and blood, with *our own private bodies;* we're ashamed of it, and we long to turn ourselves into something hypothetical called the average man. We're stillborn, and for a long time we've been brought into the world by parents who are dead themselves; and we like it better and better. . . . Soon we'll invent a way to be begotten by ideas altogether. [28]

The passage touches a theme that will dominate literary treatments of identity, the theme of "the walking dead." I take the phrase from Ford Madox Ford's *The Good Soldier* (1915)—a novel that anticipates Eliot's *The Waste Land* in connecting sexual with spiritual sterility—where the narrator intones after his wife's suicide: "I thought nothing; absolutely nothing. . . . I felt no sorrow, no desire for action. . . . I was the walking dead." [29]

A related theme is that of the mask. Dostoevsky's antihero

cannot among his other problems find a mask to wear. The theme of the mask is central to Rilke's novel *The Notebooks of Malte Laurids Brigge* (1910), where it is treated with a complexity that answers the question Goffman will raise whether masks are necessarily inauthentic. Rilke answers the question by distinguishing between modern, inauthentic, and traditional, authentic, masks. Malte is an impoverished young Danish nobleman who, down-and-out in early-twentieth-century Paris, notes that each of the big-city walking dead has several "faces," but that "the naked flayed head without a face" would be worse than such inauthentic modern masks. Since he lives near a hospital, Malte notes that "a death of one's own is growing ever rarer" and will soon be "as rare as a life of one's own"; for in hospitals death takes the character of one's disease rather than one's own character. He then records memories of the aristocratic Danish world of his childhood—which are mainly memories of impressively characteristic deaths, deaths so vital that the dead person often returned in his own character as a ghost. His grandfather, who died impressively, is referred to by his title of Count, and is described "as though he wore a mask" because he inhabits the sphere of permanent communal values: "Chronological sequence played no role whatever for him, death was a trifling incident which he utterly ignored." Malte instead fears death, for he knows "that out there, too, there was nothing but my loneliness." [30]

Since in Paris Malte has no place in society and therefore no assured sense of identity, he understands himself by finding his doubles among outcasts. One such double whom he understands to be "withdrawing from everything" makes him understand that he too is withdrawing. The theme of the double, which dramatizes without penetrating the mysteries of identity, does not emerge conspicuously in the authors I shall discuss; though the folklore connection between doubles and guardian spirits suggests that Yeats's Daimons could be considered doubles. Suffice it to say that Otto Rank, in his psychoanalytic

study *The Double*, attributes the importance of the theme in
modern literature to modern narcissism. After dealing with such
fictions as E. T. A. Hoffman's tales, Poe's "William Wilson"
and Dostoevsky's *The Double*, Rank cites as the clearest example
of narcissism Wilde's *The Picture of Dorian Gray*, in which the
narcissistic Dorian shares his "defective capacity for love with
almost all double-heroes." [31]

Malte reads two stories about deaths that explain the difference between modern and traditional masks. The first story is
about the seventeenth-century false Czar Dmitri, who wore in
death a discredited imperial mask so that they "pierced through
his night-shirt and stabbed all around in him, to see whether
they would strike the hard core of a personality." The second
story is about the fifteenth-century Duke of Burgundy, Charles
the Bold, whose identity was "hard and unalterable as granite"
and distributed throughout his body. Killed in battle, he had his
face torn by wolves so that he was hardly identifiable. But because his ducal mask remained valid, his identity remained intact. At his laying-out, one knew the corpse had a head "as soon
as one saw the crown" that needed a head to rest upon. "Death
seemed . . . a puppet-master in instant need of a duke."

Masks are authentic so long as the social values they represent
are generally accepted as valid. Malte contrasts the medieval
with the modern sense of identity: we, instead, "do not know
our part, we look for a mirror, we want to rub off the make-up
and . . . be real." We dare not don artificial masks because we
dare not assert values: we are "a mere half-thing: neither existing, nor actors." In the Roman theater at Orange, Malte imagines the performance of an ancient "superhuman drama" that
distills "the strong, all-covering antique mask, behind which the
world condensed into a face," the superhuman mask that gave
the ancients their sense of identity. Our present-day theater, instead, is as devoid of reality as our streets. "We have no theatre,
any more than we have a God: for this, community is
needed." [32] And for community, it is implied, a God is needed.

Here we have the ultimate reason for the difference between traditional and modern masks, the difference between societies in which values are and are not supernaturally sanctioned. Rilke comes close to Yeats for whom the mask gives us identity by combining the individual and the social, the human and the superhuman.

Erikson arrives at a similar insight when he says that "we are truly conscious only insofar as we can say I and mean it," mean that "I am the center of awareness in a universe of experience in which I have a coherent identity," that "I am alive, that I *am* life. The counterplayer of the 'I' therefore can be, strictly speaking, only the deity who has lent this halo to a mortal" from His numinous identity.[33] This recalls Martin Buber's famous distinction between the "I-It" identity that conceives itself as the only living reality in a world of objects and the "I-Thou" identity that understands the living reality of the other and therefore of God.[34]

These are some of the concepts that will come into play as I show how modern literature treats the theme of identity. I shall let literature speak for itself in its own terms, which means that I shall not mine literary works for ideas but will let these works speak through the inextricable combination of ideas with forms, words, imagery, emotion and with those critical judgments on our part that are inseparable from the experience of literature. I could not of course discuss these works in the way I shall discuss them without concepts drawn from philosophy, psychology, sociology and anthropology and without the method of analyzing unconscious motivations that we have all imbibed from Freud and Jung. But then literary criticism is the application of concepts to literature, and literature has inspired so many insights of philosophers, psychologists and social scientists that the debts are reciprocal. I hope that this book will reciprocally illuminate the subject of identity and illuminate through the subject of identity the literary works under discussion.

I am indebted to the many fine critics who have discussed the theme of identity in literature either as a main subject or incidentally to other concerns. Their influences on me have been too numerous and subtle to be distinguishable one from the other; indeed the theme of identity is inherent in so much modern critical discussion, no matter what its subject, that it would be difficult to draw up a bibliography of critical works treating identity. If I make any advance on what has already been written, it will be through my attempt to schematize the theme, to organize it on a larger scale than has yet been done, while discussing in depth relatively few authors.

My problem was one of selection, since the theme of identity appears almost everywhere in modern literature. I have selected six major English and Irish writers who form a coherent tradition and who treat the theme of identity with a cogency that moves it forward. It is only within a coherent tradition that one can trace the development of a literary theme. I have preferred to use these writers as a center for passing references to other writers rather than drop too many names lightly and thus run the risk of making literary works mere illustrations of an idea. Through treatment in depth, I hoped to convey the *Gestalt* of modern literature and the way in which the theme of identity is involved in that wholeness and helps to make it distinctively modern. What I am offering with the few writers I discuss is a model which should generate concepts that the reader can apply to other writers and literary traditions and to his observations of himself and other people. This book will have fulfilled its purpose if the reader goes on writing the rest of it in his own mind or in a book of his own, and if it appeals not only to literary readers but to all readers interested in the mysteries of identity as well as in the authors I am discussing.

Part I
THE ROMANTIC SELF

_____

Chapter 1
WORDSWORTH:
THE SELF
AS PROCESS

Identity is "the sameness of a person or thing at all times or in all circumstances." [1] As a term in philosophy *identity* used to apply mainly to the unity of objects, especially through an expanse of time: "a single object, plac'd before us, and survey'd for any time without our discovering in it any interruption or variation, is able to give us a notion of identity." [2] The word did not take on its current psychological denotation, it did not begin to be applied to the self, until the unity of the self became problematic. As long as men believed in a soul created and sustained (continuously *known* and *seen*) by God, there could be no question about the unity of the self. It is significant that *identity* is first used to mean personal identity by the empiricist philosophers Locke and Hume, who use the word *identity* to cast doubt on the unity of the self.

The term in this sense is not used by Descartes, who might be considered the founder of modern philosophy and the last philosopher to take the unity of the self as axiomatic. But Descartes' "*I think, hence I am*" so amputates the self by reducing it to

consciousness that, despite his intention to substantiate the self,
Descartes has probably done more than Locke and Hume to kill
it off, as Beckett's use of Descartes suggests. Most of the nine-
teenth- and twentieth-century writers I shall discuss recur to one
or another of these Enlightenment philosophers or their successors (Bradley on his empiricist side serves Eliot the way Locke
and Hartley serve Wordsworth), as defining the self in a way
they both accept and resist.

Hume, in his section "Of Personal Identity," raises most of
the issues about identity that I shall discuss in this book. "There
are some philosophers," Hume begins,

> who imagine we are every moment intimately conscious of what we call
> our Self; that we feel its existence and its continuance in existence; and
> are certain, beyond the evidence of a demonstration, both of its perfect
> identity and simplicity.

But the self, Hume argues, is not experienced. What we experience are successive, changing impressions all of which are sup-
posed to refer to the self:

> Pain and pleasure, grief and joy, passions and sensations succeed each
> other, and never all exist at the same time. It cannot, therefore, be from
> any of these impressions, or from any other, that the idea of self is
> deriv'd; and consequently there is no such idea.

The issue here, which we will see repeated over and over, is
whether we experience successive selves rather than any one
self.

"I never can catch *myself* at any time without a perception,
and never can observe any thing but the perception." The self
then is equivalent to the contents of its perceptions and ceases to
exist when it ceases to perceive, as in sleep or death. Hume has
no concept of unconsciousness, and therefore does not allow for
a sense of self in sleep or dreams.

We "are nothing," he says, "but a bundle or collection of different perceptions, which succeed each other with an incon-
ceivable rapidity, and are in a perpetual flux and movement."

We arrive at the sense of self through error, through the process of association; we pass insensibly from the idea of succession to the idea of identity, because the imagination *feels* the same in conceiving these opposite ideas (here Hume anticipates nineteenth-century dialectical thinking). In order to justify this absurdity, "we feign the continu'd existence of the perception of our senses, to remove the interruption," or we imagine "something unknown and mysterious, connecting the parts" (here Hume anticipates romantic organicism), and thus "run into the notion of a *soul*, and *self* . . . to disguise the variation." [3] The self, in other words, is a necessary fiction. Hume anticipates and rejects the dialectical logic and the organicism by which later generations will try to solve the problem of the self as he defines it.

Hume concludes that identity is not in the different perceptions themselves, uniting them, "but is merely a quality, which we attribute to them, because of the union of their ideas in the imagination, when we reflect upon them." The self is a retrospective construction of the imagination, and for this reason "memory not only discovers the identity, but also contributes to its production." Only through memory can we create the self by seeing continuity between past and present perceptions; only through memory can we conceive "that chain of causes and effects, which constitute our self or person." [4] Hume does not deny the self as an operative presence; like Locke he insists that it is a fabrication achieved through association, imagination, memory—especially memory. These terms will not change, though their meanings will expand, contract and expand again as I proceed in this book. Memory above all will remain the creator, the artist-fabricator, of self. Hume says that we can through logical inference extend the self beyond the confines of our memory, that we would not, because we have forgotten the incidents of a past day suggest that our present self is not continuous with the self of the forgotten day. His need to supplement memory with logical inference shows that he lacks a notion of unconscious memory. He lacks the Wordsworthian notion that the forgotten past comes suddenly alive in the present and establishes when it does the only continuity of self that matters.

Hume and Wordsworth make mainly negative contact, in that *association* and *imagination* which for Hume have a negative value, as fabricators of illusions, take on in Wordsworth a positive value as ways of knowing reality. But Hume comes close to Wordsworth when, in the next section, he falls into philosophical despair from the realization that reason acting alone "entirely subverts itself, and leaves not the lowest degree of evidence in any proposition, either in philosophy or common life," so that we have to "save ourselves from this total scepticism" by means of fancy. "We have, therefore, no choice left but betwixt a false reason and none at all." Only nature can cure him through some "lively impression of my senses" or through the pleasures of social intercourse which make such destructive speculations seem "cold" and "ridiculous." Overcoming the temptation to renounce philosophy for the pleasures of life, he concludes that philosophy can expect "a victory more from the returns of a serious good-humour'd disposition, than from the force of reason" alone. He is saying that reason must be motivated by feeling, by what he calls "propensity": "Where reason is lively, and mixes itself with some propensity, it ought to be assented to. Where it does not, it can never have any title to operate upon us."

He gives a Wordsworthian example of how, after tiring of company, "[I] have indulg'd a *reverie* in my chamber, or in a solitary walk by a river-side, I feel my mind all collected within itself, and am naturally *inclin'd* to carry my view into all those [philosophical] subjects." He is acknowledging that thought originates in sensation and feeling, and that he prefers some ideas over others because of their "vivacity," [5] their emotional power and association with himself. His analysis points to the Wordsworthian view that the self cannot be known as an isolated entity, that it disappears if abstracted, that it can only be known through experience, and that its unity is to be found precisely in the change, the flux of perceptions that so disturbs Hume. Hume seems to anticipate Wordsworth when he says that "vegetables and animals endure a *total* change, yet we still attribute identity to them." But he goes on to say that the identity we ascribe to these organisms is as "fictitious" as "the identity we ascribe to the mind of man." [6] Hume *experiences* the self—he says several times that "the idea of ourselves is always intimately present to us" [7]—but he does not *trust* the experience. Hume considers continuity a fiction; whereas for Wordsworth, who takes over the problem of identity less from Hume than from Locke and Hartley, continuity is the fundamental reality. The empiricist philosophers try, and fail, to find a *static* continuity through the flux of perceptions. But for Wordsworth, Keats and the other romanticists, continuity is *dynamic*; it is the continuity of change, growth, the continuity that comes of the faith that enables us to live by absorbing the individual perceptions into an intuited whole.

More completely than the other English romanticists, Wordsworth works out in his poetry the new romantic concept of self. When Keats in a letter calls this world "The vale of Soul-making," [8] he comes close to Wordsworth's thinking and helps us understand how Wordsworth, by answering the empiricist attack on the Christian concept of soul, is able to use the word *soul* in a new way. For Keats says that we come into the world as pure potentiality or "Intelligence" and that we acquire a "Soul" or "sense of Identity" through "Circumstances." And it is the main purport of Wordsworth's poetry to show the spiritual significance of this world, to show that we evolve a soul or identity through experience and that the very process of evolution is what we mean by *soul*.

To understand the implications of Wordsworth's view and

why it is distinctively modern, we have to go back to the psychological assertions of Locke and Locke's disciple Hartley that Wordsworth was both absorbing and answering.[9] The best analogy to the challenge raised by Locke is the challenge raised in our time by computers. For Lockean man is like a computer in that everything inside him comes from outside, through sensation; so that Lockean man gives back only what has been "programmed" into him. Even his choices are no evidence of free will; for once the idea of choice has entered his head, he must choose—and he must choose between predetermined alternatives. "A man that is walking," says Locke, "to whom it is proposed to give off walking, is not at liberty, whether he will determine himself to walk, or give off walking or not: he must necessarily prefer one or the other of them; walking or not walking." [10] One would use the same line of reasoning to show that a computer, for all its ability to make choices, is not free; for its choices are limited.

Although Locke lays great emphasis on self-consciousness, in that he shows that the greatest part of mental life consists of reflections on our own ideas, his system does not, as Blake pointed out in "There is No Natural Religion," allow for anything new to come into the world, since Locke's "complex ideas" merely complicate a fixed number of sensations.[11] Lockean self-consciousness is the sort we may well predict for the formidable computers of the future.

As computers become increasingly complex, as they become capable of making choices, learning, and giving orders, we inevitably wonder at what point of complexity they can be considered human, as having a soul. Now in *The Prelude* Wordsworth was trying to answer some such question as this regarding Lockean man. If we consider that the human psyche is built up of sensations, then at what point do sensations add up to soul, or how do we jump from sensations to soul? We can understand Wordsworth's answer to Locke if we imagine him answering the question in regard to computers. His answer would be that computers will never be human—will never have continuity or identity—until they are born and grow up and can therefore have the changing memory of change that constitutes awareness of one's own identity.

If sensations turn into soul—into an ineffable quality that can never be accounted for by the sensations themselves—it is because the sensations reach an ever-changing mind that transforms them, as a merely passive receiver, the sort of mind Locke likens to blank paper, could not. No two succeeding sensations from the same object can be the same, because the later sensation reaches a mind already modified by the earlier sensation. Locke recognizes all this, but it remains for Wordsworth to draw the necessary conclusions in his poetry and for Coleridge to formulate them in his theory of imagination. The necessary conclusions are summed up in the idea of interchange between man and nature—the idea that the mind modifies sensation as much as sensation modifies the mind.

It may be argued that computers, too, as they learn, offer a changing receiver to external data. This brings us to the second important point in Wordsworth's answer to Locke. Wordsworth portrays the mind as itself part of the nature it perceives; and it is this connection, sensed through what Wordsworth calls *joy*—an intensification of Hume's "vivacity"—that gives us confidence in the reality of ourselves and the external world. Dare one predict that no computer is likely to have this organic connection or to sense it through *joy?*

In *The Prelude,* Wordsworth tells us that his life began to the sound of the Derwent River that "loved / To blend his murmurs with my nurse's song" and "sent a voice / That flowed along my dreams," making

> ceaseless music that composed my thoughts
> To more than infant softness, giving me
> Amid the fretful dwellings of mankind

> A foretaste, a dim earnest, of the calm
> That Nature breathes among the hills and groves.
>   (I. 270–81) [12]

There, in the best Lockean fashion, Wordsworth traces all his mature thoughts back to the sound of the river. But unlike Locke, Wordsworth presents the perceiving mind as active. The fact that the nurse's song blends with the river suggests a correspondence between mind and river; that is why the river's voice flows along the dreams of the growing Wordsworth. When we read that the river "loved / To blend," we understand that the baby did not merely receive but loved the river's sound, reached out to it as a flower reaches out to the sun and air and rain it has the potentiality to receive. The blending and interchange turn sensation into experience, an experience of joy that will in future years spread around the mature man's thoughts an affective tone—a tone objectified in "the calm / That Nature breathes." This tone, this atmosphere of the mind, sensed as at once inside and outside the mind, is what the mature man will call *soul*.

The river received on its "smooth breast the shadow of those towers" of Cockermouth Castle (I. 283). The reflection of the towers was perceived, we gather, at a somewhat later age than the sound of the river. Visual sensations are in Wordsworth more intellectual than sensations of sound. The composite experience of river and towers—which might be understood as an experience of female and male principles—stands behind the experiences of beauty and fear described in the rest of Book I, which are composite experiences of natural and moral power.

In Book II, the mature man's capacity for love is traced back to the contentment of the infant

>   who sinks to sleep
> Rocked on his Mother's breast; who with his soul
> Drinks in the feelings of his Mother's eye!

Through his connection with his mother, he gains a sense of connection with nature, a connection portrayed through the imagery of flow and blending:

> No outcast he, bewildered and depressed:
> Along his infant veins are interfused
> The gravitation and the filial bond
> Of nature that connect him with the world.

The infant is from the start an active agent of perception who "drinks in" feelings. Because he inhabits the loving universe circumscribed for him by his mother's "Presence," he loves or reaches out to all that he beholds. That sense of "Presence," the baby's first apprehension of Deity, is produced by the sympathetic relation of mind to universe which is, says Wordsworth, the "Poetic spirit of our human life." The mind is portrayed as a relation and a process—a process *growing* from feeling through power, sense, thought, into the one great Mind and between subject and object, in such a way that the parts flow one into the other and can hardly be discriminated.

> For feeling has to him imparted power
> That through the growing faculties of sense
> Doth like an agent of the one great Mind
> Create, creator and receiver both,
> Working but in alliance with the works
> Which it beholds.

This poetic spirit, says Wordsworth, is in most people "abated or suppressed" in later years. But in some few it remains "Preeminent till death," and those few are, we gather, poets (II.235–65).

We have here a psychological accounting for affect, for the value or "glory" we find in the world, which seems to contradict the Platonic accounting in the "Immortality Ode." The accounting in *The Prelude* is the authentically Wordsworthian one, because it is naturalistic, psychological and sensationalist.

The Platonic idea of pre-existence is advanced in the "Ode,"
Wordsworth tells us in the Fenwick note to that poem, merely
as a figure of speech, as a fanciful and traditional way of generalizing the psychological phenomenon revealed to him by his
own life—that "the Child is Father of the Man," that spirit is to
be found in the primitive. "I took hold of the notion of pre-existence," says Wordsworth, "as having sufficient foundation in
humanity for authorizing me to make for my purpose the best
use of it I could as a Poet." The Platonic idea is used with fine
artistry in the "Ode" as a counterpoint to the primitivist idea. It
is the primitivist idea that takes over when in stanza IX Wordsworth gets down to the serious business of answering the question of the poem, the question posed by the adult's sense of loss.
His answer is that nothing is lost. Even if we no longer experience the "glory" we experienced in childhood, "nature yet remembers." Our souls, he concludes in a strikingly primitivist
image, can in a moment travel backward

> And see the Children sport upon the shore,
> And hear the mighty waters rolling evermore.

Yet the Platonic idea is not lost sight of even here. It is so
blended with the primitivist idea that we can see its function all
along has been to ennoble and spiritualize the primitivist idea.
Thus the sea is the physical sea where all life began; but the sea
is also immortal, through its very age ageless and transcendent:

> Hence in a season of calm weather
> Though inland far we be,
> Our Souls have sight of that immortal sea
> Which brought us hither.

Growing up has been mainly compared to a journey of the sun
across the sky; now it is compared to a journey inland from the
sea. Wordsworth explains the adult's sense of loss by telling us
that we come down from the sky and up from the sea, and by
blending the two directions to evoke an original spiritual source
that is unlocatable.

The blending goes even farther in the imagery through which Wordsworth tells us that the adult responds to the objects before him because he sees them through the lens of his memory of childhood experiences. Those "first affections" and "shadowy recollections," he says,

> Are yet the fountain light of all our day,
> Are yet a master light of all our seeing.

There is an inextricable blending here of light and water, the ideal and the primitive, Platonic metaphysics and Lockean psychology.

We find the same blending in two adjacent passages of *The Prelude*, Book I. In the first, Wordsworth speaks of experiences that cannot be accounted for by the Lockean theory of memory and association he has been developing—experiences which would seem to require, to account for them, some Platonic theory of "first-born affinities" (I.555), of archetypes, of innate ideas. He had such an experience when gazing over an expanse of sea,

> Of shining water, gathering as it seem'd
> Through every hair-breadth in that field of light
> New pleasure—   (I.578–80)

new, because not deriving from association with earlier pleasures. Wordsworth evokes the transcendent quality of the experience by turning shining *water* into a *field* of light, by dissolving both water and land into light. But in the next passage, he says that he loves to travel backward down through the corridors of memory, from forms down through sensations, to recover at the point where conscious memory fades out just such a vision of light:

> Those recollected hours that have the charm
> Of visionary things, those lovely forms
> And sweet sensations that throw back our life,
> And almost make remotest infancy
> A visible scene, on which the sun is shining.
>   (I.631–35)

We have only to recall Locke's description of the mind as a dark closet penetrated by certain rays of light from the outside word [13]—a comparison even more revealing of Locke's outlook than his better known comparison of the mind to white or blank paper—to understand the sense in which Wordsworth answers Locke. Yet it is Locke who supplies the concepts of memory and association through which Wordsworth can give psychological substantiation to his experience of his own mind as light or music. And it is important to note that the mind recognizes itself in an external sensation, that Wordsworth arrives at his concept of mind by tracing his life back to an original sensation—to "A visible scene, on which the sun is shining" or to the sound of the Derwent River. Wordsworth is moving toward a notion of external self.

Much ink has been spilled over the question whether Wordsworth believed that his apprehension of spirit came from outside or inside, whether he was a Lockean empiricist or a Platonic believer in innate ideas. [14] The answer is that Wordsworth, when he is writing his best poetry, uses both doctrines as possibilities, blending them in such a way as to evoke the mystery he is talking about—the mystery of life, vitality, organic connection. The case should teach us something about the proper relation of ideas to poetry. And, indeed, Wordsworth himself pronounces on the subject in his first "Essay Upon Epitaphs," where he speaks of the antithetical ideas of two Greek philosophers about the value of body in relation to soul. In spite of their opposite ideas, says Wordsworth, modulating from talk of thought to talk of feelings,

> Each of these Sages was in sympathy with the best feelings of our nature; feelings which, though they seem opposite to each other, have another and a finer connection than that of contrast. It is a connection formed through the subtle progress by which, both in the natural and

the moral world, qualities pass insensibly into their contraries, and things revolve upon each other.[15]

Wordsworth praises the insensible passing between contraries that Hume calls error; for Wordsworth employs dialectical thinking.

He no sooner tells us in *The Prelude* how nature through "extrinsic passion" or association first peopled his "mind with forms sublime or fair," than he speaks of other pleasures

> Which, if I err not, surely must belong
> To those first-born affinities that fit
> Our new existence to existing things,
> And, in our dawn of being, constitute
> The bond of union between life and joy.
>
> (I.554–58)

Note the tentativeness of "if I err not," and how even innate affinities are traced back to a primitive origin which one may still understand to be natural. Such blending evokes "the bond of union betweeen life and joy" that is Wordsworth's answer to the question at the heart of *The Prelude*, the question that no simply rational account of life can answer. I mean the question, why live at all, why bother to get up in the morning? As so often in Wordsworth's best lines, the answer is couched in words that are general, even vague. Yet the "Presence" evoked, to use that other vague but potent Wordsworthian word, is definite enough and is the only answer to the question "Why live?" We can infer that "the bond of union between life and joy" is the thing that will always distinguish human beings from computers. We can also infer that the philosopher's question, "Why live?" can only be answered by the poet. For the answer is that we take pleasure in the world we behold because we are one with it. And it is only the poet who can make pleasure and oneness real for us by just such blending as Wordsworth employs.

F. R. Leavis and Donald Davie have shown, through an analysis of Wordsworth's syntax, how he gives us poetry by blurring the thought.[16] One can say even more specifically that

Wordsworth gives us poetry by being both Lockean and anti-Lockean at the same time. For Wordsworth answers Locke by using the Lockean concepts of memory and association. It is only through memory, says Locke, that the mind has any effectiveness, and he equates the self with the sum of conscious memory ("whatever has the consciousness of present and past actions, is the same person to whom they both belong"). But Locke does not speak of memory as modifying the actions remembered; these actions remain fixed, like the data "remembered" by a computer. It is in speaking of the accidental association of ideas that Locke recognizes a modifying and transforming process. Locke accounts for our irrational behavior and for affect—for what he calls our "sympathies and antipathies"—by the connection through *chance* or *custom* of ideas that have no correspondence in nature or logic. Through association, in other words, sensations and ideas are transformed into something other than they would be in themselves, with a value they would not have in themselves.

The difference between Locke and the romanticists is that Locke deplores the process of association as unamenable to reason; [17] whereas the romanticists glory in it because it shows the mind as creative and carries them over from sensation to value. It is significant that Wordsworth and Coleridge were especially interested in the eighteenth-century medical doctor David Hartley, who builds his whole system on the theory of association that is in Locke only one proposition. From association, Hartley derives the affective responses of pleasure and pain which lead to Christian values and faith. Hartley must have seemed to Wordsworth and Coleridge to have transcendentalized Locke. In "Religious Musings," Coleridge hails Hartley as "of mortal kind / Wisest," because he is the first to establish value on a materialistic and therefore scientific basis— the "first who marked the ideal tribes / Up the fine fibres through the sentient brain" (368–70). Hartley comes close to calling this world a vale of soul-making when he says: "Some degree of spirituality is the necessary consequence of passing through life. The sensible pleasures and pains must be transferred by association more and more every day, upon things that afford neither sensible pleasure nor sensible pain in themselves, and so beget the intellectual pleasures and pains." [18] In other words, we grow spiritually by conferring spirituality upon the world. The issue between the Locke-Hartley doctrine and the Platonic doctrine of pre-existence is whether we gain or lose spirituality by living.

Nevertheless, Hartley's system remains mechanical because he does not recognize that the crucial element in Locke's theory of association is this—that only in speaking of association does Locke allow for any unconscious mental process. Wordsworth and Coleridge modify Hartley by dwelling on the unconscious aspects of the associative process. Thus Coleridge, in turning against Hartley, says that "association depends in a much greater degree on the recurrence of resembling states of Feeling, than on Trains of Idea," and that "Ideas *never* recall Ideas . . . any more than Leaves in a forest create each other's motion—The Breeze it is that runs thro' them . . . the Soul, the state of Feeling." [19] "*Consciousness*," Freud will declare, "*arises instead of a memory trace.*" [20] Wordsworth says much the same thing when, in *The Prelude* he describes the delayed effect of epiphanies:

> the soul,
> Remembering how she felt, but what she felt
> Remembering not, returns an obscure sense
> Of possible sublimity, whereto
> With growing faculties she doth aspire,
> With faculties still growing, feeling still
> That whatsoever point they gain, they yet
> Have something to pursue.   (II. 315–22)

Association takes place not through the ideas or manifest content of an experience but through the affective tone, which can then be communicated to experiences with quite different manifest contents. Wordsworth makes clear what is implied by Coleridge's "Breeze"—that this affective tone is a feeling of infinity which connects the individual mind with the Great Mind and cannot be entirely accounted for by present, or even recollected, experience.

For Locke, we apprehend infinity as an idea of quantity—the result of our understanding that we can count indefinitely and can indefinitely add line segments to a given line segment. The idea is inapplicable, in the same way, to quality: "nobody ever thinks of infinite sweetness, or infinite whiteness." For Wordsworth, instead, we apprehend infinity as a feeling having to do with quality and organic wholeness—we cannot add to an organism as to a line segment. For Locke, the idea of infinity follows from our experience. For Wordsworth, we not only bring the feeling of infinity to later experiences through associated memory of earlier experiences, but the feeling somehow both rises out of and is anterior to even our primal experiences. This original feeling of infinity envelops all subsequent experiences, giving the sense that they all fold into the same self.

The ambiguity is suggested through the use of both memory and the fading-out of memory. Because the soul remembers not what but how she felt, we carry with us a feeling larger than anything we can remember of our primal experiences; and the soul grows, in this vale of soul-making, toward a feeling of wholeness that seems recollected though we cannot say from where. Locke refutes the theory of pre-existence by saying that if a man has no memory at all of his previous existence, if he has "a consciousness that *cannot* reach beyond this new state," then he is not the same person who led the previous existence since "personal identity"—here Locke is at one with Descartes and Hume—reaches "no further than consciousness reaches." [21] Wordsworth's answer is to blur the line between remembering and forgetting, to introduce a notion of unconscious memory.

By combining memory and association, Wordsworth sets the Lockean system in motion, infusing it with vitality, surrounding it with mystery, and carrying the mind back beyond conscious memory to the "dawn of being" where it is undistinguishable from its first sensation.

Memory becomes in Wordsworth the instrument of the associative or transforming power. It is because we see with stereoscopic vision—as Roger Shattuck puts it in speaking, in *Proust's Binoculars*, of Proust's use of memory—it is because partly we see the tree before us and partly we see all the trees we have ever seen that we see from outside and inside and have not sensations but experiences.[22] With the "impressions" before him, says Wordsworth in *The Excursion*,

> would he still compare
> All his remembrances, thoughts, shapes and forms;
> And, being still unsatisfied with aught
> Of dimmer character, he thence attained
> An active power to fasten images
> Upon his brain; and on their pictured lines
> Intensely brooded, even till they acquired
> The liveliness of dreams.   (I. 141–48)

That is the meaning of the crucial line in "Tintern Abbey": "The picture of the mind revives again." Wordsworth sees the present landscape through his mental picture of the landscape five years earlier. Because he discovers continuity in the disparate pictures through a principle of growth, he becomes aware of the pattern of his life—he binds his apparently disparate days together. He may be said to evolve his soul in becoming aware that his soul evolves. Included in the present experience is Wordsworth's sense that he will in future feed upon it, just as in the intervening five years he has fed on his last visit to this place. The experience includes, in other words, the consciousness of laying up treasure—not in heaven but in the memory.

It is the point of "Tintern Abbey," "Immortality Ode," and *The Prelude* that this spiritual storehouse of memory *is* our soul.

In one of the earliest written passages of *The Prelude*, one of those passages that must have helped Wordsworth find his theme, the poet thanks nature, in a tone of religious solemnity, for having from his "first dawn / Of childhood" intertwined for him "The passions that build up our human soul" (I.405–7).[23] The whole poem traces this building-up process, but the words *soul* and *imagination* are used interchangeably and Wordsworth speaks more often of the building up of imagination. That is because the poet or man of imagination is being used to epitomize a psychological process.

The poet, we are being told, is more spiritual than the rest of us because he *remembers* more than we do—though his remembering is often spoken of as a kind of forgetting: "By such forgetfulness the Soul becomes, / Words cannot say how beautiful" (*Recluse* I.297–98). The poet filters a present experience back through memory and the unconscious river in his veins—Wordsworth habitually speaks of thought as flowing in and out of the veins—to the external river that was his first sensation. That is why the poet can respond to the world and see it symbolically. That is why seeing is better than faith—it is revelation. "Nor did he believe,—he *saw*," says Wordsworth of the poetical Pedlar in *The Excursion* (I.232).

Wordsworth achieves his symbolic effects through a regression in the mind of the observer and in the object observed. He makes the human figure seem to evolve out of and pass back into the landscape—as in "The Thorn" and the Lucy poems, including "Lucy Gray." And he makes the landscape itself, in his most striking effects, seem to evolve out of water. In "Resolution and Independence," the old leech-gatherer is seen by a pool. He is so old that he seems to hang on to life by a thread;

and the observer understands this by carrying the old man's existence back to the line between the inanimate and the animate. The observer sees the old man as like a huge stone that seems almost alive because you cannot imagine how it got where it is, or as like a sea beast that at first seems part of the rock on which it lies. He is—if you assimilate this poem, as Geoffrey Hartman has so beautifully done, to the recurrent imagery of *The Prelude*—like something left behind by the inland sea that once covered the landscape.[24] Because the old man is seen through the eye of unconscious racial memory, he is transformed into an archetype of human endurance capable of alleviating the observer's distress.

In one of the epiphanies or "spots of time" of *The Prelude*, Book XII, Wordsworth recalls how as a boy he fled in terror from a low place, where a murderer had been hanged, to a hill where he saw a pool and a girl approaching it, bearing a pitcher on her head, her garments blowing in the wind. Through the conjunction with water and wind, the girl turns for the boy into an archetypal figure who transforms the unpleasant experience into a pleasant one; so that in later years, when Wordsworth was courting Mary Hutchinson, he often returned with her to this place, finding in "the naked pool and dreary crags" a "spirit of pleasure and youth's golden gleam" (264, 266). Here and elsewhere in Wordsworth—the same female figure with a basket on her head is remembered through water imagery in "The Two April Mornings"—water and memory, water as perhaps the counterpart of memory, turn the individual event into an archetype. And it is through archetypalization that turbulence and pain are turned into spiritual treasure, into the recognition of that surrounding aura of pleasurable tranquility which is soul. "How strange," says Wordsworth in speaking of soul-making,

> that all
> The terrors, pains, and early miseries,
> Regrets, vexations, lassitudes interfused
> Within my mind, should e'er have borne a part,

> And that a needful part in making up
> The calm existence that is mine when I
> Am worthy of myself!   (I. 344–50)

The transformation of pain into pleasure is achieved through externalization as well as archetypalization. The terrifying boyhood experience of Book XII passes into the landscape, making it a pleasant and spiritually rewarding place to return to. Wordsworth says that "The sands of Westmoreland, the creeks and bays / Of Cumbria's rocky limits" can tell of his boyhood epiphanies; and that, conversely,

> The scenes which were a witness of that joy
> Remained in their substantial lineaments
> Depicted on the brain,
>
> (I. 567–68, 599–601)

—that he remembered those early experiences as places.

The pleasurable tranquility that is soul exists outside us as well as inside; it exists in those places hallowed by significant experiences. Place, in Wordsworth, is the spatial projection of psyche, because it is the repository of memory.[25] We can understand the relation in Wordsworth between mind and nature, once we understand that Wordsworth evolves his soul or sense of identity as he identifies more and more such hallowed places. We can understand the relation in Wordsworth between the themes of memory and growing up, once we understand that for Wordsworth you advance in life by traveling back again to the beginning, by reassessing your life, by binding your days together anew.

The old Pedlar of *The Excursion* shows that he has bound his days together; for age has

> not tamed his eye; that, under brows
> Shaggy and grey, had meanings which it brought
> From years of youth; which, like a Being made
> Of many Beings, he had wondrous skill

> To blend with knowledge of the years to come,
> Human, or such as lie beyond the grave.
>
> (I.428–33)

The phrase, "like a Being made / Of many Beings," both states and solves the problem of identity. The Pedlar makes an identity of his many Beings, because he possesses his past and thereby his future too: he seems to transcend time.

In *The Prelude*'s climactic "spot of time," the epiphany on Mt. Snowdon in Book XIV, the whole world seems under moonlight to be returned to water. The mist below is a silent sea, the hills around static billows; and this illusory sea stretches out into the real Atlantic. The optical illusion is substantiated when, through a rift in the mist, Wordsworth hears the roar of inland waters. The movement from sight to sound is always in Wordsworth a movement backward to the beginning of things, to sensation and the sentiment of Being; later in Book XIV, Wordsworth says that he has in *The Prelude* traced the stream of imagination back from "light / And open day" to "the blind cavern whence is faintly heard / Its natal murmur" (195–97). Wordsworth understands, therefore, that he has had on Mt. Snowdon an epiphany of pure imagination or pure potentiality. He has beheld, in the moon over the waters, "the emblem of a mind" brooding over the abyss—waiting, like God in the opening passage of *Paradise Lost*, to bring forth the world. We have here an image of externalized self repeating God's act of creation. We have only to compare this image with the image Beckett draws from Descartes of a mind surrounded by void to realize that for Beckett the self reverses God's act of creation by withdrawing through an act of thought from nature, leaving it dead and mechanical. The self is thus imprisoned, cannot go forth to create the world because "of the impenetrability (isolation)," as Beckett puts it, "of all that is not 'cosa mentale.' " [26]

The Wordsworthian self goes forth, achieves transcendence, because it connects with the external world through sensation.

On Mt. Snowdon, Wordsworth transcends even the beginning
of things by moving back from sight to sound and then to an
inextricable blending of sight and sound:

> the emblem of a mind
> That feeds upon infinity, that broods
> Over the dark abyss, intent to hear
> Its voices issuing forth to silent light
> In one continuous stream.   (70–74)

"This," says Wordsworth, "is the very spirit" with which
"higher" or imaginative "minds" deal "With the whole compass
of the universe" (90–93). Confronted with sensory experience,
the poetical man travels back *that far* in order to perceive it
imaginatively. He re-creates the world in his imagination; [27] so
that he can return to the scene before him, imposing upon it
the picture in his mind and thus finding there the surrounding
aura of calm that is his soul.

Thus Wordsworth establishes, on naturalistic, psychological
grounds, a self as transcendent as the old Christian self created
and sustained by God. He establishes a new certainty about self
and the self's perceptions, after the dissolution of the old Christian certainty had been articulated by Locke and the other empiricists. Wordsworth's answer to Locke (which serves also as an
answer to the rationalist Descartes) is that the mind belongs to,
and therefore *actively* connects with, the nature it perceives. It
is this connection, sensed through what Wordsworth calls *joy*,
that gives us confidence in the reality of ourselves and the external world. For Wordsworth the self is memory and process—the
memory of all its phases and the process of interchange with the
external world. The movement of thought into sensation and
back again corresponds to the circular movement of self into nature and back again and to the circular movement from the sub-
jectively individual to the objectively archetypal phases of identity and back again. Each such circular movement, which could
be conceived as starting from outside as well as inside, is a new
creation, a new confirmation, of self—and is impelled by joy.

Wordsworth establishes the model of the modern self-creating, self-regarding identity, which draws its vital force from organic connection with nature. I shall now trace the running down of the Wordsworthian self through loss of joy—loss of the sense of vitality in nature and self, loss of confidence in the connection between nature and self. This loss of joy is a main theme in Arnold's poetry, where it is expressed through the elegiac tone that denotes depleted energy.

Part II
LOSS OF SELF

Chapter 2
ARNOLD:
WANING ENERGY

Matthew Arnold was not nearly so good a poet as his two great contemporaries, Tennyson and Browning. But he was a finer critic than they, not only of literature but of his time. He understood and felt the way things were tending, and the understanding shows up even better in his poetry than in his prose. For one thing, Arnold held a regular job; and it was, significantly, a bureaucratic job. As Inspector of Schools, he fought for increased state control of education; politically he favored stronger government. In these ways, as well as in a certain air in his poetry of the fatigue that comes of self-doubt, Arnold emerges as an urban intellectual in the modern sense.

The thing Arnold as a poet can give us that the romanticists cannot, and that even Tennyson and Browning cannot, is a convincing rendition of modern urban numbness and alienation. Neither the numbness Coleridge complains of nor Tennyson's melancholy has anything to do with the plight of clerks in offices, who give "Their lives to some unmeaning taskwork,"

> And as, year after year,
> Fresh products of their barren labour fall
> From their tired hands, and rest
> Never yet comes more near,
> Gloom settles slowly down over their breast.
>   ("A Summer Night")

Nor has anyone in English before Arnold rendered the mental atmosphere of the modern intellectual—his sense of psychological pathos:

> But often, in the world's most crowded streets,
> But often, in the din of strife,
> There rises an unspeakable desire
> After the knowledge of our buried life—
>   ("The Buried Life")

and historical pathos: "Wandering between two worlds, one dead, / The other powerless to be born" ("Stanzas from the Grande Chartreuse").[1]

Arnold is the first Victorian poet to deal with the modern problem of loss of self, and it is clear from what Arnold says on the subject that the self lost is the Wordsworthian or romantic self. For the romanticists, and for a Victorian poet so preoccupied with character as Browning, wars within the self are our glory—a sign of richness in the interior life. But for Arnold the problem is that the interior life is thin, that it is all too often, when we want to fall back upon it in the romantic manner, simply not there. My self-analysis, he wrote to Clough, is unlike that of "Werter, René, and such like [for] none of them analyse the modern situation in its true *blankness* and *barrenness*, and *unpoetrylessness*."[2]

Among the Victorians, it is Arnold who gives us the clearest idea of what the personality ought to be like and of how far it falls short due to the unprecedented conditions of the nineteenth century. When Browning, in his best dramatic monologues, portrays the richness of personality in Renaissance Italy, he seems to see the Renaissance as leading to the tremendous explosion of energy in Victorian England. And we have only to read the historians (G. M. Young, for example, on the personal exuberance of the early Victorians),[3] or the novelists of the time, to realize that Browning was right about what he saw around him. But with hindsight we have to admit that Arnold saw what was coming, at least in literature. For English literature has, since Arnold's time, increasingly lamented the loss of vitality and an assured sense of self.

More clearly than Browning and Tennyson, Arnold was conscious of living in a postromantic era. He had this awareness because he understood the main stream of nineteenth-century literature. He understood, for one thing, the crucial importance of Wordsworth. Arnold, who spent his boyhood summers in the Lake District and knew the old poet, can, as critics have long noted, be considered Wordsworth's heir *manqué* in that he takes off in so many poems ("To a Gipsy Child," "Resignation") from a Wordsworthian situation in order to state his own divergence from it.[4] Yet much that is positive in Arnold's vision of life and personality comes from Wordsworth; the problem of identity is always stated in Wordsworthian terms—as a problem of self-consciousness leading to loss of feeling—even if Wordsworth's solution is rejected as no longer possible. Arnold understood that Wordsworth was the figure to be wrestled with, because Wordsworth had offered the most powerful solution to the problems left by the dissolution of the Christian idea of soul.

In the "Memorial Verses" for Wordsworth, one of his finest poems and finest pieces of criticism, Arnold shows what Wordsworth's answer is. Byron offered an example of courage to defy our modern misery; Goethe taught us to recognize and endure it, counseling art as the only solace. But Wordsworth transformed us inside; he caused us to be born anew by leading us back to nature and helping us to find in our roots there a new source of vitality and spirituality, by showing us how to start again from the beginning:

> He found us when the age had bound
> Our souls in its benumbing round;
> He spoke, and loosed our heart in tears.
> He laid us as we lay at birth
> On the cool flowery lap of earth,
>
> . . .
>
> Our youth returned; for there was shed
> On spirits that had long been dead,
> Spirits dried up and closely furled,
> The freshness of the early world.

Now that Wordsworth is dead, his answer seems the most elusive: "But who, ah! who, will make us feel?" Byron, too, made us feel. Why is it only Wordsworth's power to make us feel that is irrecoverable? Byron was a spectacle: we felt *him*. But Wordsworth accomplished something more magical. He gave us back our own identities; he went down like Orpheus among the walking dead and brought them back to life.

The problem of the modern or iron age is waning energy; this can be seen when Goethe, as "Physician of the iron age," looks down upon "The turmoil of expiring life." The theme of expiring life continues through the covert imagery of hell in Arnold's allusion, when praising Goethe, to Virgil's praise of Lucretius: "Happy is he who has been able to know the causes of things, and has trod under his feet all fears and inexorable fate and the din of greedy Acheron" (*Georgics* ii, 490–92). Goethe looked down with Olympian comprehension upon the hell of modern life, but Wordsworth sang among the dead:

> And Wordsworth!—Ah, pale ghosts, rejoice!
> For never has such soothing voice
> Been to your shadowy world conveyed,
> Since erst, at morn, some wandering shade
> Heard the clear song of Orpheus come
> Through Hades, and the mournful gloom.

Arnold anticipates the theme of the walking dead, showing how Wordsworth staved off for us that modern fate. But it is unlikely that so primitive a power as Wordsworth's, having been miraculously reborn once, can be reborn again in "Europe's latter hour."

The movement that we now call romanticism (Arnold never used the term) was in Arnold's view a miraculous rebirth, an attempt to provide a substitute for Christianity. But now that both faiths have been exploded, we cannot see what is to follow. Therefore we wander, as Arnold tells us in "Grande Chartreuse," his finest poem on the modern historical situation, "between two worlds, one dead, / The other powerless to be born." Arnold dramatizes the modern historical situation by comparing his own meditation over the Carthusian monastery to that of a Greek of Greece's latter hour who, having lost faith in the Greek gods, stands before the ruined monument of another lost religion, "some fallen Runic stone," feeling "pity and mournful awe"—"For both were faiths, and both are gone."

The monks' religion seems to Arnold as alien as the northern religion to the Greek. For Arnold was educated in a liberal tradition of rationalism and romanticism that estranged him from Christianity. His situation, however, is complex. As a romanticist, he feels kinship with the monks; for he feels like them the sadness of life, and, unlike those who are only rationalists, he grieves for the loss of faith and can appreciate the beauty of the monks' observances. Just as the world tells the monks: "your faith is now / But a dead time's exploded dream;" so "sciolists," those who are arrogant in their rationalism, tell the poet his melancholy "Is a past mode, an outworn theme." Monks and poets have this in common, that they represent an enduring elite of sensibility. But it is particularly in this age, when both are under attack, that the poet, who wanders between two worlds, "With nowhere yet to rest my head," feels that to protect his sensibility he must like the monks seek seclusion—the ivory tower:

> Their faith, my tears, the world deride—
> I come to shed them at your side.

Oh, hide me in your gloom profound,
Ye solemn seats of holy pain!
Take me, cowled forms, and fence me round,
Til I possess my soul again.

Romantic melancholy may be outdated, but the pain of life remains. The pseudo-scientific sciolists have taken away "the nobleness of grief," leaving us "the fret alone," the anxiety. It is here that Arnold strikes the elaborate posture—a posture to be characteristic of aestheticism—with which he concludes the poem. "If you cannot," he says to the sciolists,

give us ease—
Last of the race of them who grieve,
Here leave us to die out with these
Last of the people who believe!

We poets, we romanticists—Arnold in this poem equates the two—are, like the monks, obsolete men who would rather die with the old order than be reborn with the new. We prefer to be "Silent—the best are silent now."

This line is echoed by Yeats's "The best lack all conviction," in "The Second Coming." Yeats breaks through Arnold's impasse by declaring that the new era must be born through miracle, a new revelation; whereas Arnold in his prose says the new era must be brought into being through a great critical effort. "Grande Chartreuse" is in its main thrust negative or critical; for Arnold turns in the end on the romantic melancholy he has been defending. He admits that nothing came of "all the noise / And outcry" of the romantic poets. They have bequeathed us only their pangs; and we lack the energy and assured sense of self to dramatize the pangs as did Byron, who paraded through Europe "The pageant of his bleeding heart."

In fact Arnold does dramatize his pangs according to a new posture conspicuous in aesthetic and decadent poetry and in such early-twentieth-century poems as Eliot's "Prufrock," "Gerontion," *The Waste Land*. This is the self-pitying posture of depleted energy, which covertly admires depleted energy as a mark of sensibility while ostensibly disapproving of it. We men of sensibility are, says Arnold in the beautiful extended simile that concludes "Grande Chartreuse," like cloistered children, "Forgotten in a forest-glade," who glimpse through the trees passing soldiers with banners calling us to action, and hear from another direction hunting horns calling us to pleasure. We reject both action and pleasure, because the calls come "too late," because we are—and the cry is particularly affecting since these are paradoxically not old men but children—obsolete. Already conditioned for a forgotten way of life, a cloistered life of reverie and prayer, "How should we grow in other ground? / How can we flower in foreign air?" Since the foreign air is modernity, the contrast in the last two lines between men of action and recluses becomes also the historical contrast between modern men and men whose affinities are with an earlier age: "—Pass, banners, pass, and bugles, cease; / And leave our desert to its peace!"

"Desert" is surprising since the children are cloistered in a forest; and indeed "forest" was the word in the original published version. By changing to "desert," Arnold accomplished a complex criticism of romantic melancholy. Romantic melancholy is sterile, he implies, it locates us in a spiritual waste land; but the desert is all we are capable of desiring. We do not want fertility ("April," as Eliot will say, "is the cruellest month"), we do not want real life because something has happened to real life that renders it unpalatable to modern sensitive intellectuals. In other words, we desire something we cannot approve of but which our historical situation and the psychological deficiency engendered by it make us desire. The historical irony is powerfully dramatized through the transposition into children of feelings appropriate to old age. Having been born too late, the children are alienated from their own childhood and from old age; they have taken upon themselves the old age of a culture to which as children they do not belong. Their sensitivity, appropriate to children, makes them all the more aware of the anomaly.

There is at work in all this historical awareness, this trick of understanding and undercutting all positions as historical phenomena, a critical consciousness that paralyzes action and creates a problem of identity. For the person endowed with such a critical consciousness cannot foreclose possibilities by being one thing to the exclusion of another. This historically engendered psychological problem is the main subject of Arnold's poetry. Arnold deals with the peculiarly modern personality that, caught between two or more worlds without feeling at home in any, must be perpetually choosing among cultures and therefore perpetually living in the intellect. Such a person is beset by fatigue—the fatigue that characterizes Arnold's poetry and Eliot's—because he can never find repose in impulse or tradition.

This historical and psychological dilemma is most famously expressed in "The Scholar-Gipsy" which, like "Grande Chartreuse" and *Empedocles,* dramatizes the conflict in Arnold between modern intellect and premodern sensibility. "The Scholar-Gipsy" tells the story of a seventeenth-century Oxford scholar who joins the gipsies not because he is tired of the intellectual life, but because he is poor and "tired of knocking at preferment's door." It is Arnold who is tired of dissociated intellectualizing and who therefore gives Glanvill's story a modern psychological and historical significance. He contrasts the scholar's traditional Unity of Being after he has joined the gipsies, joined intellect and impulse, with our modern head-centered identity cut off from impulse so always making conscious choices. "Thou hadst," he says to the scholar-gipsy, "*one* aim, *one* business, *one* desire"; whereas we modern men have "tired upon a thousand schemes our wit." By joining the gipsies and learning their magic lore, the scholar preserved from change those youthful powers that become a metaphor for the early era to which he belonged:

> For early didst thou leave the world, with powers
> Fresh, undiverted to the world without,
> Firm to their mark, not spent on other things;
> Free from the sick fatigue, the languid doubt,
> Which much to have tried, in much been baffled, brings.

In the climactic stanza Arnold makes explicit the historical contrast to be drawn from the metaphor of youthful freshness:

> O born in days when wits were fresh and clear,
> And life ran gaily as the sparkling Thames;
> Before this strange disease of modern life,
> With its sick hurry, its divided aims,
> Its heads o'ertaxed, its palsied hearts, was rife—
> Fly hence, our contact fear!

"The Scholar-Gipsy" is a pastoral poem in which the countryside stands for the past and for the protected area in which the wandering scholar-gipsy can maintain his immortality as a legendary figure. His is a fruitful wandering between the worlds of intellect and emotion because he combines both. With Unity of Being he has become a Wordsworthian archetypal Wanderer, a genius of the landscape intermittently glimpsed by those who at rare epiphanic moments have attained Unity of Being. "In seeking the Scholar-Gipsy" Arnold, as A. Dwight Culler puts it, "seeks himself as poet" [5]—seeks the phase of identity which would make him a poet. Fly our contact, says Arnold to the scholar-gipsy, because you could not maintain that phase of identity in an era afflicted by self-consciousness, in which "each half-lives a hundred different lives."

This poem, too, ends with a beautiful extended simile. "Fly our greetings," says Arnold, as "some grave Tyrian trader," a former master of Mediterranean trade, would upon the approach of a "merry Grecian coaster" sail to the end of the known world, to Iberia, to avoid the new men, the "young light-hearted masters of the waves." The joyous scholar-gipsy corresponds to grave Tyrians while perplexed worn-out modern men correspond to light-hearted Greeks. The transposition of temperaments, like the transposition in "Grande Chartreuse" between childhood and old age, dramatizes the irony of the nineteenth-century situation where it is the inheritors who, contrary to the Greek inheritors, seem old and nontriumphant.[6] Arnold initiates a symbolical characterization, intensified by Eliot and Beckett, according to which modern men are represented as old to suggest diminished identity and the old age of an era.

The joyous Greeks could stand well enough for modern men of *action*; however Arnold is saying that the imaginative scholar-gipsy must necessarily feel alien to *insensitive* modern men of action, but must also fly the "feverish contact" of *sensitive* modern men who carry the disease of self-consciousness. He must combine his intellect with the sensibility of primitives to achieve Unity of Being. Hence he has flown to the gipsies as the Tyrians flee to the "dark Iberians" ("shy traffickers" who recall the shy children of "Grande Chartreuse"). Once again Arnold is counseling, as the refuge against modern conditions, that ivory tower in which, if we include primitive and Bohemian cloisters, so much recent literary history has transpired.

What comes most powerfully through Arnold's treatment of the modern problem of identity is his poignant awareness of what a properly constituted personality ought to be. Arnold portrays the modern personality with the authority of first-hand knowledge, but the pathos comes from the implied portrait of what the modern personality is not. The negative portrait is vivid, though accomplished through such comparisons as: "O born in days when wits were fresh and clear, / And life ran gaily as the sparkling Thames"—where nature and the past combine to make a model for personality. Arnold's main model for personality is nature. "One lesson, Nature, let me learn of thee," he says in an early sonnet ("Quiet Work"), the lesson "Of toil unsevered from tranquillity! / Of labour . . . accomplished in repose."

The antithesis of exertion and repose derives from Wordsworth, who in *The Prelude* sees identity-making as a process of composing and transforming disparate and turbulent elements into an all-encompassing tranquility: "The calm existence that is mine" (I. 349).

Far more than Wordsworth, Arnold sees identity-making as a *problem* which he examines in detail. "Weary of myself, and sick of asking / What I am, and what I ought to be," the speaker of "Self-Dependence" looks to sea and stars as models of personal tranquility. " 'Calm me, ah, compose me,' " he cries to them. And he hears through the night air the answer: " 'Wouldst thou *be* as these are? *Live* as they.' " For

> "with joy the stars perform their shining,
> And the sea its long moon-silver'd roll;
> For self-poised they live, nor pine with noting
> All the fever of some differing soul."

The first two lines are Wordsworthian, in that unconsciousness is the means and joy the sign of proper function. But the last two lines are distinctive of Arnold; for he sees as a modern problem the excessively conscious man of critical intellect who cannot *be* one thing to the exclusion of another.

"The disease of the present age," says Arnold in a note written in the Yale manuscript of this poem, "is divorce from self." [7] And in a letter to his friend Clough—who often exemplified for Arnold the side of himself he wanted to correct—Arnold wrote: "You ask me in what I think . . . you going wrong: in this: that you . . . could never finally, as it seemed—'resolve to be thyself'—but were looking for this or that experience, and doubting whether you ought not to adopt this or that mode of being." [8] " 'Resolve to be thyself' " is the moral of "Self-Dependence." But to resolve is to have half-lost the battle, since sea and stars did not have to *choose* to be themselves.

Wordsworth, too, contrasts consciousness and unconsciousness. But in Wordsworth consciousness can through communion with nature achieve a state of being equivalent to that of unconsciousness. In his sonnet "It is a Beauteous Evening," Wordsworth contrasts his own apprehension of spirit in nature with his little daughter's lack of conscious appreciation, but realizes that the child has always the unconscious relation with God that he has only in moments of heightened consciousness. Arnold, instead, though he uses nature as metaphor for a perfect state of being, learned from Spinoza that nature's case is not relevant to man's. If in the early sonnet "Quiet Work," he asks to learn a lesson of nature, he casts scorn, in the still earlier sonnet "In Harmony with Nature," on that Wordsworthian phrase. "Nature and man can never be fast friends," he says. "Man hath all which Nature hath, but more, / And in that *more* [in culture] lie all his hopes of good." In a still earlier poem, "To a Gipsy Child by the Seashore," Arnold takes off from Wordsworth's "Immortality Ode," to see in the sad eyes of a gipsy child—who ought as gipsy and child to have been in harmony with nature—forgetfulness of prenatal happiness not because the child has been wooed away by nature's gentle charm, but because he has been shocked by the pain of life. In "Religious Isolation," Arnold finally declares the discontinuity of man and nature: "Live by thy light, and earth will live by hers!"

These three poems appear in Arnold's first volume, *The Strayed Reveller* of 1849, where the dialogue with Wordsworth begins. Wordsworth achieved his solution by ignoring—as Arnold says in *"Obermann,"* written though not published that same year—"half of human fate," the tragic half. It is the pain of life that separates us from nature—the pain that comes of consciousness and pity, pity that is always a projection of self-pity. "I never saw a wild thing / sorry for itself," says Lawrence in the little poem "Self-Pity" that clarifies Arnold's meaning. It is the pain deriving from self-consciousness that the poet of "The Strayed Reveller" must overcome in order to achieve a godlike vision analogous to nature's calm.

Already in this volume Arnold advances, as an alternative to a solution based on nature, a solution based on art and culture. Thus Sophocles, the most tragic of poets, had as the finest flower of Greek culture an "even-balanced soul" that could absorb the utmost pain into a vision analogous to nature's calm, a vision that "saw life steadily, and saw it whole." This sonnet, "To a Friend," deals with poets and philosophers (the other two are Homer and Epictetus) who make Unity of Being a cultural achievement. Greek culture produced a man like Sophocles, whom "Business could not make dull, nor passion wild," but our culture offers unacceptable alternatives—either the wild-eyed romantic alienated from society or the antlike collective man (the "madman or slave" of "A Summer Night"). In the sonnet "Written in Butler's Sermons," however, Arnold sees Unity of Being as a natural endowment. Bishop Butler analyzes the human personality into separate faculties; whereas underneath, defying analysis, lies the single source of our identity:

> Deep and broad, where none may see,
> Spring the foundations of that shadowy throne
> Where man's one nature, queen-like, sits alone,
> Centred in a majestic unity.

The various aspects of personality are like "sister-islands" that show separate surfaces while "Linking their coral arms under the sea." This is another recurring theme—that our identity lies in an unconscious life symbolized by water.

Arnold plays a dialectic between these opposite ideas—that Unity of Being derives from the highest culture and that it is original, natural, unconscious. He resolves the contradiction with the synthesizing idea that culture helps us recapture through the highest consciousness our original and unconscious Unity of Being. This synthesis, central to German romanticism,[9] is also, more than Arnold himself realized, Wordsworthian; for nature is in Wordsworth the starting-point for a complete theory of society and culture. (Note, for example, the relation of nature with language, literature, mathematics in Books V and VI of *The Prelude*, with communal memory in "The Brothers," with communal memory, sorrow and religion in *The White Doe of Rylstone*.) The difference between Arnold and the romanticists is that in Arnold consciousness can hardly achieve the goal it sets for itself. When the speaker of "Self-Dependence" is told that if he would *be* as the sea and stars he must *live* as they, the model seems hardly relevant to the self-conscious person who is "sick of asking / What I am, and what I ought to be." And certainly the kind of culture that might bring so morbid a consciousness to a state analogous to that of sea and stars would have to be radically discontinuous with nature.

"Self-Dependence" belongs, however, to the *Empedocles* volume of 1852, the volume in which Arnold explores the modern identity problem with the most concentration and pessimism. In the earlier volume, *The Strayed Reveller*, he is somewhat more optimistic about the possibility of achieving a solution through art. The youthful poet of the title poem wanders into Circe's palace after having participated in a Dionysian rout; he drains a bowl of Circe's wine. In answer to Ulysses who associates him with Apollonian poetry about gods and heroes, the youth distinguishes between the Apollonian view possible to gods, who survey the human spectacle with a detachment that gives them pleasure, and that possible to poets who share the pain of the human beings they behold:

> such a price
> The Gods exact for song:
> To become what we sing.

Because he is intoxicated, the youth is, like the gods, released from pity; but the release is temporary and accomplished at the price of the outward view—he sees only "eddying forms, / Sweep through my soul!"

The gods' vision is, like nature's calm, an unattainable

model. The wholeness of vision Arnold counsels goes with a wholeness that requires a certain hardness of personality. The personal defects Arnold deals with are not those of antique literature—the excessive passion or pride that causes sin; they are the modern defects that stem from insecure identity. Thus in a poem named at one point "Desire," a monk, in a distinctively modern prayer that the ancients would hardly have understood, prays for the desire that can save us from "That torpor deep / Wherein we lie asleep," and "From that fierce anguish / Wherein," curiously enough, "we languish." Such energy-draining anguish we would call anxiety or depression. "The soul" in this poem, as J. Hillis Miller puts it, is "an empty desire," desiring the desire that would prove its substantiality.[10] Desire for the ancients was to be curbed not encouraged, and they would hardly have understood how desire could save us "From tears that bring no healing, / From wild and weak complaining," and "From doubt, where all is double." [11] These are all symptoms of dissolution; desire is the single impulse or energy—what Freud was to call libido—that binds together an identity. The lack of single impulse seems to Arnold a specifically modern weakness.

Another modern weakness is pity—understood as an excess of humanitarian or empathic projectiveness, an unwillingness to rest secure in your own identity and let the other man rest secure in his. In "The Sick King in Bokhara," we are surprised to learn that the King is wrong to grieve so intensely for the criminal whom he has had, by the criminal's own demand, to condemn to death. The Grand Vizier is right in saying that a King could not bear the burden of his office "If he for strangers pained his heart" as for parents, wife, child, for whom pain "*must* be borne." "But other loads than this his own / One man is not well made to bear." The world is so full of suffering that if we do not place some limit on empathy, we can hardly live. In Arnold's Persian source, the King's pity is treated as a virtue.[12] It is only in the context of modern identity problems, problems created by the conflict between conscious and unconscious motivation, that pity can be seen—the way it is seen in Blake, Nietzsche, Lawrence—as unconsciously destructive of its object and its subject, as a morbid condition that threatens its subject's Unity of Being.

The word "sick" in the title suggests that the King's sensibility, even though the story takes place in an unchanging Persia, is to be understood as modern European, specifically romantic. The King is "sick" because he cannot accept the fact that reality is unamenable to human wishes: "I am sick," because "what I would, I cannot do." "But what I can do," he continues, "that I will." What he can do is humanize reality through art. He memorializes and monumentalizes the executed criminal by burying him in his own "fretted brick-work tomb." The poem's point is that the King must play his role, even as the criminal insisted on fulfilling his role by demanding punishment. The role that prevented the King from saving the criminal's life now glorifies his death. Romanticism had carried so far the individualizing projectiveness that for the sake of experience dons and casts off roles at will, that postromantic literature has the task of teaching impersonality, the reconciliation of the sense of self with the roles tradition and society impose.

Romanticism itself gave birth to the ideals of both personality and impersonality. It was German romanticism that taught the ideal of impersonality through its worship of Greece and Greek art as the antidote to modern subjectivity. For Winckelmann and Goethe, sculpture was the representative art of Greece; and they drew from the figures of Greek sculpture, from their impassivity, serenity and generality of expression, a model for art and personality. It was Pater who in *Studies in the History of the Renaissance* (1873) introduced Winckelmann's sculpturesque aesthetic into England; and we can understand through Pater that Greek sculpture seemed to romanticists remarkable because the figures were not individualized and because the interior life, whatever had to be expressed, was objectified in the form. Since expression lay not in the face but in bodily form, we can see here a model for unified identity, with no division between inner and outer, self and body. The postromantic taste for the impassive static forms of Greek sculpture led to Rilke's use of Rodin's sculpture as a model for identity and art; to Yeats's taste for Byzantine mosaics and masked actors; and to Lawrence's description of his style, after the naturalistic *Sons and Lovers*, as having "a bit of stillness, like the wide, still, unseeing eyes of a Venus of Melos. . . . There is something in the Greek sculpture that my soul is hungry for—something of the eternal stillness that lies under all movement." [13] The extension of interest in our own time beyond classical sculpture to the archaic sculpture of Greece and other "primitive" cultures carries even farther the anomalous taste, in an age that grows ever more psychologically minded, for expressionless figures that give no sign of an interior life.

Although Arnold showed little interest in the visual arts, he undoubtedly knew about Winckelmann, if not directly then through his reading of Goethe and of Schelling's oration "Concerning the Relation of the Plastic Arts to Nature"—the essay in which Schelling explains that Winckelmann's dictum, "the loftiest beauty is without character," means that the loftiest beauty has archetypal "character": the sculptor "fashions the individual into a world of its own, a genus, an eternal prototype." [14] Arnold employs Winckelmann's aesthetic in his use, in the Preface to *Poems* (1853), of Goethe's word *Architectonicè* to denote the poet's power of assimilating to an all-encompassing form the poem's individual thoughts, images, verbal felicities. This assorts with Arnold's description, in *On Translating Homer*, of Homer's style as assimilating plain thoughts and diction to the noble generality of "the grand style." *Architectonicè* and "the grand style" are Arnold's equivalent to the concept of *Allgemeinheit*, of "breadth, generality, universality," that Pater will so lovingly borrow from Winckelmann to describe the genius of Greek sculpture. [15]

In "Resignation: To Fausta," Arnold offers as solution to life's sorrows assimilation to just such generality—found this time in nature rather than art. Since "Resignation" is modeled on and takes off from "Tintern Abbey," it makes clearer than any other poem in *The Strayed Reveller* Arnold's break with Wordsworth's ideas about nature and the organic connection between nature and human identity. The poet and his sister Jane, here called Fausta, have returned to a place in the Lake District where ten years earlier they and a family group had a Wordsworthian experience of pure joy in nature. Now the two are alone; and the unchanged scene suggests to the poet, despite his sister's protestations to the contrary, how much they have changed. The poem does not tell us what we know from biographical sources, that Jane's fiancé has broken off their engagement and that their father has died. The implied question is what consolation can nature offer.

Only the poet can draw nature's lesson; for only he has the mixture of involvement and detachment necessary to perceive its general laws. The gipsies (suggested by Wordsworth's "vagrant dwellers in the houseless woods") are too immersed in nature, too absorbed by problems of survival, to be aware of nature. Like Wordsworth, Arnold sees into "the life of things," into what he calls "the general life," but he sees with "tears"; for the lesson he draws from nature differs from Wordsworth's in "Tintern Abbey." Arnold's poet sees

> That general life, which does not cease,
> Whose secret is not joy, but peace;
> That life, whose dumb wish is not missed
> If birth proceeds, if things subsist;
> The life of plants, and stones, and rain,
> The life he craves—if not in vain
> Fate gave, what chance shall not control,
> His sad lucidity of soul.

It is difficult to connect "The life he craves" with the "if" clause that follows; but Arnold seems to be saying that the poet should know, if he has not in vain been given his sad lucidity, that he

cannot share nature's life, that he must "admire uncravingly"
the phenomenal world.

Arnold calls his sister Fausta because she still believes in
romantic or Faustian experience, in the possibility of fulfillment
within the natural world. He tells her you do not need to learn
"through experience" what "insight can discern"—that nature's
"Far regions of eternal change" devalue human desires; so that
the solution to personal sorrow is to resign one's self to natural
process, to "Draw homeward to the general life" by losing the
self and its desires. If the poet of "Resignation," says Lionel
Trilling, "identifies himself with the life of others, it is not
to increase his sense of selfhood but rather to lose it. Unlike
Keats and certainly unlike Byron, like the later Goethe or
Wordsworth, the chief characteristic of the Poet of 'Resignation,' is that he lives without *personal* feeling or desire." [16] It is
tempting to connect "Resignation" with the Wordsworth who
began to develop a more tragic view of nature in "Resolution
and Independence" and "Elegiac Stanzas." But Wordsworth
never wanted to *lose* the self; nor did he ever cease to believe in
the organic connection between nature and personal identity.
He moved toward impersonality, as I have shown, through archetypalizations that evolve from unconsciousness and nature in
an unbroken continuum.

Spinoza, Goethe, Senancour, the *Bhagavad Gita*, were influences that separated Arnold from Wordsworth. But an even
sharper separation comes from what in this poem seems a geo-
logical perspective. When Arnold speaks of the world as "neutral space," when he speaks of "mute turf," "lonely sky" and
"strange-scrawled-rocks," rocks with glacial striations, he is describing a god-abandoned nature that gives no support to personal identity. And when he carefully says that were he to *lend*
a voice to a mute and meaningless nature the voice would teach
us "to bear rather than rejoice," the lesson he draws, with its
emphasis on endurance and survival, anticipates, as does Tennyson in *In Memoriam*, a Darwinian view of nature.

The poem ends on a note of haunting ambiguity. Is "The

something that infects the world" (the obverse of Wordsworth's "spirit" rolling "through all things") the necessity that thwarts desire, or is it desire? Arnold is saying that the world remains tragic, with tragedy's inextricable tangle of fate and will, even if we, "In action's dizzying eddy whirled," forget that it is so. The "sad lucidity" of Arnold's poet comprehends the tragic half of life that, according to Arnold, Wordsworth ignored. If the lucidity is sadder than that of Sophocles in Arnold's sonnet, it is because the tragic is comprehended here and in all Arnold's best poems as infection or sickness, and because "Resignation" deals with man versus nature without the humanizing mediation of culture.

During the years he was composing the volumes of 1849 and 1852, Arnold lived through what we might call an identity crisis if we are willing to extend the term beyond Erik Erikson's definition of it as a crisis of late adolescence. The term seems justified because Arnold made during these years a complex of fundamental choices that determined the kind of person he was to be. The crisis can be considered to have begun with the death of Arnold's father in 1842, when Matthew was nineteen, and to have mainly resolved itself when at thirty he published and then withdrew from circulation *Empedocles on Etna, and Other Poems.*

These are the years during which Arnold wrestled spiritually with Clough; the two were so intimate that Clough at times represented for Arnold the moralizing tendency they had both learned from Arnold's father (Clough's mentor at Rugby) and that Arnold was trying to expunge from himself by playing the aesthete and dandy. In 1846 or '47 Arnold first read the book that was crucially involved in his identity crisis—Senancour's novel *Obermann*, whose hero expresses amidst gorgeous Swiss settings his alienation from nature and society and his nihilistic inertness in a world without values. The Swiss setting of *Obermann* connects with the Swiss setting of the affair with "Marguerite," the French girl whom, according to the poems, Arnold loved during two brief Swiss vacations in 1848–49. The Swiss novel and the Swiss love affair (even if the account of it is partly fictitious) figured as radically liberating experiences. Switzerland stood in Arnold's psychic life for subjectivity, sensuality, poetry as against English objective moralizing responsibility.

We can trace through the best of the Marguerite poems a Lawrencean story about the failure of modern love. According to the poems, "Marguerite" showed Arnold the way to an emotional freedom not sanctioned by his Victorian background. Her too abundant experience of love is, in "Parting," offered as the reason he gave her up: "But a sea rolls between us— / Our different past!" He feels guilty about the parting, praising her loving heart as superior to his own reserve. The Marguerite poems do not tell a consistent story; in "Isolation: To Marguerite," it is she who with her self-sufficiency "lov'st no more." But in the most beautiful of the Marguerite poems, "To Marguerite— Continued," he generalizes his own reserve into the human condition: "Yes! in the sea of life enisled, / . . . We mortal millions live *alone*." We are islands who at rare privileged moments remember we were once "Parts of a single continent." How did we become so isolated?

> Who ordered, that their longing's fire
> Should be, as soon as kindled, cooled?
> Who renders vain their deep desire?—
> A God, a God their severance ruled!
> And bade betwixt their shores to be
> The unplumbed, salt, estranging sea.

Despite the rhetorical flourish of "A God, a God," Arnold is really talking about the locked-up ego that prevents men and women from loving. In this affair, the locked-up ego is clearly male.

In "A Farewell," Arnold attributes the failure of the affair to his own lack of male force, of an assured identity. Women seek in their lovers "Stern strength, and promise of control / . . . a soul which never sways"; and "I too," he admits, "have longed for trenchant force, / And will like a dividing spear." In some remarkably vacuous stanzas, he goes on to hope that in the next life, when we "Shall see ourselves, and learn at last / Our true affinities of soul," women will not mistake "hardness" for "force," will value "gentleness"; but the next life will be asexual, he will address Marguerite as "sister." Although these stanzas point forward and up rather than backward and down, they are trying to say the same thing as the lines in "To Marguerite—Continued" about islands that recall their forgotten union. In both poems Arnold connects the problem of love with the problem of identity, saying we can meet in love only through our true selves. This is the point of "The Buried Life," one of Arnold's most powerful poems, which locates the true self in the unconscious. Related to the Marguerite series, "The Buried Life" says we can gain access to our true, our buried, self only through love, and implies that love is possible only at the unconscious phase of identity.

Arnold's parting from "Marguerite" apparently led to the courtship of a proper English girl and to the need, if he was to marry her, to take in 1851 a steady job as Inspector of Schools. By the time *Empedocles on Etna, and Other Poems* appeared in October 1852, Arnold had already made the choices that were to lead away from poetry toward criticism, away from the character of melancholy, languid young exile from an uncongenial age to the maturely urbane, energetic public figure who debated the major questions of the day. Only after the appearance of the 1852 volume did Arnold seem to realize that he had settled his identity crisis; he soon withdrew the volume from circulation, and when in the following year he republished his poems, he dropped from the volume just the poem *Empedocles* in which he brings his identity crisis to a conclusion opposite to the one he in fact adopted. For Empedocles commits suicide rather than yield the lonely fidelity to self that Arnold in fact renounced when he renounced the complex of Switzerland, "Marguerite," Obermann.

Arnold also in the 1852 volume says farewell, in "Stanzas in Memory of the Author of *Obermann*," to Obermann's alienated stance: "I in the world must live," he announces. He will not, however, betray Obermann's lonely purity; for he will use as model the heavenly band Obermann has joined, "The Children of the Second Birth," from whom Obermann has learned that one can combine meditation with action, can remain "Unspotted by the world." [17] This synthesis, which recalls Blake's recovered Innocence and points toward the Christian way Eliot will evolve for being in the world but not of it, reappears in Arnold's poetry as a model of realized identity. But the synthesis did not after all work for Arnold; for he had to abandon one thing for another—subjectivity for objectivity, poetry for criticism. In the Preface to his next volume, the 1853 *Poems* from which he dropped *Empedocles*, Arnold repudiated not only his own best poetry, but as it turned out his own career as poet, though he went on *planning* to make poetry his main occupation. Since in order to resolve his identity crisis Arnold had to repudiate the introspective youth who wrote his poetry, he had in effect to cease being a poet.

For the truth is that not only Arnold's best but most of his poetry was written during 1842–52, the years of his identity crisis, and that once he resolved the crisis he lost his most fruitful subject matter and his creativity. The volumes after 1852 are mainly reprints of the first two volumes. The new departures are the epics, *Sohrab and Rustum* (1853) and *Balder Dead* (1854), and the tragedy *Merope* (1857)—all imitations of classical forms and more or less academic performances. Of the famous melancholy poems that appeared after 1852, "The Scholar-Gipsy" (1853) had been planned by 1848 and is based on a story known to Arnold in 1845, a story that had, as is indicated in "Thyrsis," Arnold's elegy for Clough, special significance for the two poets while they were still at Oxford. The fact that Arnold planned to write "Scholar-Gipsy" in 1848—the year he and Clough came to an intellectual parting of ways—suggests that the poem grew out of Clough's involvement in Arnold's identity crisis; "Thyrsis" (1861), not one of Arnold's best poems, reverts to the intellectual parting of 1848. "Grande Chartreuse," one of Arnold's best poems, did not appear until 1855, but would seem to have been mainly written by 1852 after Arnold's honeymoon visit to the monastery in 1851. Even "Dover Beach," the most famous expression of Arnold's melancholy, which did not appear until 1867, was probably composed in 1851. The early date is indicated by the fact that part of the manuscript is on the back of a sheet of notes, probably of 1849–50, about, significantly, the Greek philosopher Empedocles.[18]

Empedocles on Etna, written during 1849–52, is the poem that most powerfully dramatizes Arnold's identity crisis. Like Arnold, Empedocles has a modern mind and a premodern sensibility. As a philosopher he is behind his time ("thou art come too late, Empedocles!" he cries); he represents an earlier mode of thought and feeling living on into an alien world. But he is also ahead of his time with his realism and skepticism, his insistence on seeing things as they are, on comprehending the world with the intellect alone. When in his most beautiful speech— "And yet what days were those, Parmenides!"—he recalls his youth with the elder philosopher, he recalls that sensibility was then united with thought:

> then neither thought
> Nor outward things were closed and dead to us;
> But we received the shock of mighty thoughts
> On simple minds with a pure natural joy.

Now instead he is

> Nothing but a devouring flame of thought—
> But a naked, eternally restless mind!
>   (II.16, 235, 240–44, 329–44, 329–30)

Those last lines suggest that Empedocles shares, has indeed helped to make, the modern dissociation he abhors of sensibility from thought. The difference between him and his contemporaries, as exemplified by Pausanias, is that Empedocles at least, like Arnold in "Grande Chartreuse," understands what has been lost.

Empedocles' problem is both personal and historical. Depleted feeling and abstractness of thought characterize the old age of an individual and a culture. The historical problem is evidenced in the fact that not only the young Empedocles, but also the older Parmenides and all their circle shared the unified sensibility described in the lines quoted above, lines that might have been written by Wordsworth. It is as though Parmenides were Wordsworth, as though Parmenides-Wordsworth had lived on into a new age that turned him into Empedocles-Arnold.

The personal problem is evidenced in the use of the young harpist Callicles as Empedocles' alter ego, representing Empedocles' youthful sensibility. For Empedocles was a great musician in his youth; and it becomes clear that music and philosophy are two phases of the same activity, phases appropriate respectively to youth and age. Callicles sings on the lower wooded slopes of Mt Etna in the hope of giving solace to Empedocles who continues alone to the barren upper region where lies, as the final antithesis to youth and verdure, the fiery crater into which he will leap. Callicles' disembodied voice seems, as it intertwines with Empedocles' doubts and self-questionings, an earlier phase of Empedocles' own thought and (here the personal and historical merge) of Greek culture generally.

Although Callicles chants myths, he shares Empedocles' contempt for superstition. That is because superstition uses knowledge for personal advantage, whereas art and philosophy are disinterested. The common people applaud Empedocles as a magician. Even Empedocles' friend, the physician Pausanias, is attracted by what he considers to be Empedocles' power to manipulate nature: he has come to Etna because Empedocles promised to tell "what might profit" him. What Pausanias gets from Empedocles is a purely philosophical disquisition, which Empedocles delivers while accompanying himself on the harp.

We see in the accompaniment the continuity of philosophy with music; but we see also in the crabbed, didactic verses the difference from Callicles' way of simply rendering a myth or a description of nature. Empedocles teaches what, according to Arnold's essay "Spinoza and the Bible," is the distinctive lesson of modern philosophy—that the world does not exist for our welfare and that nature's laws do not mirror either our hearts' desires or our imaginings. Empedocles de-anthropomorphizes and de-mythologizes nature. We invent myths to cheer ourselves up, he says, but that does not make them true. Let us, therefore, "not fly to dreams, but moderate desire," and take pleasure in the limited joys and scope for effort that are real. "Because thou must not dream," he concludes, "thou need'st not then despair!" (I.ii.386, 426).

But, and here is the crux of his identity crisis, Empedocles—whose view represents that of modern science, a view he at first, as Arnold wrote in his outline for the poem, "started towards . . . in hope . . . with joy"—cannot live by his advice to Pausanias. For his emotions are with Callicles and cannot sustain the knowledge of "things as they are" without the humanizing drapery of myths and "parables." [19] After a long pause, during which Empedocles' despair makes itself felt, Callicles sings the story of Cadmus and Harmonia who escaped despair through metamorphosis into "two bright and aged snakes." The only way through the impasse Empedocles poses is rebirth in-to· a new identity, or—it is an incidental theme in the poem since the historical Empedocles taught the doctrine—reincarnation.

The lesson, however, is designed for Pausanias who can live by it; for he is a literalist. He is the sort of person who in Victorian terms is either an orthodox Christian or a sciolist, who chooses between simple alternatives—either totally accepting or totally rejecting Christianity. The literalist can live with only one alternative at a time, but he can accept either alternative— as the man of imagination, the sort of man who is the speaker of "Grande Chartreuse," cannot. Arnold's prose works are devoted to defining a middle or romantic position between the orthodoxies of religion and science—a position by which, through reading the Bible symbolically, as we read poetry, we can understand supernatural events, beings, concepts as symbols of moral and psychological realities.

Empedocles' failure to achieve such a position is purely psychological. He cannot achieve it because he cannot organize his mind and feelings, his various roles, and the various phases of his life into the internal unity that could create, as its own reflection, the unity of the external world. Once he had the "poise" (II.234), the assured identity that could assimilate diverse experiences into unity. But the movement of history has broken up the old organization of self, has created the modern problem of identity: his "youth fell on a different world / From that on which his exiled age is thrown" (II.262–63). "Thou canst not," he soliloquizes, "live with men nor with thyself." He lays aside his magician's robes, because he canot bear the *public* role that absents him "from himself." But he lays aside also his musician's laurel, because he cannot bear the artist's *solitude* that fences him from society: "Who will fence him from himself?" (II.23, 225, 212). He is left only with his role as philosopher, with the critical intellect that rejects the other roles. Far from projecting his own life into nature, he projects into nature his "own deadness" (II.322).

Along with his roles as magician and musician, he gives up powers of ordering nature that derive from Zeus and Apollo. Callicles sings the stories of Zeus's victory over Typho, the titan whom Zeus imprisoned within Mt. Etna, and Apollo's victory in a contest between lyre and flute over the faun Marsyas who was then skinned alive. Both songs set out to celebrate the victor, but there occurs before the end a covert shift of sympathy to the loser that reflects Empedocles' identity crisis. For Empedocles, who owes his philosophy and harp to the victorious Olympian gods of reason, nevertheless identifies himself with the vanquished representatives of the instinctual life, with the defeated old order.

This dissociation between modern mind and premodern sensibility can be healed only through oblivion, through return to the elements, loss of individual self in the unity of nature. The question arises whether mind, once alienated from nature in the act of consciousness, ever can return to nature:

> But mind, but thought—
> If these have been the master part of us—
> Where will *they* find their parent element?
> What will receive *them*, who will call *them* home?
> But we shall still be in them, and they in us,
> And we shall be the strangers of the world,
> And they will be our lords, as they are now;
> And keep us prisoners of our consciousness,
> And never let us clasp and feel the All
> But through their forms, and modes, and stifling veils.
>
> (II. 345–54)

"Strangers of the world," "prisoners of our consciousness"—these are terms that will define the modern problem of identity in Yeats, Eliot, Lawrence, Beckett and so many other twentieth-century writers. Arnold uses modern philosophical and psychological concepts of alienated consciousness to account for the belief of the historical Empedocles that the guilty soul, rejected by the elements, must pass through a thirty-thousand-year cycle of reincarnations. Here, as in Yeats, the modern literary interest in reincarnation derives from the preoccupation with identity problems. Arnold's Empedocles interprets reincarnations the way Yeats will interpret them, as successive chances to discover our true selves.[21] "We shall unwillingly return," says Empedocles,

> To see if we will poise our life at last,
> To see if we will now at last be true

> To our own only true, deep-buried selves,
> Being one with which we are one with the whole world.

But progress, modernity, makes self-realization ever more difficult:

> And each succeeding age in which we are born
> Will have more peril for us than the last;
> Will goad our senses with a sharper spur,
> Will fret our minds to an intenser play,
> Will make ourselves harder to be discerned.

Empedocles goes on to describe what one recognizes from Arnold's other works as the nineteenth-century situation:

> And we shall struggle awhile, gasp and rebel—
> And we shall fly for refuge to past times,
> Their soul of unworn youth, their breath of greatness;
> And the reality will pluck us back,
> Knead us in its hot hand, and change our nature.
> And we shall feel our powers of effort flag,
> And rally them for one last fight—and fail;
> And we shall sink in the impossible strife,
> And be astray for ever.   (II. 364–90)

It is because Empedocles sees history as steadily diminishing the chances for self-realization, because he thinks that for historical and personal reasons he has more chance now than later of being received by the elements, that he leaps into Etna's fiery crater.

In arguing the question of Empedocles' motive for suicide, Walter Houghton reminds us that the suicide is prepared for at the beginning of Act II [22] when, after reflecting that "something" in this new age "has impaired thy spirit's strength," Empedocles decides that "the one way left" is to turn to "the elements" and ask "this final service" of them before things get even worse, before we arrive at a situation like that of the Victorians when the "sophist-brood" will with their reasonings have killed off the self and nature:

> Ere quite the being of man, ere quite the world
> Be disarrayed of their divinity—

> Before the soul lose all her solemn joys,
> And awe be dead, and hope impossible,
> And the soul's deep eternal night come on—
> Receive me, hide me, quench me, take me home!
>
> (II. 21–36)

Arnold himself explained Empedocles' personal reasons in the outline to the poem, where he said that Empedocles commits suicide in order to forestall depression and the complete death of self:

> *Before* he becomes the victim of depression & overtension of mind, [of] the utter deadness to joy, grandeur, spirit, and animated life, he desires to die—to be reunited with the universe *before*, by exaggerating his human [intellectual] side, he has become utterly estranged from it [the universe].[23]

This explains the ending where Empedocles can still see that *nature* is alive though he is reading into "all things my own deadness." "Oh, that I could glow like this mountain!" he wishes.

> But no, this heart will glow no more; thou art
> A living man no more, Empedocles!
> Nothing but a devouring flame of thought—
> But a naked, eternally restless mind!
>
> (II. 322–30)

He leaps into the crater *before* the death of self blots out even this much apprehension of nature's life, while he can still find in the crater the vitality he no longer finds in himself and can, as a last desperate expedient, merge with that vitality. He chooses to conclude quickly the death of his individual self while he can still believe that he will merge through nature's life with a universal self.

"It hath been granted me / Not to die wholly," he says in his final speech. "I breathe free, / " he continues. "Is it but for a moment?" His plunge is an act of existential freedom that rolls back for him the encroaching death of self, but does not roll back the historical process that is killing the self. His act occurs in a single moment salvaged from the historical process, a moment in which his life flames up again. "My soul *glows* to meet you," he says to the boiling vapors.

> *Ere* it flag, *ere* the mists
> Of despondency and gloom
> Rush over it again,
> Receive me, save me!
> (II.405–16; my italics)

Empedocles' final speech is so triumphant and Callicles' closing lyric so exquisitely serene that Arnold's attack on the poem, as offering no relief for the pain it causes, seems unfair. *Empedocles* offers the same, and indeed more beautiful, lyrical compensations for pain as *Sohrab and Rustum*, the exemplary poem of the 1853 volume. In the Aristotelian 1853 Preface, Arnold speaks of the need in poetry for action as an outlet for mental distress. This he had failed to provide in *Empedocles* and presumably had provided in *Sohrab*. But the duel in *Sohrab* produces the pain rather than the relief, while Empedocles' plunge is more obviously than the killing of Rustum a "vent in action" for mental distress. "There is," as Lionel Trilling puts it, "a *catharsis* of expression . . . as well as of action," [24] and the former is more effective nowadays. Arnold's critical condemnation of *Empedocles* would seem to mask his disturbance over the psychic conflict that generated the poem; if he overlooked the poem's objectification of this conflict, it was probably because he felt the depression out of which the poem grew must be as apparent to his readers as to him. The thing Goethe said of *Werther*, that in writing it he purged his sickness, applies to Arnold with *Empedocles*; Arnold may have feared he would spread his infection, as did Goethe whose *Werther* caused a wave of suicides. He may have been embarrassed to exhibit in the poem a self he had outgrown through a solution less pure than Empedocles'—a compromise.

It is because the pain in *Empedocles* is more dangerous, more potentially destructive than in *Sohrab*, and is objectified through a much larger intellectual framework, that *Empedocles* not *Sohrab* is Arnold's major poem, ranking with Tennyson's *In Memoriam* and Browning's *The Ring and the Book* among the three major Victorian poems. All three poems are historicist in outlook and define—though Arnold's and Browning's are set in the past—certain new manifestations of their age. *Empedocles* is not necessarily the best of these poems, but it does seem the most modern in sensibility and in its concepts of modernity. For neither Tennyson's religious doubts nor Browning's moral relativism seem revolutionary this far into the twentieth century. But *Empedocles* is about an intellectual's confrontation with an emerging modern period, with "the spectacle of a vast multitude of facts awaiting and inviting his comprehension" [25] and with his failure to comprehend them adequately because he has lost, in the face of such bewildering heterogeneity, the secure identity that could assimilate multifarious possibilities into a unity not of idea but of being, a unity he could live by. In recognizing the modern problem as a problem of identity, Arnold has touched the issue of our time that most excites us.

Above all Arnold's poem is prophetic. For Empedocles, like all superior poets and intellectuals, finds the future of society incipient in himself. He senses the depletion of the Wordsworthian self—which flourished, as he puts it, in Parmenides' time—because he no longer draws vitality from nature but can only contrast nature's vitality with his own deadness. It is a sign of his prescience that the story he tells about the encroaching death of self is continued ever more drastically by so many twentieth-century writers, of whom Eliot and Beckett will serve us as examples.

Chapter 3
ELIOT:
THE WALKING
DEAD

Eliot in his early poems takes up Arnold's elegiac note, adding to it his own note of irony. There is the historical pathos of speakers who still wander in Arnold's limbo "between two worlds," but the cry has become more poignant—for these speakers have even less energy than Arnold's. In *The Waste Land*, they fear rebirth and, with the Sibyl of the epigraph, long to die. Of Arnold's speakers, only Empedocles desires death. But there is in Empedocles' utterance an energy of rage and the intellectual energy to explore the hopelessness of his situation that is quite different from the listless understatement of Eliot's speakers, their pathos of monotone. In *The Waste Land*, only the narrating consciousness has Empedocles' coherent sense of the past in its contrast with the present. The disparity between the narrating consciousness and that of the speakers makes *The Waste Land* ironical as *Empedocles* is not. But since the narrating consciousness slides imperceptibly into the speakers' consciousness, the relation between them is complex and central to Eliot's new modes of characterization in *The Waste Land*.

Both Arnold and Eliot wrote in their twenties poems in which they dramatized their personal crises through elderly speakers; they put on—like Tennyson, who wrote "Ulysses" and "Tithonus" in his twenties—"the mask of age." [1] Empedocles and Prufrock give age as the reason they lack sufficient appetite for life to be reborn. Prufrock, who in "The Love Song of J. Alfred Prufrock" ought to change his life by proposing to the lady at the party, draws as he ascends the stairs such an acute self-portrait of enervated middle-age as to prepare already for failure. When he has failed to "Disturb the universe" by proposing, his way of leaping into the crater is to put on, with all the force of Arnold's self-pity mixed with Eliot's irony, the mask of old age: "I grow old . . . I grow old . . . / I shall wear the bottoms of my trousers rolled." [2]

Aside from the mixture of self-mockery with self-pity, Prufrock differs from Empedocles in his deliberate putting on and taking off of masks. Empedocles never fails to believe that he has a true self even though it is buried. He casts aside the masks of magician and musician not to put on new masks but to recover a naked self that can be finally achieved only through complete unconsciousness, complete merging with nature. Prufrock, instead, conceives only such selves as can be deliberately constructed for his own and others' observation. He is an ineffectual proper Bostonian who becomes, after "beheading" (psychically castrating) himself before a woman, a bald John the Baptist. He could have been, had he the courage to be reborn, "Lazarus, come from the dead"; but no, he is not to be taken seriously, he is not Hamlet, only Polonius. He settles in the end for the mask of a ridiculously timid old gentleman whose *real* life is fantasy.

These new features show that self-consciousness has gone even farther in Prufrock than Empedocles, and been even more destructive of identity. The romantic theme of self-consciousness reaches a climax in this dramatic monologue, where one aspect of the self addresses the other: "Let us go then, you and I." Self-consciousness splits the ego between the self that experiences and the self that watches, but the romanticists usually allegorize the split by objectifying one side of the self as an alter ego—Mephistopheles is Faust's watching self; Callicles is Empedocles' lost experiencing self. There is more realism and pathos in Eliot's portrayal of the split as frankly psychological, as Prufrock's conscious performance before his own consciously watching self. The things Prufrock says to the other guests at the party are blotted out, while we get his actually unspoken words to himself as the action proceeds. Eliot's method dramatizes the disengagement from the external world produced by extreme self-consciousness. The hell where the epigraph from Dante locates the poem becomes, in the poem's context, the hell of modern self-consciousness. Self-consciousness produces the emotional and moral blankness that in *The Waste Land* makes Dante's hell the setting for the walking dead.

Eliot's method in "Prufrock" has caused many readers to doubt that anything external is going on. The main evidence for the externality of the action is Prufrock's sensuous apprehension which, proceeding independently of his understanding and will, seems unequivocally real. Prufrock does not know why he wants to pass on his way to the party through the bad part of town, but the sensations he registers—"Of restless nights in one-night cheap hotels / And sawdust restaurants with oyster shells"—tell us why. These sensations connect with the yellow fog rubbing itself sensuously like a cat against the house where the party takes place:

> The yellow fog that rubs its back upon the window-panes,
> The yellow smoke that rubs its muzzle on the window-panes,
> Licked its tongue into the corners of the evening,
> Lingered upon the pools that stand in drains,
> Let fall upon its back the soot that falls from chimneys,
> Slipped by the terrace, made a sudden leap,
> And seeing that it was a soft October night,
> Curled once about the house, and fell asleep.

Prufrock senses his own repressed sexuality in the fog and the bad part of town. Fog and oyster shells come from the ocean;

they are symbols, though soiled by city dirt, of our unconscious libidinal life.

By shifting tense in the fog passage, Prufrock suggests first desire, then retreat from desire. The metaphorical cat has fallen asleep, just as "the evening is spread out against the sky / Like a patient etherised upon a table." Eliot has devised a method— the method of the "objective correlative" [3]—for telling us, through what Prufrock sees, things about him that Prufrock does not himself know. Wordsworth's speakers are aware of their projected self in what they see. But Prufrock's consciousness is cut off from his unconsciousness; he therefore projects upon the evening sky his own unrecognized neurotic inclination to fall asleep in order, as we come to understand through the metaphorical cat and the poem's action, to avoid sex. The sleep theme returns just after that cry of failure: "I should have been a pair of ragged claws / Scuttling across the floors of silent seas," which repeats, even more piercingly, Arnold's cries of desire for unconsciousness and for—desire. Prufrock's sensuous apprehension reveals also a buried libidinal self that he cannot make operative in the social world, cannot reconcile with the constructed self seen by "The eyes that fix you in a formulated phrase." In the end he makes the split complete by constructing for the regard of his other conscious self a Prufrock as removed as possible from the libidinal self:

> I grow old . . . I grow old . . .
> I shall wear the bottoms of my trousers rolled.
>
> Shall I part my hair behind? Do I dare to eat a peach?
> I shall wear white flannel trousers, and walk upon the beach.

The timid, sexless old man does, however, walk upon the beach, where—in the final passage that brings to a climax the imagery of ocean as suggesting sex and unconsciousness—he hears in the sounds of the waves mermaids singing, not to him, but to each other. By relegating his libidinal self to fantasy, Prufrock makes the split wider than ever. He thus avoids sex through a recourse to drowning ("We have lingered in the chambers of the sea") that anticipates the drowning theme in *The Waste Land*. He sings his love song to his other conscious self, while the sea-girls sing to each other.

This is Eliot's way of portraying character in the early poems. The bifurcated conscious self is mechanical, constructed, dead; but it has, as its one last sign of vitality, sudden, momentary accesses to a buried libidinal life—accesses that only deepen the split between unconsciousness and the consciousness that watches itself in action. Even the utterly blank young man in the satirical "Portrait of a Lady"—who puts on "faces" to cover his lack of response to the lady's advances, just as he keeps his "countenance" before the miscellaneous, spectacular happenings in the newspapers—even this emotionally dead young man has momentary access to a libidinal life recalling at least things *other* people have desired:

> I keep my countenance,
> I remain self-possessed
> Except when a street-piano, mechanical and tired
> Reiterates some worn-out common song
> With the smell of hyacinths across the garden
> Recalling things that other people have desired.
> Are these ideas right or wrong?

The pattern, distinctively postromantic, is to be found in a poem like Arnold's "The Buried Life." The romanticists portray the conscious self as connected with the unconscious and suffused with its vitality. In "The Buried Life," however, Arnold portrays our conscious existence as an unenergetic "Eddying at large in blind uncertainty." "Tricked in disguises, alien to the rest / Of men, and alien to themselves," men are cut off from their unconscious self—except for an inexplicable nostalgia:

> But often, in the world's most crowded streets,
> But often, in the din of strife,
> There rises an unspeakable desire
> After the knowledge of our buried life.

And sometimes, in rare erotic moments, we have access to our
buried self:

> A bolt is shot back somewhere in our breast,
> And a lost pulse of feeling stirs again.
> The eye sinks inward, and the heart lies plain,
> And what we mean, we say, and what we would, we know.
> A man becomes aware of his life's flow,
> And hears its winding murmur; and he sees
> The meadows where it glides, the sun, the breeze.

The buried self is nonindividual; it is the life force. It is better
buried, for man would with his meddling intellect "well-nigh
change his own identity," but is in spite of himself carried, by
the unregarded river in his breast, to the fulfillment of his biological destiny and "genuine self."

In Eliot, the self is buried even deeper than in Arnold and is
even less individual. Prufrock finds the buried self in an external
ocean; the buried self is, in *The Waste Land*, extended in time
through unconscious racial memory. When the nervous upper-
class lady (Eliot's neurotic first wife Vivienne), aware of inner
vacancy, asks: " 'What shall I do now? What shall I do? / . . .
What shall we do tomorrow? / What shall we ever do?' "—the
protagonist answers by describing the routine of their life:

> The hot water at ten.
> And if it rains, a closed car at four.
> And we shall play a game of chess,
> Pressing lidless eyes and waiting for a knock upon the door.
>   (II.131–38)

On the surface, his answer confirms her sense of vacancy; we
shall fill our lives, he is saying, with meaningless routines. But
there is also a positive implication, deriving from the poem's
underlying patterns, that these routines are unconscious repetitions of ancient rituals. The morning bath recalls rituals of purification and rebirth through water. The game of chess recalls
not only the game played in Middleton's *Women Beware
Women* while destiny works itself out behind the door, but also

all the games, including the Tarot cards, by which men have tried to foresee and manipulate destiny while waiting for its inevitable arrival. It is the consciousness of the poem blending imperceptibly with the protagonist's consciousness that makes us aware of what the protagonist can only know unconsciously.

As in Arnold's poem, the characters are, in spite of themselves, living their buried life; but they do this through racial as well as personal memory, through unconsciously making rituals even when they think they have abolished all rituals. Similarly, the personal libidinal associations of music and hyacinths in "Portrait of a Lady" become in *The Waste Land* unconscious memories of ancient rituals and myths. The poem's awareness makes us remember consciously what the protagonist, in recalling the Hyacinth garden, remembers unconsciously—that Hyacinth was a fertility god.

When Eliot in reviewing *Ulysses* said that Joyce had discovered in the "continuous parallel between contemporaneity and antiquity" a way of giving shape and significance to modern "futility and anarchy," he surely had in mind his own method in *The Waste Land*, published like *Ulysses* the year before and possibly influenced by it since Eliot must have read the earlier chapters in the *Egoist* and *Little Review* and did read, according to his own testimony, the latter part in manuscript in 1921 when he was just beginning *The Waste Land*.[4] This "mythical method," as Eliot called it, allows the writer to be naturalistic, to portray modern chaos, while suggesting through psychological naturalism a continuing buried life that rises irrepressibly into those shapes which express the primal meeting of mind with nature. Since the parallel with antiquity appears as unconscious memory, it is psychologically justified and cannot be dismissed as mere literary *appliqué*. The parallel is grounded in that conception of mind as shading off into unconsciousness which, having come from romantic literature, was articulated by Freud and Jung and remains still our conception, indeed our experience, of mind. The mythical method gives a doubleness of language to parallel our doubleness (doubleness between the apparent and buried) of consciousness and selfhood.

This doubleness of language reaches a climax at the end of Part I, "The Burial of the Dead," which deals with both the refusal of rebirth and the sprouting of seed and tubers in spring. On the surface the characters are the walking dead, who mythologize Eliot's "aboulie" or neurotic apathy; they are Dante's neutral spirits in *Inferno* IIII, who never were alive because they never awakened into moral action either good or evil. Since hell itself disdains them, they suffer in a long line on that dark plain outside hell which makes an analogue to the waste land. Eliot's paraphrase of Dante's lines 55–57, applying as it does to London clerks going to work in the City as Eliot did, renders powerfully the theme of the walking dead:

> A crowd flowed over London Bridge, so many,
> I had not thought death had undone so many.
> Sighs, short and infrequent, were exhaled,
> And each man fixed his eyes before his feet.
>   (I.62–65)

Among these living dead the protagonist recognizes, in Dante's manner, an old acquaintance; and just as in "Prufrock" we are to infer the small talk at the party, so here we are to infer an ordinary conversation about gardening. But the language tells us what is unconsciously transpiring:

> There I saw one I knew, and stopped him, crying: "Stetson!
> "You who were with me in the ships at Mylae!
> "That corpse you planted last year in your garden,
> "Has it begun to sprout? Will it bloom this year?
> "Or has the sudden frost disturbed its bed?"   (69–73)

The shocking substitution of "corpse" for "seed" reminds us that corpses are a kind of seed, and that this truth was symbolized in the old vegetation rituals. We find gardening satisfying because we unconsciously repeat the ritual by which gods were killed and buried in order that they might sprout anew as vege-

tation. Even more surprising is the connection of Stetson with
the ships at Mylae—the naval battle in which the Carthaginians
or Phoenicians were defeated by the Romans. The passage is a
haunting recognition scene in which conscious recognition
derives from unconscious recognition of another life. The protagonist unconsciously recognizes his fellow gardener as also a
fellow sailor and Phoenician; for they are devotees of rebirth,
and it was the Phoenician sailors who carried the Mysteries or
vegetation cults around the Mediterranean.

The heavily ironic final lines return us to the modern situation:

> "Oh keep the Dog far hence, that's friend to men,
> "Or with his nails he'll dig it up again!
> "You! hypocrite lecteur!—mon semblable,—mon frère!"
>
> (74–76)

Instead of Webster's "keep the wolf far thence that's foe to men"
(*White Devil* V.iv.113), the friendly Dog (perhaps, as Cleanth
Brooks has suggested, modern humanitarianism) [5] is the more
likely animal and the more likely danger. Webster's dirge says it
is good for the dead to be buried, and Eliot tells why—by dig-
ging up the corpse, the Dog would prevent rebirth. But we are
all, protagonist and hypocrite readers, with our advanced ideas
that cut us off from the natural cycle, engaged in a conspiracy
against fertility and rebirth. So we return to the theme with
which Part I began: "April is the cruellest month, breed-
ing / Lilacs out of the dead land" (1–2)—the fear of sex, of
burying the seed that will sprout.

In *The Waste Land*, the buried life manifests itself through
the unconscious memory of figures from the past. There is already some reaching toward this method in "Prufrock," where
Prufrock *consciously* thinks he might have been John the Baptist, Lazarus, Hamlet. But the emphasis is on the ironical disparity between these legendary figures and Prufrock's actual
character or lack of character. Prufrock does not in fact fulfill

the destinies of these legendary figures. In *The Waste Land*, however, the speakers do in spite of themselves unconsciously fulfill destinies laid out in myth; and their unconscious identification with the legendary figures who have already walked through these destinies gives them the only identity they have.

Compared to the characters in *The Waste Land*, Prufrock, for all his lack of vitality, has the sharp external delineation of a character in, say, Henry James. He has a name (a characterizing one), a social milieu to which he genuinely belongs, a face (we all have our idea of what he looks like, probably like Eliot). Prufrock has—his deliberate trying on of masks is a sign of this—a clear idea of himself. The characters in *The Waste Land*, however, are nameless, faceless, isolated, and have no clear idea of themselves. All they have is a sense of loss and a neural itch, a restless, inchoate desire to recover what has been lost. But in this very minimum of restless aliveness, they repeat the pattern of the Quest. And it is the archetypal Quest pattern, exemplified in the Grail legend, that gives whatever form there is to the protagonist's movement through the poem.

We would not know what to make of the characters were it not for the intrusion of a narrating consciousness that assimilates them to figures of the past. This is done through the double language of the Stetson passage. The same purpose is accomplished in Part II through shifting references. Part II opens with an opulently old-fashioned blank-verse-style description, not so much of a lady as of her luxurious surroundings. The chair she sits in reminds us of Cleopatra's "burnished throne" and the stately room of Dido's palace, while a picture recalls the rape of Philomela. The shifting references—showing how Eliot mythologizes his unhappy marriage—suggest that the lady is seductive, but that she is also, like Cleopatra with Anthony and Dido with Aeneas, one of those who is in the end violated and abandoned by a man. The theme of violation takes over; for the picture shows Philomela's change, after her rape, into a nightingale whose wordless cry rings down through the ages:

> So rudely forced; yet there the nightingale
> Filled all the desert with inviolable voice
> And still she cried, and still the world pursues,
> "Jug Jug" to dirty ears.   (100–3)

The nightingale's *voice*, the story's meaning, is inviolable; but the violation of innocence in the waste land goes on.

When the lady finally speaks, she utters twentieth-century words that her prototypes of the past would not have understood: " 'My nerves are bad to-night. Yes, bad. Stay with me.' " We gather from the passage that the lady is rich, that her house is filled with mementoes of the past which she understands only as frightening ghosts, that the protagonist to whom she speaks is her lover or husband, and that he has in some special modern sense violated her. The violation would seem to lie in his inability to communicate with her:

> "Speak to me. Why do you never speak. Speak.
>   What are you thinking of? what thinking? What?
> I never know what you are thinking. Think."
>   (111–14)

The modern situation is unprecedented and meaningless; therein lies the poem's negative impulse. But deep down these people are repeating an ancient drama with ancient meanings; therein lies the poem's positive impulse. The shifting references to various ladies of the past evoke the archetype that subsumes them—the archetype already revealed in Part I, where the protagonist has his fortune told by Madame Sosostris. "Here," she says, pulling a card from the ancient Tarot deck, "is Belladonna, the Lady of the Rocks, / The lady of situations" (49–50). Because all the ladies referred to are Belladonnas, we understand the character of our modern rich lady and the character —in the abrupt shift to a London pub—of the working-class Belladonna who tells a friend of her efforts to steal away the husband of another friend, another Belladonna, who has ruined her health and looks with abortion pills. Beneath the meaningless surface, the underlying tale tells again of violation in the desert—violation of innocence, sex, fertility.

The protagonist's card is "the drowned Phoenician Sailor." This explains not only the Stetson passage, but also the protagonist's reflection after his card has been drawn: "Those are pearls that were his eyes" (I.47–48). The line is from Ariel's song in *The Tempest*, addressed to Prince Ferdinand, who thinks his father, the King of Naples, has been drowned. Lines from *The Tempest* keep running through the protagonist's head, because *The Tempest* is a water poem in which all the human characters are sailors, having sailed to the island. Drowning and metamorphosis, the consolation in Ariel's song, relate to drowning and resurrection in the cult of the Phoenician fertility god Adonis (an effigy of the dead Adonis was cast upon the waves, where resurrection was assumed to take place).[6]

Among the other Tarot cards named is "the one-eyed merchant"; he turns up in Part III as the Smyrna merchant who makes the protagonist a homosexual proposition. Eliot in a note (III.218) explains his method of characterization:

> Just as the one-eyed merchant, seller of currants, melts into the Phoenician Sailor, and the latter is not wholly distinct from Ferdinand Prince of Naples, so all the women are one woman, and the two sexes meet in Tiresias. What Tiresias *sees*, in fact, is the substance of the poem.

The figures either on the Tarot cards, or in some cases frankly imagined by Eliot to be on them, provide the archetypes from which the nameless, faceless modern characters derive identity. Tiresias, not a Tarot figure but the blind hermaphroditic prophet of Greek mythology, appears only once—in the Part III episode about another violated Belladonna, the typist whose mechanical fornication with a clerk leaves her neither a sense of sin nor a memory of pleasure.

The central consciousness, which intruded through the double language of the Stetson passage and the cultural memory of Part II's introductory passage, now takes on the name of Tiresias: "I Tiresias, old man with wrinkled dugs / Perceived the scene, and foretold the rest." After the scene has been enacted, Tiresias interjects:

> (And I Tiresias have foresuffered all
> Enacted on this same divan or bed;
> I who have sat by Thebes below the wall
> And walked among the lowest of the dead.)
> (III. 228–29, 243–46)

Again we are enabled to understand the contrast between the passionate auspicious fornications of the past and this modern perfunctory performance. Again we are reminded that this scene is nevertheless a *re*-enactment. Sexual union was used in the fertility ceremonies to promote by sympathetic magic the fertility of the soil. But modern sexuality is sterile.

Through the Tiresias consciousness in him, the protagonist repeatedly finds an underlying ancient pattern but also sees that in the modern situation the pattern does not come to the preordained conclusion. This gives a direction to his Quest—to complete the pattern by restoring fertility. It is a sign of their connection that Tiresias appears as a stand-in for the protagonist in just the scene the protagonist can only have imagined.

To say that all the characters meet in Tiresias is to suggest that archetypal identities emerge from larger archetypes, in the way smaller Chinese boxes emerge from larger. The Smyrna merchant, identified with the Tarot one-eyed merchant, propositions the protagonist, who is identified with the Phoenician Sailor. Yet we are told that the one-eyed merchant melts into the Phoenician Sailor; so that the protagonist really stands on both sides of the proposition. In the same way the protagonist is identified with the Quester of the Grail legend, who sets out to find the Grail and thus cure the ailing Fisher King whose wound, symbolizing a loss of potency, has caused the land to lose fertility. The protagonist is the Quester inasmuch as he moves through the episodes of the poem to arrive at the Perilous Chapel. But in the following lines he is the Fisher King, whose

illness is in some Grail romances assigned to the King's brother
or father:

> While I was fishing in the dull canal
> On a winter evening round behind the gashouse
> Musing upon the king my brother's wreck
> And on the king my father's death before him.
>   (III.189–92)

He is also—according to the method of shifting references—Prince Ferdinand (from whom, in *Tempest* I.ii.390–91,
the last two lines derive), Hamlet, Claudius: all of whom have
to do with dead kings who in turn recall the murdered kings of
vegetation ritual. All this combines with the modern industrial
setting to portray the modern moment with modern voices and
collapse them into timeless archetypes. At the end of the poem,
the protagonist is both Quester and Fisher King; he is the Fisher
King questing for a cure: "I sat upon the shore / Fishing, with
the arid plain behind me" (V.423–24).

Since the protagonist plays at one and the same time both active and passive roles, we must understand all the characters as
aspects or projections of his consciousness—that the poem is essentially a monodrama. It is difficult to say just where the
various characters melt into the protagonist and where the protagonist melts into the poet. We have to distinguish the scenes
in which the protagonist himself plays a part—the recollection
of the Hyacinth garden, the visit to Madame Sosostris, the
meeting with Stetson, the scene with the rich Belladonna—
from the scenes in the pub and at the typist's. We can either
consider that the protagonist overhears the first and imagines the
second, or that at these points the poet's consciousness takes
leave of the protagonist to portray parallel instances. I prefer the
first line of interpretation because it yields a more consistent
structure on the model of romantic monodrama. In *Faust* and
Manfred, the other characters do not have the same order of existence as the protagonist because the protagonist's conscious-

ness blends with the poet's. We must understand the other characters, therefore, as ambiguously objective, as only partly
themselves and partly the projection of forces within the protagonist and ultimately within the poet. If we take the line that
Eliot's poem is what the protagonist *sees*, then Tiresias becomes
the figure in which the protagonist's consciousness blends perfectly with the poet's so that the protagonist can *see* imaginatively more than he could physically. (Tiresias' hermaphrodi-
tism characterizes the all-inclusive poetic imagination; Pound in
one of his annotations to the manuscript calls Eliot Tiresias.) [7]

But the poet's consciousness is itself an aspect of the age's.
We get the overheard scraps of conversation, miscellaneous literary tags, and incoherent cultural recollections that would
stock a cultivated mind of 1920—an agitated mind in which the
fragments recur compulsively. This is where Western culture
has come to, the poem is telling us, as of 1920. The protagonist's consciousness emerges from the collective consciousness
of the time as another nameless, faceless modern voice. The
protagonist has no character in the old-fashioned sense; for he
acquires delineation or identity not through individualization,
but through making connection with ancient archetypes.

Eliot's new mode of characterization derives from the romantic attempt to deal with the increasingly problematic nature of
the self. Eliot's nameless, faceless voices express the sense—
which by the twentieth century has come to prevail—that the
self, if it exists at all, is changing and discontinuous and that its
unity is as problematic as its freedom from external conditions.
We have seen how Wordsworth solved the problem of identity
through archetypalizations that evolve continuously from vital
individualizations. But in Eliot the individual is blotted out;
there is a jump from vacancy to archetype, with continuity
minimally residual in the buried life. In *The Waste Land*, and
in his earlier poems, Eliot is preoccupied with the mechanical,
automatic quality of existence. In "Rhapsody on a Windy
Night," he had written:

> I could see nothing behind that child's eye.
> I have seen eyes in the street
> Trying to peer through lighted shutters,
> And a crab one afternoon in a pool,
> An old crab with barnacles on his back,
> Gripped the end of a stick which I held him.

In *The Waste Land,* he says of the clerk: "Exploring hands encounter no defence"; and of the typist afterward: "She smoothes her hair with automatic hand, / And puts a record on the gramophone" (III.240, 255–56). The solution, toward which he had been finding his way through the early poems, is the breaking out from and enlargement of self through archetypalization. Behind the solution lie the demonstrations by Freud and Jung that when we delve deep into the psyche we find an archetypal self and a desire to repeat the patterns laid out in the sort of myths described by Frazer and Jessie Weston.

The Waste Land opens with scraps of cosmopolitan conversations that the protagonist might be understood to overhear, but which have enough in common to project an upper-class tourist mentality, out of touch with and afraid of life's rhythms: "I read, much of the night, and go south in the winter"—yet still feeding on recollected moments of genuine experience:

> And when we were children, staying at the arch-duke's,
> My cousin's, he took me out on a sled,
> And I was frightened. He said, Marie,
> Marie, hold on tight. And down we went.
> In the mountains, there you feel free.

There follow Biblical recollections—"I will show you fear in a handful of dust" (I.13–18, 30)—that establish in the image of the dry waste land the spiritual habitat of the previous speakers. (An early version of these lines, in "The Death of Saint Narcissus" bound with *The Waste Land* manuscript, establishes the waste

land as the scene of Saint Narcissus' self-aggrandizing martyrdom—suggesting the necessity, even in the spiritual life, of a
journey from narcissism.) This is a new prophetic voice, the
Tiresias consciousness, which goes on through a recollection of
the Sailor's song that opens Wagner's *Tristan* to establish also
the opposite theme of water and hope for redemption. There
follows a personal memory of love; and only here, in the lines
introduced by a dash, can we single out a voice that we come to
recognize as the protagonist's.

> "You gave me hyacinths first a year ago;
> "They called me the hyacinth girl."
> —Yet when we came back, late, from the Hyacinth garden,
> Your arms full, and your hair wet, I could not
> Speak, and my eyes failed, I was neither
> Living nor dead, and I knew nothing,
> Looking into the heart of light, the silence.
> *Oed' und leer das Meer.*   (I.35–42)

The protagonist had in the past his chance for love; he had like
Marie his perfect moment, his vision of fulfillment. But he was
unable to reach out and take what the moment offered, and
thus break through to fertility, creativity. We know he failed
only through the last line from the opening of Wagner's tragic
Third Act: "Desolate and empty the sea."

   This way of rendering the protagonist's failure makes it also
collective; as does the reference to the Hyacinth garden, since
Hyacinth was a fertility god. (Eliot capitalized the small *h* of the
original draft but restored it in the final edition of 1963, having
presumably lost interest by then in vegetation myths.) It is the
vision and loss of vision that sets the protagonist in motion; insofar as *The Waste Land* has a plot, it tells the story of the protagonist's attempt to recover his lost vision. All his subsequent
memories are transformations of the scene in the Hyacinth garden. This observation is confirmed by the words, which I have
bracketed, that Eliot deleted from the original draft. When in
Part II, lines 122–23, the rich lady asks: " 'Do you remem-

ber / Nothing?' "—the protagonist answers: "I remember / [The hyacinth garden.] Those are pearls that were his eyes [,yes!]" (*Facs.* II. 47–50). A note to this passage (II. 126) refers us back to I.37, 48—to the Hyacinth garden (love) and Ariel's song (drowning), which are related as forms of natural salvation (love is a kind of drowning). This attempt at recovery is the pattern of the Grail Quest; in most versions, a vision or fleeting sight of the Grail leads to the Quest to recover it.

The Waste Land is about sexual failure as a sign of spiritual failure. This is made especially clear by the deleted opening passage about a rowdy Irishman on an all-night binge, who lands in a brothel but is too drunk to have intercourse. The original draft then shifts to "April is the cruellest month" (*Facs.* I.55)—about upper-class people who, like the Irishman, fail in sex not because they are practicing Christian abstinence but because of spiritual torpor. The vegetation myths are better than Christianity for diagnosing modern sexual failure; for the myths make clear that sex and religion spring from the same impulse and that sexual and religious fulfillment are related. In *Eliot's Early Years* (1977) Lyndall Gordon gives a convincing account of *The Waste Land* as Eliot's spiritual autobiography, but she minimizes the sexual theme. Eliot approved I. A. Richards' observation of his "persistent concern with sex, the problem of our generation, as religion was the problem of the last." But Richards' "contrast of sex and religion," Eliot added slyly, "is too subtle for me to grasp." [8] Eliot was suggesting that sex and religion are inextricably related.

To understand how far Eliot has come in his treatment of sex and in his concepts of character and identity, we have only to compare the memory of the Hyacinth garden with a corresponding memory in the early poem, written in French, "Dans le Restaurant." In the French poem, a dirty broken-down waiter recalls an amorous experience under a tree in the rain when he was only seven and the little girl was even younger. She was soaking wet, he gave her primroses and tickled her to make her laugh. He experienced a moment of power and ecstasy. But he too lost his vision, for a big dog came along and he became scared and deserted her; he has never fulfilled the promise of that moment. The customer to whom he has insisted on telling this story remarks on his physical filthiness as a way of separating the waiter from himself: "What right have you to experiences like mine?" The customer gives the waiter ten sous for a bath.

The poem escapes from this sordid situation by taking a leap to the cleansing by drowning of Phlebas the Phoenician, a character for whom we have not been in the least prepared. The sudden contrast affords welcome relief. Since Part IV of *The Waste Land* is an English revision of this passage:

> Phlebas the Phoenician, a fortnight dead,
> Forgot the cry of gulls, and the deep sea swell
> And the profit and loss,   (312–14)

we are justified in connecting certain details preceding it with "Dans le Restaurant." The dog may stand behind " 'Oh keep the Dog far hence,' " and the customer who wants to separate himself from the waiter may stand behind " 'You! hypocrite lecteur!—mon semblable,—mon frère!' " But most important, the connection with the waiter's memory suggests that the protagonist betrayed the hyacinth girl through nonconsummation. The experience took place *after* "we came back, late, from the Hyacinth garden," presumably in the rooms of one or the other (I.74, 76, 37). In both scenes, sexuality is associated with rain and flowers; the hyacinth girl came back with her arms full of flowers and her hair wet.

Having failed to consummate a union that would have combined love with sex, the protagonist turns to the fortune-teller and then proceeds to live out his fortune by experiencing dry, sterile lust. He fails the rich Belladonna, overhears the dialogue in the pub, is propositioned by the Smyrna merchant, conceives the typist's fornication and the lament of the girl seduced on the

Thames. Finally the imagery of dryness and burning comes to a climax: "Burning burning burning burning" (III. 308), and we are afforded the welcome relief of Phlebas's "Death by Water."

> A current under sea
> Picked his bones in whispers. As he rose and fell
> He passed the stages of his age and youth
> Entering the whirlpool.   (IV. 315–18)

The passage holds out to the protagonist the possibility of a natural or pagan salvation, the kind suggested by the song from *The Tempest* in which Ariel makes drowning seem so desirable because it is "a sea change / Into something rich and strange" (I. ii. 401–2).

"Fear death by water," said Madame Sosostris. "Here, said she, / Is your card, the drowned Phoenician Sailor"; at which point the protagonist recalled "Those are pearls that were his eyes" (I. 55, 45–47), another line from this same song of Ariel's. Thus Eliot does in *The Waste Land* what he has not done in "Dans le Restaurant": he prepares for the drowning of Phlebas. He retains on the surface the vacant characters of the earlier poem, but he prepares beneath the surface archetypal identities that give the characters positive force. We must read the protagonist's development in self-understanding through the shift in the archetypes with which he identifies himself. In identifying himself with Phlebas, the protagonist fulfills in Part IV his natural fortune. Part V, "What the Thunder Said," moves beyond Madame Sosostris, who could not find the Hanged Man (I. 55). Part V explores the possibility of a supernatural answer through the unpredictable miracle of revelation.

The drowning of Phlebas must be understood as the equivalent of a psychological and ritual experience—as a *rite de passage* or psychic dying through which the protagonist can be reborn into the identity that enables him to continue his Quest. The protagonist has after Part IV outgrown pagan archetypes;

the references now are to Christianity and the higher ethical Hinduism of the Upanishads. The Hyacinth garden turns into the garden of Gethsemane. The missing Hanged Man of the Tarot deck turns into the hooded figure whom the disciples on the journey to Emmaus saw but did not recognize as the risen Christ:

> Who is the third who walks always beside you?
> When I count, there are only you and I together
> But when I look ahead up the white road
> There is always another one walking beside you
> Gliding wrapt in a brown mantle, hooded
> I do not know whether a man or a woman
> —But who is that on the other side of you?
>   (V. 359–65)

Eliot so suggestively avoids specification that he eludes an exclusively Christian reading, thus making the personages and situation archetypal. He makes the passage refer also to an account he read of an Antarctic expedition where the explorers, as he says in his note to these lines, "at the extremity of their strength, had the constant delusion that there was *one more member* than could actually be counted." Because of the new concept of identity advanced in *The Waste Land*, we have had to learn how to read a passage in which the twentieth-century London protagonist exhibits his identity by melting into other quite remote characters—a disciple of Christ, an Antarctic explorer. We find a similar method in Joyce's *Ulysses* where the Bloom-Dedalus relation is rendered archetypal through shifting analogues with Odysseus and Telemachus, King Hamlet and Hamlet, Jew and Greek, God the Father and God the Son, and where Bloom undergoes metamorphoses in appearance corresponding to the shifting aspects of his identity. We are to understand by the identifications in *The Waste Land* that the protagonist has reached the point where he has intimations of Godhead.

It is in Part V that the Grail legend becomes most explicit, and explicit in its Christian interpretation. The protagonist might be said to repeat in his own progress the evolution of the Grail legend, as described by Jessie Weston, from pagan ritual to Christian romance (in *From Ritual to Romance*, 1920). When in the final passage the protagonist becomes both Quester and Fisher King, there is a powerful recapitulation of the disorder that has been the poem's main theme. As he sits upon the shore fishing, with the arid plain behind him, we are given a poignant sense of the incoherent fragments that stock the cultural memory of Europe:

> Shall I at least set my lands in order?
> London Bridge is falling down falling down falling down
> *Poi s'ascose nel foco che gli affina*
> *Quando fiam uti chelidon*—O swallow swallow
> *Le Prince d'Aquitaine à la tour abolie*
> These fragments I have shored against my ruins
> Why then Ile fit you. Hieronymo's mad againe.
> Datta. Dayadhvam. Damyata.
>   Shantih shantih shantih.   (V.423–33)

Yet all these apparently miscellaneous fragments speak of purgation—whether through the refining fire of Dante's line, or the melancholy of Nerval's ghostly Prince, or the purposeful madness of Kyd's Hieronymo—or else they speak of desire for salvation, as in the line from the Latin *Pervigilium Veneris*: "When shall I become as the swallow?"

"These fragments I have shored against my ruins." The line turns to a positive purpose the fragmentation upon which the poem has been built. They point to a tradition which, though in disarray, is all we have to draw on for salvation. The fragments are in many languages because all European culture is being tapped, going back to its earliest origins in the Sanskrit Upanishads. As the protagonist, through memory and association, makes his identity, he is able to give the fragments a new order. They are made to issue in the three Sanskrit precepts—

give, sympathize, control—upon which the protagonist has already meditated, and which are to guide him toward that peace, signified by *shantih*, which passes understanding.

Once we see that *The Waste Land* dramatizes the making of an identity, that the Quest is for personal order that leads to cultural order and cultural order that leads to personal order, the poem turns out more positive than we used to think it. The deadness and disorder that made the biggest, indeed the only, impression on the poem's first readers [9] are seen as a phase through which the poem passes to point toward the Christian poems that are to follow Eliot's conversion in 1927. We can now see from *The Waste Land* that Eliot was by 1922 farther along toward conversion than we had thought. Eliot—"Fishing, with the arid plain behind me," and wanting to set "my lands in order"—has by now put behind him all liberal humanitarian modern answers: he is fishing, waiting for revelation. He has by now seen the need for Christianity, though he still cannot believe.

To understand the modern problem of identity that Eliot is trying to solve in *The Waste Land*, we have to look back not to "Prufrock" or "Portrait of a Lady," whose speakers are still, as I have suggested, Jamesian in their delineation, but to "Preludes" and "Rhapsody on a Windy Night," which were written during those same years, 1909–11. The characters of these poems are not, like Prufrock and the lady, separated from external reality by an unspoken ideal; they are, on the contrary, undistinguishable from the images of external reality that make up their consciousness.

II

The morning comes to consciousness
Of faint stale smells of beer
. . .

III

You dozed, and watched the night revealing
The thousand sordid images
Of which your soul was constituted;
They flickered against the ceiling.
And when all the world came back
And the light crept up between the shutters
And you heard the sparrows in the gutters,
You had such a vision of the street
As the street hardly understands;
. . .

IV

His soul stretched tight across the skies
That fade behind a city block,
Or trampled by insistent feet
At four and five and six o'clock.

In all these instances from "Preludes," there is a minimum of
that distinction between perceiver and perceived, and hence of
that will and organizing power, which constitute an identity.
Yet the validity of the sensations and the vision of the street
suggest some minimal awareness.

The Laforguian "Rhapsody on a Windy Night" reads like a
parody of Wordsworth in that it opens up, under the transforming influence of moonlight, the flow of memory and association. But moonlight in an urban setting does not yield beauty.
Reinforced by the light of a street lamp, it transforms the streetwalker into a grotesque:

> "Regard that woman
> Who hesitates towards you in the light of the door
> Which opens on her like a grin.
> You see the border of her dress
> Is torn and stained with sand,
> And you see the corner of her eye
> Twists like a crooked pin."

The twisted eye recalls the memory of twisted things:

> The memory throws up high and dry
> A crowd of twisted things;
> A twisted branch upon the beach . . .
> A broken spring in a factory yard,
> Rust that clings to the form that the strength has left
> Hard and curled and ready to snap.

Perception again stirs memory when the sight of a cat slipping out its tongue to devour butter recalls, in the passage quoted earlier, the equally automatic reach of a child's hand for a toy: "I could see nothing behind that child's eye." [10]

This vacancy, this automatic action without reserve of thought and feeling, fascinates Eliot in his early view of character. Prufrock, who is paralyzed by too much reserve of thought and feeling, longs for such automatism: "I should have been a pair of ragged claws." But the speaker of "Preludes" sees the automatism as blotting out individuality. "The morning comes to consciousness" means there is no distinction among all the people who come to minimal consciousness because it is morning:

> One thinks of all the hands
> That are raising dingy shades
> In a thousand furnished rooms.

In "Preludes" IV, the soul of the clerk returning from work at evening is trampled like the street "by insistent feet." His soul is also "stretched tight across the skies," suggesting perhaps his taut nerves.

> And short square fingers stuffing pipes,
> And evening newspapers, and eyes
> Assured of certain certainties,
> The conscience of a blackened street
> Impatient to assume the world.

The certainties of such people, certainties derived from the mass media and from urban sensations, are as determined and insensitive as the street blackened by trampling. Their certainties are almost as automatic as the grasping reflex of the crab in "Rhapsody."

In "Rhapsody," the speaker on his way home late at night recognizes the number on his door. " 'Memory!' " says the street lamp sardonically, contrasting the mechanical memory of one's address with Wordsworthian memory. The indoor lamp " 'spreads a ring on the stair,' " giving another kind of light from the moon's.

> "Mount.
> The bed is open; the tooth-brush hangs on the wall,
> Put your shoes at the door, sleep, prepare for life."
>
> The last twist of the knife.

If the moonlight has yielded such mechanical sensations and memories, what can be expected of ordinary life? The speaker's thoughts are given him by moon and lamps—a sign that perceiver and perceived are not distinguished.

The view of the self in these two poems was either influenced by Bradley, or else, what is more likely, Bradley confirmed for Eliot a view of the self he had already arrived at on his own. We do not know when Eliot first read Bradley, but he did not begin to study him until he returned from Paris to Harvard in autumn 1911 to work for a doctorate in philosophy. F. H. Bradley, the turn-of-the-century English philosopher on whom Eliot wrote a doctoral dissertation, taught that the self can be known only through experience; for the self cannot be distinguished from its psychical contents, its sensations and memories of sensations. For the same reason, the self is in experience hardly distinguishable from the not-self—each fills and determines the other. "We have no right, except in the most provisional way," says Eliot, explaining Bradley in his dissertation, "to speak of *my* experience, since the I is a construction out of experience, an abstraction from it." [11] Bradley speaks, therefore, not of subjective perceivers but of subjective-objective centers of experience—"finite centres." There are as many universes as there are finite centres; for as Bradley puts it: "My external sensations are no less private to myself than are my thoughts or my feelings. In either case my experience falls within my own circle, a circle closed on the outside; and, with all its elements alike, every sphere is opaque to the others which surround it. . . . In brief, regarded as an existence which appears in a soul, the whole world for each is peculiar and private to that soul." [12] Eliot quotes this passage in a note to *The Waste Land* V, 411–13—lines in which the self as so described is the thing to be overcome. Through an analogy to the prison in which Dante's Count Ugolino was locked up to starve to death, Eliot, in meditating on the Sanskrit precept *Dayadhvam* (sympathize), is saying we must break out of the Bradleyan prison-house of self.

In "Preludes" and "Rhapsody," the Bradleyan view of self as opaque and discontinuous ("The usual self of one period is not the usual self of another") [13] is presented as true but awful. In both poems, the word *I* is severely repressed. But we can tell from the perceived details that the *speakers*—as distinguished from the characters they perceive—have in reserve an unacknowledged ideal by which they judge the mechanical life they portray. In "Preludes," the speaker finally uses *I* to express through the trampled souls on trampled streets an accumulating sense of violation, and to suggest that even these mechanical registers of sensation may obscurely feel some core of self that has been violated:

> I am moved by fancies that are curled
> Around these images, and cling:
> The notion of some infinitely gentle
> Infinitely suffering thing.

But no, this is only fancy; the universe is as sordid and meaningless as the urban scene:

> Wipe your hand across your mouth, and laugh;
> The worlds revolve like ancient women
> Gathering fuel in vacant lots.

Yet the fancy of some other possibility remains with us here and in "Rhapsody."

Having dissolved the distinction between subject and object, Bradley himself acknowledges a "limit of this interchange of content between the not-self and the self." He admits that we do nevertheless entertain obscure sensations of an essential self-hood, which derive from "our ability to feel a discrepancy between our felt self and any object before it. This . . . gives us the idea of an unreduced residue." [14] It is out of this unreduced residue, sensed in spite of the problematical nature of the self, that modern literature generates the mysteries of identity. And it is this unreduced residue—sensed as a mere perceptual bias in "Preludes" and "Rhapsody," and in the blank young man in "Portrait" who responds to the street piano and the smell of hyacinths—that develops into a positive force in *The Waste Land*.

The structure of "Preludes" anticipates that of *The Waste Land*. Both present separate vignettes of city life; yet the vignettes are unified by the central consciousness which must be understood as perceiving or imagining them all. The speaker of "Preludes," having thought of all the morning hands "raising dingy shades / In a thousand furnished rooms," imagines himself in the furnished room where the streetwalker wakes up alone. In the same way, the protagonist of *The Waste Land* imagines himself at evening in the furnished room where the typist receives the clerk; and he does this after envisioning, like the speaker in "Preludes," the city's taut nerves at the end of a working day:

> At the violet hour, when the eyes and back
> Turn upward from the desk, when the human engine waits
> Like a taxi throbbing waiting.   (III. 215–17)

Not rest but stimulation is wanted; hence the intercourse that turns out as mechanical as the taxi's throbbing. This typist and clerk, too, have had their souls trampled by the "insistent feet" returning from work.

"Preludes" gives us a world where people live alone in furnished rooms; the speaker of "Rhapsody" returns to such a room. *The Waste Land* gives us a world in which people do not communicate. Dialogues are one-sided; the answer, when there is an answer, is thought rather than spoken and does not answer the question:

> "Speak to me. Why do you never speak. Speak.
>   What are you thinking of?" . . .
>
>   I think we are in rats' alley
>   Where the dead men lost their bones.
>   (II.112–16)

But this isolation is counteracted by the ability of the speaker in "Preludes" and the protagonist in *The Waste Land* to project into the other characters. Hence the speaker's fancy in "Preludes" is of a compassionate humanity they all share, and his view remains general when he reverses himself to see that our general fate, instead, is as loveless as the force that moves the stars. The final lines may invoke an ironical comparison with Dante's final line in *Paradiso*: "Love that moves the sun and other stars." And, indeed, the minimal "notion of some infinitely gentle / Infinitely suffering thing" is just the unreduced residue of feeling out of which Christian mythology takes shape.

In *The Waste Land*, the speaker's projection into the typist's room takes shape in the figure of Tiresias. Bound up with the original draft of *The Waste Land* are some poems that demonstrate the projective sensibility that was to produce Tiresias. In "The Death of Saint Narcissus," the saint felt he had been a tree, a fish, "a young girl / Caught in the woods by a drunken old man"; finally he embraced martyrdom as the ultimate sensation. "Song" speaks of "Bleeding between two lives"; and some untitled lines help us understand how the protagonist of *The Waste Land* can be both Quester and Fisher King:

> I am the Resurrection and the Life
> I am the things that stay, and those that flow.
> I am the husband and the wife
> And the victim and the sacrificial knife.

The protagonist's projective imagination, which sees or creates the connections among the characters, sees in them a memory of and yearning for a communal identity, and that communal identity is expressed through the mythical figures in the poem, most notably the figures of the Tarot cards. In a 1916 paper, "Leibniz' Monads and Bradley's Finite Centres," Eliot threw light on the method of establishing identities he was to use in *The Waste Land*: "Nothing is real, except experience present in finite centres. The world, for Bradley, is simply the *intending* of a world by several souls or centres. . . . For Bradley, I take it, an object is a common intention of several souls, cut out (as in a sense are the souls themselves) from immediate experience. The genesis of the common world can only be described by admitted fictions." [15]

Thus the mythical figures and patterns—the Grail Quest, the vegetation myths leading to the Christian myth—are the admitted fictions rising out of the characters' memories and desires, their unreduced residue of feeling. The vision encountered and lost of the hyacinth girl leads to a desire for recovery expressed through the fiction of the Quest. The longing everyone has for water recalls the seasonal alternation of drought and rain; while winter and spring are recalled by the longing for death that leads in the end to the longing for rebirth. The whole connection of human emotions with the cycle of the seasons is expressed through the fictions of the vegetation myths.

The sense of violation we detected in "Preludes" permeates the first three parts of *The Waste Land*. The theme is established through the fiction, represented in the rich Belladonna's painting, of Philomela's rape; and that fiction applies to all the women in the poem, including such recollected victims as Dante's La Pia and Ophelia (III.293–94, 306). The Christian

imagery of Part V makes explicit our accumulating sense that all
the violations come together in the figure of Jesus, the arch-vic-
tim.

The movement from the fire of Part III to the relief, in Part
IV, through water prepares the sensuous texture out of which,
in Part V, the figures of Jesus and other redeemers take shape.
They take shape because the senses require them to take shape,
the senses and the sensuous images as objective correlatives to
the protagonist's emotions:

> Ganga was sunken, and the limp leaves
> Waited for rain, while the black clouds
> Gathered far distant, over Himavant.
> The jungle crouched, humped in silence.
> Then spoke the thunder—
>
> (V.395–99)

of revelation. Earlier, a similar rendition of thirst gives rise to
the figure of Jesus:

> If there were the sound of water only
> Not the cicada
> And dry grass singing
> But sound of water over a rock
> Where the hermit-thrush sings in the pine trees
> Drip drop drip drop drop drop drop
> But there is no water.   (V.352–58)

The longing for water, for even the sound of water, together
with the hope offered by the lovely water-dripping song of the
hermit-thrush, leads to "Who is the third?" The third, as we
have seen, is the unrecognized apparition born of the Antarctic
explorers' despair, and the unrecognized apparition of Jesus
born of the disciples' grief over the Crucifixion. In both cases
the apparition was a deliverance. *The Waste Land*'s positive
force derives from the characters' ability to generate, from an
unreduced residue of feeling, an archetypal identity which de-

livers them from the closed circle of the Bradleyan self and the
immediate historical moment.

After Eliot's conversion in 1927, the Bradleyan self becomes the
unredeemed self for which Christianity is the cure—a cure that
is miraculous, spiritual, moral, quite different from the steps in
The Waste Land toward a psychological cure through the asso-
ciationist evolution of archetypes within the psyche. In *Four
Quartets* and even in the Dantesque *Ash-Wednesday*, which
allegorizes Eliot's conversion experience, the self is no longer
problematical. The self is there to be decomposed in *Ash
Wednesday* II and finally, in Part VI, recomposed into a self
that has broken out of its prison ("Suffer me not to be separated"), having united its will with God's ("Our peace in His
will"). The speaker can now be in the world but not of it
("Teach us to care and not to care"), because his will is no
longer individual, no longer defined by its opposition to the
general order of things ("Teach us to sit still"). The cure has
been accomplished through visions of archetypes and symbols
external to the speaker—the leopards, the purgatorial stairs, the
lady in the garden—that confirm a unified and continuous self.

It is in his last three plays—*The Cocktail Party*, *The Confidential Clerk*, *The Elder Statesman*—that Eliot again treats the
self as problematical and tries to *solve* the problems of identity
raised in the early poems. His exploration begins when he aban-
dons the spiritual elitism that followed upon his conversion—
the idea, advanced in *Ash-Wednesday* and in his first two plays,
Murder in the Cathedral and *Family Reunion*, that there can be
redemption only through the saint's complete transformation of
self, and indeed only, in the first two plays, through the martyrs'
deaths chosen by Becket and Harry. The other characters, who
constitute the choruses of the two plays, remain (except for

Agatha and Mary in *Family Reunion*) the vacuous walking dead of *The Waste Land* who have no spiritual existence.

Eliot begins to answer his own earlier questions when, starting with *The Cocktail Party* (1949), the most successful of the last three plays, he comes to realize that every self is redeemable according to its own character. Even the worldly Chamberlaynes, who relate to the upper-class voices of *The Waste Land*, enter into a spiritual existence when they discover who they really are and what they really want—when they consciously choose to make "the best of a bad job," to carry on as people who can never really love or understand each other, and to face the consequences of that choice: which is to be decent and tolerant and to cooperate in giving the very best cocktail parties possible. The important thing is to humbly acknowledge our deficiencies and our low place in the spiritual scale, rather than practice the self-justification and self-deception that causes neurosis and unhappiness. "The best of a bad job" (II, p. 410) is all we can accomplish unless we are saints, says the Christian psychoanalyst Reilly. In a mad, violent world, the way of decency and duty is a good life. Reilly is even unwilling to tell Celia that the saint's way she chooses is better. Both ways are necessary; but you must choose between them, discover what you really want, what kind of person you are.

The characters of the last three plays come to understand themselves by coming to understand other people; and they start by misunderstanding other people, by using them to sustain their own false images of themselves. Edward Chamberlayne flatters himself, in his affair with Celia Coplestone, into thinking himself capable of returning the kind of love Celia gives. When his wife Lavinia leaves him and gives him the freedom he thought he wished for to marry Celia, Edward recovers his own sense of identity by *choosing* to have Lavinia back. Because she has like Alcestis (the model is Euripides' *Alcestis*) been lost and recovered, he sees her as "a stranger" (I.3, p. 385), recog-

nizes her otherness or intrinsic reality. Edward complains of
being locked up in the Bradleyan prisonhouse of self. Celia
complains that in their affair neither she nor Edward broke out
of their prisons, that each made use of the other for his own
purpose. This means—it is the essence of the modern sexual
problem as defined by Lawrence—that we can "only love /
Something created by our own imagination," so that "one *is*
alone" and "unreal" (II, p. 416).[16] Only through communion
with others, through belief in their reality, can we, says Eliot in
answer to Bradley, break through appearance to reality.

Eliot's prescription for breaking through could derive from
Bradley's conclusion that "Personal identity is mainly a matter
of degree." [17] Edward and Lavinia have in common "the same
isolation" (II, p. 410), and the realization of this provides a certain amount of shared consciousness. They can also achieve
some continuity of self through consistent social action. Celia,
instead, by choosing the saint's way, achieves continuity of self
and communion with others through a love that is not self-
projection because it derives from love of God. Both ways of
self-recognition lead out of the prisonhouse of self, away from
anxiety and neurosis.

Eliot uses the Chamberlaynes' adjustment to mediocrity to
solve the identity problems in his next two plays. Taking off
from Euripides' *Ion*, a tragicomedy of mistaken identity in
which identity is determined entirely by parentage, Eliot shows
in *The Confidential Clerk* how people find out who they are by
finding their true parents and true children. Colby, in the process of finding his true self and parents, discovers that his ultimate parent is God. His self-discovery through unraveling mistaken identities provides Eliot's Christian answer to Bradley's
empiricist skepticism about the phenomenal self in Book I, "Appearance." Eliot's Christian answer also derives from Bradley's
romantic or idealist reinvalidation of the self in Book II, "Reality," where his argument, as Eliot explains it, is that "the self

. . . is an interpretation of experience by interaction with other selves," and that philosophy is founded on the

> felt identity between appearance and reality. . . . The only real truth is the whole truth. . . . the felt background against which we project our theories. . . . We all recognize the world as the same "that"; it is when we attempt to describe it that our worlds fall apart.[18]

Bradley settles for a split between the felt and analyzed worlds.

But to break through to reality the romantic split between the two worlds and the two selves that apprehend them must, in Eliot's Christian view, be healed, the felt or imaginary must be substantiated; we must have, as we have been told in *The Cocktail Party*, both loneliness *and* communion. Colby wants "not to be alone" in the garden of his inner life:

> If I were religious, God would walk in my garden
> And that would make the world outside it real
> And acceptable, I think.   (II, p. 474)

Colby's work in the Church will make his garden as substantial as the vegetable garden of Eggerson, the play's other authentic character, who finds fulfillment in a cozy domestic life in the country. In *The Cocktail Party*, we can hardly believe Reilly's assertion that Celia's way of redemption is no better than the Chamberlaynes' way. But there is so little distinction between Colby's churchly and Eggerson's ordinary way of redemption that Eggerson can be considered Colby's spiritual father and, as Eliot suggested in a manuscript note, the play's "Only real Christian." [19]

In Eliot's last play, *The Elder Statesman*, the dying ex-statesman, Lord Claverton, has sacrificed his friends, his children and his own authenticity in order to sustain too elevated an image of himself. In a purgatorial experience, he acknowledges a betrayed friend and a betrayed mistress as specters from the past, thus exorcizing them as ghosts haunting his conscience and turning them into ordinary people. Now that he understands and confesses his sins, now that he has become a person rather than a public image, he can love and be loved and can—like the aged Oedipus in Sophocles' *Oedipus at Colonus*, the play's model—die serenely, freeing his children for love and self-fulfillment.

Although the story is Christian, the vocabulary comes from the psychology of identity. Original sin is the denial of one's true identity; salvation is the recovery of it. As in the two earlier plays, sin is using other people to sustain one's false self-image; love can only flow between people who have found their true selves. The solutions in all three plays do not require conversion, only self-knowledge. The beginning of self-knowledge is the sense of sin, and Eliot is in these plays concerned with the sense of sin in ordinarily upright people like us, his readers—people whose sins are as pallid as their virtues. It is as though he were mainly concerned to redeem the neutral spirits of *The Waste Land*.

We can take to heart Eliot's prescriptions for finding ourselves, we can try to live by his solutions. And yet, and yet his answers do not make the imaginative impact of his earlier negative portrayals of a vacancy and walking death that come as stark illuminations just because they do not *at first* seem applicable to ourselves but only to a general cultural condition. The happy adjustments to mediocrity of the Chamberlaynes and Colby, even Lord Claverton's exaltation rising out of his willingness to settle for his own mediocrity and his son's—none of these "happy endings" can compete poetically with such early portrayals as: "We are the hollow men"; or "A crowd flowed over London Bridge, so many, / I had not thought death had undone so many." Lord Claverton cannot compete poetically with that dried-up old man in "Gerontion," to whom age reveals only his own increasing deadness and who has not even on his conscience the ghosts ("I have no ghosts") that could redeem him.

Whatever his religious convictions, Eliot's imagination—like

Arnold's and Beckett's, but unlike Yeats's and Lawrence's—
remains engaged with the *loss* of self. Even in the last plays he is
most moving when showing how little self-realization can be expected:

> They may remember
> The vision they have had, but they cease to regret it,
> Maintain themselves by the common routine,
> Learn to avoid excessive expectation,
> . . .
>
> Two people who know they do not understand each other,
> Breeding children whom they do not understand
> And who will never understand them.
>
> (*Cocktail Party* II, p. 417)

It is because these last three tragicomedies—with their attempts
to offer generally applicable solutions as the first two tragic
plays, and as *Ash-Wednesday* and *Four Quartets* do not—seem
products of will rather than imagination, that the continuator in
drama of early Eliot is not Eliot but Samuel Beckett.

Chapter 4
BECKETT:
ZERO
IDENTITY

Beckett's plays project and intensify the atmosphere of early Eliot. Beckett's living dead do not even walk—in the novels they hobble and crawl, in the plays they are remarkably stationary. Beckett presents in his plays unindividuated characters with stylized faces, whose single names do not name them, give no clue to family, class, nation (we do not identify Vladimir as Russian or Pozzo as Italian). His characters come from nowhere, belong nowhere, have no occupation or place in society. There is no society. Society appears as the small band that beats Estragon when he sleeps nights in a ditch. Godot beats his messenger's brother; Pozzo beats Lucky. Beating seems the last vestige of the social principle; and for certain pairs (Pozzo-Lucky, Hamm-Clov) the tyrant-victim relation is all that remains of love. Beckett goes farther than early Eliot, who portrays the breaking down of our civilization; Beckett portrays the period after the wreck.

His plays are set on the waste land—*Waiting for Godot* on a country road with only a bare, black tree; *Happy Days* on an

"expanse of scorched grass"; [1] *Endgame* in a room into which
are carried reports of a lifelessly gray sky and sea. This waste
land, like Eliot's, signifies sexual and spiritual sterility; but it
also signifies the site of a vanished civilization, where a few survivors exist in scattered pairs. The pair is the minimum unit
necessary for human existence, since human existence is dialectical: these people need to be seen, heard, remembered, need
above all to talk, in order to assure themselves they exist. "We
always find something, eh Didi, to give us the impression we
exist?" says Estragon in *Godot*. [2] In *Happy Days*, Winnie, isolated with her husband, speaks of the couple who once beheld
them as the "last human kind—to stray this way." The last vestiges of self are maintained by a few final habits—Winnie's
brushing her teeth and hair—and by ceaseless talk. Winnie
dreads her husband's death; for the impression that "Something
of this is being heard, I am not merely talking to myself. . . .
enables me to go on, go on talking that is." [3] The waste land is
the void over which the self puts forth its few threads, precariously.

The waste land is also a spatial extension without landmarks
and therefore without direction, without distinctions of place
and therefore without locations. To Vladimir's question in Act
II, "Where were we yesterday" if not here, Estragon replies:
"How would I know? . . . There's no lack of void." The place
we're at is "indescribable," says Vladimir to Pozzo, who doesn't
remember being here yesterday. "It's like nothing. There's nothing. There's a tree." [4] Since the tree is the one landmark,
there's no place to go from it; just as there is no place to go from
the room in *Endgame*, or from the mound in which Winnie is
buried to the waist. That is why the characters are largely stationary, and why even when they *intend* to go—as Vladimir
and Estragon do finally, also Clov in *Endgame*—they remain.

Nature has not been restored by the disappearance of civilization; for whatever catastrophe destroyed civilization also destroyed nature. "There's no more nature," says Clov. [5] The

blind Hamm, whom he serves, longs atavistically to feel a ray of sunshine on his face and hear the sea, but there is no sun and the tideless sea makes no sound. "What a blessing nothing grows," says Winnie.[6] The waste land represents a condition beyond civilization and nature.

The props in these plays are like the random artifacts dug up by archeologists; one has to read back through them to the coherent civilization that gave them meaning. Though only *Krapp's Last Tape* specifically takes place in the future, all these plays suggest the future of the last men—especially *Endgame*, where Hamm controls the last supplies of food and fuel and the cry is "no more nature," "no more pain-killer," "no more coffins." [7] The bowler hats worn by the four men in *Godot* contrast comically with the ragged clothes of the slave Lucky and the tramps Vladimir and Estragon. The hats represent an anachronistic notion of human dignity, of man as thinker: Lucky can only think with his hat on, but then Lucky's garbled speech suggests that thought itself is anachronistic. Vladimir and Estragon are tramps in a metaphysical rather than a social sense; they are not tramps because they occupy the bottom rung of the social ladder, but because there is no ladder and no rung for them, no social function that might make them respectable. "A million years ago, in the nineties" they "were respectable," because there was then a society (the world wars apparently made the difference). In the end Estragon's trousers fall to his ankles because he has offered his belt as a cord for hanging themselves. Vladimir takes off the hat he got from Lucky, "*peers inside it, feels about inside it, shakes it, knocks on the crown,*" as though searching for its meaning. Then donning his hat preparatory to departure, he bids Estragon pull on his trousers. "You want me to pull off my trousers?" asks Estragon, not realizing they are down. "Pull ON your trousers," says Vladimir.[8] The comic business is Chaplinesque and means, as with Chaplin whose little tramp is never without a bowler hat, that whatever humanity is salvaged will not depend on such social signs as hat and trousers.

Winnie pulls out of her comically capacious bag toothbrush, comb and brush, mirror, lipstick—implements for preparing to meet a society that does not exist. She is aware of the absurdity. "There is so little one *can* do. One does it all. All one can. Tis only human. . . . (*Smile.*) To speak in the old style. The sweet old style." These last two sentences are her refrain whenever she refers to the humanistic values of the old civilization. If she could not make her toilette, take the things out of her bag in the morning and put them back at the end of the day, if she could not talk, "what *could* I do, all day long, I mean between the bell for waking and the bell for sleep?" [9] Time in Beckett is the other void represented by the waste land, a void to be deliberately filled.

The revolver Winnie so incongruously takes out of her bag corresponds to the tree from which Vladimir and Estragon plan to hang themselves. Both denote "life as," in one critic's phrase, "the non-committing of suicide." [10] "We'll hang ourselves tomorrow," says Vladimir in the end; then, after a pause, "Unless Godot comes." [11] Godot will not come and they will not hang themselves; they will *wait*, which is to say *live*. Vladimir, the rationalist, uses the word "waiting" for what we do in time, and the name Godot for the direction of our wait. Estragon, the irrationalist and former poet, remains skeptical. In this pair the rationalist gives such direction as there is. In the other pair, the thinker Lucky enslaves himself to Pozzo, the man of power; the two are traveling, and Pozzo gives so strong a sense of direction that Estragon wonders whether Pozzo is Godot. (Traveling and waiting are Beckett's two images of existence; waiting predominates in the plays.) By Act II, however, Pozzo has disintegrated; he has grown blind, Lucky has grown dumb, and all four in their physical decrepitude fall into the same heap. Bodily decay marks time—but faintly, because Beckett's characters are old and decayed at the start; the rapid decline of Pozzo and Lucky is exceptional, an example of dramatic compression. Pozzo's refusal to name the day when disaster struck suggests that the decline is to be understood as the slow inevitable work of time.

Time moves slowly and irregularly. It is moved forward by such events as the entrances and exists of Pozzo and Lucky and of Godot's messenger boy in Acts I and II, and by the few leaves that have miraculously appeared on the tree for Act II. Time is moved forward by Winnie's additional burial from waist to neck, and by the death of Hamm's mother and Clov's sight of the boy outside that makes Hamm decide the end has come, that Clov can leave. Clov's refrain, "Something is taking its course," [12] evokes the movement of time in all these plays. Times moves cyclically, as we see by the repetitions; but because memory fails, the cycles cannot be exactly perceived. Neither Godot's messenger nor Pozzo and Lucky remember, when they return, having been there or having seen Vladimir and Estragon the day before. Because the tree now has leaves, Estragon denies that this is the same place; so the rationalistic Vladimir, for whom continuity is essential, points triumphantly to the boots Estragon left there yesterday. But Estragon finds they are not his boots. Tell Mr. Godot, says Vladimir in the end to the messenger boy, "that you saw me." Then violently, "You're sure you saw me, you won't come and tell me to-morrow that you never saw me!" He springs forward, the boy exits: *"As in Act I, Vladimir stands motionless and bowed."* [13] The mime in *Act Without Words* (*Endgame* volume) ends with just such motionlessness after he has failed to rationalize the absurdity of objective phenomena.

Continuities of place, time, identity are connected, and depend upon memory. Because of the characters' lack of memory, time in Beckett's plays has a limited backward extension, which relates to a lack of depth in space and identity. Krapp, in *Krapp's Last Tape*, is the only character who dwells on memory and remembers in detail; but he remembers by playing tapes—

through what Beckett in his book on Proust calls, using Proust's terms, "voluntary" or mechanical rather than "involuntary" or organic memory.[14] Krapp therefore establishes no connection with the past: "I wouldn't want [those years] back," he says in the last line.[15] As a character he has no depth, since the memory is not inside him; he moves only a little within his "den" and, accordingly, little present time elapses. In Beckett's plays, the counterpart to the characters' lack of depth is their immobility or near-immobility within a very limited extension of space-time. Beckett's characters lack the unseen third dimension of memory and unconsciousness; they exist almost entirely in what they do and say. This is curious in a writer who has praised Proust for accomplishing just the opposite, for creating infinite depths of character through extensions of time, memory, unconsciousness. Like the movement in painting that starts with post-Impressionism, Beckett's dramatic art strives to be statically two-dimensional in order to evoke sheer existence— "presence," as Robbe-Grillet calls it in his essay on Beckett's plays.[16]

There is as little forward as backward extension in time. The characters only dimly remember the last cycle and do not anticipate the rebirth that would bring round the next. Winnie sinks into the mound through her cycles of day and night. The arrival of Godot would be an end not a beginning, and the leaves on the tree betoken no general rebirth: "Everything's dead but the tree," says Vladimir.[17] The question of cycles comes clearest in *Endgame*, when Hamm refuses to bring in the boy whom Clov, dismayed, spies through his telescope and calls "potential procreator." Hamm will do nothing to bring on the new cycle except send Clov away and, by covering his face with the bloody handkerchief he took off it in the beginning, prepare to die. Hamm has been telling the story of a Christmas Eve when a desperate father begged him to feed his starving boy and Hamm argued against fostering new life: "But what in God's name do you imagine? That the earth will awake in spring? That the

rivers and seas will run with fish again?" The story is never finished, Clov may be that boy; but the implication is that Hamm
should have let the boy die, if he didn't. "Are there still fleas?"
he asks when Clov finds one. Kill it, for "humanity might start
from there all over again!" [18] In the radio play *All That Fall*, an
old man, blind and sick like Hamm, pushes a boy off a train.
"Did you ever wish to kill a child?" he asks. "Nip some young
doom in the bud." [19] We are back to "April is the cruellest
month," the reversal of natural instinct in fear of rebirth and
longing for death. Although there are echoes of Eliot throughout Beckett—his main characters are "hollow men"; like the
speaker in "Gerontion," they are old, with ruined senses, disembodied consciousnesses representing the old age of a culture—such echoes are particularly noticeable in *Endgame*.

The following conversation parodies the conversation with
Stetson in *The Waste Land*. Here is Eliot:

> "That corpse you planted last year in your garden,
> "Has it begun to sprout? Will it bloom this year?
> "Or has the sudden frost disturbed its bed?"
>
> (I.71–73)

Here is Beckett:

> HAMM: Did your seeds come up?
> CLOV: No.
> HAMM: Did you scratch round them to see if they had sprouted?
> CLOV: They haven't sprouted.
> HAMM: Perhaps it's still too early.
> CLOV: If they were going to sprout they would have sprouted. (*Vio-
> lently.*) They'll never sprout!

Hamm's "Then let it end! With a bang!" [20] echoes the last lines
of "The Hollow Men": *"This is the way the world ends / Not
with a bang but a whimper"*—lines that turn all the games and
rituals of the poem into an endgame. The whole theme of lost
memory, individual and cultural, recalls Eliot—though Beckett
is even more satirical than Eliot. The past is represented by
Hamm's father and mother, Nagg and Nell, who are relegated

to ash cans and pop their heads up to talk. They lost their legs when their tandem crashed in the Ardennes (scene of fighting in both world wars) on the road to Sedan (recalling the 1870 Franco-Prussian War). Nagg and Nell represent the pre–World War I world of sensuality, sex, joy; they still laugh, tell jokes— they try to kiss but can't reach each other from their separate ash cans. Hamm, who despises their sensuality, can't forgive his father for begetting him. Nell's recollection of happiness one April afternoon, rowing on Lake Como, parodies the opening recollections in *The Waste Land* of prewar romantic experience. *The Waste Land*'s " 'Do you remember / Nothing?' " is echoed by Vladimir's appeal to Estragon to confirm the continuity of Acts II and I: "Do you not remember? . . . Do you not remember?" Estragon's reply: "I remember a lunatic who kicked the shins off me" [21] parodies the sense and rhythm of: "I remember / Those are pearls that were his eyes."

Even the positive impulse of these plays, the unaccountable vestigial tenderness that ties into pairs these almost unfeeling characters, can be compared to the unaccountably minimal "notion" in "Preludes" of "some infinitely gentle / Infinitely suffering thing." Vladimir and Estragon suddenly embrace; Clov, who is always threatening to leave and can speak no words of affection, nevertheless takes good care of Hamm and in the end returns at least temporarily; the mute, apparently unheeding Willie whispers in the end Winnie's name, giving her a "happy day." [22] Beckett does not, like Eliot, develop this minimal intuition, because he does not acknowledge the enduring underlife and the archetypes emerging from it. He reverses the direction running from Wordsworth through Eliot, in that he deliberately avoids the archetypalization of characters; his characters are symbolic only negatively, since they symbolize the *lack* of life: Hamm does *not* fulfill the God-King-Father archetype suggested. In the trilogy of novels, the personae and fictions tried and discarded suggest archetypes—Ulysses, Hermes, Jesus; but the shifting references do not, as in *The Waste Land*

and *Ulysses*, reinforce the characters' identity—they reduce it. The shifting references that in *The Waste Land* produce an accretion of contents produce in Beckett's trilogy a "gradual reduction of contents," which in Dieter Wellershoff's words "appears as a progressive process of de-mythologization." [23]

That is why identity in Beckett approaches zero, with the difference between life and death almost imperceptible. How shall I know, asks Hamm, whether you have left or died. If I have died, "I'd start to stink," says Clov. Hamm: "You stink already. The whole place stinks of corpses." When Hamm asks Clov to see if Nell is dead, Clov, raising the lid of her ash can, says: "Looks like it."

> HAMM: And Nagg?
> CLOV: Doesn't look like it.
> HAMM: What's he doing?
> CLOV: He's crying.
> HAMM: Then he's living. [24]

This recalls Eliot's "infinitely suffering thing," and Beckett's description in *Proust* of periods of transition between an old self and a new "when for a moment the boredom of living is replaced by the suffering of being." [25] There is certainly no rebirth of self in these characters; they are all locked into an old self, they are all, to borrow Beckett's terminology in the Proust book, prisoners of habit. When they do suffer because they have for a moment broken through to an awareness of their suffering, the release is not, as in Proust, involuntary memory—it is a glimpse, through the structured world of habit, into the void: a momentary awareness of their own nothingness. The discarding of selves in the trilogy leads to the same void; the process is not rebirth.

Hamm reveals himself most genuinely when he cries—as Clov describes his view of nature through a window—"Clov! . . . I was never there!" [26] I never lived, he is saying, never got outside myself, never made contact with reality. "We are bored," says Vladimir of his rationalized world. But "in an instant," as we dispel not fantasy but habit, "all will vanish," he continues, reversing the metaphysics of *The Tempest* when Prospero says that the spirits he conjured up for the masque "Are melted . . . into thin air," restoring us to reality (IV.i.148–58). Vladimir says, instead, that when the habitual world has vanished, "we'll be alone once more, in the midst of nothingness!" [27]

Despairing of Willie's attention, Winnie feels "that someone," her equivalent to Godot, "is looking at me," and that she passes in and out of being as she passes in and out of his gaze: "I am clear, then dim, then gone, then dim again, then clear again, and so on, back and forth, in and out of someone's eye." Buried now up to the neck, she wonders what remains of her identity: "To have been always what I am—and so changed from what I was. I am the one, I say the one, then the other." She counts up the bodily features that still constitute *me*—face, nostrils, lip, tongue—even as she realizes where being finally resides: "If the mind were to go. It won't of course. . . . It might be the eternal cold." [28] Winnie is most poignant at this moment of self-reduction. Beckett's characters have most "presence," are existentially most powerful, when their being is reduced to the one last flicker of self-consciousness.

Beckett has described his epistemology as Berkeleyan: "*Esse est percipi* [To be is to be perceived]. . . . Search of non-being in flight from extraneous perception breaking down in inescapability of self-perception." Hence, as Martin Esslin puts it, "the *compulsiveness* of the voice" throughout Beckett, "the inescapability and painfulness—through its failure to achieve non-being —of the process of self-perception." [29] Hence the disintegration of bodies in the plays and fiction—as a way of reducing the self to its last vestige, of discovering how closely one can approach zero. I do not agree with Esslin that all Beckett's characters desire non-being. Hamm does (he calls repeatedly for pain-killer), but Winnie does not (her love of life is parodied); Vladimir and Estragon are pulled both ways, but incline I think toward life. I do agree that being is portrayed at bare minimum. The compulsive talking wards off non-being; so does the pairing, which makes the characters feel they are seen and heard. Hamm prepares to die when he bids Clov leave him. He predicts to Clov—who cannot return his gestures of affection because "the words you taught me. . . . don't mean anything any more"—a future in which even this last social unit, the pair, will have disappeared because tenderness will have disappeared: "you'll be like me, except that you won't have anyone with you, because you won't have had pity on anyone and because there won't be anyone left to have pity on." [30]

Although all these plays approach the quality of Winnie's monologue in that the characters speak mainly to hear themselves, only Krapp is alone. That may be why *Krapp's Last Tape* is the only one of the plays discussed so far to end on a purely negative note, without any sure sign of tenderness. Krapp, who has been recording each year's events on annual tapes, creates company by playing tapes of his former selves, selves with which he feels no connection so that they seem like other people. Yet Krapp's comments and the tape we hear—an utterance of thirty years ago—do not make a true dialogue since the earlier self, in repudiating a still earlier idealistic self of ten years back (whose recording he reports having just played), has already made the choice for discontinuity which the onstage Krapp merely repeats. We have here Proustian and Wordsworthian layers of time; but because the memory represented by tapes is mechanical or voluntary, Krapp does not in Wordsworth's phrase bind his days together—except for moments of involuntary memory, memories of women's eyes and his mother's death.

The Krapp of thirty years ago—the year he was thirty-nine and his mother died—had a "vision": "clear to me at last that the dark I have always struggled to keep under is in reality my most—unshatterable association." The "dark," as Vivian Mercier suggests, is the source of Krapp's literary talent. For the sake of literature Krapp renounced love, presumably in this year but it may have been earlier. He recurs over and over to a moment when he and his girl lay motionless together in a punt with the water rocking them. This was a moment of perfect communion with another person and nature. But Krapp, like so many modern people, does not want communion; he prefers isolation in the locked-up ego, he thinks in accordance with the Proust book that the darkness of isolation is good for his writing. There in the boat he told the girl "it was hopeless and no good going on." The Krapp of thirty years ago chose over love the confinement of his den—that is, himself: "I love to get up and move about in it, then back here to . . . me. Krapp." [31] *Krapp's Last Tape* projects an image of complete solipsism.

"Just been listening," says the onstage Krapp, "to that stupid bastard I took myself for thirty years ago. . . . Thank God that's all done with anyway." Yet he adds involuntarily (the involuntary memory shows a last minimal touch of humanity): "The eyes she had!" The voice on the tape, who repudiates the idealistic self of ten years ago ("Hard to believe I was ever that young whelp") ends the play by saying: "Perhaps my best years are gone. When there was a chance of happiness. But I wouldn't want them back. Not with the fire in me now. No, I wouldn't want them back." He has sacrificed the fire of passion for the fire of literary ambition; but the onstage Krapp, whose book failed and who throws away the envelope on which the taped Krapp scrawled notes for some great work, has not even that fire. His final posture of immobility and silence suggests that he has enough humanity left to question the taped Krapp's cocksureness. We are left wondering how much involuntary memory remains.

The onstage Krapp cannot make his last tape, because he has no present life to record; there is only the pleasure he takes in the word "spool," denoting the tape spool. [32] The onstage Krapp can only refer compulsively, through replaying the tape, to the moment in the boat when he was alive. Such compulsive memory is not, like involuntary memory, a release from the prison-house of self but a cyclical trap within it—a trap that Freud calls anxiety and Beckett, Eliot, Dante call hell. Nevertheless, there is Krapp's final stillness—always in Beckett an image of being. Because *Krapp's Last Tape* is the only play that employs the discarding of selves so conspicuous in the trilogy, Krapp's final powerful stillness confirms Wolfgang Iser's argument that the "negativity" of the novels is fruitful: that by taking us through the successive rejections of selves, fictions, language, of all conscious structures, Beckett makes us finally "experience the unknowable." In distinguishing himself from the still romantic Joyce, who tended "toward omniscience and omnipotence as an artist," Beckett said: "I'm working with impotence, ignorance. I don't think impotence has been exploited in the past." [33]

In the radio play *Embers*, produced a year later, we see how a writer who started with a family has, through retreat into the ego, annihilated other people and turned himself into a solipsistic monologuist like Krapp. Alone by the sea, whose sounds haunt him as they did his father, Henry summons the ghosts of his father, who does not engage him in dialogue, and then of his wife, who does. His father is dead, but his wife and daughter are not; yet all are ghostly memories because he has annihilated them as objective realities. His wife recalls how she warned him to see a doctor about the compulsive talking to himself that frightened their daughter. Feeling nothing for wife and daughter, he talked not to communicate but to keep from hearing the sounds of the sea; those undistinguishable sounds are the void compared to distinguishable sounds, like "thuds," which are "life." "The time will come," his wife predicted in a prophecy like Hamm's to Clov, "when no one will speak to you at all, not even complete strangers. You will be quite alone with your voice, there will be no other voice in the world but yours."

As she disappears, Henry begs her to "Be with me" [34] to con-

firm his existence; but she cannot perform this function since he
has himself destroyed her otherness. He returns to the endless
fiction he has been narrating to himself about an old man,
Holloway—the name of the physician who was to have cured
Henry's compulsive talking—who is summoned by an old man,
Bolton, the projection of Henry. Finding only existential
death—"Fire out, bitter cold, white world, great trouble, not a
sound"—Holloway wonders why he was summoned. Bolton
holds a lighted candle over his own face, revealing: "Tears?
(*Pause. Long laugh.*) Good God no!"—revealing that he is still
alive enough to suffer. "Holloway: 'If you want a shot say so and
let me get to hell out of here.' (*Pause.*) 'We've had this before,
Bolton, don't ask me to go through it again.' " The shot recalls
Hamm's pain-killer; the last sentence fits Beckett's pattern of
movement toward insight or communion, which is then aborted
by oblivion or the return to awareness of nothingness. Holloway
is driven frantic by Bolton's trick of opening and closing cur-
tains, letting moonlight in then restoring darkness—"white,
black, white, black": the cycles of awareness and unawareness
the two men are trying to escape. Bolton's " 'Please Holloway!' " suggests a desire for the opposite of pain-killer, for the
communion that would release them from the cycles; Bolton's
plea modulates into Henry's to Ada, Father, Christ—to the
other—to save him from nothingness.

Consulting his appointment book, Henry like Krapp finds
that he has no present life: "All day all night nothing. Not a
sound." [35] The play ends with the sounds of the sea. Henry has
made his life a void to match that of the sea. But consciousness
remains, and therefore sound (speech), suffering and cycles.
Bolton will forever summon Holloway, who will offer not communion but oblivion; Henry will forever summon Ada who will
forever leave him. Henry can never break out of the cycle because he has destroyed the objective world; he has drawn the
whole world into his skull.

Since consciousness can never know its own extinction, since "the individual," as Martin Esslin puts it, "can never become aware of his own cessation, his final moments of consciousness must remain, as it were, eternally suspended in limbo and can be conceived as recurring through all eternity." [36] This is the point of the Dantesque stage work *Play*, where the dead are locked into the cyclic memory of their passionate lives. They evolve purgatorially toward a higher understanding of their lives; hell is the aborting of illumination and the inescapable return in memory to the way they thought and felt in life.

Play is unusual for Beckett in that it presents *three* main characters—M, the man; W1, his wife; W2, his mistress. In their memories of life, there are never more than the usual two on-stage; M imagines all three, after death, drifting idyllically in a rowboat—the rowboat is a recurring image of happiness in Beckett. *Two* seems to be the number for life, *three* for heaven, *one* perhaps for hell; these characters partly inhabit all three places. They are described in the stage directions as three heads protruding out of *"three identical grey urns"* that touch one another. *"They face undeviatingly front throughout the play. Faces so lost to age and aspect as to seem almost part of urns. But no masks."* This is a model of all Beckett's characterizations, since character, even being, comes so close to zero. Identity is reduced even farther in *Not I* (1972), a monologue in which only a mouth is visible. The characters of *Play* are almost undifferentiated consciousnesses: *"Faces impassive throughout. Voices toneless."* [37] The specific exclusion of masks shows Beckett as even more impersonal than Yeats; for even the stereotypes portrayed by masks have too much personality.

The utterances are monologues. The three are not present to each other; each thinks the other two still alive. Yet the touching urns suggest that the three are united through pattern. (In the novel *Molloy*, the tramp Molloy and the proper citizen Moran are similarly united through a cyclical pattern of which they are unaware.) The inquisitorial spotlight, which plays Dante's questioning role, solicits each character individually, leaving the other two in darkness. When in the moving choral passages all three faces are illuminated, they speak in unison but say different things—a sign that only pattern unites them.

The faint light with which the play opens indicates their awareness that they are now shades; the strong light that follows indicates that they are remembering their former lives; the return to faint light indicates that they are back in the present as shades. Their life story of lust, betrayal, hatred is unusually passionate for Beckett; *Play* follows the cyclical structure of Noh drama, in which ghosts relive their passionate lives then fade back into death. But the point is as usual in Beckett's plays: the characters have more "presence" now that they have less vitality, they understand each other better now that they speak monologues than when they spoke to each other. Now they pity each other, wish each other well. M says: "When first this change I actually thanked God. I thought, It is done, it is said, now all is going out. . . . peace is coming." W2 says: "I had anticipated something better. More restful. . . . At the same time I prefer this to . . . the other thing. Definitely. There are endurable moments."

The better state seems to be an oblivion equivalent to complete understanding. W1 speaks of "Hellish half-light," and adds: "someday somehow I may tell the truth at last and then no more light at last, for the truth?" The remaining light is the remaining consciousness: "How the mind works still!" she says twice. In the crucial speech that explains the title, M says: "I know now, all that was just . . . play. And all this? When will all this . . . have been . . . just play?" To see phenomena as play is to deprive them of being by reducing them to pattern. When will some higher understanding reduce to pattern their present state so that they can pass out of existence? In the end M feels himself scrutinized by a higher understanding represented apparently by the spotlight: "Looking for something. In my face. Some truth. In my eyes. Not even." He feels himself passing out of existence either because he is completely under-

stood, or because the spotlight as absolute eye is mindless so
that he does not feel himself perceived: "Mere eye. No mind.
Opening and shutting on me. Am I as much—." There is a
blackout, then spot on M. "Am I as much as . . . being
seen?" [38] There is a blackout, then the faint spots on three faces
with which the play began. The play is repeated. Neither complete understanding nor complete oblivion—perhaps they are
the same—can be attained, because consciousness cannot conceive its own extinction. Since there is only consciousness reflecting on itself, the thought of breaking through to an outside
reality is only a thought that leads back to the round of consciousness.

   Is this usurpation of the world by consciousness the catastrophe that seems to have preceded all these plays, making Beckett's characters seem survivors of some terrible wreck? The catastrophe is to some extent the world wars (there are hints of this in
Godot and *Endgame*); it is to a greater extent old age when, with
wreck of body, life retreats into a consciousness that is itself failing. But the clue to the catastrophe's main meaning is Vladimir's statement: "What is terrible is to *have* thought." To Estragon's question: "But did that ever happen to us?" Vladimir
replies: "Where are all these corpses from?" [39] Hamm, too,
says: "The whole place stinks of corpses," [40] and tells of a madman who, looking upon a lovely scene, sees only ashes. The catastrophe is in Blake's terms a fall in perception. To *have*
thought is to have killed off the world, to have drawn it all inside the skull. After that no more thought is possible (Vladimir:
"We're in no danger of ever thinking any more"); for genuine
thought is about something other than itself. All we can do now
is invent the talk, games, rituals necessary to cover the void.
Talk has become a substitute for thought. "We are incapable of
keeping silent," says Estragon. "It's so we won't think."

   In the play's most lyrical passage, they hear the past as talk, as
"all the dead voices" rustling over the void:

VLADIMIR:	To have lived is not enough for them.
ESTRAGON:	They have to talk about it.
VLADIMIR:	To be dead is not enough for them.
ESTRAGON:	It is not sufficient.
	Silence.
VLADIMIR:	They make a noise like feathers.
ESTRAGON:	Like leaves.
VLADIMIR:	Like ashes.
ESTRAGON:	Like leaves.
	Long silence.
VLADIMIR:	Say something!
ESTRAGON:	I'm trying.
	Long silence.
VLADIMIR:	(*in anguish*). Say anything at all!
ESTRAGON:	What do we do now?
VLADIMIR:	Wait for Godot.
ESTRAGON:	Ah! [41]

"Ah!" parodies revelation. Beckett's art is distinguished by such powerful images as this of human existence suspended over a void made palpable.

The destructive thought alluded to would seem to be Descartes'. For it was Descartes who, after dismissing the inherited world by an act of doubt, reestablished the world on the principle "*I think, hence I am.*" He thus cut mind off from body, especially since he did not recognize that thought requires a sensuous object. He made mind the center of life and identity in an otherwise mechanical world; he gave us the image, which haunts Beckett, of mind surrounded by void:

> I thence concluded that I was a substance whose whole essence or nature consists only in thinking, and which, that it may exist, has need of no place, nor is dependent on any material thing; so that "I," that is to say, the mind by which I am what I am, is wholly distinct from the body, and is even more easily known than the latter, and is such, that although the latter were not, it would still continue to be all that it is. [42]

Beckett's first published poem, *Whoroscope*, is a dramatic monologue spoken by Descartes; and the Cartesian split defines the geography of self which, in the manner of Wordsworth with Locke and Eliot with Bradley, Beckett accepts and fights throughout his work—perhaps because he feels his own self-hood that way, and feels Descartes' amputation of self predictive of our time. "Murphy," he tells us in his first published novel,

> felt himself split in two, a body and a mind. They had intercourse apparently, otherwise he could not have known that they had anything in common. But he felt his mind to be bodytight and did not understand through what channel the intercourse was effected nor how the two experiences came to overlap. He was satisfied that neither followed from the other.[43]

To the dissociated mind, body seems a mere mechanical appendage. Hugh Kenner has brilliantly analyzed Beckett's recurrent image of man on bicycle as a "Cartesian centaur," replacing animal body with a machine.[44] It is because Beckett modifies Descartes by treating body as a disintegrating rather than as an efficient machine that so many Beckett characters drag around old inadequate bodies that seem hardly to belong to them and require the aid of bicycles, crutches, wheelchairs. Beckett assumes romanticism has failed in its attempt to answer Descartes by establishing the organic connection of mind with body and of the mind-body self with nature. "We should turn resolutely toward Nature," says Estragon, modulating, as he and Vladimir often do, from personal into cultural experience. "We've tried that," says Vladimir.[45] We have tried romanticism.

One might draw the opposite conclusion—one might say that Beckett is a romanticist working negatively through satire of the isolated self. But it is likelier—since Beckett apparently resembles the heroes of his fiction—that he could not square with his experience of his own self romantic accounts of the self's infinite possibilities for expansion and for transforming the external world. The best evidence of Beckett's antiromanticism is this: that whatever positive impulse he does generate comes from reversing the Wordsworthian direction, from withdrawal rather than projection of self. Beckett's "salvation" or self-realization is, as John Fletcher says, "a negative one: not an expansion but a contraction, into oneself and into a more barren, if truer, existence"; Beckett counsels "retreat towards" the nothingness that is reality.[46]

Beckett's reversal of the Wordsworthian direction is curious, since in his book on Proust he uses Wordsworthian categories to describe Proust's achievement in a direction that we recognize to be Wordsworthian. As in Wordsworth, habit is the villain. Habit and the ego represented by an habitual organization of the world screen us from reality. We break through in periods of transition "when for a moment the boredom of living is replaced by the suffering of being"—when, lifting the veil of familiarity, we experience world and self as flowing, alive and threatening because unrationalized. The insight fades as we proceed to rationalize that experience into a new habitual organization of the world. Life in Proust (and Wordsworth) proceeds through such cycles of birth, death and rebirth of self and the world it perceives. The breakthrough is accomplished by "involuntary memory," which is as in Wordsworth a form of forgetting that leads us to the permanent self underlying the "succession of individuals" that accompany the "succession of habits":

> We can only remember what has been registered by our extreme inattention and stored in that ultimate and inaccessible dungeon of our being to which Habit does not possess the key. . . . Here, in that "gouffre interdit à nos sondes," is stored the essence of ourselves, the best of our many selves and their concretions that simplists call the world.

Our permanent self is unconscious; we have access to those unplumbable depths where it resides only through unconscious memory; only the unconscious is creative: "From this deep source Proust hoisted his world." [47]

Having described so precisely and sympathetically what Proust is doing, Beckett in his plays and fiction does the opposite. In the plays his characters remain prisoners of habit, in the trilogy they have little conscious memory; in both plays and novels they have no unconscious memory, no unconscious, no depth—which is why his mode is comic rather than psychological. Depth is projected as action and landscape.

In his remarks on Proust's solipsism, however, Beckett does describe his own practice. Since neither love nor friendship "can be realized because of the impenetrability (isolation) of all that is not 'cosa mentale,' . . . the attempt to communicate where no communication is possible is . . . horribly comic." Friendship, which according to Proust, negates our "irremediable solitude," is a "social expedient" with "no spiritual significance. For the artist . . . the rejection of friendship" is

> a necessity. Because the only possible spiritual development is in the sense of depth. The artistic tendency is not expansive, but a contraction. And art is the apotheosis of solitude. There is no communication because there are no vehicles of communication. Even on the rare occasions when word and gesture happen to be valid expressions of personality, they lose their significance

as they emerge. " 'One lies all one's life long,' writes Proust, 'notably to those that love one, and above all to that stranger whose contempt would cause one most pain—oneself.' " " 'Man,' " writes Proust, " 'is the creature that cannot come forth from himself, who knows others only in himself.' " [48]

Nevertheless Beckett's characters, unlike Proust's, see—when they break through the screen of habit—not the unformed vitality of Proust's periods of transition, but the void. They have negative epiphanies ("Moments for nothing"),[49] the reverse of Wordsworth's and Proust's insights into process. Consequently there is no rebirth of self in Beckett; there is only reduction—through the discarding of false selves in the trilogy and through the lack of content in the plays. But is truth a void, or is it the power of irreducible being Robbe-Grillet discusses?

Starting with Heidegger's proposition that the condition of man is to be *there*, Robbe-Grillet suggests that the stage, where a character is necessarily *there*, provides the best medium for

Beckett. In the trilogy the protagonists deteriorate, as progressive reincarnations of each other, toward nonentity—disappearing into the cascade of words. But how better project sheer existence than with actors who have to fill an extension of space-time when they have nothing with which to fill it? Our very boredom in beholding them emphasizes the "presence" that nevertheless rivets our attention and stands in the mind afterwards. Unfortunately Robbe-Grillet thinks "presence" annihilated in *Endgame* with Hamm's cry "I was never there"; [50] but in fact Hamm has most "presence" at that poignant moment reminiscent of early Eliot. All the plays end with the assertion, through their protagonists' silent immobility, of "presence."

Beckett pursues the inaccessible self throughout his work, but never gets there as Proust and Wordsworth do, instantaneously, with the magic of memory and imagination. The plight of Beckett's protagonists confirms Wordsworth's belief that self and the world can only be known through the senses that connect them, through sensation passing into thought that passes back into sensation. Eliot surprisingly confirms Wordsworth when he says in his book on Bradley that "to inspect living mind, you must look nowhere but in the world outside," that the mind viewing itself sees only mechanism. [51] The disembodied mind can only know through analysis, and analysis kills the thing it would know, making it disappear into the vacuum of mental process, the novels' cascade of words. "I'm in words, made of words," says the voice in *The Unnamable*; yet "I'm something quite different . . . a wordless thing in an empty . . . black place" [52]—the dungeon of inaccessible self.

Beckett's characters conspicuously lack a sensuous life. Their hatred of sex confirms Lawrence's observation that sex contemplated coldly by the disembodied mind must seem disgusting. Winnie, the only Beckett protagonist who still lives in the senses and consequently enjoys getting up in the morning, is parodied and has in the end few senses left. Winnie's head protruding from the mound is, in spite of her wishes, an image of disembodied mind, of self isolated in the head. Other such images are Hamm's legless parents whose heads pop up out of ash cans, the heads protruding from urns in *Play*, and in *The Unnamable* the torso stuck "in a deep jar, its neck flush with my mouth." Death in Beckett is birth reversed; these characters have almost returned to the womb, but cannot quite die because death is a physical event whereas consciousness cannot conceive its own extinction. "If only I were alive inside," says the jarred head of *The Unnamable*, "one might look forward to heart-failure." This voice, which cannot avoid naming and renaming the unnamable self, says later: "Ah if only this voice could stop, this meaningless voice which prevents you from being nothing, just *barely* prevents you from being nothing and nowhere."

Beckett dramatizes with a force unequaled in our literature the solipsistic condition of modern man who must fabricate reality out of his own head. "I'm in a head," says the voice of *The Unnamable*; and later: "Yes, a head, but solid, solid bone, and you imbedded in it, like a fossil in the rock." [53] (Ruby Cohn suggests that Hamm's room with its two high peepholes may be the inside of a skull, and that "the interior of a skull" is "a recurrent locale in Beckett's fiction.") [54] The voice of *The Unnamable* finds not only himself but his environment a fabrication of his own words: "wherever I go I find me, leave me, go towards me, come from me, nothing ever but me." [55] "Everything was tainted with myself," writes Lawrence who, in his poem "New Heaven and Earth," breaks out by discovering through touch the otherness of his wife's body. Indeed, Beckett's characters exemplify all that Lawrence and the other writers I am discussing most feared for the future of human identity. It is from such solipsism, such final diminution and retreat of the vital outgoing Wordsworthian self, that Yeats and Lawrence try to deliver us.

Since Beckett's work—which emerged in the 1950s—follows theirs, he clearly does not think that they and others who have tried to reconstitute the romantic self have succeeded. He seems to insist that, in spite of all the fine writing, his portrayal of the diminished self remains, to quote the title of his prose poem, *How It Is.* Beckett, who thoroughly understands the romantic position, poses a problem for a literary study such as this one. For if the problem of identity is a real problem in modern life, then can literature do anything about it, can the best writing in the world make us restructure our identity? Beckett would seem to be saying that things can only get worse, seeing that God is dead and has been dead so long that Beckett's characters often seem to have forgotten His name. Nietzsche and the post-Nietzschean romanticists tell us that man can transcend himself and thus give *himself* the identity he used to derive from God's eye. Beckett says he cannot.

Yet Beckett's report on humanity is not the worst conceivable. For his characters, who belong to the idealistic side of the Cartesian split, *suffer* from their desolation; except for the parodied Winnie, they do not *think* they are happy—as do the cheery, efficient last men (the objective, mechanical men who have not transcended themselves) of Nietzsche's devastating satire.

> " 'We have invented happiness,' say the last men, and they blink. They have left the regions where it was hard to live, for one needs warmth. One still loves one's neighbor and rubs against him, for one needs warmth. . . .
>
> "A little poison now and then: that makes for agreeable dreams. And much poison in the end, for an agreeable death.
>
> "One still works, for work is a form of entertainment. But one is careful lest the entertainment be too harrowing. One no longer becomes poor or rich: both require too much exertion. Who still wants to rule? Who obey? Both require too much exertion.
>
> "No shepherd and one herd! Everybody wants the same, everybody is the same: whoever feels different goes voluntarily into a madhouse. . . .
>
> "One has one's little pleasure for the day and one's little pleasure for the night: but one has a regard for health.
>
> " 'We have invented happiness,' say the last men, and they blink." [56]

These are the machines, not Beckett's disintegrating solitaries. These collective men—who deny life's pain, rubbing against each other and taking drugs to ward it off—are more easily recognizable in the world around us than Beckett's essentially religious characters who require only one companion to assure them they exist and whose humanity resides in the awareness we share with them of what is lacking. Lawrence shows the mechanical collective man as incipient in his satirical portrait of Benjamin Franklin; he satirizes modern solipsism in Clifford Chatterley—who with his motorized wheelchair makes a super-Cartesian centaur—and modern collectivism in Clifford's ant-like miners. Both Yeats and Lawrence, in their attempts to reconstitute the twentieth-century self, take into account the two opposite manifestations of lost identity—solipsism and collectivism. Lawrence worries more about solipsism; Yeats worries more about the collectivism represented by the last objective phases on his wheel.

Part III

RECONSTITUTION OF SELF: YEATS

THE RELIGION OF ART

Chapter 5
EXTERIORITY
OF SELF

Early in his life Yeats was struck by two main ideas, which possessed and obsessed him and which account for the rest of his career as poet and thinker. Both ideas—the first about history, the second about identity—reversed what Yeats considered, rightly I think, to be the two leading beliefs of the nineteenth century—belief in *progress* and *sincerity*. In the Introduction to his late play *The Resurrection* (1931), Yeats recalls how his idea about history evolved: "When I was a boy everybody talked about progress, and rebellion against my elders took the form of aversion to that myth. I took satisfaction in certain public disasters, felt a sort of ecstasy at the contemplation of ruin, and then I came upon the story of Oisin." He wrote *The Wanderings of Oisin* (1889) as an escape from history. Oisin lives out his inner life in a timeless world; and when after three hundred years he returns to the world of time, he finds "progress." St. Patrick has Christianized Ireland, and the old gods are now devils. Oisin goes off to die, determined to stick by the old gods whether he finds them in hell or heaven. Like the nineteenth-century decadents (the last section echoes Swinburne's "Hymn to Proser-pine"), Oisin prefers to die with the old order rather than be reborn with the new.

But then around 1895 Yeats came to understand that history itself might be counted on to bring back the pagan values. "Oisin and his islands faded and the sort of images that come into *Rosa Alchemica* and *The Adoration of the Magi* [stories published in 1897] took their place. Our civilization was about to reverse itself, or some new civilization about to be born from all that our age had rejected." Yeats came to understand that history moves not in a straight line, but in cycles. The new age cannot be said to advance on the old because each age values opposite things, and because the new age brings back certain values rejected by the old. The values of the new age terrorize the old. It is through terror, as the two stories indicate, that history moves and that the revelation ushering in the new age descends.

The second idea, which struck around 1907 when Yeats was beginning work on his play *The Player Queen*, reversed the nineteenth-century idea that a man finds his identity through self-realization, through being true to himself. "Then after some years came the thought that a man always tried to become his opposite, to become what he would abhor if he did not desire it." [1] In his Note to *The Player Queen* (1922), Yeats explains that around 1907 "the thought I have set forth in *Per Amica Silentia Lunae* was coming into my head, and I found examples of it everywhere. I wasted the best working months of several years in an attempt to write a poetical play where every character became an example of the finding or not finding of what I have called the Antithetical Self." [2] This idea—that a man seeks his opposite—became the foundation for Yeats's theory of identity. He was to write the mystical little treatise *Per Amica Silentia Lunae* (1917), where he enchants us into assent, just to expound his idea of the antithetical self, which came to

him, as he says there, with the force of revelation: "When I had
this thought I could see nothing else in life." [3]

In his Introduction to *The Resurrection*, Yeats describes still a
third phase in his career—those events, starting with his wife's
automatic writing in 1917 and culminating in the publication of
the first version of *A Vision* in 1925, which produced "a symbolic system displaying the conflict in all its forms": [4] that is, as
a historical conflict between antithetical ages and a psychological conflict between antithetical selves. In *A Vision* Yeats
manages to combine his theories of history and identity, and he
combines them through the overarching idea of conflict itself.

Although *A Vision* tries to be as relativistic as possible, the
idea of conflict stands forth as the one absolute, the one acknowledged good. It was the purpose of the spirits who gave
Yeats his ideas for the book "to affirm that all the gains of man
come from conflict with the opposite of his true being." The
idea of conflict was also in his own mind: "I had never read
Hegel, but my mind had been full of Blake from boyhood up
and I saw the world as a conflict." Dante is a greater poet than
Shelley, because Dante, though a fierce partisan in life, was in
his poetry "content to see both good and evil"; whereas Shelley
"lacked the Vision of Evil, could not conceive of the world as a
continual conflict." Yeats does not of course mean that Shelley
was unaware of evil, but that as a Utopian Shelley envisioned
an end to evil or conflict: Jupiter and Demogorgon are destroyed
together in *Prometheus Unbound*. Yeats, whose own moral vision comprises unending conflict rather than evil, touches on
evil when he portrays mindless impersonal destructiveness as in
"Meditations in Time of Civil War" and "Nineteen Hundred
and Nineteen."

Yeats tries in his system to be impartial. Nevertheless, the
subjective or *antithetical* person, who is in conflict with his age
and destiny, is slightly favored over the objective or *primary* person who serves a code; and the *antithetical* pagan age, which

comprises conflict, is noticeably favored over the *primary* Christian age which rejects it: "instead of seeking noble antagonists," both of whom were as in Greek tragedy justified, Christian imagination called the antagonist evil. When Yeats says: "My instructors identify consciousness with conflict, not with knowledge, substitute for subject and object and their attendant logic a struggle towards harmony, towards Unity of Being," [5] he sees the struggle as both personal and historical. More than that, he sees the historical struggle as though it were personal. The conflict is not, as in Hegel, a conflict between ideas; rather an age struggles toward wholeness in the way a person does. There is no right or wrong, truth or falsehood—there is only growth. An age is "a stream of souls . . . all knowledge is biography."

Yeats says this in his Introduction to *The Resurrection*. The passage is worth quoting because it summarizes the relation between psychology and history in *A Vision:*

> We may come to think that nothing exists but a stream of souls, that all knowledge is biography, and with Plotinus that every soul is unique; that these souls, these eternal archetypes, combine into greater units as days and nights into months, months into years, and at last into the final unit that differs in nothing from that which they were at the beginning.

This is no mere metaphor. Once we realize that for Yeats identity-making goes on not only in this life but between lives as well, and that individual identities merge into archetypal or communal identities, we can understand how the historical cycles reflect these personal dynamics. In the course of one life and many lives, our individuality frees itself from, then returns to, a communal matrix; and the historical periods chart in their varying characteristics the phases of this cyclical movement. The purpose of it all? "All things," says Yeats drawing the moral of this passage, "have value according to the clarity of their expression of themselves, and not as functions of changing economic conditions or as a preparation for some Utopia" [6]—not inasmuch as they contribute to progress. The question we will have to consider is why Yeats found it necessary to reverse the nineteenth-century belief in sincerity as a way of returning to the romantic ideal of self-expression.

The answer is to be found in the connection he drew between psychology and history—a connection already apparent in *The Player Queen* where Yeats could hardly advance his new idea about antithetical selves without carrying over his slightly older idea about antithetical ages. The newer idea would seem to have been born out of the older; the two would seem to be inextricable. Although not one of Yeats's best, *The Player Queen* is a very interesting play and is especially important for understanding Yeats's career since the ten years during which he wrestled with the play were the crucible in which he remade his ideas and prepared the way for *Per Amica*, *A Vision* and the major poems and plays. It is here we find the statement that sums up his theory of identity: "Man is nothing till he is united to an image." [7] Not only is this to be Yeats's answer whenever, as in "Among School Children," he confronts the mysteries of identity, but it is also his criterion for judging a civilization. Does the civilization provide the antithetical images with which we can unite? We may in the process of identity-making be unconsciously looking toward a new civilization for the saving image.

This is what happens in *The Player Queen* to the actress Decima who, in a play about Noah's ark, refuses to accept the role assigned her of Noah's wife. Decima must help usher in a new age before she can play the role that shows forth her identity, that of Queen. Yet this role is antithetical to her, since she is a harlot's daughter. The role of Noah's wife *seems* suitable since her husband Septimus, the poet who wrote the play, is to act Noah. But Decima does not really love Septimus, whose mistress willingly takes over the role of Noah's wife. Thus Decima's search for the antithetical self is a search for the identity that can fulfill her deepest desire—for a new and deeper sincerity.

Septimus foresees in his poetry the Queen she is to be. Because she treats him badly, she can serve as the antithetical image that inspires his poetry—as his "mask," his " 'hollow image of fulfilled desire.' " [8] She sings the first stanza of a song by Septimus, the whole of which, appearing in Collected Poems as "The Mask," is a source from which we deduce Yeats's theory of the mask. In earlier drafts the man wears the mask, but in the final version the woman, as Decima makes clear, wears the mask.[9] The man says: "Put off that mask of burning gold / With emerald eyes," and the woman replies:

"O no, my dear, you make so bold
To find if hearts be wild and wise,
And yet not cold."

The implication is that beauty, if it is to move lovers, poets and saints, must project terror and mystery. In the subsequent stanzas, the man wants to know what lies behind the mask, whether love or deceit—whether or not the woman is his enemy. It is the mask, she answers, that "set your heart to beat," [10] so rest content with the enigma. The implication is that a knowledge of her sincere or "real" self might produce friendship but would kill passion—that love, like art, requires aesthetic distance.

The "real" self the man wants to fathom is the woman as unreconstructed individual, before she has been united to an image. But it is the woman as archetype, the woman united to an image, who awakens passion and whose true individuality shines forth—as we see when Decima finally assumes her role as Queen—with renewed force and clarity. The old sincerity reveals the unreconstructed self, the new sincerity the reconstructed self. The distinction between these two orders of identity determines everything Yeats has to say on the subject.

The distinction explains that puzzling artifact in The Player Queen, the mask of the sister of Noah. Septimus explains the symbolic meaning of Noah and the flood, when he says:

It is necessary that we who are the last artists—all the rest have gone over to the mob—shall save the images and implements of our art. We must carry into safety the cloak of Noah, the high-crowned hat of Noah, and the mask of the sister of Noah. She was drowned because she thought her brother was telling lies.[11]

As opposed to popular poets, who confirm the mob in the prejudices of the age, the true poet speaks symbolically of the coming era ("The arts," says Yeats elsewhere, "lie dreaming of things to come").[12] The true poet is a Noah who foretells the end of the present era, and salvages from the flood the stock of eternal images that will enable other poets to do the same job in the coming era. Noah's sister is the unreconstructed individual who, because she cannot read symbols, is entirely immersed in her own age and drowns with it. Yet her type appears in every age giving each age its own character; the poet needs her as the eternal flesh-and-blood antithesis to the image.

Queen Decima, in preparing in the end to announce to her fellow actors their banishment, dons the mask of the sister of Noah. The mask represents Decima's previous unreconstructed self, the self that was destructive because not fulfilled, and not fulfilled because the age had not yet arrived that could supply the image of queenship with which she could unite. As in all traditional comedy, the final dance celebrates a banishment— the banishment of her unreconstructed self—and a marriage— her union with her image of queenship, objectified in the marriage to the Prime Minister that politically confirms her reign. The dance, as always in Yeats, celebrates that union of individual with archetype which Yeats was to call Unity of Being.

But why must Septimus and the players be banished? Septimus, who read the symbols rightly and foresaw the coming queenship of Decima, now insists she is his wife. Having projected the archetype, the poet returns to fact; he is always ahead in the cyclical movement, therefore always in opposition. Having sung in the new era, Septimus must be banished so he can prepare to sing it out. The players too must be banished because they always act plays about the ends of eras, and the Queen would rather not witness their new prophecy. There is no right or wrong in historical issues; history is a play: "Why must I think the victorious [historical] cause the better? . . . I am satisfied, the Platonic Year [the historical cycles] in my head, to find but drama." [13]

The present Queen, who desires sainthood and martyrdom, has the Christian virtues but not the courage to sustain them—a sign that the Christian era is on the way out. Another sign is that her chastity and seclusion make her seem to the mob not a saint but a witch. When the mob murderously pursues her, the Queen is glad to yield her identity, to allow Decima to face the mob in the Queen's clothes. Because she risks her life, Decima can assert to the mob: "I am Queen. I know what it is to be Queen." Her heroic assertion of an antithetical identity signals a new pagan era. It is a sign of the new pagan values that the mob accepts her as Queen because of the self-assertion, and because she is not good but beautiful. Yeats cannot say whether Decima ushered in the new age or the new age made her Queen.

As *poet* Septimus does not have to remake his identity. He plays out the conflict in his poetry; while the *saint*, the former Queen, and the *heroine*, Decima, play out the conflict in life. After she breaks with Septimus, Decima looks for a beast to rut with so she can remake herself and, like Leda with the swan, inaugurate a new era. She plays the harlot in order to become Queen. On her first appearance she sang the lovely song of the harlot's daughter that foretells the destiny she now fulfills. Her antithetical image had just been revealed to her: "The moment ago as I lay here I thought I could play a queen's part, a great queen's part; the only part in the world I can play is a great queen's part." [14] In finding her antithetical self, Decima finds her deepest self, the self laid out for her from the beginning.

Are these eccentric ideas about identity intrinsically interesting, or are they interesting only inasmuch as they help us un-

derstand Yeats's artistically successful poems and plays? Let me
say first that no major work can, in my experience of literature,
be founded on shoddy ideas. The ideas may seem obsolete or
eccentric, but the great writer will be using them to shock himself and us into new insights. Thus the arcane diagrams of *A
Vision* turn up in William Irwin Thompson's recent sociological study, *At the Edge of History* (Ch. 4), as a structural model
of conflict and change. Yeats's ideas about identity are likewise
valid as a model, if only because they systematize his response
to a modern problem that must really be there since so many
modern writers have noted it. The problem is the loss of personal force that goes with the loss of spiritual force, and vice
versa. As an example of what Yeats saw when he looked at modern personality, let me quote the little poem about a bureaucrat
which was written in 1907 or 1908 and first published in
1909—the years during which Yeats began his long struggle
with *The Player Queen.*

> Being out of heart with government
> I took a broken root to fling
> Where the proud, wayward squirrel went,
> Taking delight that he could spring;
> And he, with that low whinnying sound
> That is like laughter, sprang again
> And so to the other tree at a bound.
> Nor the tame will, nor timid brain,
> Nor heavy knitting of the brow
> Bred that fierce tooth and cleanly limb
> And threw him up to laugh on the bough;
> No government appointed him.
>   ("An Appointment")

The contrast between the squirrel's self-delighting life and the
bureaucrat's meagerness corresponds to Yeats's comparison, in
the *Autobiography*, between Sargent's portrait of Woodrow Wilson, where the body is wooden and all life concentrated in the
head, and Strozzi's Baroque portrait in which the Venetian gentleman's life is distributed throughout his body: "his whole body

thinks." [15] The problem is self-consciousness which brings anxiety, that corrosive of self-delight. The life of the bureaucrat in
the poem is too simply individual, which is to say too simply
conscious. Nothing comes from instinct, race, archetypal pattern.

This is a poem Lawrence might have written. Arnold could
have portrayed the bureaucrat, but probably not the squirrel.
Arnold diagnosed the disease and saw joy as the cure, but he
could not portray joy because he had not the concept of the two
orders of identity. It is because the nineteenth century took into
account only the unreconstructed individual self that it made
what Yeats considered its mistake—that it thought love comes
from compatibility and that poetry, to quote Arnold, is "a criticism of life" and religion, "morality touched by emotion." Although its best poets (Wordsworth, for example, in his archetypalizations) had intuitions beyond this, and Blake stepped
right across the century into our own, the nineteenth century
still, when it formulated its thoughts, equated the desirable with
the gentle and rational—Arnold's "sweetness and light." In
other words, the nineteenth century did not fully articulate the
idea of conflict it had invented. Although preoccupied with the
divided self, it thought division lay *within* the unreconstructed
individual self. Because Yeats saw conflict as coming from *without,* he understood physical love as founded upon spiritual hate,
poetry as the revelation of an antithetical image, and religion as
hatred of God that brings the soul to God. He saw that the
conflict was with a self, an image, that has not yet come into
being; so that the struggle was part of a movement that would
bring into being a new age governed by new images.

Yeats knew he was but rediscovering premodern identity, an
identity he rediscovered perhaps through some face seen on
Byzantine mosaics when he visited Ravenna for the first time in
1907 before starting *The Player Queen*—a face archaic, expressionless, mysterious. This experience, the return of the archaic,
would have resembled Picasso's when he first gazed upon Afri-

can masks and found them beautiful though they were in their ferocity antithetical to all that European art had stood for since Phidias. Both Yeats and Picasso stepped into the twentieth century when they recognized the return of the archaic (described in Pound's poem, "The Return," quoted in *A Vision*), saw beauty united with its opposite—terror.

To account for the sense of identity that derived from this new aesthetic experience, Yeats made a philosophy that he considered to be thoroughly revolutionary in its regressiveness. Like Lawrence, he felt that a mere change in the economic and social system would not be enough to usher in the new age, that nothing less than a complete change in the constitution of self would do. Arnold understood that the problem of self was linked to the problem of the culture, but he did not want to change the culture; he wanted more of the same—more humanism. Yeats saw as necessary a reversal of culture that he half wanted and half dreaded; he wanted a culture that would provide images antithetical to those of the present culture—images with which we could remake ourselves. Then all the rest would follow; we would remake our ideas about love, art, religion, nationality.

In the introductions to the four plays collected in 1934 as *Wheels and Butterflies*, Yeats addresses the Garrets and Cellars, by which he means the two main revolutionary forces of his time. The Garrets are the artistic avant-garde which reacted against the bourgeoisie by going Catholic; the Cellars are the Communists. Yeats proposes his own philosophy as a third way that is even more revolutionary, because it upsets the relatively recent assumptions maintained by Catholics and Communists that history is linear and the self simply individual and fixed in its identity. " 'To Garret or Cellar a wheel I send.' " The wheel means not only that history is cyclical, but that it is "a stream of souls" [16]—and that the cycles are moved by the need of these souls to individuate, find their archetypes, pass back into the matrix, then individuate again. "The wheel where the world is butterfly," this phrase from *Per Amica*,[17] meaning the cycles which show the world as reincarnated soul, suggests that our identity is not single but many-layered, that we have lived many lives. So seriously does Yeats take the idea of reincarnation that he expects in a few years "we may have much empirical evidence, the only evidence that moves the mass of men to-day, that man has lived many times."[18]

We cannot blink the fact—as some of Yeats's more rationalistic critics have tried to do—that Yeats believed in reincarnation. To read Yeats properly we need not ourselves believe in reincarnation; but we must not be so confirmed in old-fashioned prejudices as to be embarrassed by his belief in it, or to forget how complexly modernist thought treats the problem of belief.[19] We must be ready to entertain the idea of reincarnation as a serious and worthy speculation. We must, in other words, be able to respect Yeats's intelligence and perception of life—in his prose as well as in his verse. We need not believe in reincarnation to understand that so many of our authors touch on it, because the idea is at least one attempt to account for the deepest and subtlest manifestations of psychic life and the complex layers of identity. The idea of reincarnation explains perhaps better than any other hypothesis the feeling, which is at the core of our sense of identity, that we include all the identities we have tried and rejected in order to become what we are—that to be a saint requires the psychic experience of having known what it is to be a great sensualist, and vice versa.

"We can satisfy in life," says Yeats in *Per Amica*, "a few of our passions and each passion but a little, and our characters indeed but differ because no two men bargain alike." We are what we are because we have bargained differently to be this at the price of not being that or the other. Identity is always threatened by the return of excluded passions, and if we keep identity going at all it is through catharsis—through living and thus exhausting the banished passions in dreams. The passions that return in dreams are those of which we are not conscious. But the excluded passions of which we are conscious, "when we know that they cannot find fulfillment, become vision," and vision is objective as dream is not, because vision bears the mark of conscious arrangement: "and a vision, whether we wake or sleep, prolongs its power by rhythm and pattern." The question is whose consciousness creates the pattern: "Whether it is we or the vision that create the pattern, who set the wheel turning, it is hard to say." Thus, the passions we have excluded in order to make an identity return as an unconscious-conscious projection that challenges the old identity and helps us make a new one. Yeats calls this projection the antiself or Daimon.

Yeats draws the connection between identity and history when he considers, as in *The Player Queen* and *A Vision*, that the projected vision belongs to the new era, so that in making and remaking our identity we dream of the future even as the arts do. In *Per Amica*, however, he confines himself to questions of identity.

Per Amica Silentia Lunae (1917) makes the large, bold statement that our unconscious mind lies outside us; hence our identity comes from without. We discover who we are by looking outside not inside. Since this idea is only implicit in *The Player Queen*, *Per Amica* in formulating it represents a giant step forward in Yeats's thinking about identity. It is this idea about the external source of identity that Yeats refers to here as the idea that obsessed him when he began work on *The Player Queen*.

> Saint Francis and Caesar Borgia made themselves overmastering, creative persons by turning from the mirror to meditation upon a mask. When I had this thought I could see nothing else in life. . . . I was always thinking of the element of imitation in style and in life, and of the life beyond heroic imitation. I find in an old diary: "I think all happiness depends on the energy to assume the mask of some other life, on

a re-birth as something not one's self, something created in a moment
and perpetually renewed." [20]

Yeats discovered a new sense of identity by rediscovering the ancient process of identity-making through imitation. But the object of imitation for Yeats is an image not a person, and he
added the idea that the reconstructed self must be perpetually
renewed through perpetual conflict with the object of imitation
and with the temptation to rest in the unreconstructed self.

We can understand the significance of this development by
considering the parallel development in the career of Thomas
Mann. In an essay of 1936 called "Freud and the Future,"
Mann describes the transition in his fiction from the psychological and naturalistic *Buddenbrooks* to the mythical *Joseph and
His Brothers*; and he attributes the change in his subject matter
"from the bourgeois and individual to the mythical and typical"
to psychoanalysis, which teaches in new terms the ancient
"mystery of the unity of the ego and the world." For psychoanalysis teaches that "the apparently objective and accidental" is "a
matter of the soul's own contriving," that "the giver of all given
conditions resides in ourselves." When we remember, Mann
explains, all Freud has revealed about "error, the retreat into illness, the psychology of accidents, the self-punishment compul-
sion," we realize that we make connection with external events
through our deepest desires.

We pass from the individual to the archetypal order of identity at that psychological depth where we desire to repeat mythical patterns. Life at its intensest is repetition. Thus the ego of
antiquity, Mann tells us, became conscious of itself by taking
on the identity of a hero or a god. Caesar trod in the footsteps of
Alexander; and Cleopatra manifested in dying her mythical self,
for "there exists a statuette of Ishtar holding a snake to her
bosom." Jesus quoted on the Cross the Twenty-second Psalm,
" '*Eli, Eli, lama sabachthani,*' " to say in effect, " 'Yes, it is
I!' " of whom the psalm speaks. [21] Sophocles' Oedipus, I would

add, discovers to his horror that it is he who, because of his efforts to avoid it, fulfills the predicted pattern—has in fact killed
his father and married his mother.

When in *Per Amica* Yeats says, "We meet always in the deep
of the mind . . . that other Will," he is describing without
benefit of psychoanalysis the same psychological experience
Mann describes of external identity. Yeats derives from Goethe's
Wilhelm Meister the Freudian idea that "accident is destiny,"
and he understands the unity of the ego and the world by understanding why the self unconsciously contrives its own destiny, "why there is a deep enmity between a man and his destiny, and why a man loves nothing but his destiny." The reason
is the struggle with that external self, "the Daimon who would
ever set us to the hardest work among those not impossible." [22]

Although we have no documentary evidence of Yeats's reading in Freud and Jung, it is obvious from his allusions that he
was aware of their work. But if Yeats read the psychoanalytic literature and did not simply rely on hearsay, he read it sparsely;
for he was far too busy reading Plotinus and the other Neoplatonists who gave him a terminology that explained his own experience of the external self and carried authority just because it
was ancient and mystical rather than innovative and scientific.
Since Yeats felt that he was in his revelations about history and
identity rediscovering ancient tradition, he is closer to Jung than
to Freud—he and Jung drew on the same Neoplatonic sources.
He is also closer to Jung in that Jung lays more emphasis than
Freud on the collective unconscious and therefore on the externality of self.

The term for the external self which Yeats took over from the
Neoplatonists, and which he introduces for the first time in *Per
Amica*, is *Daimon*. According to Plutarch, Yeats's main source,
the souls of certain illustrious dead men become purified to the
point where they "are exalted into Daimons" and champion
those living men who "strive for the same attainments"—communicating with them in sleep or waking trance. [23] To Plutarch

and Platonism generally, "I add," says Yeats, "another thought: the Daimon comes not as like to like but seeking its own opposite, for man and Daimon feed the hunger in one another's hearts." [24] Yeats added to Plutarch Blake's theory of opposites. Why? To solve the twin problems bequeathed him by romanticism, the problems of the divided self and solipsism—the claustrophobic fear that the struggle played out within the prisonhouse of self has nothing to do with external reality. By adding the concept of the Daimon, Yeats could assert that the conflict was actually with an external force and therefore connected with external reality.

That is what he means when he says in his Introduction to *The Resurrection:* "Even though we think temporal existence illusionary it cannot be capricious; it is what Plotinus called the characteristic act of the soul and must reflect the soul's coherence." [25] In other words, Yeats does not agree with Descartes that mind is cut off from matter as another order of existence. He insists that the process we sense as within is continuous with an external process. He is making the same assertion when in *Per Amica* he says that no poet has ever "been a sentimentalist," that "the sentimentalists are practical men" who believe that only the material world is real and therefore take pleasure in holidays from what they call reality. Poets, instead, take pleasure in revelations of a reality combining mind and matter: "The other self, the anti-self or the antithetical self, as one may choose to name it, comes but to those who are no longer deceived, whose passion is reality." [26]

"Ego Dominus Tuus," the poem that opens *Per Amica*, deals with such revelations to poets. The poem answers the question in literary theory raised by the romanticists, who claimed that poetry is expressive rather than mimetic, that poets write about themselves and their experience. Yeats stands by the expressive theory but revises it. "A poet writes always of his personal life," he says elsewhere, but "he is never the bundle of accident and incoherence that sits down to breakfast; he has been reborn as

an idea, something intended, complete." [27] The nineteenth
century did not understand the *sense* in which the poet writes
about himself, because it did not understand the two orders of
identity.

The two orders are exemplified by Yeats's title, with its reference to the appearance in *La Vita Nuova* of Love as a Daimon,
"a lord of terrible aspect" who said to Dante "I am thy lord"
and gave him a "new life," a new identity. Yeats's poem is a dialogue between Hic, the poet Yeats started out as, and Ille, the
poet he was in the process of becoming. Ille wants to write poetry by looking outward for the antithetical self that will help
him create the identity poetry expresses: "By the help of an
image / I call to my own opposite." Hic, instead, wants to write
poetry by looking within, by being true to his simply individual
self: "And I would find myself and not an image." Ille's reply
sums up all that Yeats and Arnold thought was wrong with
modern personality and art, that it was emasculated by self-
consciousness and, as the last line suggests, by isolation:

> That is our modern hope, and by its light
> We have lit upon the gentle, sensitive mind
> And lost the old nonchalance of the hand;
> Whether we have chosen chisel, pen or brush,
> We are but critics, or but half create,
> Timid, entangled, empty and abashed,
> Lacking the countenance of our friends.

Ille goes on to explain that Keats praised luxurious sensuality
because his senses were starved, and that Dante exalted the
purest lady ever loved because he was a lecher—that the "hollow face" we think we know from the *Commedia* is not the
Dante his friends knew. Being a Westerner, Dante "fashioned
from his opposite" an Oriental mask—made hollow by "A hunger for the apple on the bough / Most out of reach." Here we
see the difference from the classical mode of identity-making
through imitation. For antiquity the self imitated was simply external and similar—Caesar imitated Alexander. But here the

other self is an antithetical projection of our unfulfilled desires—we meet this projected self in the deep of our minds.

Hic in the end asks a question more classical than romantic.
Why do you leave your books to pursue occult practices when
everyone knows a style is found through study and imitation of
the great poets? "Because I seek an image, not a book," Ille
replies. I call to my Daimon,

> to the mysterious one who yet
> Shall walk the wet sands by the edge of the stream
> And look most like me, being indeed my double,
> And prove of all imaginable things
> The most unlike, being my anti-self,

which shall "disclose / All that I seek."

This is the expressive theory with a difference. Men had
always recognized that certain kinds of poets are—as Plato put it
in the *Ion*—possessed, that a god or muse speaks through them.
The expressive theory began with the romanticists, who insisted
that the source of inspiration lies within, that poets exceed their
usual capacity for insight and expression when imagination
takes over. Imagination, as Wordsworth's poetry demonstrates,
so transforms the world perceived by the poet that he sees as
coming from without a vision that started within. The implication is that the poet's true self is expressed through imaginative
activity (Coleridge defines the poet as the man who uses imagination), and that the poet writes well only when he expresses his
true self. But the emphasis is on the distinction between faculties—reason versus imagination. It is when that distinction is
turned into a distinction between selves—as in Blake's *Four
Zoas* and his short poem about Spectre and Emanation ("My
Spectre around me")—that the expressive theory takes a new direction.

According to Blake's distinction, which may be the greatest
single influence on Yeats's theory of identity, the Spectre (male)
is the ordinary conscious self that sits down to breakfast; it is the
abstracted self conceived as subjective, as cut off from the exter-

nal world. The Emanation (female) would seem to be the unconscious, the true self that is not cut off from the external world; hence the Emanation can also be considered the external world as loved or imagined. To the Spectre, which understands self as inside, the Emanation seems not a self but an elusive external ideal to be pursued. "My Spectre," says the speaker of the short poem to the Emanation, "follows thee behind. / . . . When wilt thou return again?" Only when the speaker is redeemed will the Emanation return and the two selves be one self existing both inside and outside the speaker.[28]

Yeats—who rewrote Blake's poem in his lovely "Song of Wandering Aengus"—aimed to create just such an internal-external self. He revises expressive theory by insisting it is the reconstructed self that poetry expresses, and that to be a great poet you have to find and make manifest this other self. Better than earlier expressive theorists, Yeats accounts for the artifice of art by saying, in "A General Introduction for My Work" (1937), that the poet "never speaks directly as to someone at the breakfast table, there is always a phantasmagoria. Dante and Milton had mythologies, Shakespeare the characters of English history or of traditional romance; even when the poet seems most himself," when he is Byron whose " 'soul wears out the breast' . . . , he is never the bundle of accident and incoherence that sits down to breakfast." Even when the poet uses as material his own life and personality, he turns his life into a myth and lends his name to an archetype. "He is more type than man, more passion than type. He is Lear, Romeo, Oedipus, Tiresias; he has stepped out of a play. . . . He is part of his own phantasmagoria and we adore him because nature has grown intelligible, and by so doing a part of our creative power." [29] The artistic process exemplifies the mysteries of identity, in that transformations of identity account for the artist and his personae.[30]

Yeats opens Part I of *Per Amica*, called "Anima Hominis" ("The Soul of Man"), by describing his own discovery of the two orders of identity. When he comes home from a party, he feels he has not been himself; for in the spirit of argument he has said many things he does not believe. When he sits down to write, he feels he is himself; then realizes he is no more himself under the spell of revelation than under the spell of argument, but that the antitheses are different. When in conflict with others, he assumes the false individuality necessary to counter-act their false individualities. When he takes antithetical revelation inside himself, he discovers a new archetypal identity. "We make out of the quarrel with others, rhetoric, but of the quarrel with ourselves, poetry." [31] The difference between imaginative literature and the rest depends on the different orders of identity out of which they are written.

Of imaginative literature Yeats says in the "General Introduction": "Talk to me of originality and I will turn on you with rage. I am a crowd, I am a lonely man, I am nothing." There are only masks and their expression; or if we start with the various passions, there are only the traditional types deliberately assumed in order to express them. Masks are not false, because we *know* they are artifices. Great acting is obviously artificial; it is stylized and cold. "The heroes of Shakespeare convey to us through their looks, or through the metaphorical patterns of their speech"—but not through what they overtly say—"the sudden enlargement of their vision, their ecstasy at the approach of death. . . . They have become God or Mother Goddess, . . . but all must be cold." [32]

> Eternity is passion, girl or boy
> Cry at the onset of the sexual joy
> "For ever and for ever"; then awake
> Ignorant what Dramatis Personae spake.

Our deepest passions in sex, art, religion are felt and articulated by selves that seem to be using our bodies to play out a personal and historical drama of which we are ignorant.

> A passion-driven exultant man sings out
> Sentences that he has never thought;
> The Flagellant lashes those submissive loins
> Ignorant what that dramatist enjoins,
> What master made the lash. Whence had they come,
> The hand and lash that beat down frigid Rome?
> What sacred drama through her body heaved
> When world-transforming Charlemagne was conceived?
> ("Whence Had They Come?")

The cold expressionless artifice of the mask is a sign that it prefigures the identity we have not yet achieved. Its very deficiency invokes the Daimon, who descending into us completes our identity by making us act out the unknown drama.

Thus Yeats, without resorting to a concept of God, restores the old supernatural confirmation of identity. He restores it here through the analogy with drama: the unknown dramatist and plot are equivalents for the direction and motivation of an unconscious mind that in its rhythm and pattern takes on the objective existence of a cosmic system. Elsewhere the aesthetic analogy is with the artist's self-transcendence while creating. Only while creating does the artist put on the mask, summon the Daimon (transcend, in other words, his ordinary self) and objectify the mask in poem or statue. Afterwards he returns to his ordinary self; the transcendence remains in the work of art. The saint or hero, instead, maintains transcendence, makes *himself* into a work of art: "he works in his own flesh and blood and not in paper or parchment."

The idea that it is possible and desirable to turn yourself into a work of art came to Yeats from Pater and Wilde. By adding the imperative of struggle, Yeats evolved an ethic for art and life. To keep producing great art, the aging artist cannot settle into a mask won in some earlier struggle, but must perpetually renew the struggle, change masks and sometimes rediscover old ones. Nor can we in life feed on moral principles abstracted from the insights of an earlier self; to be authentic our morality must go on being characteristic, the expression of a newly won self. "Active virtue, as distinguished from the passive acceptance of a code, is therefore theatrical, consciously dramatic, the wearing of a mask." One feels Yeats has Wilde in mind and is thinking that active virtue is experimental, exuding an air of charlatanism and apparent immorality rather than the stale odor of righteousness. Wordsworth's "moral sense," instead, "has no theatrical element." [33] Wordsworth *thought* he was sincere, and therefore became insincere.

The problem for Yeats was how to maintain sincerity in art and life, as Wordsworth through his lengthy and visible decline did not. Yeats uses the mask, which for Wilde promoted a doctrine of insincerity, to promote a renewed doctrine of sincerity. For Wilde masks were alone interesting and various; they concealed dreary, undifferentiated selves: "What is interesting about people in good society . . . is the mask that each one of them wears, not the reality that lies behind the mask." [34] Yeats, instead, uses the mask to penetrate through the ordinary self to remote depths where the real interest lies.

The historical implication, to be worked out in A *Vision*, is that magical values belong to ages that believe—as present-day bourgeois democracy does not—in the possibility of magical or self-transcended personalities. Anticipating A *Vision*, Yeats in *Per Amica* suggests that it is repeated gain and loss of self-transcendence that creates the cycles from which the saint, who pursues the "straight line" out of nature, is exempt (the hero's transcendence, like the artist's, remains within the "winding movement of Nature").

> I think that we who are poets and artists, not being permitted to shoot beyond the tangible, must go from desire to weariness and so to desire again, and live but for the moment when vision comes to our weariness like terrible lightning. . . . I do not doubt those heaving circles, those winding arcs, whether in one man's life or in that of an age, are mathematical, and that some in the world, or beyond the world, have foreknown the event and pricked upon the calendar the life-span of a Christ, a Buddha, a Napoleon: that every movement, in feeling or in

thought, prepares in the dark by its own increasing clarity and confidence its own executioner.[35]

History is the reification of identity-making.

There are, however, only two references in *Per Amica* to the
historical cycles already described in the "Rosa Alchemica"
stories and *The Player Queen*. Yeats takes up instead, in the second part of *Per Amica*, called "Anima Mundi" ("The World
Soul"), a new subject—the exteriority of the self, which is accounted for by the completion of identity in the life after death,
the life between lives. In the "General Introduction" Yeats says,
"I hated and still hate with an ever growing hatred the literature
of the point of view. I wanted . . . to get back to Homer. . . .
to cry as all men cried, to laugh as all men laughed." [36] He
opens "Anima Mundi" by saying, "I have always sought to
bring my mind close to the mind of Indian and Japanese poets,
old women in Connacht, mediums in Soho . . . to immerse it
in the general mind where that mind is scarce separable from
what we have begun to call 'the subconscious.' " [37]

He wants another kind of mind because he wants another
kind of identity. Modern point-of-view literature is about the
unreconstructed individual; it concentrates on idiosyncrasy, on
all that sets one person apart from another. The sign of this in
the dramatic monologue—and Yeats alludes to Browning and
Browning's admirer Pound as architects of this new form in
poetry—is the limited perspective which tells us that the story
will not be completed, that it will fade out where the limited
self loses sight of things. Since these new poets "express not
what the Upanishads call 'that ancient Self' but individual intellect," they are right to choose the man in the subway as their
model of personality.[38]

"Anima Mundi" explains the way discovered by Yeats for
completing the story, for getting over from the limited, entirely

interior modern self to the completed self, which is an equivalent for God. The first step is to release the unconscious through free association. So far Yeats is with the psychological school of Wordsworth; but he parts company with Wordsworth, he moves beyond psychology, in dreading "any confusion between the images of the mind and the objects of sense," for Wordsworth aims at just such blending. Yeats takes the step that leads beyond psychology when he realizes that the images derive not from "forgotten personal memory" but from "a Great Memory passing on from generation to generation." The step is Jungian, and the evidence that caused Yeats to take it is Jungian. His dreams revealed symbols such as those of alchemy, before he had any knowledge of alchemy. "Our daily thought," he concludes, "was certainly but the line of foam at the shallow edge of a vast luminous sea." So far he is with the romanticists, as he suggests by alluding to Wordsworth's portrayal of memory in the "Immortality Ode" as a "sight of that immortal sea / Which brought us hither." For Wordsworth, the conscious thought we call ours and by which we define the ego is a tiny emanation from the unconscious; the unconscious simply grows in vastness and impersonality as we move on to Jung and Yeats. All three want to discover a self larger than the ego, which can embrace consciousness and unconsciousness and is both inside and outside our skins.

Yeats prepares his step beyond romanticism and psychology by alluding also to the seventeenth-century Platonist, Henry More. Wordsworth has merely *intimations* of immortality: his "Children sport upon the shore." But More's *Anima Mundi* refers to the immortals: "in that sea there were some who swam or sailed, explorers who perhaps knew all its shores." [39] Jung remains psychological in that he considers the images or archetypes to be contents of the collective unconscious; whereas Yeats gives them an independent existence, considers them to be spirits, souls of the dead who use our minds in order to complete their identity between lives. This makes Yeats what?—

mystical, occult—depending on the name we give to the ancient science that dealt with those phenomena of the inner life now dealt with under the rubric of psychology. Before "empirical psychology," writes Jung in explaining the world-view of the alchemists, "everything unconscious, inasmuch as it was activated, was projected upon corporeal things—that is, confronted the human being from without."

> Science began with the stars, and mankind discovered in them the dominants of the unconscious, the so-called gods, as well as the curious psychological qualities of the zodiac: a complete doctrine of character, wholly projected. . . . Such projections always repeat themselves when man tries to investigate an empty darkness and then unwittingly fills it with living form.

That darkness, Jung feels, now that physics and psychology have led us back to mystery, has come again and may restore a non-psychological world-view that knows "no either-or . . . but an intermediate realm between matter and mind, a psychic realm of subtle bodies" that "ceases to exist as soon as one seeks to investigate matter in and for itself, apart from all projections." [40]

The model for the next life is the romantic epiphany—Wordsworth's "spots of time," Pater's "moments," and in "Anima Hominis" those visionary moments of self-possession, lost and then regained, that give mortal life its cyclical character. In "Anima Mundi," those moments are hypostatized into spirits seen as completed identities. Yeats cites St. Thomas's description of spirits as having "entered upon the eternal possession of themselves in one single moment," and illustrates with Coleridge's little-known lines on a phantom:

> All look and likeness caught from earth,
> All accident of kin and birth,
> Had passed away. There was no trace
> Of aught on that illumined face,
> Upraised beneath the rifted stone,
> But of one spirit all her own;
> She, she herself and only she,
> Shone through her body visibly.

Taken alone, the last two lines might be a romantic epiphany of self-possession; but the whole superb poem seems more Yeats than Coleridge just because it distinguishes so sharply between "the images of the mind and the objects of sense"—between, for example, "illumined face" and "rifted stone." [41]

Yeats plays the same subtle trick with Coleridge's theory of imagination. The power of imagination to manifest itself through images becomes the model for the real materialization of souls, who according to the Platonists need a vehicle or body and use "animal spirits" (a luminous substance midway in materiality between spirit and matter) and the minds of men. "The soul has a plastic power, and can after death, or during life, should the vehicle [as in witchcraft] leave the body for a while, mould it to any shape it will by an act of imagination, . . . and make it visible by showing it to our mind's eye." Yeats equates art and ghost-making when he asks, "But how does it follow that souls who never have handled the modelling tool or the brush make perfect images?" [42] He answers by alluding to the imaginative free association by which the romanticists accounted for artistic miracles beyond the reach of mere technical accomplishment. "We have come to understand," says Yeats in "Swedenborg, Mediums, and the Desolate Places" (1914), "why the Platonists . . . confused imagination with magic." [43] Both create a phantasmagoria; but in imagination the suggestion comes from within, in magic from without.

Here is how Yeats in *Per Amica* takes off from Wordsworthian imagination:

> Communication with *Anima Mundi* is through the association of thoughts or images or objects. . . . A glove and a name can call their [dead] bearer; the shadows come to our elbow amid their old undisturbed habitations, and "materialisation" itself is easier, it may be, among walls, or by rocks and trees, that bring before their memory some moment of emotion while they had still animate bodies. [44]

In both poets the phenomenon is the same, memory and the sense of a presence evoked by place. But they explain the phenomenon differently. Wordsworth imagines *his* memory and *his* self-presence in the landscape; whereas the object's or landscape's memory is imagined *through* Yeats—Yeats feels his imagination to be the vehicle for another's memory. After the demythologizing Enlightenment, Wordsworth starts empirically to mythologize the landscape by recalling spots where the vision came upon him and thus restoring the ancient sense of holy places; but the holiness is equivocal, resting only on Wordsworth's memories of his own experiences. Yeats completes the process by circling back to the ancient sense of holy places as objectively sacred. In that last phrase about " 'materialisation' . . . by rocks and trees," we move from Wordsworth back to Noh plays in which place evokes the ghost who in life had some overwhelming experience there. Both Wordsworth and Yeats are dealing with an area of psyche beyond what the ego can lay claim to. Wordsworth deals with it as inexplicable, Yeats as explicable, mystery.

Yeats's explanations lead in "Anima Mundi" to the astounding conclusion that "the dead living in their memories are, I am persuaded, the source of all that we call instinct, and it is their love and their desire, all unknowing, that make us drive beyond our reason, or in defiance of our interest." In other words, our unconscious life is external; the dead are working out their destiny through us. The notion that our spontaneous thoughts are not really ours must inevitably change the idea of the self. And Yeats, in another astounding statement, changes the whole geography of self and not-self that has shaped the European sense of identity at least since Descartes' time: "Though images appear to flow and drift, it may be that we but change in our relation to them, now losing, now finding with the shifting of our minds."

Descartes identified the self with the thoughts of which we are conscious, the thoughts we call ours. For Descartes, thought was subjective and incorporeal; it went on entirely inside the head. For Yeats, thoughts are subtly corporeal and are out there "in the general vehicle of *Anima Mundi*"; instead of thoughts passing through us, we pass through thoughts, mirroring them "in our particular vehicle." Moreover, thoughts have their own autonomous laws of growth. When Yeats says, "I think of *Anima Mundi* as a great pool or garden where [thought] moves through its allotted growth like a great water-plant," he is pointing already to the historical cycles and the characterology of opposites in *A Vision*.

"A seed is set growing, and this growth may go on apart from the power, apart even from the knowledge of the soul." A thought, once set in motion, completes itself out of reach of consciousness. So does an identity.

> We are always starting these parasitic vegetables and letting them coil beyond our knowledge, and may become like that lady in Balzac who, after a life of sanctity, plans upon her deathbed to fly with her renounced lover. After death a dream, a desire she had perhaps ceased to believe in, perhaps ceased almost to remember, must have recurred again and again with its anguish and its happiness.

Since the desires we renounced in order to delineate an identity are still there, the concept of a completed identity requires the concept of successive lives in which to complete it. If we can't complete it in the life after death, then we must be reborn. "The mask," says Yeats, "is but my imagination of rhythmic body," of the completed identity that enables us to pass into the condition beyond conflict, the condition of fire. Yet the process by which the dead refine themselves involves no loss of identity: "this running together and running of all to a centre, and yet without loss of identity." [45] To complete an identity is to be saved, to find what Christians call God.

Chapter 6
THE SELF
AS A WORK
OF ART

Writing in 1919 when he was fifty-four, Yeats recalled that when he was twenty-four the following sentence formed in his head without his willing it: " 'Hammer your thoughts into unity.' " The sentence became the ruling principle of his life. His three interests—in literature, Irish nationality and the occult—seemed, he says, to have nothing to do with each other. But now "all three are a discrete expression of a single conviction. I think that each has behind it my whole character and has gained thereby a certain newness—for is not every man's character peculiar to himself?" [1]

Actually Yeats had already connected literature and nationality; for the Fenian leader John O'Leary, who made him an active nationalist, also influenced him to turn in his writing to Irish subjects. In 1886, when he was twenty-one, he began *The Wanderings of Oisin*, based on Gaelic epics. In 1887 he began the short story "Dhoya," an amazingly successful feat of original mythmaking; and in the next year he began the novel *John Sherman*, in which the dreamy, indolent hero—Yeats before he discovered activism—has to choose between Sligo and London (Yeats's boyhood was divided between them) and chooses Sligo.

It was through his research into Irish folklore that Yeats developed the concepts necessary to reconcile his three interests. Yeats's collection *Irish Fairy and Folk Tales* (1888) and the two volumes of his own stories derived from folklore—*The Celtic Twilight* (1893) and *The Secret Rose* (1897)—celebrate the folk imagination. The conclusion he drew from his research was that any genuine high art would have to issue from the same kind of mind that had produced the folklore. The folklore had been produced by many minds operating as though they were one mind—not a universal mind in a vacuum but one *characteristic* mind of a particular nation. The connection between literature and nationality was fully articulated when Yeats came to understand that the maker of high art must have character and could have this only if his character were rooted in national character.

The connection with occultism came with Yeats's realization, expressed in the dedication of *The Secret Rose* to his mystical friend George Russell, that so far "as this book is visionary it is Irish; for Ireland, which is still predominantly Celtic, has preserved with some less excellent things a gift of vision, which has died out among more hurried and more successful nations." In the argument leading to this assertion, we find the incipient theory of identity that will forge the reconciliation of Yeats's literary, nationalist and occult interests. My friends, he says, believe that a national poetry and romance can be made by historical research. But a writer "may choose for the symbols of his art [his people's] legends, their history, their beliefs," [2] only if these things really symbolize his own emotions. Antiquarianism won't do. To revive a national mythology poets must recover the kind of mind that saw the world that way. Yeats had already, in the Introduction to *Irish Fairy and Folk Tales*, said that he had not in his notes "rationalized a single hobgoblin" [3] because, like Socrates in Plato's *Phaedrus*, he realized that the

more we, with our modern skeptical intellects, delve into the
mysteries of the self the more valid seems the literal understanding of myth.

The Secret Rose, with its dedication, Rosicrucian title and
cosmopolitan epigraphs, turns our attention to the occult meaning of the Irish contents. The volume was originally to have
ended with the three stories "Rose Alchemica," "The Tables of
the Law," "The Adoration of the Magi," which are overtly occult and minimally Irish (the last two, because the publisher
feared they were heretical, came out in a separate volume).
These stories introduce two characters, Michael Robartes, an
occultist, and Owen Aherne, a heterodox Catholic, follower of
Joachim de Flora, who are important because they turn up in
other works, notably *A Vision*, and represent opposing sides of
Yeats himself.

Richard Ellmann, who in *Yeats: The Man and the Masks*
(1948) has shaped our understanding of the development of
Yeats's personality, sees Yeats as starting with the characteristically romantic division between a subjective or inward-looking
self and an objective or outward-looking self. Yeats's subjective
self is, according to Ellmann, dramatized by John Sherman in
the novel and Robartes in the stories; while his objective self is
dramatized in the novel by the fashionably High Church English
curate William Howard and by Aherne in the stories. Howard,
however, is too English and too consistently satirized to represent Yeats or correspond to Aherne. For Aherne's Catholicism is
as intensely felt and imaginative as Robartes's occultism; Aherne
is no less attractive than Robartes. Robartes and Aherne represent, I think, not Sherman-Howard but two sides of Sherman.
They represent the two directions in which Yeats as Sherman
could advance after he awakened through Oisin into adulthood
and began to flourish in the aesthetical London of the nineties
—a London quite different from the middle-class commercial
city Sherman rejects, the city of the middle-class boys Yeats
hated at his London school.

Oisin's three hundred years in fairyland can be considered, as
Ellmann suggests, three phases of Yeats's boyhood, with the return to Ireland or reality the shock of maturation: he is suddenly
an old man.[4] Having left a pagan Ireland, Oisin awakens to an
Ireland that has a pagan past and a Christian present. By choosing paganism, making it a conscious stance, he turns from
dreamer to poet. In the next stage of his development, Yeats
takes the pagan-Christian conflict inside himself, projecting it as
the equally attractive Robartes and Aherne and relating both
sides through what was by then his main preoccupation—art. In
"Rosa Alchemica," "The Tables of the Law" and "The Adoration of the Magi," Yeats contains the pagan-Christian conflict
by means of the aestheticism he learned from Pater, the French
symbolists—and Blake, whose works he edited in the early nineties and from whom he derived, as he put it in an essay of 1897,
"the religion of art."[5] Robartes, Aherne and the narrator of
these stories started together as aesthetes in Paris.

Yeats is also represented in these stories by the first-person
narrator, whose continuing presence gives the stories sequence.
The stories trace the narrator's development. Robartes and
Aherne show the opposite extremes to which aestheticism leads;
each expounds his religion as the religion of art. Together they
expound the mixture of pagan and Christian ideas and symbols
that Yeats found in alchemical writings, in the ritual of the Hermetic Order of the Golden Dawn which he joined in 1890, and
in all great poems. The timid, prudent narrator retreats from
both extremes into a conventional Catholic orthodoxy that repudiates the extremes and the aestheticism from which they
derive. Although Yeats disapproves of the narrator's final position
and wants us to distinguish the narrator's philistine orthodoxy from
Aherne's art Catholicism, the narrator does represent the prudent reserve that kept Yeats from losing over occultism his common sense and his grip on practical affairs. The nineties was the
decade in which Yeats was most aesthetical, most engaged in

occultist sects, and most active as an initiator and manager of nationalist organizations. He kept enough reserve from each commitment to leave room for the others; and he was to maintain this prudent reserve even toward his own system in A Vision.

Robartes and Aherne represent positions in advance of the narrator's and therefore the *direction* of Yeats's development—a direction made clearer by the fact that the narrator retreats where Yeats advances. Yet the narrator seems in some underlying sense to have advanced too, because he is ready to receive the more advanced revelation of the third story, "The Adoration of the Magi." Inspired by a vision of the by then dead Robartes, three old men take the narrator to witness a nativity that will usher in the new era foretold in their different ways by Robartes and Aherne. It is significant that the nativity takes place in Paris, capital of aestheticism, where the dying prostitute, who as opposite to the Virgin of the Christian era gives birth to a unicorn, murmurs " 'the name of a symbolist painter. . . . who taught her to see visions.' " [6] Retreating again, the narrators utters an early Christian Gaelic prayer, asking Mary and Christ to save the suppliant from the pagan gods. Yeats wants us to understand that the terms of the prayer ought *now* to be reversed. By his retreat at the end of each story, the narrator tells us in reverse what Yeats means.

Robartes and Aherne are in different ways destroyed by their extreme commitments. Human life is possible only where the narrator stands, between the extremes, pulled by them in opposite directions yet exercising a prudent reserve toward both. It is amazing how far Yeats had gone by 1897 toward conceiving the circular diagram of A Vision, where human life takes place between opposite poles. If Yeats assumes in these stories opposite stands—for Robartes, for Aherne, for both against the narrator, for the narrator against both—it is because he is dialectical not only in thought but in personality: he is in all three characters, though he inclines toward Robartes. His problem was to evolve a system of thought and a personality that could contain contradictions without annihilating them.

In "Rosa Alchemica," the narrator moves from aestheticism toward occultism through a transformation of identity. He starts as an aloof Paterian, experiencing "every pleasure because I gave myself to none, but held myself apart, individual, indissoluble, a mirror of polished steel." The mirror is Yeats's recurrent image for the modern Western egocentric individuality, which derives from the separation of subject and object: the ego, a bundle of sensations, merely reflects a world from which it is separated—thought is in the subject, matter in the object. The narrator falls into a trance in which voices cry that the mirror must be shattered, the line between subject and object dissolved. Robartes has already explained that the forms of our thought, the figures of myth and literature, are not inside us but outside; we do not make them, " 'they are always making and unmaking humanity.' " And the narrator has already defended his egocentric identity: " 'You would sweep me away into an indefinite world which fills me with terror; and yet a man is a great man just in so far as he can make his mind reflect everything with indifferent precision like a mirror.' "

On their trip to the occultist temple, the narrator falls in and out of trances through which he "felt fixed habits and principles dissolving before a power, which was *hysterica passio* or sheer madness." *Hysterica passio* recurs in Yeats as the force of dissolution suppressed by the ego, which in *Per Amica* becomes the antiself or Daimon that is integrated into the self when it returns after objectification, returns through the Daimon's descent into the self. By the time Robartes and the narrator arrive at the temple, the narrator has broken through to a new sense of identity: "I was so changed that I was no more, as man is, a moment shuddering at eternity, but eternity weeping and laughing over a moment." His identity has been inverted; its center is now outside. He has achieved the perspective Yeats will discover again in Noh, where the character does not possess the emotion but is possessed by it, is called up as a ghost to embody the emotion. This perspective, systematized in *A Vision*, will yield a world anything but indefinite. It is thought withdrawn into the ego that leaves the world terrifyingly empty.

Now the narrator sees Robartes's sleeping face as "more like a mask than a face. . . . The man behind it had dissolved away," [7] and supernatural beings spoke through it. Robartes, because his identity is centered outside, has become all mask. The same will be true of Aherne when, in "The Tables of the Law," he reappears as "a lifeless mask"; his "inner life had soaked up the outer life" [8] and come back to him as outer. In his final dream in "Rosa Alchemica," the narrator sees himself as "a mask, lying on the counter of a little Eastern shop." When he becomes all mask, he will have inverted his Western into an Oriental sense of identity.

In the alchemical writings that at first interested him only aesthetically, the narrator finds the doctrine that explains the inversion of identity he has actually experienced. "The independent reality of our thoughts," he reads, is "the doctrine from which all true doctrines rose." "Bodiless souls . . . what men called the moods" descend into our bodies, determining our identity and even our appearance. "In this way all great events were accomplished," he reads, as if in answer to his erroneous linking of great men with indissoluble egos; "a mood, a divinity, or a demon, first descending like a faint sigh into men's minds and then changing their thoughts and their actions." In seeing events, too, as vehicles of spirit, Yeats gets over from personality to history. " 'Into the dance! into the dance!' " an adept calls to the narrator, " 'that the gods may make them bodies out of the substance of our hearts.' " [9] This sentence helps us understand the famous last line of "Among School Children," in which Yeats both poses and answers the mysteries of identity: "How can we know the dancer from the dance?" The answer, here as in the poem, is that we cannot know them apart from each other, because an identity is an incarnation.

There is a straight line from this concept of identity to the 1925 *A Vision*. Indeed, the fiction with which that book begins is a sequel to these three stories. The Introduction is supposedly written by Owen Aherne, who tells of his meeting in 1917, after a separation of some thirty years, with Michael Robartes. Robartes wants to see Yeats to tell him about a book, printed in Cracow in 1594, which contains "curious allegorical pictures . . . and many diagrams where gyres and circles grew out of one another." Later near Mecca, he "saw certain markings upon the sands which corresponded almost exactly to a diagram" in the book; he learned that these markings were made by the Judwalis, whose doctrines were founded upon a lost book by Kusta Ben Luka, a Christian philosopher at the court of Harun Al-Raschid. Thus, non-Christian doctrine had a Christian origin; and Robartes, who joined the Judwalis to learn their doctrine, became convinced that their doctrine did not originate with Kusta Ben Luka but had, in wheel-like fashion, an even older pagan origin.

They travel together, passing Yeats's tower where "words were spoken between us slightly resembling those in 'Phases of the Moon.' " [10] In "The Phases of the Moon," the poem that opens Book I of *A Vision*, Robartes and Aherne—now old men, angry with Yeats for what he wrote about them "in that extravagant style / He had learnt from Pater"—tell each other the meaning of the twenty-eight phases in the system's circular diagram. They stand by the tower, where a light at the top shows Yeats at his occult studies—seeking "in book or manuscript / What he shall never find." Again Yeats projects himself into three characters, with Robartes and Aherne ahead of the character closest to Yeats. The appearance of Yeats's tower shows how Yeats used *A Vision* to bind together his life and work. The binding is completed in the revised version, where Yeats discloses what he here only hints at in the poem "Desert Geometry"—that Mrs. Yeats's automatic writing and speech transmitted the revelation Robartes and Aherne deny him. *A Vision* originated in the three 1897 stories and evolved through the drafts of *The Player Queen* begun in 1907, through Yeats's study of Noh in 1913, and through the 1914 essay "Swedenborg, Mediums, and the Desolate Places" that led to *Per Amica* in 1917.

Although not so completely articulated as the revised version, the 1925 version reveals more about *A Vision's* roots in Yeats's earlier work and about his original intentions in writing the book. The introductory story is written in the oracular style of the 1897 stories, and the chapter titles are romance-like: "What the Caliph Partly Learned," "What the Caliph Refused to Learn." In the revealing dedication to Vestigia (Mrs. MacGregor Mathers's occult name), Yeats says that he and his occultist friends were attracted by a "phantasy" that "did not explain the world to our intellects which were after all very modern." *A Vision's* complexity of tone derives from the experience of an intellect that, having rejected the orthodoxies of religion and science, is amazed to find how many preposterous things it has come to believe. Yeats indicates that the system is not so much true as useful: "I had a practical object. I wished for a system of thought that would leave my imagination free to create as it chose and yet make all that it created, or could create, part of the one history, and that the soul's. The Greeks certainly had such a system, and Dante." In other words, Yeats could not unify his life and work, combine as Dante had the personal and universal, without a system that would give coherence to his symbols and thus unify matter and mind, fact and value. By alluding to such a system he could save his poetry from abstraction and the arbitrariness of metaphors generated merely by sensibility. Poem would lend strength to poem and all his short poems become one great poem, unified by his personality in Dante's rather than Wordsworth's manner. He would have to invent such a system, since his culture could not provide it.

Swedenborg and Blake invented systems, but theirs are figurative. "I am the first," Yeats says in a revealing statement that he does not repeat in the revised version, "to substitute for Biblical or mythological figures, historical movements and actual men and women." [11] The statement reminds us not only that Yeats admired *The Ring and the Book,* in which Browning retrieves the pattern of Christian mythology from real events, but that one of his favorite authors, ranking in importance for him with Blake, Shelley and Dante, was the realist Balzac: "the only modern mind which has made a synthesis comparable to that of Dante." [12] In the 1925 A *Vision,* the cyclical pattern is danced on the sand in order to "explain human nature [to the Caliph] so completely that he should never be astonished again" [13]—for it will have become predictable.

Yeats's own personal development leads along with his writings to A *Vision.* That development has been outlined by Yeats himself in the autobiographical writings and letters where, consciously and unconsciously, he created the legend of his life. We know that Yeats had to establish his Irish identity against the contrary attraction of England, of the literature, the very language to which he owed his career as a writer, and that he had to assimilate his Irish into a cosmopolitan identity by finding continuity among his literary, nationalist and occult interests. As he came to appreciate the Anglo-Irish writers and his own Anglo-Irish heritage, he was able to feel that "the mind of my family merges into everybody's mind," to feel himself "a part of some national mythology." [14] To overcome shyness and social awkwardness, he forced himself to speak at public meetings and to take tea at refined houses—to do, as he says in *Per Amica,* the hardest task among tasks not impossible. His theory of the mask evolved from the deliberate self-reconstruction by which he made himself into the public figure of the nineties—the impresario of the Irish renaissance—who was at the same time writing poetry of withdrawal, indulging in occultist extravagances, and failing with Maud Gonne because, as he himself analyzed the failure, he lacked the self-confident diffidence necessary to the successful lover. His theory of the mask evolved from the realization that success in poetry, love and nationalist politics would require the same ability to make connection with the general mind and present himself as an artifice, to present his passion under an antithetical surface of cool control.

Yeats never triumphed as a lover, but with marriage love at least ceased to be a problem (though sex became one in old age). By the time of A Vision, however, he had fashioned the mask that served for his life and his poetry, because he had by then made his life almost as much a work of art as his poetry. He had established by then the public legend to which he could allude in his poetry—the legend of the poet champion of Ireland, disappointed lover of Ireland's beautiful heroine, friend of the model aristocrat Lady Gregory, and owner of the tower where he revived the ancient life of Ireland and explored occult mysteries. A Vision, especially when he revealed his wife's hand in it, appeared as capstone to the legend because it showed occultism as the link between his life and his work. It was the assimilation of his personality to certain publicly acknowledged roles that enabled him to speak in his poems with a voice that grew increasingly personal while gaining in authority.

If Blake and Shelley were the main influences on Yeats's poetry, and Pater on his prose, Oscar Wilde was the main influence on the work of art we call his life. Wilde taught him that "a man should invent his own myth," become, in Yeats's words, "mythological while still living." [15] Yeats seems from the start, however, to have understood self-mythologizing in a sense deeper than Wilde's. Wilde thought insincerity made you more interesting and attractive. But Yeats understood that the fiction of creating a fiction freed you from the necessity for self-deception; it provided the disguise under which you could afford to be sincere. When he writes in his essay on Shakespeare (1901) that "there is some one myth for every man, which, if we but knew it, would make us understand all he did and thought," [16] he is extrapolating the myth from Shakespeare's plays not his life, and suggesting that Shakespeare did not choose the myth but that the myth chose Shakespeare. In other words, he is finding the link between a man's life and art at that unconscious level where artifice is the agency of the deepest self-expression, an expression carried on through the rituals and symbols that art and the occult have in common. Yet a man can mythologize himself in his life or his art, seldom in both. Wilde, triumphant as a personality, failed as an artist; while for Yeats the "interior personality created out of the tradition of myself" is "alas, only possible to me in my writings." [17] Actually Yeats succeeded more than he cared to admit in creating reciprocally nourishing myths of himself in his life and art.

If Yeats made his own interpretation of Wilde's self-mythologizing, it was because he became convinced through experiments in telepathy "that mind flows into mind." [18] Having learned from magic "the power of many minds to become one," [19] he urges his contemporaries to apply the lesson to art. A nation, too, he came to realize, is a collective mind. In his essay "The Autumn of the Body" (1898), Yeats says that the faint outlines and energies of character in so-called decadent art point not to an end but a beginning; they point toward a total historical change—the dissolution of the body as container of the individual self. Recalling elsewhere Pater's archetypal interpretation of the Mona Lisa, Yeats asks: "Did Pater foreshadow a poetry, a philosophy, where the individual is nothing, the flux" everything—"human experience no longer shut into brief lives?" [20] In turning from the individual back to the collective self, our era is reversing the evolution of European art and personality. "We are, it may be," says Yeats in a sentence so important that he repeats the idea in A *Vision,* "at a crowning crisis of the world, at the moment when man is about to ascend, with the wealth he has been so long gathering upon his shoulders, the stairway he has been descending from the first days." [21] Modern "character," he says in the *Autobiography,* is "the revolt from all that makes one man like another"; whereas "the old art, if carried to its logical conclusion, would have led to the creation of one single type of man, one single type of woman; gathering up by a kind of deification a capacity for all energy and all passion, into a Krishna, a Christ, a Dionysus." God is the ultimate phase in this unification of identity, the One Self of which all other selves are aspects.

A conversion experience made him realize that it is the surrender of ego that makes devotion to any religion possible, that the religious life begins with rebirth of self. During 1897 and 1898, when the ideas of A *Vision* first came to him, Yeats experienced the revelation of the other self.

> I woke one night to find myself lying upon my back with all my limbs rigid, and to hear a ceremonial measured voice, which did not seem to be mine, speaking through my lips, "We make an image of him who sleeps," it said, "and it is not him who sleeps, and we call it Emmanuel."

This is the language of religious revelation: "Behold, a virgin shall conceive, and bear a son, and shall call his name Immanuel" (Isaiah 7:14). But Yeats gives the experience a psychological meaning: "After many years that thought, others often found as strangely being added to it, became the thought of the Mask [or antiself], which I have used in these memoirs to explain men's characters." Yeats's *masking* resembles Nietzsche's *unmasking* psychology in that both penetrate self-deception by analyzing unconscious and contrary motivations. Nietzsche himself wrote: "Everything that is profound loves the mask" because the self's uniqueness cannot possibly find social expression. [22] It is significant that the revelation to Yeats of antiself refers to Jesus' birth; for incarnation, the descent of the other self, is the central image by which Yeats solves the mysteries of identity.

Yeats's character analyses are so brilliantly modern because he uses the traditional doctrine of the other self to justify a dialectical logic that is distinctively modern. A good example is his treatment in the *Autobiography* of his aesthetical London friends of the nineties. Why should men, he asks, who were so traditional in dress and manner, so scholarly, timid and, in the cases of Johnson and Dowson, so religious, live private "lives of such disorder"? What looks like incoherence takes on a dialectical coherence once we understand that a man's actions may express a self opposite to the one he knows and exhibits. Thus Dowson could pursue innocence through alcoholism and debauchery, and Beardsley could draw "lascivious monstrous imagery" because his intellect was virginal. With his new idea that "mind flows into mind," Yeats sees Beardsley as a kind of saint who cures others by taking upon himself their disease, who exhausts sin by taking upon himself the full knowledge of it. These aesthetes of "the tragic generation"—who dove so low in their private lives because their idealism was too high and pure—remind us "that the Holy Infant shared His first home with the beasts."

Incarnation means for Yeats the sharpest possible conflict between the known and unknown self. The transforming descent of the antithetical other self accounts for the evolution of personality and art. After showing how knowledge of all sin is absorbed in Beardsley into something opposite, "frozen passion, the virginity of the intellect," he asks:

> Does not all art come when a nature, that never ceases to judge itself, exhausts personal emotion in action or desire so completely that something impersonal, something that has nothing to do with action or desire, suddenly starts into its place, something which is as unforeseen, as completely organized, even as unique, as the images [also externally derived] that pass before the mind between sleeping and waking?

This crucial sentence is about the escape from self-consciousness through the miraculous transition from the indi-

vidual to the archetypal. It explains the movement of the great
meditative poems—poems like "Meditations in Time of Civil
War" and "Nineteen Hundred and Nineteen"—where the personal drama leads to an impasse that is resolved by a sudden
change of perspective, the impersonal perspective of the system.

The psychological problem is also a historical problem in that
idealism—Yeats quotes as illustration Johnson's shattering poem
"Dark Angel"—is the aesthetes' poison. Even their Christianity
"but deepened despair and multiplied temptation. . . . Why
are these strange souls born everywhere to-day? with hearts that
Christianity, as shaped by history, cannot satisfy." Yeats alludes
by way of answer to the cyclical system that would soon appear
in A Vision: "Our love letters wear out our love; no school of
painting outlasts its founders, every stroke of the brush exhausts
the impulse. . . . Why should we believe that religion can
never bring round its antithesis?" [23]

The objectification of an emotion exhausts it; the emotion
must then seek a new objectification. The religious impulse
turns to poison in Christianity—expresses itself subversively
through sexual excess, alchoholism, drug abuse—because it is
now seeking an opposite, neopagan, objectification. "No mind
can engender till divided in two." A creative man lives between
the self that he is and the self that he is becoming. He lives with
one foot firmly planted in this age and the other lifted, ready to
step into the next age. But the next age means an earlier age
that is returning. Thus the "doctrine of 'the mask' " convinces
Yeats "that every passionate man . . . is, as it were, linked with
another age, historical or imaginary, where alone he finds
images that rouse his energy"—images through which his other
self can emerge. This is the process—the process of drawing on
outside powers—by which the genius in life turns himself into a
myth: "Napoleon was never of his own time . . . but had some
Roman emperor's image in his head." The genius in art likewise draws upon "some knowledge or power [that] has come
into his mind from beyond his mind. It is called up by an
image," just as, when Yeats hung on one side of a bird's cage a

saucer, and a bundle of hair and grass on the other side, the image called up in the bird's mind a nest-building revelation: "our images must be given to us, we cannot choose them deliberately."

"I know now," says Yeats summing up the biological, psychological half of what *A Vision* will say about the mysteries of identity, "that revelation is from the self, but from that age-long memoried self, that shapes the elaborate shell of the mollusc and the child in the womb, that teaches the birds to make their nest; and that *genius is a crisis that joins that buried self for certain moments to our trivial daily mind.*" Except for the dialectical concept of crisis, the passage is so far Jungian. The Platonic combines with the psychological when Yeats speaks of "personifying spirits," the Daimons of *Per Amica*, who personify the unconscious as contriver of events since "through their dramatic power they bring our souls to crisis."

> They have but one purpose, to bring their chosen man to the greatest obstacle he may confront without despair. They contrived Dante's banishment, and snatched away his Beatrice, and thrust Villon into the arms of harlots, and sent him to gather cronies at the foot of the gallows, that Dante and Villon might through passion become conjoint to their buried selves, turn all to Mask and Image, and so be *phantoms* in their own eyes.

To become conjoint with your buried self, that is the purpose of life. Fulfillment means that you turn your body and your known self into a vehicle for the archetype, which is sometimes conceived as buried, sometimes as descending from outside. You turn into Mask and Image, into a *transparency* through which the archetype is manifested. This happens through a transformation in self-perception: Dante and Villon become "phantoms in their *own* eyes." Suddenly you see your life as phantasmagoria or myth, the repetition of a preconceived pattern; just as in art you suddenly see the details as symbol, as the image or repetition of a pattern.

In his boldest statement on the link between life and art,

Yeats goes on to say that the greatest artists fulfill themselves in life and art by using their art to mythologize their lives. By passing certain events of their lives (e.g. Dante's banishment) through the medium of art, they acquire a perspective analogous to the Daimon's; they view themselves and their lives the way a playwright views his dramatis personae. They become both dramatis personae and playwrights; hence they become transparencies, since they know and accept everything about themselves. As dramatis personae they suffer; but as playwrights, they "would not, when they speak through their art, change their luck." "The two halves of their nature"—the dramatis persona and playwright halves—

> are so completely joined that they seem to labour for their objects, and yet to desire whatever happens, being at the same instant predestinate and free, creation's very self. We gaze at such men in awe, because we gaze not at a work of art, but at the re-creation of the man through that art, *the birth of a new species of man*, and, it may even seem that the hairs of our heads stand up, because that birth, that re-creation, is from terror.[24]

"Predestinate and free"—this is the polarity by which events are recreated into art and individual artists are recreated through their art into those gigantic archetypal figures that haunt our cultural memory. "The hairs of our head stand up" when we recognize the archetype.

Yeats also found in Noh the perspective that turns individuals into phantoms or transparencies; for in Noh, where the view is backward from the grave, passion *re*played by a ghost is transparently suffered and understood. The passion that in life seemed so important is, in Noh's retrospective view, no longer important in one sense yet enduringly important in another. Repetition does not devalue, it revalues passion under an eternal aspect. It is this trick of reseeing the single incident through repetition that Yeats took from Noh for his system and for those later poems and plays where the personal and historical impasse is resolved through a vision of the cycles. The Noh perspective

is personified by the moveless gaze (the gaze of Byzantine mosaics and Noh masks) of Old Rocky Face in "The Gyres" who,
like the *waki*, the beholder in Noh of the ghostly manifestation,
sees the events before his eyes as phantasmagoria, repetition,
and thus assimilates history to a pattern of movement that is itself unchanging.

It was to dramatize his developing concept of transparent
identity, an identity untouched by progress, that Yeats—as he
says in "Certain Noble Plays of Japan"—went "to Asia for a
stage convention, for more formal faces," and for that concluding dance which, by replacing facial expression with "movement of the whole body," expresses Unity of Being. "In poetical
painting and in sculpture," he says extending Pater's observations on Greek sculpture, "the face seems the nobler for lacking
curiosity, alert attention, all that we sum up under the famous
word of the realists, 'vitality.' It is even possible," he continues
in the awe-inspiring statement that, summing up the Oriental
ideal of identity fulfillment, leads beyond Pater and Pater's aesthetic appreciation of dead faces to the eschatology of *A Vision*—the statement "that being is only possessed completely by
the dead." [25] Through the Nohlike plays Yeats collected in
1921 under the title *Four Plays for Dancers*, we can trace his
development toward the 1925 *A Vision*. The last three prefaces,
which were written well after Mrs. Yeats had begun her automatic writing, are more concerned with the developing *A Vision* than with the plays themselves.

To explain human nature and its re-creation, and to explain it
through the analogy of art—that is the design of *A Vision*. In *A
Vision*, Yeats comes to see that the perfection of self, which the
artist portrays in the figures of art and achieves for himself
through the artistic process, cannot always in life be achieved

within a single lifetime, that self-realization may require a succession of historical periods and a succession of lives.

In *Per Amica* Yeats discovered the struggle between self and
antiself, and assumed that the struggle and the goal were the
same for all men—to achieve Unity of Being or self-fulfillment.
But by the time he wrote the 1925 *A Vision*, Yeats had come to
realize

> that there are men who cannot possess "Unity of Being," who must not
> seek it or express it—and who, so far from seeking an anti-self, a Mask
> that delineates a being in all things the opposite to their natural state,
> can but seek the suppression of the anti-self, till the natural state alone
> remains. These are those who must seek no image of desire, but await
> that which lies beyond their mind—unities not of the mind, but unities
> of nature, unities of God—the man of science, the moralist, the hu-
> manitarian, the politician,

the saint. [26] Yeats had discovered objective or *primary* man who,
in contrast to subjective or *antithetical* man, is content to find
unity in the external world. The discovery enabled Yeats to
chart in *A Vision* differing personalities who inhabit differing
realities involving differing values. He could establish for each
type its own authenticity.

Yeats could now explain his psychological and historical insights by each other; he could characterize the alternating historical cycles as *primary* and *antithetical*. In the revised *A Vision* (1937)—the latest edition of which I shall cite unless I
specify otherwise—"nations, cultures, schools of thought" have
their personalities, "their Daimons. These Daimons may move
through the Great Year [the two-thousand-year cycle of personalities and historical periods] like individual men and women
and are said to use men and women as their bodies." The
Daimons who stage-manage our lives also stage-manage history.
"Every action of man declares . . . that reality is a congeries of
beings and a single being." [27] Plotinus, we are told elsewhere,
was the first to see reality as a "timeless individuality" that "contains archetypes of all possible existences . . . , and as it tra-

verses its circle of allotted lives, now one, now another, pre-
vails." [28] Thus the personified reality, the earth teeming with
phantoms, that poets project in metaphor is literally true—it is
the underlying religion of the world. As a young man Yeats
proposed for the consideration of the occultist Hermetic Society
"that whatever the great poets had affirmed in their finest moments was the nearest we could come to an authoritative religion, and that their mythology, their spirits of water and wind
were but literal truth." [29]

The whole system of A Vision—the unfolding of personality
through history and the life between lives—is held together by
the analogy with art. Yeats sees art as organized by two principles—incarnation and conflict—and these are the principles
that govern the movement of the system. Literature embodies "a
mood, or a community of moods, as the body is wrought about
an invisible soul," [30] and just as art seeks perfect embodiment,
the complete physical manifestation of idea, so the personality
moves through its phases in history and in the life between lives
in order to achieve perfect embodiment. Phase 15, where such
perfection exists, is described in terms that apply to both art and
personality: "every beloved image has bodily form, and every
bodily form is loved. . . . all thought has become image. . . .
All that the being has experienced as thought is visible to its
eyes as a whole"; and because its knowledge is perfectly embodied, "it perceives," not as generalization, "not as they are to
others, but according to its own perception, all orders of existence." All that it perceives is, as with the figures of great art,
made visible in its own body, which is why

> Its own body possesses the greatest possible beauty, being indeed that
> body which the soul will permanently inhabit, when all its phases have
> been repeated according to the number allotted: that which we call the
> clarified or Celestial Body—

what I have called transparent identity.

There can be no human life at Phase 15; but the phase's
perfection is approximated historically by civilizations, like

Byzantium, which express all their ideas through visible symbols accessible to all and expressive of a collective identity —civilizations whose perfection can be understood through the perfection of their art, an art in which idea is completely incarnate. The figures of great art also help us understand the Celestial Body achieved in that final stage of the life between lives called the Purification: "during the *Purification* those forms copied in the Arts and Sciences are present as the *Celestial Body.*" In the Purification, as in art, the identity embodied is collective or archetypal. Yeats connects the spirits at this stage "with an early conviction of mine, that the creative power of the lyric poet depends upon his accepting some one of a few traditional attitudes, lover, sage, hero, scorner of life." The figures in art represent a phase of identity that most of us achieve only after death, though the artist can achieve it through his art.

Vision is another way to apprehend Celestial Body while living. Yeats interprets his Emmanuel dream (recounted in the *Autobiography*) of the self seeking incarnation in him as really about Celestial Body: "A living man sees the *Celestial Body* through the *Mask*" [31] or other self. It is because art gives us the visionary eye to see the Celestial Body potentially incarnate in our bodies that Blake, as Yeats explains elsewhere, insisted "that 'Christianity is Art,' and that 'the whole business of man is the arts.' " [32] Yeats, who also learned the principle of conflict from Blake, quotes him: " 'There is a place at the bottom of the graves where contraries are equally true.' " [33] The greatest art is located in that place.

In a letter to Dorothy Wellesley, Yeats describes personality as the "holding down" of "violence or madness," of "Hysterica passio." [34] In A *Vision* he says the same thing about a civilization: "A civilization is a struggle to keep self-control, and in this it is like some great tragic person." [35] Personality and civilization are linked by a Nietzschean concept of tragedy, and indeed of all art, as an uneasy balance of Apollonian and Dionysian elements, of control and unarticulated energy. By naming the contraries and locating them in art, "Nietzsche," Yeats felt, "completes Blake." [36] In analyzing his new poem "To D. W. [Dorothy Wellesley]," Yeats says that in his poem, as in personality and the actor's portrayal of personality, "all depends on the completeness of the holding down, on the stirring of the beast underneath." The conflict in the poem is not planned; "conflict is deep in my subconsciousness, perhaps in everybody's." [37] Conflict is the organizing principle of nature, history, personality and art.

The analogy between personality and art is clearest when Yeats uses the *commedia dell' arte*—the improvised drama of Italy in which actors wear the masks of a few conventionalized types—to explain the variations of personality charted on his Great Wheel. The analogy explains the Four Faculties as four poles across which the personality unfolds itself through twofold conflict. The Faculties are: Will or ego, as against the object of will, Mask or the desired opposite self; Creative Mind or thought, as against the object of thought called Body of Fate or circumstances.

> The stage manager, or *Daimon*, offers his actor an inherited scenario, the *Body of Fate*, and a *Mask* or role as unlike as possible to his natural ego or *Will*, and leaves him to improvise through his *Creative Mind* the dialogue and details of the plot. He must discover or reveal a being which only exists with extreme effort.

This is *antithetical* or subjective man, who makes his identity through struggle against an inherited archetype. For *primary* or objective man, "I go to the *Commedia dell' Arte* in its decline. The *Will* is weak and cannot create a role, and so, if it transforms itself, does so after an accepted pattern." Objective man makes his identity, not through self-expression, but through service, fulfillment of a code.

Phase 1, midway on the left side of the Wheel, represents complete objectivity; Phase 15, midway on the right side, represents complete subjectivity (see Diagram A, p. 197). In Phase 8,

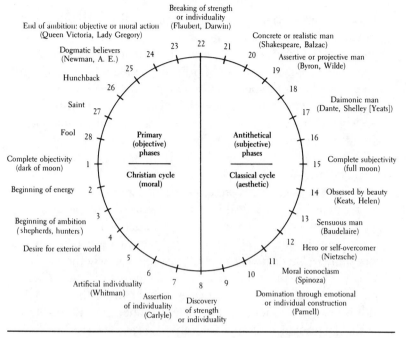

A. The Great Wheel
(The Phases of the Moon)

Breaking of strength
or individuality
(Flaubert, Darwin)

End of ambition: objective or moral action
(Queen Victoria, Lady Gregory)

Dogmatic believers
(Newman, A. E.)

Hunchback

Saint

Fool

Complete objectivity
(dark of moon)

Beginning of energy

Beginning of ambition
(shepherds, hunters)

Desire for exterior world

Artificial individuality
(Whitman)

Assertion
of individuality
(Carlyle)

Discovery
of strength
or individuality

Concrete or realistic man
(Shakespeare, Balzac)

Assertive or projective man
(Byron, Wilde)

Daimonic man
(Dante, Shelley [Yeats])

Complete subjectivity
(full moon)

Obsessed by beauty
(Keats, Helen)

Sensuous man
(Baudelaire)

Hero or self-overcomer
(Nietzsche)

Moral iconoclasm
(Spinoza)

Domination through emotional
or individual construction
(Parnell)

Primary
(objective)
phases

Christian cycle
(moral)

Antithetical
(subjective)
phases

Classical cycle
(aesthetic)

23 22 21
24
25
26
27
28
1
2
3
4
5
6 7 8 9 10
20
19
18
17
16
15
14
13
12
11

This diagram is an elaboration of Yeats's in *A Vision*, p. 81. For the sake of
clarity, I have filled in only the phases most relevant to my discussion and have
sometimes paraphrased Yeats's description of the phases in the text.

midway on the bottom, the Will as it moves toward subjectivity
can no longer take its world-view from a code, but is not yet
strong enough to impose its own view on the world. People at
this stage may destroy themselves through drink, sex, drugs.

In Phase 22, midway on the top, the Will, moving away from
subjectivity, submits entirely to "external fact (*Body of Fate*)"
and desires "the death of the intellect." This is what we call the
scientific view. The phase is represented by Darwin, whose
theory of natural selection makes evolution a mindless process;
by Flaubert who wanted a scientific art ("all must be impersonal; he must neither like nor dislike character or event"); by
Swedenborg, who made a scientific study of Heaven; and also—

surprisingly, yet on reflection rightly—by Dostoevsky, whose characters must yield personality and intellect to "some ungraspable Whole to which they have given the name of God." Dostoevsky's Christianity is specifically modern, because it reveals to his characters the full horror of the identity crisis it cannot solve: "For a moment that fragment, that relation, which is our very being, is broken; they are at Udan Adan 'wailing upon the edge of nonentity, wailing for Jerusalem, with weak voices almost inarticulate'; yet full submission has not come." [38]

This example alone shows the fruitfulness of Yeats's terminology, and the way psychological leads inevitably to historical analysis. Although the representatives of a phase do not always cluster in a single historical period, one can usually pick out the period to which the description of personality mainly applies. Yeats never explicitly poses or settles the question whether all personality types can exist in all periods, or whether certain types exist only in certain periods. He seems to incline toward the latter possibility, but apparently cannot make the idea gibe with other requirements of the system. When he says of Phase 14 that "Thought is disappearing into image," we see that he is talking not only about Wordsworth and Keats, but also about romanticism as it extends throughout the nineteenth century. At Phase 14 "the greatest human beauty becomes possible," because the man disengages from thought and circumstance his images of desire so he can impress upon them the full character of Mask or desire. This accounts for Keats's doctrine of Negative Capability, in which "intellectual curiosity is at its weakest," and for the disengagement from thought and circumstance of Wordsworth's solitary figures, who are seen momentarily amid a space that is half an image in the poet's mind: "in Wordsworth the soul's deepening solitude has reduced mankind, when seen objectively, to a few slight figures outlined for a moment amid mountain and lake." "The being," says Yeats in a stunning combination of psychological, historical and literary criticism that carries us from Wordsworth to Proust, "has almost reached the end of that elaboration of itself which has for its climax an absorption in time, where space can be but symbols or images in the mind."

Even Giorgione and Helen fit into Phase 14, because Giorgione's figures along with Helen, as Yeats describes her, exhibit the self-absorbed detachment of the women painted by the late-nineteenth-century Burne-Jones, also in Phase 14. Although Giorgione is not discussed, we can assume by his placement that Yeats is following Pater's assimilation of Giorgione's paintings to nineteenth-century symbolist art. If Yeats cannot always make his insights gibe with the symmetry of the system, it is because he is writing mainly about his own time; whereas the system requires an evenhanded treatment of history. Yeats's interest is mainly on the *antithetical* or subjective side of the Great Wheel, and the figures here are predominantly nineteenth century.

Unlike Hegel, who in *The Philosophy of History* distinguishes between organic nature and the dialectical progress of mind, Yeats sees historical process as both organic and dialectical, as moving like natural organisms toward wholeness not knowledge: "Logical and emotional conflict alike lead towards a reality which is concrete, sensuous, bodily." The natural cycle is the model of all truth: "That bird signifies truth when it eats, evacuates, builds its nest, engenders, feeds its young; do not all intelligible truths lie in its passage from egg to dust?" [39]

This sentence connects with, and is complicated by, the curious story about birds in the rewritten fiction that introduces the revised version—the story about Mary Bell who has an illegitimate child by the ornithologist John Bond. She makes her husband happy by passing the child off as the fruit of their hitherto childless marriage. Through another deception, using this time John Bond's expertise rather than his sexual power, she makes her husband happy on his deathbed. Having devoted his life to teaching the cuckoos to build nests, the husband thinks he must die unfulfilled when Mary presents him with a

simulated cuckoo's nest. Nature is unchanging; only man produces novelty or history, but this novelty is illusion. The historical cycle is a cycle of changing illusions, which are, however,
congruent with the unchanging natural cycle.

Art, Yeats says in the *Autobiography*, derives from the same
mind that tells the birds how to build their nests. But "all civilization," he says in a brilliant paragraph of the same book, "is
held together by . . . artificially created illusions. The knowledge of reality. . . . is a kind of death"; for it reveals the void
beneath the illusions. That is the point of the late poem
"Meru"; but here, in spite of Yeats's concluding sentence, the
illusions seem to cover a vibrant reality.

> Every symbol is an invocation which produces its equivalent expression
> in all worlds. The Incarnation invoked modern science and modern ef-
> ficiency, and individualised emotion. It produced a solidification of all
> those things that grow from individual will. The historical truth of the
> Incarnation is indifferent, though the belief in that truth was essential to
> the power of the invocation.[40]

We can see why the reading of history in *A Vision* is largely a
reading of art history, since it is in their artifices that civilizations differ and since each civilization's characterizing idea is
most clearly incarnated in its art. The modern relativist view
that each personality and historical period perceives its own
characteristic reality suggests that personalities and historical
periods have to be read as we read works of art—for their self-
coherence as images of truth.

Mary Bell's story converges with the preceding story of Denise
de l'Isle Adam, who loves the painter Duddon but, since Duddon is impotent, sleeps with Huddon, the man who buys all
Duddon's pictures.[41] By taking care of the physical side, Huddon makes possible Duddon's art and love affair with Denise.
The triangles in this story and Mary Bell's teach the principle of
incarnation. Spirit alone produces nothing, but must have a
vehicle, a body. God needed Leda's egg and Mary's womb to

bring forth new eras (Robartes gives Mary Bell Leda's third egg, which she must lay in a shallow hole where it will hatch the post-Christian era); just as the artist needs images to embody truth.

Incarnation takes on added complexity in Yeats, because it soon becomes reincarnation. The Four Faculties are "the result of the four memories of the *Daimon* or ultimate self of that man." This external memory differs from Jung's in that it belongs to a distinct personality that is tied by antithesis to the man's personality. Hence the sense of being puppets, of repetition, which informs our psychic life at its profoundest, producing the intuition of reincarnation. The analogy is still to a play, where the characters half act out their own purposes as though they did not know the outcome, and half move, with the author's consciousness of the outcome inside them, to fulfill the design. "Life is an endeavor, made vain by the four sails of its mill [the conflicting Four Faculties], to come to a double contemplation, that of the chosen Image, that of the fated Image." [42]

Thus each man finds his characteristic way to the same kind of people and events. "We walk through ourselves," says Stephen Dedalus in *Ulysses*, "meeting robbers, ghosts, giants, old men, young men, wives, widows, brothers-in-love. But always meeting ourselves." [43] Sometimes an encounter produces the sense of repetition without recalling to the conscious memory a definite precedent, and then we get as a widespread psychological phenomenon the inexplicable sense that we are repeating a pattern from another life. In a passage that might apply to recurring encounters in *The Waste Land, Ulysses, The Rainbow*, Yeats passes without modulation from patterns within the one life to patterns within the many lives of the same soul:

> We all to some extent meet again and again the same people and certainly in some cases form a kind of family of two or three or more persons who come together life after life until all passionate relations are

> exhausted, the child of one life the husband, wife, brother or sister of
> the next. Sometimes, however, a single relationship will repeat itself
> . . . especially . . . where there has been strong sexual passion.[44]

One sees the usefulness here of the word *identity*; for the same
identity can manifest itself through shifting roles, names and
even personalities. It is antithesis that locks people into recurring relationships; and where antithesis is strongest, as in sexual
passion (Yeats cites Lawrence to prove the cruelty and deceit in
love), that conflict must be exhausted before the relationship
can be continued through other roles.

This passage comes from Book III, "The Soul in Judgment"—
the most difficult and for many readers the most repugnant
chapter of A *Vision*. "Soul in Judgment" deals with the life between lives, where the spirit prepares for its reincarnation; and
such subject matter passes for many readers beyond the bounds
of intellectual respectability, especially since Yeats claims to
have knowledge of this realm through his "communicators."
The "communicators," however, mainly confirm knowledge
drawn from the Neoplatonic tradition reaching from Plotinus
through Henry More to Swedenborg, and from a religious-
literary tradition reaching from Irish folk tales through the Bible
and the Upanishads to Noh plays. The chapter has, therefore,
sufficient weight of authority to deserve, when you consider its
author's commanding intelligence, some measure of the re-
spectful attention we give to Dante whose other world, if more
familiar, is no more susceptible than Yeats's of scientific proof.
Since Yeats himself believed in doctrines the way one believes
in works of art, the question of belief should not keep us from
appreciating "Soul in Judgment" as the book's boldest stroke of
imagination. One does not have to believe in the life between
lives to admire the power and subtlety of an imagination that
has laid out the soul's development in such fine gradations,

visualizing all it describes. We must in any case read the chapter for its psychological perspicuity; for it draws out the ultimate, most rarified implications in Yeats's theory of identity.

We can see from a passage in Jung how close Yeats's spirits come to Jung's strictly psychological archetypes. Jung defines the collective, as distinguished from the personal, unconscious as that "deeper layer of the unconscious where the primordial images common to humanity lie sleeping." These primordial images or archetypes

> are the most ancient and the most universal "thought-forms" of humanity. They are as much feelings as thoughts; indeed, they lead their own independent life rather in the manner of part-souls, as can easily be seen in those philosophical or Gnostic systems which rely on awareness of the unconscious as the source of knowledge. The idea of angels, archangels, "principalities and powers" in St. Paul, the archons of the Gnostics, the heavenly hierarchy of Dionysius the Areopagite, all come from the perception of the relative autonomy of the archetypes.[45]

Not only does Yeats consider the archetypes as persons, he considers them to be spirits of the dead who are completing between lives the identity only partially manifested in one life. These discarnate spirits work out their destinies through incarnation in our unconscious; they *are* our unconscious thoughts and feelings, "the *Dramatis Personae* of our dreams." Our mind gives to the dream its manifest content, the meaning *we* understand, that seems to apply to *our* life. But the dream's latent content lies in the concrete images that tell quite another story, the story of the spirit's life.

Since the other self is for Yeats an ultimate self, he needs another realm where the ultimate self can become fully manifest. Hence he gives to the ultimate self its own structure of Four Principles that correspond and provide in life a ghostly accompaniment to the Four Faculties. Of the Four Principles, Husk and Passionate Body correspond to Will and Mask; Spirit and Celestial Body correspond to Creative Mind and Body of Fate. Husk and Passionate Body, which prevail during life, must pass between lives into Spirit and Celestial Body. The transformation takes place through six states following death that objectify the stages of memory through which we grow in self-realization during life.

In the first state, The Vision of the Blood Kindred, one's earthly life flashes before one for the last time as unordered sensation. The second state has four stages. There is the Meditation, during which "the *Spirit* has its first vision and understanding of the *Celestial Body.*" In the next stage, the Dreaming Back, "the *Spirit* is compelled to live over and over again the events that had most moved it. . . . They occur in the order of their intensity or luminosity, the more intense first." In a higher stage, the Return, "the *Spirit* must live through past events in the order of their occurrence, because it is compelled . . . to trace every passionate event to its cause until all are related and understood . . . made a part of itself." [46] Through the Return, the Spirit gains that complete understanding of its life for which the model is art.

The psychological source of Dreaming Back and Return is portrayed in the powerful short poem "The Cold Heaven" (1912), where Yeats, "Riddled with light," understands in a moment of destructive recollection that he was responsible for the failure with Maud Gonne. Is this what the afterlife is like, he asks, this purgatorial experience of remorse and illumination, this compulsive memory? The play *Purgatory* (1939) portrays simultaneously the realms of the living and the dead. The dead woman, "Driven to it by remorse," [47] relives through the mind of her living son, the Old Man, the passionate error, her lustful marriage to a groom, that has ruined her aristocratic house and family. Only now, through the Old Man's mind and experience, she understands the consequences of her error. The Old Man, who killed his drunken father when the house burnt down, kills with the same knife his own ignorant brutal son, in order to end the chain of consequences and release his dead mother from memory. But her memory, as the Old Man real-

izes, returns; this second murder has only increased her remorse.

There remains the Phantasmagoria, through which the Spirit
completes its moral life: "if the life was evil, then the *Phantasmagoria* is evil, the criminal completes his crime." As in art,
the Phantasmagoria completes not only what the man did, but
also what he imagined he did. "It is indeed," says Yeats in a
puzzling but important sentence, "a necessary act of the human
soul that has cut off the incarnate and discarnate from one
another, plunging the discarnate into our 'unconsciousness.' "
Yeats is, I think, saying that all value like all art derives from
the disjunction between the potential and the manifest, between
the unconscious image and its conscious meaning.

Thus far the Spirit is in a realm equivalent to Purgatory, for it
is still tied to earthly events and to whatever moral code it held
in life. The third state, the Shiftings, reverses the Phantasmagoria, in that the Spirit enlarges its moral consciousness by
playing the moral role opposite to the role it played in life: "In
so far as the man did good without knowing evil, or evil without
knowing good, his nature is reversed until that knowledge is ob-
tained." This is how we enlarge our moral consciousness
through art, by sympathizing with points of view opposite to
ours, by taking into our consciousness the full measure of moral
conflict. Having acknowledged conflict, the Spirit reconciles it
in the fourth state, the Marriage or Beatitude, to achieve that
vision beyond good and evil, where "good and evil vanish into
the whole," which Yeats in many places announces as the ultimate liberating vision of art.

In the fifth state, the Purification, the Spirit discovers its true
identity; and it does this at a state where "all memory has vanished, the *Spirit* no longer knows what its name has been." It
"becomes self-shaping, self-moving, plastic to itself, as that self
has been shaped by past lives." We see here how "Soul in Judgment" carries Yeats's theory of identity to its logical conclusion.
For we see that the other or true self exists below the level of

names, roles, personalities, that it unfolds itself through the changing circumstances of the Spirit's many lives. There is only the ultimate self now, the phenomenal self having been purged away; so the Spirit no longer knows itself through its opposite but through itself. Celestial Body is no longer its opposite, but its image. It is Celestial Body at this state that Yeats envisioned in his Emmanuel dream of the other self, and which is equivalent to the luminous *images* of art (whose *meaning* would still be disjunctive). The self externalized in art is at the point in identity formation equivalent to the Purification—a point where identity is collective: "Their perfection is a shared purpose or idea." These five states can be understood to trace the evolution of identity as the self passes from the artist into his work, or as the artist himself changes from the individual who sits down to breakfast into the man of collective identity who creates a great work of art.

In the sixth and final state, the Foreknowledge, the Spirit sacrifices the achievement of the Purification in order to prepare its next incarnation. Almost united to the shadow of its next body,

B. Reversed Cones

Primary
(objective)

Antithetical
(subjective)

the Spirit now understands the consequences of its future life as it previously understood the consequences of its past life. With the assistance of the mysterious Thirteenth Cone (which introduces into the system an uncertain quantity of free will), the Spirit shapes the circumstances that suit, and therefore make possible the rebirth of, its "unique nature." The Spirit composes its future life the way art is made—out of existing conditions.

There appear here the two most profound sentences in the chapter. "The *Spirit* cannot be reborn until the vision of [its future] life is completed and accepted." "During its sleep in the womb the *Spirit* accepts its future life, declares it just." [48] These sentences account in Yeats's terms for all that ancient wisdom and modern depth psychology have revealed about man's relation to his destiny—that the pattern of events is there before we fulfill it. In some deep sense we know in advance the things that will happen to us and are the contrivers of those events; in some deep sense we desire our destiny, even the suffering—we would not, as Yeats put it in the *Autobiography*, change our luck. We even derive a satisfaction, which gives the structure to art and religion, from seeing the plot or ritual played out, from fulfilling the preordained pattern.

"Book III: The Soul in Judgment" is the second of the three most important chapters in *A Vision*. "Book I: The Great Wheel" deals with cycles of personality; "Book V: Dove or Swan" deals with cycles of history. Behind all three stands the central cyclical idea of reincarnation and the idea that the dead and the living work out their destinies in antithetical relation to each other: " 'Dying each other's life, living each other's death.' " The words are Heraclitus's. Yeats diagrams Heraclitus's principle as two reversed spirals or cones, one inside the other, which show one life winding outward as the other winds inward (see Diagram B, p. 206). A series of such pairs—each pair representing a personality and its antithesis—compose the Great Wheel.

The cones and the Wheel derive from the post-Kantian dichotomy between subject and object, but Yeats adds the idea that one side waxes as the other wanes. Our aim is to objectify the subjective. By the time we have accomplished that, we are depleted and the objective world has grown rigid with custom. That is why the man in "Nineteen Hundred and Nineteen," who knows no objective work can endure, has the one comfort that "all [objective] triumph would / But break upon [deplete] his ghostly solitude [subjectivity]." That is why, as Yeats explains in *A Vision*, the rigid sky figures of his poem "The Magi" journey toward a new incarnation: "The world of rigid custom and law" must be broken up by "subconscious turbulent instinct. . . . 'the uncontrollable mystery upon the bestial floor.' "

The Wheel charts the increase and decrease of self-consciousness, the extent to which self or the principle of unity is incarnate. In the *antithetical* or subjective phases (8–22), while self-consciousness increases, the man seeks unity within himself and imposes that unity upon the external world by giving it form and giving his own body form (see Diagram A, p. 197). *Antithetical* man increases in bodily beauty until Phase 15; afterwards such increasingly objective incarnations as merchant, statesman, scientist, seek their unity in the external world and thus lose forming power and bodily beauty. The last three *primary* or objective phases are represented by such extremes of "deformity" and minimal self-consciousness as Hunchback, Saint, Fool. The first three *primary* phases, with their animal-like unself-consciousness, start the move back toward subjectivity and forming power.

"This wheel," says Yeats obscurely, "is every completed movement of thought or life, twenty-eight incarnations, a single incarnation, a single judgment or act of thought." We can understand how the Wheel represents a completed movement of thought if we remember that thought is characteristic, that certain thoughts are possible only at certain phases of personality and history; so that the progression of personalities and historical periods is necessarily a progression of thoughts, and the world of thoughts is conversely "a congeries of beings."

Yeats gains precision and power by placing illustrious men and their thoughts along a scale of subjectivity-objectivity, because the scale indicates that the men and thoughts are being judged by the same criteria and in relation to each other. I find Yeats's insights convincing because they seem to come from direct observation yet are satisfyingly confirmed by their conformity to the system. It is satisfying to see the characterization of Spinoza—in Phase 11, "Moral iconoclasm"—analyzed in antithesis to Phase 25—the phase of dogmatic believers like Newman and A.E. (George Russell)—which draws its *Mask* from Phase 11 as "Consciousness of self." [49] Since one had always suspected that the personalities of iconoclast and believer are related, it is convincing to see a structural analysis which shows the conflict in both as composed of the same elements with the only difference the side of the conflict on which self and antiself are located. [50] The iconoclast has to struggle against inherited belief in order to sustain his self-motivated iconoclasm, while the believer has to struggle against the consciousness of self that subverts belief. Similarly, the most sophisticated criticism having taught us to regard Baudelaire with his exploration of sensuality and evil as an obverse saint, it is satisfying to see Baudelaire's sensuous Phase 13 opposite on the Wheel to the Saint's Phase 27.

It remains difficult to understand how the Wheel represents the completed movement of a *single* incarnation or act of thought. Yeats says he himself did not understand, until after he had written his account of the twenty-eight incarnations, that "every phase is itself a wheel," that to experience antithesis completely at any point on the Wheel is to experience the whole Wheel and thus achieve at least temporary Unity of

Being. This is the romantic doctrine of epiphany, the doctrine that intensification of the particular opens insight into the whole.

If personality results from the oscillations between antitheses, where does the image of the other self come from? Yeats offers two parallel explanations. One says that the antiself is the Daimon, a soul of antithetical personality. The other says that the antiself exists as an unconscious memory of the man's own personality in another life. Thus the Saint was once a man of the opposite Phase 13, Baudelaire's phase: "the love [the Saint] brings to God at his twenty-seventh phase was found in some past life upon a woman's breast." Our latest personality is an accrual of all our past personalities.

In some of his most stunning analyses by contraries, Yeats demonstrates the mysteries of identity; for the man is so divided that the question arises where his identity lies. The men of Phase 17 are, like Dante, Shelley, and we gather Yeats, "partisans, propagandists and gregarious," yet "hate parties, crowds, propaganda." Their Mask from Phase 3 holds up as an ideal the unself-conscious "solitary life of hunters." Thus Shelley (like Yeats as Irish nationalist) "writes pamphlets and dreams of converting the world," yet returns again and again in his poetry to self-consciously conceived "images of solitude." Shelley's mask—whether as the ancient Ahasuerus or as the young Prince Athanase "whose hair has grown white from the burden of his thoughts"—projects a presence at once definite and mysterious, mysterious because containing opposite personalities. Conflicting tendencies do not negate, they manifest identity; for an identity, like a historical period (the inverted cones apply to both) is strung across oscillation. It is where conflict is minimal, in the very early and late phases where the poles are too close, then too far, for much attraction and repulsion, that identity is least vivid.

Identity is most vivid at those phases where Yeats describes nineteenth-century dissociation of sensibility from thought—as in his description of romantic projection and role-playing. The

being "adopts a personality which it more and more casts outward, more and more dramatises. It is now a dissolving and violent phantom which would [through self-dramatization] grip itself and hold itself together." In Phase 19, the phase of Byron
and Wilde, "the being is compelled to live in a fragment of itself and to dramatise that fragment." [51] The Wheel describes
the different strategies by which the self achieves integration and
the self's varying degrees of wholeness.

The last three phases—phases that precede the complete objectivity of Phase 1—deal with human possibilities so extreme,
yet so psychologically valid, that they are best exemplified in literature. For Phase 26, the Hunchback, Yeats gives no examples, but he describes the walking dead of so much modern
writing. When he says "the deformity may be of any kind," one
recalls the sexual impotence of Clifford Chatterley and Faulk-
ner's Popeye: "He commits crimes, not because he wants to
. . . but because he wants to feel certain that he can; and he is
full of malice because, finding no impulse but in his own ambition, he is made jealous by the impulse of others." His malice
stems from the sense of his own nothingness. When Yeats describes the man's pitiless clarity of moral self-judgment, we are
reminded of those motiveless malignities in Dostoevsky whose
moral understanding places them next door to the saints: "He
stands in the presence of a terrible blinding light, and would,
were that possible, be born as worm or mole."

Since the Saint, Phase 27, envisions the total life, his desire
for self-annihilation goes even farther than the Hunchback's:
"His joy is to be nothing, to do nothing, to think nothing; but to
permit the total life, expressed in its humanity, to flow in upon
him and to express itself through his acts and thoughts." He differs from the Fool, Phase 28, only in that last minimum of self-
awareness which tells him he is not identical with the whole:
"for if he were he would not know that he is nothing." The
Fool exemplifies complete lack of self, of resistance to external
reality: "He is but a straw blown by the wind, with no mind but

the wind." [52] Since he is unconsciously attuned to reality, his randomness can produce along with nonsense complete wisdom. Yeats's model is probably the Fool in *King Lear*; but we, noticing that the diagram opening "Dove or Swan" charts the years after 1927 as moving into the last phases, may also see as symptomatic of Phase 28 the twentieth-century aesthetic of free association—stream-of-consciousness, surrealism.

In *A Vision* and elsewhere, Yeats makes little distinction between persons in art and in life. He considers persons in art potential phases of human identity, as are fairies, ghosts, gods. This is evidence of Yeats's essential paganism; for in the pagan as distinguished from the Judeo-Christian world-view, there is no absolute gap between human and divine: human identity contains the potentiality for apotheosis. It is this return to paganism, to the renewed possibility for self-transcendence now that the transcendent Christian God is dead, that Nietzsche announced in *Thus Spoke Zarathustra* (1892). The change from transcendent to immanent Spirit leads in Nietzsche, as in Yeats, to a change from linear, teleological time to the ancient doctrine of Eternal Recurrence.

Just as "The Great Wheel" implies, though unsystematically, that personalities are historically determined, so "Dove or Swan" implies that historical periods more or less derive their character from the kind of personality dominant at the time. Since "The Great Wheel" deals mainly with personalities, the examples are mainly characterizations of writers and their works. The emphasis in "Dove or Swan," instead, is on the visual arts; statues and paintings are made to yield a quintessential face or posture that personifies their age's culture. As history of art and culture the chapter has validity, especially since Yeats adopts fairly standard notions about styles and periods. The coincidences with Spengler's *The Decline of the West*, which Yeats had not seen when he first published *A Vision*, indicate that both drew on the same organicist ideas that cultures grow and have the unity we call character—ideas also drawn on by Yeats's

model for writing cultural history, Pater. "We have learned to
understand arts," says Spengler, "as prime phenomena. . . .
[as] *organisms* of the Culture, organisms which are born, ripen,
age and *for ever* die." [53]

Yeats is frank about his need to juggle dates to make history
fit his system. He juggles a little to "make Phase 15 [on the
opening diagram, 560 A. D. the middle of the first Christian
millenium] coincide with Justinian's reign" in Byzantium (Jus-
tianian died in 565). Yeats's description of early Byzantium parallels his description of Phase 15 as a phase of personality in
which "all thought has become image." In "Dove or Swan" we
are told that "some philosophical worker in mosaic" could make
Christian dogma "show as a lovely flexible presence like that of
a perfect human body." Because they embodied the thought of
the age, the Byzantine visual arts spoke "to the multitude and
the few alike," reflecting a unity of culture to match Phase 15's
Unity of Being. With the birth of a Christian *art*, civilization itself turns *primary*; earlier Christianity was imposed on a still
Classical or *antithetical* civilization.

"I imagine the annunciation that founded Greece as made to
Leda," says Yeats, "remembering that they showed in a Spartan
temple . . . an unhatched egg of hers." This is the unhatched
egg of the introductory story, the egg that must produce still
another pagan civilization. The sentence explains the title
"Dove or Swan" and the corresponding poems "Leda and the
Swan" and "The Mother of God." Just as the union of Leda
with Zeus, who came to her as a swan, ushered in Classical civilization, so the union of Mary with the Holy Ghost (symbolized as a Dove) ushered in Christian civilization. Yeats's vision
of "bird and woman" [54] says that a civilization is structured by
the union of God or idea with body. A civilization is, like a personality, an incarnation.

Comparative mythology has taught us to view the gods of different civilizations as different incarnations of the same ritual
roles—often the role of sacrificial victim. In "Two Songs from a

Play," Yeats, who had read *The Golden Bough* and assimilated
it to Nietzsche, uses a technique like Eliot's in *The Waste Land*
to make the same words refer to the death and resurrection of
Dionysus, Christ, and all the murdered gods of the spring fertility rituals that gave rise to Greek tragedies and Christian Passion
plays: "As though God's death were but a play." In *The Resurrection*, the play where the songs appear, the worshippers of
Dionysus, awaiting the resurrection of their god, hear instead
about Christ's resurrection.[55] Art provides the pattern of incarnation and repetition that can be applied to a civilization as to a
personality. The role is there, and gods, civilizations, pass
through it because individual men have preceded them. It is the
revived sense of personality as the filling in of a pre-existing role
that, coming after an age of self-conscious individualism, generates the twentieth-century sense of identity as a mystery. For
how separate the individual from the role? Both the mystery and
the static permanence of the role are portrayed through expressionless faces ("I saw a staring Virgin stand / Where holy Dionysus died") and ritualized movements ("And lay the heart upon
her hand / And bear that beating heart away").[56]

In the last stanza Yeats, who throughout his poems oscillates
between empiricism and Platonism, gives a surprisingly empirical answer to the mysteries of identity. Here as elsewhere he
makes the individual the fundamental reality. When the subjective has been objectified, life passes from the individual to
art—"The painter's brush consumes his dream"—and to civilization: "Whatever flames upon the night / Man's own resinous
heart has fed." Civilization, like art, must return for renewal to
its source in the individual: "In the foul rag-and-bone shop of
the heart," as Yeats says later in "The Circus Animals' Desertion." The need to return means that civilizations like persons
oscillate between subjectivity and objectivity, that the character
of an age is determined by antithesis to the preceding age:
"Each age unwinds the thread another age had wound." East-
ward-moving Byzantium developed its character by fleeing all

that was Roman, and our westward-moving Renaissance developed its character by fleeing all that was Byzantine.

"A civilization," says Yeats, in the analogy with personality I have already quoted, "is like some great tragic person" struggling "to keep self-control." [57] Loss of control occurs at the end of the spiral or cone, where the oscillations have become too wide. That wide end of the cone corresponds on the Wheel to the phases of Saint and Fool, where dissolution of personality prepares for the revelation that will usher in a new era.

Yeats traces through the Christian era a cycle of periods that corresponds to the cycle of personalities charted on the Wheel. Classical civilization prepared the way for Christ by so exalting the human body (an exaltation represented by Salome dancing) that the Roman emperors could become gods and God become a man. But in the first 1000 years A. D. there is a swing, after the subjective pagan era, to the opposite view that spirit is entirely objective: "God is now conceived of as something outside man and man's handiwork." Personality is at a minimum. Meanwhile Roman decay, the decay of a civilization surrendering its own best qualities, is represented by marble heads of Senators, screwed on to pediments or standard bodies, where the eyeball is a drilled round hole to suggest "the glance characteristic of a civilization in its final phase"—the glance of "the administrative mind." All life, all character, "as with us of recent years," is in the head and the head sees power as outside itself.

In the second Christian millenium, secular culture brings back subjectivity. Yeats finds the first victory of personality in Dante, who "in the *Divina Commedia* imposes his own personality upon a system and a phantasmagoria hitherto impersonal." Masaccio, Chaucer, Villon (1380–1450) project through their realism an individualized body. There are no longer "miracles to stare at, for man descends the hill he once climbed with so great toil, and all grows but natural again." The High Renaissance in Italy (1450–1550) corresponds to the age of Phidias—in both, traditional faith is broken. When it could be felt that "the human norm, discovered from the measurement of ancient statues, was God's first handiwork," then "the second Adam [Christ] had become the first." The Fall is redeemed through *antithetical* art; the religion of art is born.

The Renaissance synthesis disintegrates as art moves toward objectivity: the painter increasingly takes his material from outside, eventually making it "a matter of pride to paint what he does not at all desire." It disintegrates through Shakespeare in whose works human personality, hitherto restrained by Christianity, "burst like a shell"; and through Milton who tries too late to restore the synthesis. "All that comes out of Bacon" leads to the eighteenth century, when the artistic life "is external, sentimental and logical," the emotion having become as simple as the thought. The modern novel emerges, and soon does away with "the happy ending, the admired hero, the preoccupation with desirable things."

> Personality is everywhere spreading out its fingers in vain, or grasping with an always more convulsive grasp a world where the predominance of physical science, of finance and economics in all their forms, of democratic politics, of vast populations, of architecture where styles jostle one another, of newspapers where all is heterogeneous, show that mechanical force will in a moment become supreme.[58]

One recalls the vision, in "Meditations in Time of Civil War," of the revolutionary mob plunging "towards nothing, arms and fingers spreading wide / For the embrace of nothing."

Toward the end of this period, 1650–1875, romanticism creates an " 'Emotion of Sanctity' " possible only "in those things that are most intimate and personal." But romanticism cannot stem the movement toward depersonalization and abstraction. The period from 1875 to 1927 is "a period of abstraction," in which applied sciences, social movements and the kind of art from which the artist has disappeared "have for their object or result the elimination of intellect"—the preference, we might add extending the period to the present, for statistics, computers and group work over ideas and individual distinction. In the latest physics, which does not like Newton's yield an "objective world intelligible to intellect," Yeats recognizes "that the limit itself has become a new dimension," that men must "for the first time since the seventeenth century, see the world as an object of contemplation, not as something to be remade." [59] We are thus preparing the ideology of the next cycle, which will resemble the eclectic occultism of A Vision.

Yeats stops here, but in the 1925 version he characterizes the young writers of the 1920s as substituting "technical research" for both abstraction and "the personal dream." He names among those who are initiating a revolt against abstraction,

> Mr. Ezra Pound, Mr. Eliot, Mr. Joyce, Signor Pirandello, who either eliminate from metaphor the poet's phantasy and substitute a strangeness discovered by historical or contemporary research, or who break up the logical processes of thought by flooding them with associated ideas or words that seem to drift into the mind by chance; or who set side by side, as in "Henry IV," "The Waste Land," "Ulysses," the *physical primary*—a lunatic among his keepers, a man fishing behind a gas works, the vulgarity of a single Dublin day prolonged through 700 pages—and the *spiritual primary*, delirium, the Fisher King, Ulysses' wandering.

Without a world-view to organize them, facts (the *physical primary*) become so meaningless that meaning (the *spiritual primary*) reenters as mythical pattern which avoids both objective abstraction and subjective dream. "It is as though myth and fact, united [by intellectual system] until the exhaustion of the Renaissance, have now fallen so far apart that man understands for the first time the rigidity of fact, and calls up, by that very recognition, myth—the *Mask*—which now but gropes its way out of the mind's dark but will shortly pursue and terrify." This parallels Eliot's salute to the new "mythical method" of *Ulysses* in a review Yeats could have read.

"I foresee a time," says Yeats—in a prophecy that applies to our increasingly collectivist age—"when all personality will seem an impurity—'sentimentality,' 'sullenness,' 'egotism.'" With that reversal of nineteenth-century individualism, we will be ready for the next cycle which, like the Christian cycle, will "find its philosophy already impressed upon the minority." The next cycle will awaken not Blake's "human form divine" nor even "Nietzsche's superman," but collectivist symbols. Are such symbols heralded by the shapes in abstract painting and sculpture and the characterless, nearly nameless figures in our latest serious fiction and drama? Is the flight from ego already manifest in young people's attraction to drugs, communes and Hindu-Buddhist religion, and the predilection of Western intellectuals for depersonalizing systems like Marxism and structuralism? From collective identity and from that final "adoration of force"—dramatized by the "rough beast" of "The Second Coming" and the even more frightening because more mindless Robert Artisson of "Nineteen Hundred and Nineteen"—will come, surprisingly, an *antithetical* or subjective cycle. That is because religion—the religion of *A Vision*—will be *antithetical*; whereas only art has, since the Renaissance, been *antithetical*. Religion will be *antithetical* because it will be, despite its abstract, collectivist symbols, the Blake-Yeats religion of art: "Men will no longer separate the idea of God from that of human genius, human productivity in all its forms." [60] This is Yeats's one hope for the future—that we may be preparing an identity more propitious for religious experience than the nineteenth-century individualism that killed off religion.

The reader must cut through the density of terminology and diagrams and overlook the sometimes clumsy mechanics of the system, in order to judge *A Vision* by the fruitfulness of its psychological, historical and critical insights, by the beauty of its prose and verse, by its imaginative power. It should be clear from my account that I consider *A Vision* a work of major importance in its own right. Others, especially Harold Bloom in his *Yeats* (1970), rate it lower. The reader must judge for himself, but judge by the right criteria. There can be no doubt, in any case, of the book's importance, especially when supplemented by the 1925 version, as an aid to understanding the later poems and plays and as Yeats's most systematized statement of his theory of identity.

Chapter 7

THE SELF
AS GOD

All through his career Yeats was concerned with the question of
how you get over from the flesh-and-blood creature to the
mythical person who puts forth those magical powers from which
all value and culture derive. In "Easter 1916," he expresses his
amazement that people whom he knew as ordinary citizens
have now been translated into an awesome sphere of being ("A
terrible beauty is born") by their participation in the heroic and
tragic Easter Rebellion. The point is that the Easter Rebellion
was, in its useless and excessive sacrifice, like a work of art; so
that these people have stepped from "the casual comedy" of ordinary life into a tragedy. In so doing they have *lost* their individual characters, assimilated to the archetype of the hero, and
passed into Irish legend. For character, as Yeats says in his essay
"The Tragic Theatre," belongs to comedy and is incompatible
with tragedy. "Tragedy must always be a drowning and breaking
of the dykes that separate man from man." "In mainly tragic art
one distinguishes devices to exclude or lessen character," to
reveal the archetype.[1]

Another mode of transformation is through the intensification of *character* to the point where it becomes a vision of itself and thus a different order of being. In "Beautiful Lofty Things," in *Last Poems*, Yeats recalls in the life of his father and certain friends one epiphanic moment in which that person was courageous in his own individual way and thus turned himself into a legendary figure. The poem closes with:

> Maud Gonne at Howth station waiting a train,
> Pallas Athene in that straight back and arrogant head:
> All the Olympians; a thing never known again.

Individuality has welled up from a depth in touch with universal force.

The next two poems show a naturalistic and an artistic mode of transformation. In "A Crazed Girl," the poet Margot Ruddock, who dances upon the shore, is so "wound" in her "desperate music," music undistinguishable fom the sea's, as to have become "A beautiful lofty thing." Her identity has been "heroically found" because "heroically lost" through complete blending with universal force. In "To Dorothy Wellesley," Yeats bids his poet friend consciously draw into herself, through the "sensuous silence of the night," universal force. Because her identity will be thus transformed, he asks, when she ascends to bed,

> What climbs the stair?
> Nothing that common women ponder on
> If you are worth my hope! Neither Content
> Nor satisfied Conscience, but that great family
> Some ancient famous authors misrepresent,
> The Proud Furies each with her torch on high.

The Furies are misrepresented as evil, but are the Daimons necessary for transformed personality (the artist's and his created characters'), which is structured on suppressed "violence or madness." [2] Margot Ruddock accomplishes the transformation only in herself because her madness is not suppressed—there is no

conflict with universal force. Dorothy Wellesley will accomplish the transformation in herself and her poems, because
there will be conflict with internalized universal force.

In "The Tower," written some ten years earlier, Yeats rages
against the abstractness of old age, and tries in Wordsworthian
fashion to bind his days together by understanding how he himself has got over from man to poet, from aging individual to
maker of a time-defying superhuman dream. The tower is the
symbol of his transformed personality, and as he paces its battle-
ments he looks out on the surrounding landscape and as-
sembles, as Wordsworth would, the elements out of which he
has made his soul and will make it in preparing for death. Yeats
differs from Wordsworth in that these elements are local
legends, rather more than personal experiences, connected with
the landscape. The elements are subtle mixtures of life and
art—like the peasant girl glorified by Blind Raftery's song, or
Yeats's own Red Hanrahan from *The Secret Rose* who now
seems a figure in legend and life, as do the previous inhabitants
of the tower and their ghosts. The elements are mixtures of cultural and personal memory. They consist of his ancestors' pride
and his belief, drawn from tradition and symbolized by the
swan's last journey, in the mysterious opening of mortality into
immortality. They consist of the heritage from Italy, Greece and
the poetic tradition, and of his own "memories of love" and
"words of women." The elements are all those human things
whereof "Man makes a superhuman / Mirror-resembling
dream."

Here, he cries "in Plato's teeth" that "Death and life were
not / Till man made up the whole." But elsewhere he takes the
opposite Platonic stance, as in the previous companion poem,
"Sailing to Byzantium," where he welcomes old age as the time
to escape nature and take form *from*, instead of giving it *to*, abstract things. The empirical romantic stance of "The Tower"
(restated in "A Dialogue of Self and Soul" and "The Circus
Animals' Desertion") is, however, his more fundamental posi-

tion and connects with his theory of identity. For just as identity
is transformed into wholeness through intensification of character, so Yeats, in "The Tower," resolves the problem of old age
by seeing the poignant awareness of its pain and loss as that intensification of mortality which opens, like the swan's last song,
into immortality.

To intensify any one phase of life is to arrive at the whole.
Yeats speaks in his *Autobiography* about "true Unity of Being,
where all the nature murmurs in response if but a single note be
touched." [3] As applied to real people in real life, the question of
identity comes down to this. Where, among the different
aspects we show to people, and among the metamorphoses we
pass through in the different stages of our life, is our identity?
Yeats deals with this question most completely in "Among
School Children," a poem that grew from a notebook entry of
March 1926 which connects it with the first of the Nohlike
plays, *At the Hawk's Well*, written in 1915–16. The entry reads:
"school children and the thought that life [live] will waste them
perhaps that no possible life can fulfill their own [this or]
dreams or even their teacher's hope. Bring in the old thought
that life prepares for what never happens." [4] The "old thought"
refers to the last sentence of *Reveries over Childhood and Youth*
(1914), the first volume of *The Autobiography*, and to the play's
first-draft ending: "Accursed the life of man—between passion
and emptiness what he longs for never comes. All his days are a
preparation for what never comes." [5] In the play the old man,
through Oriental avoidance of life (he falls asleep), and the
young Cuchulain, through Western heroic passionate engagement in it (he follows the girl as she dances offstage), miss the
vision they have been waiting for. The poem as it evolved in
June 1926 transforms the notebook entry into a question about
identity, about the unity of all life's stages, the answer to which
answers the "old thought" as *At the Hawk's Well* could not.

The poem opens with Yeats's shock, on visiting a girls'
school, that the little girls are staring in wonder at "A sixty-year-

old smiling public man," who is different from the man Yeats thinks of as himself. He feels the great distance between himself and the children until he remembers Maud Gonne as a beautiful young woman and finally, through a story she told of her childhood, has a vision of her as just such a little girl as these. "Her present image," that of a worn old woman, comes to mind, and his "heart is driven wild" by the thought of the passing stages of her life and his. Where among the metamorphoses is the real, the continuing person?

Yeats begins his answer by rephrasing a question from the opening chorus of At the Hawk's Well. What mother would think giving birth worthwhile could she see the "shape upon her lap" at sixty? Yeats uses "shape" for the same reason that he asks Dorothy Wellesley "What climbs the stair?"—to avoid saying where the real person is to be found. Yeats's notes for this stanza (V) are, according to Thomas Parkinson, "concerned with the soul's betrayal into the flesh." [6] The stanza talks further of the soul's betrayal into old age and of its "struggle to escape" the problem "As recollection or the drug decide"—through either memory or forgetfulness of its divine origin. Yeats called the poem, while writing it, his "curse upon old age"; [7] but as the poem evolved through revisions—the evolution is deftly analyzed by Parkinson—it came, as did Wordsworth's "Immortality Ode," to bless life and all its stages.

Yeats has now to account for the obvious answer to his question about mothers, that mothers do think giving birth worthwhile. He finds his explanation not in philosophical theories— for theories, like the philosophers themselves, become obsolete—but in the image. "Both nuns and mothers worship images." The mother worships the flesh-and-blood "shape," the nun the marble Holy Infant, because each object refers to the other. The nun's statue can break the heart because she refers it to living babies; the mother can love the "shape upon her lap" because she refers it to the marble archetype and therefore knows that a single identity will bind together its various phases.

Nuns and mothers worship not the object before them, but the combination of archetype and flesh, the embodied idea, the image. "Man is nothing till he is united to an image." The answer to the poem's problem is drawn from *The Player Queen*.[8]

It is also *because* they worship that nuns and mothers can see through the objects before them to the combinations—the internal-external "Presences" that account, as they do in Wordsworth, for affect. The correspondence between the objects of worship is especially clear in an earlier version of Stanza VII that speaks of both as statuary:

> the Presences
> That love, or piety or affection knows
> And *dead* or *living statuary* symbolize.[9]

By making the "Presences" in the final version symbolize "all heavenly glory," Yeats specifically locates his images in that heaven of perfect embodiment where the concluding stanza takes place. These images are "self-born mockers of man's enterprise," because they cannot be willed though they are projected by us. Like all our imaginative creations—our gods, our works of art—they mock us, their creators, because they are better than we.

"Labour," or flesh-and-blood life, says Yeats in the concluding stanza, "is blossoming or dancing where / The body is not bruised to pleasure soul"—where Adam's curse (the need to labor) is undone and conflict resolved, because all thought is incarnate. This is Phase 15 of *A Vision*, the realm of perception portrayed in art. It is in this realm, which is always with us though we cannot always perceive it, that our permanent self resides. To the extent that we perceive the self as an image, an incarnation, we can bind together its various phases. Yeats's answer to the poem's implied question about identity is couched as two gorgeous questions:

> O chestnut-tree, great-rooted blossomer,
> Are you the leaf, the blossom or the bole?

> O body swayed to music, O brightening glance,
> How can we know the dancer from the dance?

The tree refers to the relation between parts and whole; the
dance to the relation between movement and static pattern. The
tree exists in all its parts, because we bring the idea of the tree to
the perception of its parts. Similarly dancer and dance, body
and idea, can only be known through each other; the whole
dance exists in each of its phases, because the movement (the
dance is inferred, the dancer is about to take off from stillness)
adds up to stillness, to idea. Like an identity, tree and dance are
perceived as wholes because perceived as images combining nature and art, flux and fixed idea.[10]

Only the empirical artistic self is dealt with in "Among
School Children." "A Dialogue of Self and Soul" reopens
Yeats's internal debate between Platonism and empiricism—
between the *primary* Platonist-saint, who wants purity not self-
realization and would ascend in a straight line out of life, and
the *antithetical* hero-artist who, loving life's impurity, seeks self-
realization through the experiential cycle of repetition and reincarnation. Extinction alone, says the saintly *My Soul*, can "Deliver from the crime of death and birth"; but the heroic-artistic
My Self insists on the right "to commit the crime once more,"
to be reborn into life. Yeats confirms his own choice of the artist's way by showing how it is possible to achieve, in the midst
of life's foul and fecund ditch, a transcendence equal if not superior to the saint's. "Only the dead can be forgiven," says *My
Soul*. But *My Self* shows how we can forgive ourselves through
the complete comprehension of our actions that constitutes a
purgatorial experience in life:

> I am content to follow to its source
> Every event in action or in thought;
> Measure the lot; forgive myself the lot!

This is the illumination art gives, illumination to the point
where all seems justified. It is also the illumination that takes

place through the progress between lives that prepares the soul to return to life. In his sublime final lines, the most exalted he ever wrote, Yeats carries identity-making to its triumphant conclusion by portraying perfect self-realization in this life:

> When such as I cast out remorse
> So great a sweetness flows into the breast
> We must laugh and we must sing,
> We are blest by everything,
> Everything we look upon is blest.

The switch from first-person singular to plural reminds us that in the fifth state between lives, the Purification, the identity embodied is, as in the luminous images of art, collective. In "Vacillation," which again debates the saintly and artistic ways, the artistic vision of life's blessedness arrives through an understanding of symbols ("that Attis' image") and through epiphany:

> While on the shop and street I gazed
> My body of a sudden blazed;
> And twenty minutes more or less
> It seemed, so great my happiness,
> That I was blessèd and could bless.

Salvation for Yeats consists not in extinction but in transformation of self.

In the poems I have dealt with so far, Yeats moves from the living to the mythical figure. But in two of the *Last Poems*, in "The Municipal Gallery Revisited" and "A Bronze Head," he moves from the mythical back to the living figure. In "Municipal Gallery," he sees paintings of his friends and realizes that they have already passed into the legendary Ireland " 'The poets have imagined, terrible and gay,' " and that the legend is the essential truth about them and Ireland. In "A Bronze Head," Yeats sees in the Municipal Gallery a bronze-painted plaster bust of Maud Gonne in old age, a terrifying bust that makes her look "mummy-dead" and supernatural. Since the bronze head is "Human, superhuman," it exemplifies the mysteries of identity and makes him recall the full-bodied, gentle girl she once

was. He asks explicitly the question that is only implied in
"Among School Children": "Which of her forms has shown her
substance right?" The answer is that the mummy-dead head is
an image that refers to the vital girl; while the girl, as Yeats
remembers, gave signs already of turning into this supernatural,
staring, nonvital head through a "wildness" that was suppressed
hysterica passio: already "A vision of terror that it must live
through / Had shattered her soul." It is because Yeats comes to
understand Maud Gonne's identity as the repetition of a life already anticipated that he realizes she has always been an image,
a mythical figure both natural and supernatural. There is no
sharp distinction in these two poems between the people and
their portraits; their portraits were painted because the people
had already become images, mythical figures.

In "Lapis Lazuli," the greatest of *Last Poems,* Yeats combines
his concept of transformed identity with a principle of repetition
to project an attitude for confronting life's problems—an attitude, equivalent to casting out remorse or freeing one's self of
guilt, which he calls, with reminiscences of Nietzsche, tragic
gaiety or joy. In answer to politically minded women like Maud
Gonne, who taught that poets like himself were superficially gay
in the face of the pressing dangers of the times, Yeats talks first
about the tragic theater. The sum of tragedy does not increase,
Yeats says, with the number of people involved in catastrophes.
There is no greater amount of tragedy in the world than the
tragedy that happens to Hamlet or Lear.[11] It is because the
tragic poet knows this, because he collapses all the diverse trou-
bles in the world into the tragedy of a single archetypal figure
who walks through the paces of a representative action—an action representing "All men have aimed at, found and lost"—it is
for this reason that the actors who play Hamlet and Lear do not,
at the end of the play,

> break up their lines to weep.
> They know that Hamlet and Lear are gay;
> Gaiety transfiguring all that dread.

The actors know that Hamlet and Lear are like themselves actors, who are consciously—because the author's consciousness is in them, they are partly marionettes at the service of the author's consciousness—repeating the paces of a given action. Hamlet and Lear are, like actors, gay with the aesthetic satisfaction of seeing the whole play at every point of it, and of knowing finally that the action has moved toward its necessary conclusion. The mystery by which gaiety transforms dread is the mystery not only of art, but of the human mind which in all its endeavors assimilates the disorder and violence of day-to-day existence to its own triumphant patterns. Yeats makes this clear in the next stanza where he shows the same transforming principle of repetition in history itself. Through some deep historical instinct that accounts for the continuity of civilization, we know that "All things fall and are built again," which is why "those that build them again are gay."

Finally, Yeats brings history and art together by recalling the blithe wisdom of an ancient civilization like that of China—a wisdom reflected in Chinese art, in the great piece of lapis lazuli carved into the shape of a mountain that the poet has set out to celebrate. The point is that all wisdom and all art aspire to the quality of Chinese wisdom and art: Yeats having shown how tragic art transforms Western heroic action into something like Oriental tragicomic acceptance. The quality of the carved scene, as the poet brings it to life, is perfectly tragicomic. For though the Chinamen, whom the poet imagines as having progressed up the mountain, stare upon a "tragic scene" and ask "for mournful melodies," their response is the smiling, comic comprehension that includes and transcends all tragic knowledge:

> Their eyes mid many wrinkles, their eyes,
> Their ancient, glittering eyes, are gay.

Yeats is able in this poem to reconcile Western and Oriental wisdom, because Western tragedy collapses the sort of diverse

disasters that are reported in the newspapers into the single disaster that is assimilated to the pattern of the Great Mind and
the Great Memory. And it is this transformation—the transformation of perspective Yeats found in the Noh—that transforms
dread into gaiety. The final lines project a mood that in Noh is
called *yūgen*—the acceptance of life's mystery and depth, its
ineffableness. *Yūgen* describes the tone of Yeats's great affirma-
tions in "Among School Children," "A Dialogue of Self and
Soul" and "Lapis Lazuli."

Last Poems is mainly about the transformation of perspective
and identity resulting from assimilation to the Great Mind and
Great Memory. Such transformed perspective, which produces
"tragic joy," is represented by Old Rocky Face in the opening
poem, "The Gyres." "The Three Bushes"—in which the lady
deceives her lover by secretly sending her maid to be his body
mistress by night while she remains his soul mistress by day—is
about incarnation. It is about the need of body and soul for
each other, and about what Yeats in *A Vision* calls the necessary disjunction between body and soul in order that they may
be combined to produce affect or images—in order "That I may
hear," as the lady says to her maid,

>   if we should kiss
>   A contrapuntal serpent hiss,
>   You, should hand explore a thigh,
>   All the labouring heavens sigh.
>   ("The Lady's Third Song")

This is like the nuns and mothers passage in "Among School
Children"; each side produces an image that contains the other
side, and passion for the women and the lover comes of the
need to complete the image. There is always a triad, the lover
and the divided image of the beloved. But the disjunction pro-

duces a collective identity. After the deaths of the three, the three rose bushes over their adjacent graves merge into one.

In "The Statues," the mathematically measured marble or bronze figures lack character.

> But boys and girls, pale from the imagined love
> Of solitary beds, knew what they were,
> That passion could bring character enough.

Yeats considered passion antithetical to character or individualized identity. But by referring statues of the opposite sex to their passionate longings, boys and girls complete the image and thus give a collective identity to themselves and their as yet undiscovered lovers. The image in their heads will enable them to fall in love; for it is only at the phase of collective or archetypal identity that two people can be locked together in passion. The boys and girls "pressed at midnight in some public place / Live lips upon a plummet-measured face." This is the clearest representation in *Collected Poems* of the completed image, the union of body and idea.[12]

The late plays—*The King of the Great Clock Tower* and its revision, *A Full Moon in March*—are devoted to the same representation. Body is represented by the low-born man (a swineherd in *Full Moon*), idea by the Queen's coldly impassive beauty. The man is decapitated, and the Queen's dance with the severed head represents the image. The severed head suggests the sexual intimacy of the union and also the man's necessary transformation, the sacrifice perhaps of his egocentric identity, as he passes into the image. "What marvel is / Where the dead and living kiss?"[13] When the Queen, as the climax of her dance, kisses the man's severed but singing head, we can no longer say which is the dead and which the living; each has brought the other to completion in the image. For the man is now dead but singing; while the Queen's former coldness is explained by Yeats's statement in *A Vision* that the Platonic separation of "the Eternal Ideas from Nature" is "a form of death."[14]

In *Last Poems*, "Long-Legged Fly" treats with lyrical clarity the collective identity of world-historical figures. Civilization is made and moved forward by people who gather superhuman power from *"silence,"* from a collective unconsciousness outside themselves. The individual or conscious self rests *"Like a long-legged fly upon the stream"* of collective unconsciousness; the individual *"mind moves upon silence."* The world-historical work is accomplished unconsciously: Caesar's eyes before a campaign are "fixed upon nothing"; Helen's beauty attracts Paris at a moment when she thinks nobody is looking; Michelangelo's hand moves automatically across the Sistine ceiling. The poem's remarkably impersonal voice speaks in imperatives, suggesting that these figures are at such moments puppets in a world-historical drama.

The companion poems "Sailing to Byzantium" and "Byzantium," and "The Delphic Oracle upon Plotinus" and "News for the Delphic Oracle," trace the cycle from life to the sphere of images that in turn refer back to life. Yeats comes to terms with his old age according to the same cyclical perspective. He starts in "The Circus Animals' Desertion" in the sphere of images. He cannot find a theme for poetry; he is "broken," because completely objectified in his images. Yet "Those masterful images because complete" refer to the world of objects from which they rose: "A mound of refuse or the sweepings of a street"; and if Yeats is to write new poetry he must return to the concrete, subjective and individual, to "the foul rag-and-bone shop of the heart," and start the process of image-making again. In "An Acre of Grass," instead, Yeats is left at life's end with ruined body and mental faculties that cannot yield truth. His solution, as always, is to remake himself. He will return to spirit, put on the old man's mask that can call down revelation and revive the forgotten procession of images: "Shake the dead in their shrouds; / Forgotten else by mankind."

In the two closing poems, Yeats tries to make from his old man's vision and sense of collective identity a tradition to leave to his successors. "The Black Tower," which he finished a week before his death, relates in imagery and theme to Browning's " 'Childe Roland to the Dark Tower Came' "; it is about victory through failure. The obsolete soldiers of the old black tower are victorious because "oath-bound" to a lost cause. "Swear" is the first word of "Under Ben Bulben," a somewhat earlier poem which stands last because Yeats ended it with lines for his epitaph. Both poems are about loyalty to a tradition which, as "Under Ben Bulben" too didactically tells us, reads the world symbolically and understands identity as collective—as an incarnation and a repetition that combines the continuing collective identity of race with the continuing individual identity of soul:

> Many times man lives and dies
> Between his two eternities,
> That of race and that of soul.

The dead return as thoughts, as Daimons inhabiting human minds: the grave-diggers "but thrust their buried men / Back in the human mind again." It is because ancient Ireland knew all this that Irishmen must remain faithful to Irish tradition. The many Irish ballads in *Last Poems* are, I think, examples of the popular poetry proper to a symbolizing culture with a sense of collective identity.

The aim of life is to complete the image by completing your life's preordained pattern. Man "completes his partial [individual] mind" through heroic action and through the art which projects the archetypes that bring "the soul of man to God"—that help man complete his identity by filling "the cradles right," by playing pre-existing roles and incarnating pre-existing ideas. The job of modern artists is to preserve the archetypes, restoring cultural memory to men who are "base" because "unremembering." The epitaph Yeats prescribes for his tomb projects another version of Old Rocky Face and the Chinamen's "ancient, glittering eyes"; it projects the mask of an identity that can *"Cast a cold eye / On life, on death,"* because aware of the cycles.

The mysteries of identity are plumbed most profoundly in the poem completed a week before "The Black Tower." This is "Cuchulain Comforted," which Yeats described as a "strange" sequel to the "strange" play,[15] *The Death of Cuchulain*, that turned out to be his last. After the death dramatized in the play, the hero Cuchulain arrives in a Dantesque Purgatory. The dead appear as Shrouds, and one of these Shrouds asks Cuchulain to sew himself a shroud so as to resemble the others. The Shroud reveals their character: "Convicted cowards all." The revelation is not puzzling if we understand Yeats's theory of identity. Cuchulain's place is with the cowards, because his heroism has had to define itself against cowardice. The coward is Cuchulain's Daimon, antiself, or character in an earlier incarnation. In the afterlife, the antithesis is resolved through transformed identity represented by the shroud as Celestial Body and by the cowards' triumphant singing: "They had changed their throats and had the throats of birds." [16] Cuchulain will sing with the same voice; for everything is "done in common" in the higher stages of the afterlife, where identity is collective. In *The Death of Cuchulain*—where Cuchulain seems to have played the coward in allowing himself to be tied up by a woman and beheaded by a Blind Man—Cuchulain envisioned, as he was dying, the birdlike shape his soul would take after death: "And is not that a strange shape for the soul / Of a great fighting-man?" [17]

His soul must experience antithesis before it can arrive at the reconciling birdsong which is Cuchulain's "comfort" for finding himself among the cowards. Cuchulain's purgatorial state corresponds to that of the Shiftings, where the "nature is reversed"; it corresponds also to the next state, the Marriage or Beatitude, where "good and evil vanish into the whole" and the Spirit assumes the shroudlike "*Celestial Body* . . . the Divine Cloak lent to all." [18] Written in *terza rima*, "Cuchulain Comforted" is a triumph in the Dantesque style; but the ending is pure Yeats. In Dante, the afterlife brings out the moral implications of a man's character; he remains what he was, but he can, in Purgatory at least, ascend to a higher moral quality. In Yeats, however, moral quality cannot be abstracted from identity; hero and coward are inseparable parts of a complete identity. To be one or the other intensely enough is to arrive at the whole; whether a man starts as hero or coward, it comes in the afterlife to the same thing. In Dante salvation is through ascent; in Yeats through intensification. The difference between the vertical characterology of *The Divine Comedy* and the circular characterology of *A Vision* is the difference between a moralistic and an aesthetic world-view. Dante's system requires the idea of a God who distributes rewards and punishments, towards whom all things long to ascend. Yeats's system requires his theory of the image, of the reconciliation between opposites. [19]

The frenzied old man who speaks the prologue in *The Death of Cuchulain* spits upon the modern world, because it can no longer read symbols and has therefore such a different sense of what constitutes identity and reality that no compromise is possible between the old man's traditional view and the modern departure. Because this play is mythical and symbolic, the now-dominant middle class will not like it; the play will speak, as we see in the end, to outsiders like harlots and beggars whose view of life, because now obsolete, will prevail in the next age.

Cuchulain's death is tragicomic rather than tragic, because he moves toward it like a puppet without resisting. F. A. C. Wilson is right in saying that "the play, a play of rejoicing, centres about his transfiguration." [20] Cuchulain, while allowing his head to be cut off by the Blind Man from the heroic tragedy *On Baile's Strand*, ecstatically envisions his soul's transfiguration into a bird. We see by the present-day ballad at the end that Cuchulain has returned to men's minds as the Daimon that inspires sexual and nationalist passions, that he has become the symbol of Irish nationality behind the Easter Rebellion.

In *The Death of Cuchulain*, Yeats answers most completely the question about identity with which he had been wrestling

ever since *The Player Queen*—the question of how you get over
from the flesh-and-blood creature to the mythical person. He
wrote Ethel Mannin that he had put into the play his unpublished "private philosophy":

> According to Rilke a man's death is born with him and if his life is suc-
> cessful and he escapes mere "mass death" his nature is completed by his
> final union with it. Rilke gives Hamlet's death as an example. In my
> own philosophy the sensuous image is changed from time to time at
> predestined moments. . . . One sensuous image leads to another be-
> cause they are never analysed. At *The Critical Moment* they are dis-
> solved by analysis and we enter by free will pure unified experience.
> When all the sensuous images are dissolved we meet true death. . . .
> the soul and body embracing.[21]

It is difficult to see how this differs from the philosophy of "Soul
in Judgment." The self evolves toward its original model or
complete identity through a series of actions that are inadequate
images of the complete identity yet point toward it. While a
man is engaged in living, he exhausts his partial images or embodiments—living them through in sequence because he does
not understand them. When the retrospective moment of understanding arrives—a moment equivalent to the Return after
death—the man dissolves these sensuous images, as Cuchulain
does when he confronts and repudiates the images of his past
self that return to him from *On Baile's Strand*. The man is now
ready to die and thus don the Celestial Body that has walked
with him as an invisibly transparent cloak through life. He thus
completes his identity. In the Purification, he will shed even
Celestial Body to become the pure spirit with which living men
can combine to make images. Hamlet and all tragic heroes
must, as Yeats suggests in "Lapis Lazuli," desire their deaths as
a fulfillment.

Art, through the transparency of its characters, adumbrates
such completion of identity. In life, the completion of identity
is adumbrated through the opposite ways of hero and saint, who
work on themselves as the poet works on paper, thus achieving

the transparency of figures in art.[22] Cuchulain turns through the manner of his death from hero to saint. As he comes to understand his life completely, he goes willingly to his death.

The conflict between the ways of hero and saint, between King Congal and the priestess Attracta, is treated in Yeats's most curious and interesting play, *The Herne's Egg*, written the year before *The Death of Cuchulain*. *The Herne's Egg* finally achieves the method for which Yeats worked through the drafts of *The Player Queen*—the seriously farcical method for poking fun at both the saintly and heroic alternatives while asking us to take them seriously as historical alternatives. *The Herne's Egg* solves the problem by treating all truths as self-enclosed systems, potent only so long as they are generally taken for symbols of reality.

The Herne's Egg is, like *The Death of Cuchulain*, about the disparity between natural and supernatural views of reality. F. A. C. Wilson considers that here, as in *The Death of Cuchulain* (as, indeed, in all tragicomedies), the supernatural is the correct view. In *The Herne's Egg*, however, both views are problematical. That is the difference between tragicomedy and absurdist comedy. As in tragicomedy, the characters move like dancers to a divine tune—the tune is "The Great Herne's Feather." But the question arises, as it would not in tragicomedy, whether the Herne is god or plain bird, creator or creation of the tune: whether the priestess Attracta was raped by Congal and his men or, as she imagines, by the god using men as vehicles.

The last bleakly ironic scene—reminiscent of Lear on the heath (especially as seen through Jan Kott's absurdist reading of *King Lear*) [23]—is an absurdist version of Cuchulain's death. Instead of transfiguration, there is devaluation. King Congal's assertion of identity and freedom—"I am King Congal of Connacht and of Tara"—is flung into the void. For he realizes, even as he is about to fall upon the kitchen spit with which he has let the Fool stab him, that he can't escape the Herne's curse whether the curse comes from the god, as Attracta believes, or from his own actions. Either way the Herne has the last laugh. "The Great Herne knows that I have won," [24] he says at the moment when he seems to have lost. Here we come to the heart of the play's meaning. Attracta, who believes in the reality only of spirit and interprets all phenomena according to that belief, seems less admirable than Congal who, believing only in material reality, asserts his identity and freedom knowing the assertion is absurd. On the metaphysical issue between them, the play remains neutral. We are confronted in the end with King Congal's assertion of his heroic identity and with the prediction that he will be reincarnated as a donkey. The assertion strikes us as admirable if illusory; the fatality, which derives from the chance copulation of donkeys at the moment of his death, strikes us as silly yet no more or less "real" than the assertion.

Is so problematical an assertion of identity consistent with the system, in which identity is substantiated by Daimons and historical phases? The answer is that *The Herne's Egg* is not Yeats's final statement. He anticipates in this play the views and techniques of a generation twice removed from his. But he returns in his last two plays (*Purgatory* and *The Death of Cuchulain*) and in his last poems to his main position—that the self is substantial, is indeed the only reality.

The last poems and plays show, however, a changed emphasis most clearly expressed in "Meru" (1934). Although "Civilization is hooped together . . . / By manifold illusion," we are told that "man's life is thought" and that he must therefore go "Ravening, raging, and uprooting," must uproot old illusions "that he may come / Into the desolation of reality." The emphasis here is not on fabricating new illusions, but on the spiritual benefit, the self-discovery to be derived from remaining in "the desolation of reality."

In *A Vision*, the "stylistic arrangements of experience" that bind for Yeats "reality and justice" [25] seem configurations over a vital flux; but in "Meru" the configurations are projected over a void. Yeats had earlier intuitions of the void. "The knowledge of reality. . . . is a kind of death," he wrote in 1909. He entitled an early story, "Where There is Nothing, There is God," used the same line in a play of 1908, and announced to a friend that "The last kiss is given to the void." [26] But the emphasis on the void in his last phase increases the emphasis on the self as the only reality. *The Herne's Egg* is nihilistic not only because it cancels out opposite illusions by presenting them simultaneously rather than successively as in *A Vision*, but also because it does not substantiate the self that fabricates those illusions.

Yeats was preparing his answer to *The Herne's Egg* by collaborating, while writing the play, on a translation of the ten principal Upanishads. In his introduction to *The Holy Mountain*, the book on Indian religion that inspired "Meru," Yeats says: "No two civilizations prove or assume the same things, but behind both hides the unchanging experience of simple men and women." [27] Yeats in his last phase becomes at once more mystical and more materialistic than ever, because he renews and clarifies his old intuitions about void and self.

No wonder he finally found his way to Indian religion where all that is not self is void, where as F. A. C. Wilson puts it: "The Self, which is both Godhead and the core of each individual personality, is diffused into every particle of life; 'everything that lives is holy,' as Blake had said." [28] Yeats unified his life by finding that Blake and ancient Ireland, his starting points, knew it all, knew the wisdom of Swedenborg, Platonism and finally Hinduism. Hence the ancient Irish setting of *The Herne's Egg* and the wisdom of the early-Irish Druidical Christian hermit Ribh, who in *Supernatural Songs* reconciles, in the all-inclusive Indian manner, sexuality and spirituality.

Most surprising is Yeats's lifelong devotion to Balzac, whose realism one would have thought contrary to Yeats's taste. Yeats

found in Balzac, the materialist and mechanist who was nevertheless interested in Swedenborg and "supernormal experiences," the model of his own modern Western stance toward
occultism. Yeats was particularly interested in Balzac's Swedenborgian novels, *Séraphita* and *Louis Lambert*, but he admired
the whole *Comédie humaine* because it taught the acceptance of
all life. " 'Blessed are the imperfect,' " Balzac taught, " 'for
theirs is the Kingdom of Love.' " [29] That is why Balzac took on
renewed importance during Yeats's final phase, when he came
to represent the Western counterpart to Indian religion. " 'I
know nothing' " any more, Yeats wrote only half in jest, " 'but
the novels of Balzac, and the Aphorisms of Patanjali.' " [30]

We find in Yeats's last essays (*Essays 1931 to 1936*, reprinted
in *Essays and Introductions*) an illuminating consistency in that
the thought turns largely upon the twin poles of Balzac and
Hinduism, with Shelley as a consequence partially repudiated
and Blake reconfirmed. He had already in 1912 preferred the
saintly modern Indian poet Tagore to most Christian saints,
because Tagore does not separate spirituality from love of life:
"we go for a like voice to St. Francis and to William Blake"; [31]
Yeats would have added Balzac's name in the 1930s. I shall
conclude by discussing these essays, since they contain Yeats's
summarizing statements about identity. These statements read
like discoveries, because Yeats during his last years discovered in
Indian religion the ultimate implications of all he had been saying through a lifetime about identity. Balzac showed him how
he could absorb such insights while remaining European.

In the essay "Bishop Berkeley," Yeats shows how Berkeley
managed to overcome one European obstacle to self-realization—empiricism; but not the other—Christianity. Berkeley,
who faced the empiricist problem whether objects exist when
they are not perceived, sustained the reality of the corporeal
universe by asserting that the universe is perceived by God.
Yeats paraphrases Berkeley in such a way as to make Daimons
give substantiality to the identity of the perceiver and, therefore,

to the perceived object. The romanticists, he goes on to suggest, substituted for Berkeley's God the creative self as bridge between perceiver and perceived object. But the romantic movement, with its heroic "self-assertion," has been "superseded by a new naturalism that leaves man helpless before the contents of his own mind." Joyce's *Anna Livia Plurabelle* (in *Finnegans Wake*), Pound's *Cantos*, Proust cut off the operations of consciousness from the operations of the external world. As a premodern Irishman Yeats prefers a philosophy that dissolves the distinction between subject and object, "idealist and realist." He finds Berkeley reaching toward a concept of identity like his own. But to protect his Christian orthodoxy, "Berkeley deliberately refused to define personality" as reflecting "the whole act of God; his God and Man seem cut off from one another." Berkeley dared not take "the next step" [32]—the step taken by Blake and Hinduism—that conceives God as embodied in man.

In "My Friend's Book," Yeats criticizes George Russell's mysticism as vague, sensuous self-indulgence. He makes a similar criticism of Shelley, in his essay "*Prometheus Unbound*," for being neither mystical nor realistic enough. "Shelley was not a mystic, his system of thought was constructed by his logical faculty to satisfy desire, not a symbolical revelation received after the suspension of all desire." Because Shelley's idealism was sublimated sexuality, he expunged from it "whatever seemed dark, destructive, indefinite." Such idealizing led to what Yeats castigates as Shelley's Jacobinism, his hatred of all that does not fit into his Utopian system. Since Yeats says in his essay on *Louis Lambert* that Balzac saved him from Jacobinism, it is not surprising that he alludes in his essay on Shelley to Balzac, who saved him from Shelley's influence, "from the pursuit of a beauty that, seeming at once absolute and external, requires, to strike a balance, hatred as absolute." [33]

It is in his praise-singing 1900 essay on Shelley, not here, that Yeats calls *Prometheus Unbound* "a sacred book." [34] Nor does *Prometheus Unbound* appear on Yeats's 1933 list of sacred

books: "Perhaps *Faust, Louis Lambert, Séraphita* and *Axel* are
our sacred books," because they teach "man self-sufficing and
eternal"—teach that divinity is to be found in man as the fulfillment of his whole, including his sexual, nature. *Louis Lambert*
echoes the Swedenborgian dictum Yeats often quotes, "that the
sexual intercourse of the angels is a conflagration of the whole
being." [35] This concept of identity, learned from Blake, is in
the last essays restated and reconfirmed in terms drawn from Indian religion.

Thus Shelley's idealism is criticized through covert comparison with Indian religion, which is at once more mystical and
more materialistic. In contrast to Shelley's sublimation of frustrated desire, the Indian ascetic's mystical experience follows the
fulfillment and transformation of desire. If the ascetic "finds it
impossible at once to transform sexual into spiritual desire, he
may beseech the God to come as a woman" and "the God may
send some strange woman as his emblem," or may come himself as a woman, to have intercourse with the ascetic. Shelley
was trapped in the ego, "was the tyrant of his own being,"
because he seemed to know "the shortness of his life," had not
the liberating sense that the self lives many lives. "That life, and
all lives, would be unintelligible to me did I not think of them
as an exfoliation prolonged from life to life." Shelley sang not of
something returning but "of something beginning," [36] as
though he were alive for the first time. Hence his moral idealism and belief in progress—attitudes appropriate to the rationalistic, moralistic Western personality.

In "An Indian Monk," Yeats contrasts the moralistic intolerant quality of Western personality with the aesthetic tolerant
quality he calls "Asiatic courtesy." "Our moral indignation"
comes from

> the Christian conviction that the soul has but one life to find or lose sal-
> vation in: the Asiatic courtesy from the conviction that there are many
> lives. There are Indian courtesans that meditate many hours a day
> awaiting without sense of sin their moment, perhaps many lives hence,

to leave man for God. For the present they are efficient courtesans. As-
cetics . . . have lived in their houses and received pilgrims there.
Kings, princes, beggars, soldiers, courtesans, and the fool by the way-
side are equal to the eye of sanctity, for everybody's road is different, everybody awaits his moment.[37]

Modern literature, without necessarily believing in reincarnation, uses the tradition that has led from romanticism through
aestheticism to depth psychology to justify every phase of
human identity—as in Yeats's quintessentially modern approval
of love, just because "Love has pitched his mansion in / The
place of excrement." [38]

In *"The Holy Mountain,"* Yeats passes from a discussion of
the Upanishads to discussing Hegel's *Philosophy of History* as an
expression of modern European intolerant idealizing. Hegel,
who sees consciousness as the only good, teaches a philosophy
of progress in which consciousness (Europe) liberates itself from
nature (Asia) to absorb progressively more of existence into itself. Imagining Balzac's answer to Hegel, Yeats makes Balzac a
spokesman for his own system: man achieves irrational as well
as rational glory; the movement is not progressive but cyclical:
" 'I too have my dialectic,' " in which " 'the perfection of Nature' " alternates as a value with " 'the perfection of Spirit.' "
Yeats makes Balzac conclude: " 'My *Comédie humaine* will
cure the world of all Utopias,' " and again aligns him with the
Hindus as against modern European abstraction. "The Indian
would have understood the dialectic of Balzac, but not that of
Hegel—what could he have made of Hegel's optimism?" [39]

Balzac, says Yeats in *"Louis Lambert,"* is a materialist who
spiritualizes matter by seeing its essence as fire or light, and spiritualizes character by seeing its essence as will. Fascinated by
"supernormal experiences," he believed that as mere men "we
are capable of incomprehensible acts which we, in our admiration for the incomprehensible, attribute to spiritual beings." [40]
Balzac believed, in other words, in the natural-supernatural and
was thus, as Yeats says, opposite to Berkeley who, though taking

off from empiricist premises, represents the Platonic pole in the debate running through Yeats's career between Platonism and empiricism. Yeats finally found, I think, in Balzac's energized materialism, the resolution of this debate—a resolution that accounts for the remarkably increased materialist bias of his latest work: the Crazy Jane poems, *Supernatural Songs*, "The Three Bushes," "News for the Delphic Oracle," "John Kinsella's Lament for Mrs. Mary Moore," "The Circus Animals' Desertion," *The Herne's Egg*.

" 'Mind, as a form of matter,' " says Louis Lambert, " 'has brought me a new conviction of [God's] greatness.' " [41] It is likewise the refined materialism of Indian religion that attracts Yeats. He sees in *Chitta*, the objective "mind-stuff" of which mental images are formed, the concept "which most separates Indian from European thought," since we regard mental operations as immaterial. According to the Indian concept, "If I think of the table on which I am writing, my mental image is as much Matter as the table itself, though of 'a subtler kind,' and I am able to think correctly, because the Matter I call Mind takes the shape of this or that physical object." Nor is God immaterial; for every man can become God—mystical vision is spoken of as "the realisation of the Self." [42] Actually, Balzac and Indian religion confirmed for Yeats the ancient philosophy of Europe—the Neoplatonic, alchemical tradition according to which mind is continuous with matter. It was Descartes and the empiricists who split mind off from matter, thus creating modern doubt, abstraction, idealism.

Of the ten principal Upanishads that Yeats helped translate, his favorite was the *Mandukya Upanishad* which teaches the four states of the self. The first state, as Yeats describes it in his essay "The *Mandukya Upanishad*," is "the physical or waking state" that gives what we call *objective knowledge*. The second is "the dream state, where only mental substances appear"; this corresponds to our *subjective knowledge*. The third state is "deep sleep, where man 'feels no desire, creates no dream,' yet . . . is now united to sleepless Self, creator of all, source of all." In this state, called "unconscious *Samādhi*," man has *unconscious knowledge* of universal Self or ultimate reality. This *unconscious knowledge* becomes *conscious* in the triumphant fourth state, called "conscious *Samādhi*." Here the initiate achieves "pure personality . . . that bare 'I am' which is Brahma." Having passed through the "egoism, or [ordinary] personality . . . made by his Karma [sin]," the initiate is now " 'the Human Form Divine' of Blake, that Unity of Being Dante compared to a perfectly proportioned human body."

Thus Yeats finds in the Indian prescription for passing from individual to universal self the counterpart to his own ideal of Unity of Being, as opposed to modern Western individualism. The Indian, like the Japanese in Noh, inverts our sense of identity. The consciousness of the self's fourth state is "what we call, because we sit in the stalls and watch the play"—because we locate the self in the alienated individual consciousness—

> the unconscious. The Indian, upon the other hand, calls it the conscious, because, whereas we are fragmentary, forgetting, remembering, sleeping, waking, spread out into past, present, future, permitting to our leg, to our finger, to our intestines, partly or completely separate consciousness, it is the "unbroken consciousness of the Self," the Self that never sleeps, that is never divided, but even when our thought transforms it, is still the same. It is the Universal Self but also that of a civilization.

The European historicizing Yeats sees the universal self as still having character, the character of a civilization. This takes us back to *A Vision*. *A Vision* also helps us understand Indian meditation as leading to what Yeats in his system calls Phase 15, where all thought is embodied. When the ascetic begins with an object,

> this object slowly transforms and is transformed by his thought until they are one. When he meditates upon an image of God, he begins with thought, God subjectively conceived, and this thought is slowly transformed by, and transforms its object, divine reality, until suddenly superseded by the unity of thought and fact.[43]

Whether the ascetic begins with object or thought, God materializes; for God is self and both God and self are *image*, the union of object and thought. This materialization brings into consciousness what in the self's third state was intuited. The ascetic, in a process analogous to artistic embodiment, passes through an evolution of consciousness from the individual to the universal self.

Indian religion crowned with authority Yeats's lifelong accumulating thoughts on identity. His study of Indian religion accounts for the incisiveness of the statements on identity that appear in the posthumously published "A General Introduction for my Work" (1937)—the statements cited earlier that describe the poet as a man who materializes a certain phase of identity. "A poet writes always of his personal life," but

> he never speaks directly as to someone at the breakfast table, there is always a phantasmagoria. . . . he is never the bundle of accident and incoherence that sits down to breakfast; he has been reborn as an idea, something intended, complete. . . . He is part of his own phantasmagoria and we adore him because nature has grown intelligible, . . . a part of our creative power.

Nature has grown intelligible because the poet, by assuming a mythical identity and walking through the paces of his own myth or phantasmagoria, has rendered the unconscious conscious; he has materialized the universal self. Sure enough Yeats in the next sentence quotes an Upanishad: " 'When mind is lost in the light of the Self,' says the Prashna Upanishad, 'it dreams no more; still in the body it is lost in happiness' "—the happiness of consciousness and embodiment. We poets, Yeats concludes, "know everything because we have made [embodied] everything." [44]

By bringing together the three principal sources of his view of identity, Yeats has achieved his original aim—he has hammered into unity his thought, life and art. For if the poet is a man who materializes a certain phase of identity, so is the Irish nationalist when he merges with family and nation; so is the occultist when entranced in vision; and so is the lover who for success in love must become the embodiment of passion, or the old man in "An Acre of Grass," who, to triumph over age, must embody an old man's frenzy: "Myself must I remake / Till I am Timon and Lear." "We must then be artists in all things, and understand that love and old age and death are first among the arts." [45] To triumph in life, one must constantly remake one's masks—bring into consciousness each new phase through new materializations, as the artist brings into consciousness his latest unconscious perceptions. This is how one makes one's life into a work of art.

Yeats sums up his thought, life and art when he says in a letter written a few weeks before his death: "It seems to me that I have found what I wanted. When I try to put all into a phrase I say, 'Man can embody truth but he cannot know it.' " The next sentence is significant. "I must embody it in the completion of my life." It is through his personality that man embodies truth, and his art works, religions, historical periods are but projections of personality. "The abstract is not life and everywhere draws out its contradictions. You can refute Hegel but not the Saint or the Song of Sixpence." [46] You can refute ideas but not a personality or a poem. Personality and poem are analogous structures; as embodiments not statements, they are grounds of being and therefore nondiscursive models of ultimate reality. Yeats uses the model of art to restructure the modern European self after the decline in vitality of the organically natural, evolving self Wordsworth projected to replace the Christian belief in a God-created identity or soul.

Part IV

RECONSTITUTION OF SELF: LAWRENCE

THE RELIGION OF LOVE

Chapter 8
IDENTITY
AND SEXUALITY

Just as we oversimplify Wordsworth when we think of him as the poet of nature, so we oversimplify Lawrence when we think of him only as the apostle of sex. Wordsworth might just as appropriately be called the poet of mind, since he never writes about nature without writing about mind; and Lawrence might just as appropriately be called the great writer on identity, since he never writes about sex without writing about identity.

Lawrence came to realize, in the remarkable intellectual leap that carried him from *Sons and Lovers* to *The Sisters* (the first version of *The Rainbow* and *Women in Love*), that successful sexuality flows from a certain phase of identity and that the modern sexual problem is an identity problem. A properly reciprocal sexual relation is impossible so long as each partner is locked up in self-consciousness, in the modern separated ego that has worried all our authors. In *Women in Love*, Ursula and Birkin achieve relative success in love when they learn to lose their individuality and then find it again—when they are able to meet as archetypes, at the unconscious phase of identity, and then pass back to their conscious selves without the need, apparent in Gudrun and Gerald, to seek oblivion, to destroy one mode of being for the sake of the other. For Gudrun and Gerald, oblivion is the only antidote to consciousness; only by depersonalizing themselves through oblivion can they join sexually—they cannot "meet" as persons.

Ursula and Birkin's successful intercourse in Sherwood Forest merely confirms a "meeting" already achieved at the properly archetypal phase of identity. She has already, tracing with her fingertips "the straight downflow of the thighs," apprehended his male potency and seen him as one of "the strange inhuman sons of God." He has already, through her touch, apprehended her womanhood "as a new marvelous flower opened at his knees." [1] These words are not rhetorical embellishments but express actual transformations of being. As in Yeats, sexual desire derives from archetypal apprehension.

Lawrence's preoccupation with problems of identity shows clearly in the critical essays he wrote in the 1920s, after he had published *The Rainbow* and *Women in Love*. In all these essays, discussions of art turn into discussions of personality; it is simply assumed that the quality of a work derives from the identity structure of the artist and his contemporaries. Thus, in a bold little essay called "Surgery for the Novel—or a Bomb," the modern serious novel of Proust, Joyce, Dorothy Richardson is shown to be dying of the same morbid self-consciousness that is killing our civilization. Since these novelists conceive their characters as locked up in a circumscribed conscious ego cut off from objective reality, what can they do except analyze ever more minutely the thoughts and feelings that go on within that circumference while the character is doing something utterly trivial and unrelated like buttoning on gloves? Such "purely emotional and self-analytical stunts" no longer interest Lawrence because the value system behind them no longer really interests anyone—the value system that, having originally given birth to the novel, declares the importance of every last thing happening to the individual. The death rattle of that system sounds through the oversubtle analysis, and produces thoughts of the bomb that might blow up the whole existing scheme of things. The interesting question, therefore, is: "What feelings do we want to carry through into the *next* epoch? . . . What is the underlying impulse in us that will provide the motive power for a new state of things, when this democratic-industrial-lovey-dovey-darling-take-me-to-mamma state of things is bust?" [2]

Like Yeats, Lawrence sees the weakness of the identity structure produced by our democratic, industrial, humanitarian, individualist culture. And he is, like Yeats, preparing for the identity structures of the coming antidemocratic, antihumanitarian, neopagan culture; that is what *Women in Love* is about. It is about the difference between the impersonality toward which Ursula and Birkin evolve and the impersonality sought by Gerald, Gudrun, Loerke. Ursula and Birkin prepare for the next epoch through rebirth of the individual self, Gerald through its death, Gudrun and Loerke through its disintegration. Birkin says we must burst out of our old selves or else wither away inside them; and this essay suggests, in a Yeatsian analogy between art and personality, that we must do surgery on the novel and the individualist self it celebrates, or else novel and individualist culture will have to be blown up. "The novel has a future" if, instead of "inventing new sensations in the old line," it gives us "new, really new feelings," breaking "a way through, like a hole in the wall." [3] The breakthrough is a new identity structure; only from that could really new feelings emerge.

"Art and Morality" makes clear that modes of feeling and seeing derive from identity structure. Lawrence examines the "moral repugnance for a Cézanne still-life" felt by ordinary people, who rightly sense an assault on their inherited geography of self and not-self and the man-centered, ego-centered values such a geography implies. The modern visualization of self is for Yeats confirmed by the mirror of polished steel and for

Lawrence by the camera. The camera enables man to see himself as a complete entity definitely outlined against the scene; so that nature becomes mere background. This absolute separation of self and not-self is equated with reality: "even god could not see *differently.*" Against this view that "the me that is *seen,* is me," Lawrence sets the primitive man who never had a complete view of himself. If we imagine a world without mirrors, in which men saw themselves reflected only in water or shadows, we can understand why primitive men did not conceive themselves as enclosed in an outline. "Like men in a dark room, they only *felt* their own existence surging in the darkness of other creatures."

Lawrence is formulating a notion of external self, in a way that combines Wordsworth and Yeats. He is Wordsworthian in regarding the self as external because continuous with nature. He is Yeatsian in understanding that this self has been undone through humanist culture, through all that has happened to Western man "since Greece first broke the spell of 'darkness,'" and that the external self may be recovered in the coming era signaled by the sophisticated art of Cézanne. Cézanne's apples offend us because they refuse to take their significance from our man-centered view; they assert their own selfhood, their own multiplicity of relations, and therefore do not look like apples. "The universe," says Lawrence in a passage that combines Wordsworth and Yeats by way of an Einsteinian relativism,

> is like Father Ocean, a stream of all things slowly moving. We move, and the rock of ages moves. And since we move and move for ever, in no discernible direction, there is no centre to the movement, to us. To us, the centre shifts at every moment. . . . There is nothing to do but to maintain a true relationship to the things we move with and amongst and against.

Lawrence draws from this world-view a moral that is highly Wordsworthian in its emphasis on organic relatedness to nature. "And nothing is true, or good, or right, except in its own living relatedness to its own circumambient universe; to the things that are in the stream with it." The moral is also Yeatsian in that this relatedness is an ideal for culture, for Unity of Being. Works of art are cited as examples of the relatedness between various artists and their different universes; and design in art is defined as the total recognition of all possible relations among the elements depicted, as the breakthrough to a fourth-dimensional or absolute vision of relative relationships. Lawrence's fourth dimension differs from Blake's fourfold vision, which transforms life into art, because Lawrence settles for simple naturalism in attributing this breakthrough not to culture, artifice, or even imagination, but simply to the use of all our natural organs of perception. "You can't *invent* a design. You recognize it, in the fourth dimension. That is, with your blood and your bones, as well as with your eyes." [4] Although in doing without a concept of imagination Lawrence is theoretically more naïve than Wordsworth, he is certainly more Wordsworthian than Blakean or Yeatsian. He in fact reconstitutes the self by revitalizing Wordsworth's view of it as organically related to nature.

Although Lawrence was deeply read in Wordsworth and almost always refers to him with respect, Wordsworth's mode of characterization seems to have influenced him by way of Hardy. Lawrence might be talking of Wordsworth's "Michael" when, in *Study of Thomas Hardy* (written in 1914), he says that there exists in Hardy's novels "a great background, vital and vivid, which matters more than the people who move upon it." In *The Return of the Native*, "the real sense of tragedy is got from the setting. . . . The Heath persists"; the characters "are one year's accidental crop." The most admirable characters are "rooted . . . in the soil of all things, and living from the root!" [5] This also describes the relation of character to landscape in Wordsworth, except that in Wordsworth the enduring landscape *compensates* for the passing of human lives.

In "Morality and the Novel," Lawrence's view of life and art and his way of dissolving the distinction between them is remarkably Wordsworthian. Art, he says, "is a revelation of the perfected relation, at a certain moment, between a man and a sunflower. . . . And this perfected relation between man and his circumambient universe is life itself, for mankind. It has the fourth-dimensional quality of eternity and perfection. Yet it is momentaneous." The analysis applies to all those poems of Wordsworth in which the beholder transforms into significance a flower, landscape, or person through a visionary moment, an epiphany. Like Lawrence's statement, these poems are also prescriptions for life; the poems imply that in life we make our souls through privileged moments and that the poems themselves describe and derive their form from such moments in life. This transforming vision is what Lawrence means by a "pure" or "living" relationship. The relationship remains living as long as the significance remains relative to the particular relationships through which it was perceived, as long as the celandine or leech-gatherer is held in a "delicate, for ever trembling and changing *balance*" between the real flower or leech-gatherer and the significance the poet sees in it, as long as the object remains fluid, flowing into symbol then back again to perceived object.

The novel for Lawrence is the supreme genre because the most relativistic—

> the highest example of subtle inter-relatedness that man has discovered. Everything is true in its own time, place, circumstance, and untrue outside of its own place, time, circumstance. If you try to nail anything down, in the novel, either it kills the novel, or the novel gets up and walks away with the nail. Morality in the novel is the trembling instability of the balance.

Wordsworth, too, is against nailing down the "sentiment of Being" into a fixed symbol abstracted from the moment of perception and transferable to other contexts. Morality for Lawrence and Wordsworth means giving your allegiance to experience rather than theory. But Lawrence goes on to explore the conflict between characters that corresponds to the epistemological conflict between perceiver and perceived object. The novel, he says, rescues us from "the toils of old relationships" to reveal, through "the living moment," [6] real relationships that have not yet been formulated. This looks forward to the description of the novel, in *Lady Chatterley's Lover*, as leading "our sympathy . . . into new places," away "from things gone dead" [7]—as an agent of cultural change. In the greatest because most polar human relationship, that between man and woman, one partner, says Lawrence in "Morality and the Novel," tries to impose a relationship by nailing down the other as his instrument. If, however, there is a "balance" whereby each is "true to himself, herself, his own manhood, her own womanhood," [8] then a relationship emerges that is reciprocally fluid, as in a Cézanne still life where there is no center and all selfhoods remain intact.

This is the relationship Birkin describes as "star-equilibrium." Through exploring the unconscious, Lawrence justifies psychologically characterization at a depth, anterior to manners, where character has the existential potency of a natural object, of Cézanne's apples or Van Gogh's sunflowers. Wordsworth explained that he was trying to portray the leech-gatherer as an existence rather than a character: "What is brought forward? 'A lonely place, a Pond' 'by which an old man *was*' . . . not stood, not sat, but '*was*.' " [9] The old man's *existence* breaks upon us as a marvel because he is portrayed in inextricable relation to the landscape—as though he were in fluid transition between animate and inanimate, like a boulder so unaccountably alone on a bald hilltop that it seems to have moved itself there; the boulder's fluidity is then evoked through the opposite case of a sea beast that at first seems part of the rocky ledge on which it rests. The transition between animate and inanimate becomes the counterpart of the transitional state between natural and supernatural that the old man, with his frail hold on life, seems to inhabit; so that the poem establishes an organic line of existence from rock to spirit which is not hierarchical, as in the traditional concept of the Great Chain of Being, but contained within a single identity.

In "Why the Novel Matters," Lawrence opposes the division of self between body and spirit. "My hand, as it writes these words, . . . is just as much *me* as is my brain, my mind, or my soul." [10] If we compare this to the dissociated bodies in Beckett, we see that Lawrence takes over just the biological sense of identity that unites Wordsworth with Yeats; Yeats's phrase "the thinking of the body" [11] perfectly expresses this monistic view of identity. "The novel is the one bright book of life," says Lawrence, because it deals with the whole man in his aliveness, and not, like the scientist, with the parts of a man who must be posited as dead in order to be analyzed or dissected (this recalls Wordsworth's "We murder to dissect").

"We should ask for no absolutes," says Lawrence. "All things flow and change." "In all this change," however,

> I maintain a certain integrity. But woe betide me if I try to put my finger on it. If I say of myself, I am this, I am that!—then, if I stick to it, I turn into a stupid fixed thing like a lamp-post. I shall never know wherein lies my integrity, my individuality, my me. I *can* never know it. It is useless to talk about my ego. That only means that I have made up an *idea* of myself. [12]

Although he has more faith than Beckett in the self's continuity and vitality, Lawrence broaches the mysteries of identity as Beckett does in *The Unnamable*, where the self eludes the speaker every time he tries to name it.

For Lawrence, as for Blake and Wordsworth, the problem of identity begins with a fall into self-consciousness and the consequent division into a real or subjective and a false or social self. "While a man remains a man, before he falls and becomes a social individual, he innocently feels himself altogether within the great continuum of the universe." [13] Our aim is to recover the sense of connection. Sexuality is a way of recovering it; but for most modern people, locked into ego and self-consciousness, sexuality must be purchased at the price of obliterated consciousness and obliterated sense of the partner's otherness, of his or her real existence.

The closing off of mind from feeling, of consciousness from unconsciousness, of ego from archetype, produce the modern problems of identity and sexuality. There should be a reciprocal flow between consciousness and unconsciousness, a sexuality that heightens consciousness all over the body, an individuality open to connection through the interlocking relation of opposite archetypes. Instead, there is in modern people the split between consciousness and unconsciousness that makes sex a clash of hard-shelled egos, each out to dominate the other and exploit the other as an instrument for sexual gratification. This is sadomasochism. In *The Rainbow*, Lawrence traces through three generations of nineteenth-century Brangwens the developing split between consciousness and the unconsciousness that shades into universal unconsciousness. In *Women in Love*, he portrays a twentieth-century world in which all identity structures are split, both within themselves and from the universe, and all sexuality is consequently sadomasochistic. Ursula and Birkin are, in their recovery of connection through rebirth of self, miraculous exceptions.

The "carbon" identity, described in Lawrence's letter to Edward Garnett (5 June 1914), is the phase of identity that makes connection with the universe. It can be best understood if we start by recalling the way Wordsworth's leech-gatherer is characterized in continuum with the landscape. "That which is physic," Lawrence writes,

> non-human, in humanity, is more interesting to me than the old-fashioned human element—which caused one to conceive a character in a certain moral scheme and make him consistent. . . . What is interesting in the laugh of the woman is the same as the binding of the molecules of steel or their action in heat; it is the inhuman will . . . that fascinates me. I don't so much care about what the woman *feels*— in the ordinary usage of the word. That presumes an *ego* to feel with. I

only care about what the woman is—what she IS—inhumanly, physio-
logically, materially . . . what she *is* as a phenomenon.

"What she IS" recalls Wordsworth's "an old man *was*"—a
*was*ness evoked through the leech-gatherer's reduction to a
stone. The difference is that Wordsworth uses the reduction to
achieve transcendence, whereas Lawrence studiously avoids
transcendence.

Lawrence goes on to talk of egos as allotropies or variations of
a single substance contained in all nature.

> You mustn't look in my novel [a draft of *The Rainbow*] for the old sta-
> ble *ego*—of the character. There is another *ego*, according to whose ac-
> tion the individual is unrecognisable, and passes through, as it were,
> allotropic states which it needs a deeper sense than any we've been used
> to exercise, to discover are states of the same single radically unchanged
> element. (Like as diamond and coal are the same pure single element of
> carbon. The ordinary novel would trace the history of the diamond—
> but I say, "Diamond, what! This is carbon." And my diamond might
> be coal or soot, and my theme is carbon.) [14]

The "logic" of a character's action, his unity or identity, is not
to be found within the ego, in rational or moral consistency,
but in the force, the "inhuman will," that flows through him
and all matter. The unity is in the external field of energized
matter to which the character belongs. Lawrence says in this letter that he will portray the "carbon," the external inhuman
identity that the character shares with nature, rather than the
"diamond" or ego, the special temporary variation that sets the
character apart. But in *The Rainbow* Lawrence actually portrays
the "diamond" by referring it back to the "carbon." He includes
sex as part of the larger electromagnetic force that binds the
molecules in all nature.

This view of identity as a continuum, in which human
merges into animate and animate into inanimate, is most
clearly exemplified in Lawrence's best animal poems, which
offer mainly implicit models for the Unity of Being we have lost
and must recover. In the beautifully quiet "A Doe at Evening,"

the model is explicit. Beholding the doe as part of the landscape—"she pricked a fine black blotch / on the sky"—the poet regresses to the life they have in common, and *knows* her as a sexual force in an epiphany involving a transformation of his own being: he feels himself turn into an antlered stag.

The wittily magical tortoise poems celebrate life at that first verge where it moves the most unlikely of lumps into animation. "What a huge vast inanimate it is," says the poet to the baby tortoise, "that you must row against, / What an incalculable inertia." Sex among the tortoises is grotesque in its blank unconsciousness:

> He is dumb, he is visionless,
> Conceptionless.
> His black, sad-lidded eye sees but beholds not
> As her earthen mound moves on.

The inevitable question reads like a parody of "Leda and the Swan," although Yeats's poem postdates Lawrence's:

> Does she know
> As she moves eternally slowly away?
> Or is he driven against her with a bang . . .
> All knowledgeless?

The mating, even more than Leda's, is fraught with human consequences; for it recalls the organism's first loss of unified identity: the tortoise has been "crucified into sex, / . . . Divided into passionate duality" [15]—he anticipates the dismemberment of Osiris.

In the uncanny "Tortoise Shout," one of Lawrence's great poems, this dumb creature emits at orgasm a scream in which Lawrence, undergoing the regression that is his equivalent for spiritual experience ("till the last plasm of my body was melted back / To the primeval rudiments of life, and the secret"), hears the "First faint scream, / Out of life's unfathomable dawn" that anticipates all the cries of nature and civilization, of the whole bloody glorious adventure set going by the need to recover our lost unity.

Sex, which breaks us into voice, sets us calling across the deeps, calling,
    calling for the complement,
Singing, and calling, and singing again, being answered, having found.
Torn, to become whole again, after long seeking for what is lost,
The same cry from the tortoise as from Christ, the Osiris-cry of abandonment.

Lawrence finds his gods, and therefore the pattern of civilization, at this ultimate point of regression.

"Fish," instead, presents the fish as complete in himself, as
making no distinction between self and environment:

> As the waters roll
> Roll you.
> The waters wash,
> You wash in oneness
> And never emerge.

Therefore, "Never know"; for knowledge comes from separation. In a stunning feat of imaginative projection, Lawrence
evokes the fish's indissolubly internal-external sense of his being:

> To sink, and rise, and go to sleep with the waters;
> To speak endless inaudible wavelets into the wave;
> To breathe from the flood at the gills,
> Fish-blood slowly running next to the flood, extracting fish-fire.

When Lawrence infers from this that the fish is beyond
him—"*His God stands outside my God*"—he means that the
fish's organization of the sensed world is entirely different from
his, and that gods, as he says in "Art and Morality," represent
our organization of the sensed world and therefore our identity,
since we *are* what we sense. In reminding us, however, that
"Jesus was called The Fish," he reminds us that Jesus came to
restore our lost Unity of Being. In *The Man Who Died*, his
revision of the Gospels, Lawrence suggests that the ego was
nailed to the cross and that resurrection means recovery of our
primal self through "the greater life of the body" [16]—it means
Osiris recomposed, identity as continuum.

In the animal poems, Lawrence moves from animal to god
not through transcendence or transformation, the entranced

vision of "Resolution and Independence," but through intensification of the animal's being until the animal's unconsciousness
becomes, in contrast to our consciousness, the equivalent of the
god's superconsciousness. The animal's "strangeness," or existential superiority over us, becomes the equivalent of the god's
existential superiority. Godhead is for Lawrence the culminating phase of identity. All this is especially apparent in "Snake,"
another great poem, in which Lawrence comes closest to
achieving the aim of all his animal poems—to let godhead
emerge inevitably from naturalistic evocation of the animal's
nonhuman otherness.

The details, casually accumulated, all point to the snake's
"strangeness" and lordliness. He is strangely *there* at the water
trough, having taken precedence over the poet:

He reached down from a fissure in the earth-wall in the gloom
And trailed his yellow-brown slackness soft-bellied down, over the edge of the
  stone trough
. . .
He sipped with his straight mouth,
Softly drank through his straight gums, into his slack long body,
Silently.

The snake embodies the golden earth-color and earth-heat of
Sicily in July; he has awesomely come up from the underworld.
The word "god" is finally broached in the lines where the snake
fully manifests his power of identity, his nonchalance and self-
containment:

He drank enough
And lifted his head, dreamily, as one who has drunken,
And flickered his tongue like a forked night on the air, so black,
Seeming to lick his lips,
And looked around like a god, unseeing, into the air.

Earlier the unseeingness had been compared to that of cattle;
now it is godlike.

Overawed, the poet has resisted the human education that
bids him kill the golden venomous snake. But as the snake

withdraws into his hole, the poet unaccountably throws a log at him, thus destroying the image of sanctity by forcing the snake to pull in the rest of him with "undignified haste." In his immediate regret the poet thinks of the albatross. Like Coleridge's ancient Mariner, he has violated the sanctity of nature and has evolved a sense of sin from natural experience. But here the violation comes from the poet's inescapable fear of sex. As the snake "put his head into that dreadful hole, / And as he slowly drew up, snake-easing his shoulders, and entered farther," the poet is overcome by "horror, a sort of protest against his withdrawing into that horrid black hole." This image of sexual entrance fills us with horror, too, and we realize that our fear of snakes is a fear of the phallus, of the sexual power our culture has driven underground.

When Lawrence calls the snake "one of the lords of life," he uses a term that provides the model for fully realized identity in the novels. And when he calls the snake "a king in exile, uncrowned in the underworld / Now due to be crowned again," he introduces, despite his generally linear view of history, a Yeatsian idea of cycles. The chthonic or phallic god will be worshipped again in the coming neopagan era. The difference is that for Lawrence godhead is not a supernatural incarnation. The snake remains a real snake; he was worshipped because his shape is phallic and really does, like the phallus, embody life force. "In those days," when gods were really alive, says a character in *St. Mawr*, "you saw the thing, you never saw the God in it: I mean in the tree or the fountain or the animal." [17] That is the aim of Lawrence's animal poems, to evoke the god as the essence of the animal's life or identity.

This is another version of Wordsworth's aim to "see into the life of things." Lawrence revitalizes Wordsworth's sense of organic identity by rejecting those Wordsworthian visual transformations that had come to seem mere idealizing impositions of meaning upon the natural object. [18] Instead Lawrence confirms, through knowledge of Darwin and Freud, Wordsworth's evolutionary intuition of identity as continuum—as evolving from inanimate to unconscious animate to thought that passes out of and back to the blood. The "life of things" means spiritual force to Wordsworth, sexual force to Lawrence; and it is easier for us nowadays to believe in sex than spirit. Sex also seems more rudimentary and unconscious than spirit and therefore more vital—for in Lawrence, as in Wordsworth, the more unconscious the more vital. Lawrence revitalizes Wordsworth's organicism by projecting sex as the binding and creative force—a force that it requires no transformations, no concepts of the supernatural, to see as miracle and mystery. Thus he can say about the sexual intercourse of whales:

And over the bridge of the whale's strong phallus, linking the wonder of whales
the burning archangels under the sea keep passing, back and forth,
keep passing, archangels of bliss.

                                                        ("Whales Weep Not!")

This is not presented as supernatural transformation. The monumental magnitude of the whales' intercourse makes sufficiently clear that intercourse is for them and all animals a climax of bliss, heaven. The lack of transformation ("Bavarian Gentians" is the notable exception) makes Lawrence's poetry simpler, less associatively rich than Wordsworth's—and less substantial, since the assertions of archetypal or mythical identity are not substantiated by a change in the perceived reality.

It is in his fiction that Lawrence equals Wordsworth in stature; for there he explicitly transforms his people by carrying their identity back to the point in unconsciousness where it can be manifested, not through action or dialogue, but through external embodiments of life force. These embodiments may be projected by visual transformations of the characters themselves—as in the transformations of Ursula and Skrebensky into moonlight and shadow in their crucial love scenes in *The Rainbow*—or by transformations of the character through connection with a landscape: Gerald takes on godlike proportions

because the arctic landscape at the end of *Women in Love* projects his psyche. These external embodiments of life force often
take shapes that are animals in the same sense as they are gods.
When Lawrence uses animals in his fiction, he moves from
people to animals to gods as a way of moving from the ordinary
to the archetypal or mythical self, then back to a reconstructed
individuality that oscillates between animal and god.

In the short novels, *The Fox* and *St. Mawr,* and in certain
episodes in the longer novels, Lawrence poses animals on the
scene to suggest that the characters are being brought into touch
with their unconscious life. A character may find in an animal
the image of his deepest desire, and fall in love when he recognizes in the animal his lover's true self. He discovers at the
same time his own true self through its object of desire. It is
only when men and women recognize each other's unconscious
selves that they can fall genuinely in love and thus find their
own true selves. The sexual problem of our time comes from
the inability of modern people to find their way back to their
unconscious selves. But they must do more than that. In *The
Fox* and *St. Mawr,* the fox and the stallion merely start the
heroines on the road to self-discovery through discovery of their
unconscious desires; the heroines must progress to an integration of unconsciousness with consciousness, which in fact they
never achieve.

Lawrence would certainly agree with Yeats that "there is
some one myth for every man, which, if we but knew it, would
make us understand all he did and thought." [19] Once he conceived of "carbon" identity, Lawrence thought that every person
has his external self in some animal or landscape that represents
his object of desire. In *Women in Love,* Gudrun becomes sexually attracted to Gerald through her visual transformations of
him into arctic wolf and Norse god; his mastery of mare and
rabbit shows her the kind of sadomasochistic sexuality she wants
with him. Gerald and Gudrun find their psychic landscape in
the snowbound Alps; whereas Birkin and Ursula, who accom-

panied them, finally flee the snow for the flowery earth of Italy. Self-realization for Lawrence is the process by which a character comes to know what moon or water, flowery earth or frozen waste means to him, of coming to understand how all his life is a fulfillment and realization of a self that can only be symbolized since it exists prior to mentality and verbalization.

The "carbon" identity embodied as animal and god in fox or golden stallion resembles Yeats's external archetypes that are knowable through an external race memory. The difference is that Yeats's world of external souls, his *anima mundi*, is half-Platonic, half-psychological; whereas Lawrence's unconscious is entirely naturalistic, psychological, Darwinian. Lawrence dissolves the realistically conceived individual back into the elements out of which life arose, and then rediscovers those primordial shapes that men first delineated out of earth, air, water, light, as a way of evolving their own sense of identity. (The fox first emerges, in March's eyes, from copper-colored evening sunlight; then Henry emerges from the fox.) Like Yeats, Lawrence reascends the stairway that Western man has been descending since Periclean Greece; he turns from internalized individuality back to external, archetypal identity, in order to root the modern separated ego in a vibrant individuality open to connection with other people and the universe.

Yeats and Lawrence return to archetypal identity not, as many people think, to destroy but rather to renew and enlarge our withering individuality by bringing it to birth again from the shapes out of which it originally evolved. Paul Morel's problem, in *Sons and Lovers*, is that he can love Miriam only as individual or conscious soul and Clara only as archetype or unconscious body. The aim of all Lawrence's work is to heal that split through what we might call dialectical regression. For Lawrence, godhead is the existential potency of our animal life brought to total consciousness—a total consciousness as alien to us as the animal's total unconsciousness. Human individuality is the uneasy, changing fluid relation between the two poles of animal and god, and requires for its self-definition that the poles be as vivid and definite as possible. There is hope for us only if our modern self-conscious individuality can regress, in order to salvage all that is best of its freedom and sensitivity, in order to gather strength to go forward into a strangely inimical future where we will have to face conditions human beings have never faced before.

Like Yeats, Lawrence tried to reconstitute the modern self by showing how you get over from the flesh-and-blood to the mythical person. "Any creature"—he says in "Reflections on the Death of a Porcupine"—"that attains to its own fullness of being, its own *living* self, becomes unique, a nonpareil. It has its place in the fourth dimension, the heaven of existence, and there it is perfect." Lawrence's "heaven of existence" resembles Yeats's in the last stanza of "Among School Children." The difference is that Yeats's Phase 15 is an achievement of nature and art; while Lawrence's fourth-dimensional "being"—even though a dance between sun and earth, incarnating as seed the Holy Ghost—is an entirely natural achievement: "as much material as existence" in space and time [20] Yeats explains the transition from flesh-and blood as an incarnation of either supernatural or culturally determined archetypes. Lawrence, for whom the Holy Ghost is a seed, comes closer to Wordsworth in seeing the transition as a regression leading to rebirth. The "secret" to which Lawrence regresses in his moments of insight is that miraculous point in evolution where life first distinguished itself from nonlife; our unconscious is the reversion in each of us to that point.

In *Psychoanalysis and the Unconscious*, Lawrence dismisses the Freudian unconscious as "the inverted reflection of our ideal consciousness." The "true unconsciousness" is the point "where our life bubbles up in us, prior to any mentality. . . .

Where life begins the unconscious also begins." But primordial unconsciousness is not, as in Jung, collective. It is individual; so what you discover through regression is an individuality that is archetypal because original. "The first naked unicellular organism is an *individual*," an indivisible organic as opposed to a divisible mathematical unit. "Where the individual begins," the "life-motive also begins." This original individuality contains all the mystery wrapped up in the old word *soul*. "By the unconscious we do mean the soul," Lawrence admits.

> But the word *soul* has been vitiated by the idealistic use, until nowadays it means only that which a man conceives himself to be. And that which a man conceives himself to be is something far different from his true unconscious.[21]

Here is a succinct restatement of the modern problem of identity—that we have come to understand our "real" self as different from our idea of it. The consequences in art, as we have seen, are new modes of characterization, new ways of telling us things about the characters that they do not know about themselves.

In *The Fox*, identity is revealed through an animal and through visual transformations of the characters. March is subject to trances, a sign that her conscious mind is cut off from her unconscious: "her inner mind took no notice of what she saw." Her sight of the fox is visionary, the objectification of her image of desire, an image of maleness deep inside her: "She lowered her eyes, and suddenly saw the fox. He was looking up at her. His chin was pressed down, and his eyes were looking up. They met her eyes. And he knew her." Although March is playing the man's role on the farm she and Jill Banford are trying to run together, the fox sees through the man's clothes to her womanliness, knows her deepest desire.

March falls in love with the stranger Henry Grenfell when, in another visual transformation, she recognizes him as the fox: "He had a ruddy roundish face, with fairish hair. . . . His eyes

were blue, and very bright and sharp. On his cheeks, on the
fresh ruddy skin were fine, fair hairs, like a down, but sharper."
Later the same features, "the ruddy, elate face" appear godlike
or nobly human. Fox-god is an external shape from which
Henry emerges to fulfill his individuality and March's. When
March can look out at Henry from a dark corner, then, "hidden
in the shadow . . . she need not any more be divided in herself, trying to keep up two planes of consciousness. She could at
last lapse into the odour of the fox." By yielding to her unconscious desire for Henry as fox, March finds the image of her
own true self as hunted animal, as hare (hence her name).

March's dream—more poetical than most of Lawrence's
poems—transforms Henry and fox into a phallic corn god,
Dionysus singing. A singing round the house turns out to be
"the fox singing." The fox is now the color of corn (wheat). He
whisked his tail or "brush across her face, and it seemed his
brush was on fire, for it seared and burned her mouth with a
great pain." [22] As counterpoint to the fox's call, there arrives
throughout the story Banford's call reminding March that it is
teatime or bedtime. Banford's is the voice of consciousness gone
wrong, offering cozy comforts instead of sex, saying sex isn't important. Weak, nearsighted, incompetent, Banford turns vis-
ually into a witch as she fights Henry for March.

After Henry kills the fox, March seems liberated from her
phallic image of Henry. She begins to see him as an individual.
She dreams Banford's death, associating it with the fox's. She
then brings her unconscious desire to consciousness by appearing quite unexpectedly in a dress. "If she had suddenly grown a
moustache [Henry] could not have been more surprised." The
reverse comparison shows how very like a sexual transformation
this is. The revelation turns Henry from a youth into a man,
"with all a man's grave weight of responsibility. . . . Since he
had realised that she was a woman, and vulnerable, accessible,
a certain heaviness had possessed his soul. He did not want to
make love to her." They have both progressed beyond the phal-

lic. Hearing "the deep, heavy, powerful stroke of his heart, terrible, like something from beyond," she knows him now not as an animal but as that cross between animal and god, that internalized beyondness, which is distinctively human. "She was too confused to think who he was or what he was." Beyondness, mystery, the sensing in the beloved of an external identity that is deeply internal—these are signs in Lawrence of a fully human sexual relation.

In a dark shed from which she cannot see the lighted house where Banford waits, March consents to marry Henry before he leaves for Canada to earn money to support her. Returning to the house, they see Banford in her final transformation into "a queer little witch," looking "round with reddened eyes as they entered." Banford beholds with envy the glow of their nobly human sexual identities: Henry "seemed strangely tall and bright and looming"; "March had a delicate look on her face." In desiring that Henry save her from the routine of going to bed with Banford, March seems almost aware that her relationship with Banford has been latently homosexual. To consider them Lesbians—as in the otherwise excellent film version—is to miss the problem in this and the other stories where two women set up house together. The problem is not homosexuality, but the pretense that a household can be established without a sexual relation.

March almost makes it as a woman, but not quite. Once Henry is out of sight and can no longer provide a visual link to her unconscious self, she reverts to the old relation with Banford and writes him a letter breaking off their engagement. Henry reverts through visual transformation to the role of fox, and with a fox's predatory will returns to murder Banford by *willing* that she reject his warning to step away from the tree he is cutting down. The fact that Banford could have stepped away, that the murder looks like a Freudian accident, suggests that the murder fulfills her desire as it fulfills Henry's and March's (March dreamed Banford's death). It is because the real action is psychic, because for Banford there is only the choice between physical and eventual psychic death, that the reader withholds the usual moral judgment of the physical murder. March is conquered through the murder, and has unconsciously wanted to be taken that way, to have her consciousness overwhelmed. That is why she beholds Henry's return with a "helpless, fascinated rabbit look," [23] and is again entranced as when she first saw the fox. That is why their marriage begins badly. He has conquered, she has surrendered; they do not "meet" reciprocally as persons.

For conventional perfection—and *The Fox* almost satisfies conventional expectations since all is dramatized without discursive residue—the story should have ended happily, given its valuation of instinct over repression. But Lawrence, as usual in his major work, negates his own solution in order to leave the way open for evolution. He even brings back the evolutionary rainbow image from *The Rainbow* to suggest that the marriage may develop successfully in Canada. Readers misunderstand Lawrence because they oversimplify him; they do not realize that his view is always evolutionary, that he approves a kind of action or character only up to the point where it ought to be abandoned for a higher kind. The animal is a model of identity so long as the character needs to recover unconsciousness, but is abandoned at the point where the character should discover his human individuality. There are two kinds of regression in Lawrence—healthy regression where the character moves from animal to god to human, and unhealthy regression where he reverts to the animal phase after having, like Henry and March, outgrown it. Hence Lawrence's surprising disapproval of "primitivism":

> We can't go back to the savages: not a stride. We can be in sympathy with them. We can take a great curve in their direction, onwards. But we cannot turn the current of our life backwards . . . . We can only do it when we are renegade. The renegade hates life itself.

"Yet," he adds indicating the right kind of regression, "we must make a great swerve in our onward-going life-course now, to gather up again the savage mysteries." [24]

The merely tentative validity of the animal model is even clearer in *St. Mawr*. Published in 1925, two years after *The Fox*, *St. Mawr* is a masterpiece as long as it is organized around the stallion St. Mawr, whose glowing vitality provides the model of identity against which we can measure the deadness of the modern cosmopolitan characters. When halfway through, the stallion, having served his purpose, virtually disappears, the story turns discursive, sometimes tediously, sometimes brilliantly. Lawrence is, however, honestly thinking aloud, exploring beyond his certainties, even beyond, in places, his artistic powers. Although artistically less perfect than *The Fox*, *St. Mawr* has more scope—it is one of Lawrence's most complex statements on the modern problem of identity. It is—as F. R. Leavis recognized by comparing it to *The Waste Land* [25]— Lawrence's jazz-age story about the walking dead.

Lou and her mother Mrs. Witt are rich expatriate Americans, and Lou's society painter husband Rico is, as an Australian with an English title, equally rootless. The style, imaginatively satirical in Lawrence's later manner, moves from satirically rendered jazz-age patter to the profoundest poetic vision. Lou's marriage is sexless; it exists as a social convenience, for having "fun." She becomes aware of a growing numbness, "as if she couldn't feel any more." "I can't feel"; "I can't live"; "I am dying, mother"; "we don't exist"—this is her refrain. And her mother—a handsome widow who long ago died emotionally, living now only in her destructive wit—joins in the litany; for Mrs. Witt "really wanted to be defeated," but "men were never really her match." Mother and daughter make a distinctively modern tragic chorus, a chorus of upper-class Anglo-Saxon women failed by upper-class Anglo-Saxon men. The men in Lawrence who save women by bringing alive their womanliness are either foreign,

like Count Dionys in *The Ladybird* or the Armenian in
"Mother and Daughter," or else lower-class, like Henry in *The
Fox*, or the collier in "Daughters of the Vicar," or the game-
keeper in *Lady Chatterley's Lover*.

St. Mawr breaks upon Lou as the external-internal image of
her deepest desire, a model not only of maleness but of vital
identity. "At the back of her consciousness loomed a great,
over-awing figure out of a dark background: St. Mawr, looking
at her without really seeing her, yet gleaming a question at
her"—in the way the fox "knows" March. Animal and god—
god as essence of animal—St. Mawr is visualized under the
changing aspects of sun, fish, reptile—as embodying the whole
evolution of life force. Like the fox, or the snake in Lawrence's
poem, the horse is a lord of life; whereas Rico's eyes show "a
central powerlessness, that left him anxious." Lou "realized that
St. Mawr drew his hot breaths in another world," another phase
of identity, "from Rico's." It is the phase not only of Greek
horses but of Greek heroes, where consciousness and life's forms
first emerge from the matrix—the phase of prehistoric horses
newly emerged from reptiles:

> With their strangely naked equine heads, and something of a snake
> in their way of looking round, and lifting their sensitive, dangerous
> muzzles, they moved in a prehistoric twilight where all things loomed
> phantasmagoric, all on one plane, sudden presences suddenly jutting
> out of the matrix.

Yeats's phantasmagoria is here achieved through regression—"a
step . . . Rico could never take." But Lou "was prepared to
sacrifice Rico."

For she now understands that identity must flow from the
source of life, and that the identities of the people she knows
rest uneasily on mere "attitude" because "something else is lacking. . . . That black fiery flow in the eyes of the horse was not
'attitude.' It was something much more terrifying, and real."
Even in thinking, the men whose identities flow from the same
source as St. Mawr's—his Welsh groom, Lewis, and the Ameri-

can Indian, Phoenix, who works for Mrs. Witt—seem more profound than clever men whose life is concentrated in the head: if Rico's "head had been cut off," it "would not have missed the body." Lou complains about such dissociated thinking in men:

> "Why can't men get their life straight, like St. Mawr, and then think? Why can't they think quick, mother: quick as a woman: only farther than we do? Why isn't men's thinking quick like fire, mother? Why is it so slow, so dead, so deadly dull? . . . But then men always do leave off really thinking, when the last bit of wild animal dies in them."

Yeats would agree that women are generally less dissociated in their thinking than men; so that both authors consider abstract opinionated women, like Maud Gonne and Mrs. Witt, or Hermione in *Women in Love*, perverse.

So far the value system of *St. Mawr* seems simple. St. Mawr stands for all that is good—nature and unconsciousness—against all that is bad—civilization and consciousness. But there are complications even at the outset, when we hear that St. Mawr may be malevolent, has killed a man, and for all his appearance of virility will not breed. We are also asked to distinguish between Mrs. Witt's simple and Lou's complex primitivism. Mrs. Witt makes a simple dichotomy between effete thinking men and sexy brutes; while Lou understands that "A pure animal man would . . . . never cease to wonder," [26] that a genuine primitive would have a poet's mind.

These complexities come to a climax in the final visual transformations of St. Mawr—after Rico has the inevitable accident on him (there has been hostility between them from the start). By frantically reining in the rearing horse, Rico pulls him over backwards upon himself—making an inverted Blakean and Freudian image of frantic energy or id on top of frantic will or ego. St. Mawr's "great eyes starting from the naked lines of his nose" parallel Rico's "eyes also starting from his yellow-white face"—a parallel that climaxes the visualizations of Rico as a nervous untrustworthy horse no less menacing through lack of vitality than St. Mawr through overabundant vitality. "The writhing, immense horse, whose pale-gold, inverted bulk seemed to fill the universe" symbolizes a universal overturning. Struggling to his feet, the horse recapitulates the course of evolution—he is a "fish," a "lizard," and seems finally, with his "guilty, ghostlike look," to be "seeing legions of ghosts, down the dark avenues of all the centuries that have lapsed since the horse became subject to man."

Not until her own mare shies at a dead adder does Lou realize why St. Mawr reared. Wondering why her horse shies, she discovers the snake; whereas Rico ignorantly thwarted St. Mawr's natural instinct to avoid it. Riding past the dead snake, Lou has a vision of evil, not as the "mere negation of good," but as an ocean sweeping us away without our knowing it while we are absorbed with our good intentions. Lou is repeating Eve's experience, except that Lou learns about evil through a *dead* snake, learns about the evil that calls itself "good." She now recollects her sight of the inverted St. Mawr; and the recollected image, differing from the original description in places I shall italicize, turns her original vision of repressed energy into a vision of evil:

> the pale-gold belly of the stallion upturned, the hoofs working *wildly,* the *wicked* curved hams of the horse, and then the *evil* straining of that arched, *fish-like* neck, with the *dilated* eyes of the head. Thrown backwards, and working its hoofs in the air. Reversed, and *purely evil.*

The "crumpled" snake, with "gold-and-yellow back" and "bit of pale-blue belly showing," looks something like St. Mawr and something like Rico lying "crumpled," staring "from a yellow, dead-looking face." "Which was wrong, the horse or the rider [id or ego]? Or both?" Even worse than St. Mawr's savagery was Rico's "impotence as a master," his unworthiness to rule because corrupted by self-doubt (the point of Lawrence's poem "Elephant").

The choice is not, she realizes, between savagery and civilization, but between the overt aggression of animals and the subtle psychological undermining that civilized people practice upon each other. This is the answer to the attacks on Lawrence's inhumanity. The choice is between Henry's murder of Banford and the destruction Banford and March would have worked upon each other; between Lou's abandonment of Rico and the undermining that will follow Flora Manby's solicitude for him. The danger lies in allowing natural aggressiveness to go underground, which is what happens when humanitarianism, by stifling life's cycle of destruction and renewal, overpopulates earth with inwardly rotting millions whose socially organized eruptions of violence are more terrible than any animal savagery. St. Mawr, in his final transformation, represents mankind ridden to destruction by its own ideals: "Mankind, like a horse, ridden by a stranger, smooth-faced, evil rider. Evil himself, smooth-faced and pseudo-handsome, riding mankind past the dead snake, to the last break"—the last break (we infer from "death-break" in reference to the African statue in *Women in Love*) with organic connection to nature. The rider masquerades "as the [dissociated] ideal, in order to poison the real." [27]

The thought here risks escaping from the story altogether (as it escapes in later places), but can at this point be substantiated if we pay close enough attention to the spectacular evolution of the imagery. The inverted St. Mawr is pathetic, then menacing, and is finally put back upon his feet—given a newly positive if ambivalent valuation in human rather than animal terms. The story might have ended here, with Lou and her mother transporting St. Mawr to their Texas ranch to save him from the vengeance of Rico and his friends who want to geld the stallion, turn him into their kind of male. Instead, the story takes a new direction as Lou and Mrs. Witt learn that they cannot draw from St. Mawr a lesson for their own lives. Mrs. Witt tries to draw such a lesson by proposing marriage to St. Mawr's groom, Lewis; but Lewis rejects her attempt at pseudo-primitivism, realizing that she would do to him what Rico did to St. Mawr.

Later the American Indian servant Phoenix hints at his willingness to serve Lou as stud in marriage; but Lou quashes his
advance, realizing she is through with "mere sex": "Even the
illusion of the beautiful St. Mawr was gone."

St. Mawr, who in Texas began slavishly following a mare,
has already dissolved as a symbol, having become just stud. As a
symbol, St. Mawr helped Lou understand what is wrong with
our civilization. For a solution she must look beyond St. Mawr,
beyond the phallic, to a recovery and rebirth of self. "She
wanted to escape from the friction which is the whole stimulus
in modern social life. She wanted to be still: only that, to be
very, very still, and recover her own soul." Unless sex "touches
my very spirit, the very quick of me, I will stay alone . . . .
and give myself only to the unseen presences"—the way Vestal
Virgins preferred to save themselves for a god.

Mrs. Witt looks forward only to dying, which she hopes will
give her the big experience life denied her. But "even Death,"
she fears, "can't sting those that have never really lived." And
she cries with jazz-age pathos: *"O Death, where is thy sting-a-
ling-a-ling?"* Mrs. Witt is more complex than the mother in
"Mother and Daughter," who is in some ways her prototype; for
having started life on a Texas ranch, she at least knows what she
lacks, though she lives too entirely in the head to have Lou's capacity for rebirth.

Lou, instead, will develop through regression on a wildly
remote New Mexico ranch, where she will move back in her
appreciation to pines and to the "pure . . . *absolute* beauty" of
the inanimate desert—scenery described in some of Lawrence's
most gorgeous nature writing. St. Mawr taught her admiration
for nature. But this mountain ranch will teach her admiration
for civilization, for man's struggle against that natural savagery
which, glimpsed for a moment in the inverted St. Mawr, will
reappear as "some serpent-bird for ever attacking man, in a
hatred of man's onward-struggle towards further creation."

To reconcile the story's contradictory valuations of both nature and civilization, we must understand that Lawrence mixes a cyclical with a linear view of history. At the story's outset civilization is too much in control; so civilization is bad, nature good. Confronted by wilderness, however, man's desire to impose order on nature is good. When there is so much order that there is no vitality left to be ordered, then the old forms must be destroyed and man must begin again with the wilderness. Man seems happiest when his ordering impulse confronts a dangerous antagonist whose conquest can be undertaken without guilt. Thus genuine primitivism is, in its valuations of identity and life style, concerned with nature for the sake of civilization, wants us to regress in order to move forward.

> All savagery is half sordid. And man is only himself when he is fighting on and on, to overcome the sordidness. And every civilization, when it loses its inward vision and its cleaner energy, falls into a new sort of sordidness, more vast and more stupendous than the old savage sort. An Augean stable of metallic filth. And all the time, man has to rouse himself afresh, to cleanse the new accumulations of refuse. To win from the crude wild nature the victory and the power to make another start, and to cleanse behind him the century-deep deposits of layer upon layer of refuse: even of tin cans.[28]

The tin cans are the outworn forms—signs of an inorganic savagery that might be cured by confronting organic savagery (Lou's way) or by assimilating one's self to it (Kate's way in *The Plumed Serpent*).

In characterizing nature as "serpent-bird," Lawrence picks up the imagery of *The Plumed Serpent*, which had already been drafted in Mexico. *St. Mawr* and the short stories "The Woman Who Rode Away" and "The Princess" were written on Lawrence's New Mexico ranch during spring-summer 1924, before he returned to Mexico to finish *The Plumed Serpent*. The four fictions offer different solutions to the same problem—

an upper-class woman's search for rebirth through connection with a more primitive mode of existence. In "The Princess," a quintessential James story, the rich, super-refined American virgin defeats the Indian who might have saved her through sex, and lives out a walking ice-death. The aristocratic Irish heroine of *The Plumed Serpent,* instead, starts where Lou leaves off. Lou leaves off as a kind of nun—her convent the wilderness, her religion an as yet unannounced neopaganism—awaiting rebirth as an individual experience. Kate travels to Lake Sayula in a remote part of Mexico, in order to be alone and recover her soul. But it takes a revolution in culture, a revival of Aztec religion, to produce in Kate a rebirth of self, a discovery of her womanliness made possible by a culture in which women can be women because men are men. Kate is made Irish to suggest, with perhaps an allusion to Yeats, that the Irish nationalist movement, for which Kate's husband died, is trying to revive Ireland's pagan past as the aristocratic Don Ramón is trying to revive Mexico's.

The Plumed Serpent brings to a climax all Lawrence's beast fables in prose and verse. The god Lawrence finds in animals here takes human form in Ramón, the living manifestation of the Aztec god Quetzalcoatl whose symbol is the serpent and eagle combining earth and sky, sense and spirit. Quetzalcoatl, "the feathered snake," is called "lord of two ways" as distinguished from Jesus, "lord of the one way," of spirit only. In the beast fables, the animals are gods because existentially superior to men. Here we see that men, when they realize themselves completely, are gods—that godhead is the ultimate external phase of identity. To "meet in the quick," we must meet outside ourselves; but we must become gods—"without transfiguration we shall never get there"—in order to meet in love with the requisite impersonality. When the Indian Cipriano announces, " 'I *am* the living Huitzilopochtli,' " the Aztec fire god, even the ironically skeptical Kate—seeing in his eyes "an inhuman assurance, which looked far, far beyond her, in the darkness"—murmurs, " 'I know you are.' " [29] Cipriano undergoes a ritual rebirth in order to change his identity.

Kate's problem is from the start an identity problem. She wants *a life of her own;* her loyalty is to the European notion of the enclosed self. But she is forty, in the middle of her life's journey, and already disillusioned with the European notion, when she first crosses the "spermy," "fish-milk" waters of Lake Sayula which symbolize rebirth. "She had thought that each individual had a complete self"; but now realizes, "as plainly as if she had turned into a new being," that modern men and women are "assembled" fragments lacking unity because not in touch with an external self. That is why modern people merely function, "degrading the one mystery left to them, sex," and acting "with a collective insect-like will, to avoid the responsibility of achieving any more perfected being or identity." Kate finds herself "afraid, mystically," of the Mexican boatman "crouching there in the bows with his smooth thighs and supple loins like a snake, and his black eyes watching." Snake imagery pervades the novel as a symbol of the antithetical impersonal identity toward which Kate must move.

Kate's task is to acquire an individuality open to external self and to a natural and communal will that differs from the collective will of an atomized mass of egoists because community is a personality (Yeats) or a god (Lawrence)—an external self from which its members derive identity. Ramón becomes the living Quetzalcoatl to give the members of his community their individual being: " 'Quetzalcoatl is just a living word . . . . All I want them to do is to find the beginnings of the way to their own manhood, their own womanhood.' "

Kate finds her womanhood through Cipriano, who subdues her to his sexual will. The nonindividual womanhood he wants of her is signified by his desire that she become a goddess—that by marrying him she become Huitzilopochtli's consort, Malintzi. "Surely it would not be *herself* who could marry him," Kate reflects. "It would be some curious female within her,

whom she did not know and did not own." She submits to
Cipriano as an act of masochistic self-abandonment, abandonment to "the ancient phallic mystery," to "the sheer solid mystery of passivity." "Her world could end in many ways, and this
was one of them." [30] She is at this stage like the American
heroine of "The Woman Who Rode Away," who voluptuously
allows an Aztec tribe to use her as a human sacrifice.

Kate resents Cipriano's interest in her only as female, though
he says that he in turn could not achieve his manhood without her. " 'Let the Morning Star rise between us,' " he says, re-
iterating the triune pattern worked out through *The Rainbow*
and through the "metaphysical" books *Study of Thomas Hardy*
and *The Crown.* " 'Alone you are nothing, and I am *manqué*.
But together we are the wings of the Morning.' " Is this, Kate
wonders, "the final answer to man's assertion of individuality?
. . . It meant the death of her individual self."

She moves toward the realization that submission means not
the death but the rebirth of the self, that Cipriano attracts her
not by his will, but by a "living, flickering, fiery *Wish*" that they
may both serve ends larger than themselves. The will, instead,
is used by men "seeking their own ends as individuals." Cipriano is justified by his "vulnerability" or lack of self-interest. It
is not degrading, as Ramón's wife Teresa teaches her, to give
your soul to a man who is more than a mere man. Modern
men fear the responsibility of a complete relation. Kate's Irish
husband " 'didn't *want* my soul. He believed I should keep a
soul of my own.' " But, says Teresa, " 'you can no more keep
your own soul inside you for yourself, without its dying, than
you can keep the seed of your womb.' " She has summed up
the reasons for the death of self in the modern world and its
connection with the death of sexuality.

Now Kate moves toward rebirth—she can feel herself "changing . . . to another creature"—as she becomes a genuine wife
to Cipriano, enjoying the absolute rest of "strange, heavy, *positive* passivity." Intuitively aware of the "irritant quality of talk,"

Cipriano refuses to engage in serious conversation; just as he refuses to satisfy her "old desire for frictional, irritant sensation," for the kind of orgasm which is the counterpart to individual consciousness in that the woman takes her own conscious satisfaction. This kind of orgasm comes in spasms or isolated moments of pleasure that are a form of *knowing*. What happens with Cipriano, instead, is "dark and untellable"; she becomes "a fountain gushing noiseless"; she cannot isolate her own orgasm or moments of pleasure—"there was no such thing as conscious 'satisfaction.'" Once she accepts the fact that she cannot know her pleasure nor know Cipriano, that he must remain "forever as the stranger in whose presence she lived," [31] she can meet him at the impersonal phase of identity where their relation is sealed.

The quality of orgasm is important because, as we see again in *Lady Chatterley's Lover*, it is a sign of identity structure. So many modern men—Kate's Irish husband, the writer Michaelis who precedes the gamekeeper Mellors as Lady Chatterley's lover—have their orgasms too fast and thus force the woman into activity to secure her own orgasm. This reversal of roles, which upsets the relation between the sexes in all departments of life, is caused by the anxiety of modern men insecure of their manhood. "'It's because th' men *aren't* men, that th' women have to be,'" says Mellors. Nevertheless his own wife was the kind of modern woman who in intercourse fights for the active role by withholding her orgasm until the man has had his, then, keeping him inside, her vagina like a beak, brings herself off by turning him into the passive instrument of her gratification. "'Self! Self! Self! all self! tearing and shouting!'" [32] Lawrence may in *The Rainbow* be alluding to such sexual behavior when he speaks euphuistically of Ursula's female self-sufficiency and represents her, in the final destructive intercourse with Skrebensky, as a beaked harpy. Like Cipriano with Kate, Mellors refuses to allow Connie a separate orgasm, omitting in their first intercourses the foreplay that would lead to it. Yet the frustrated Lady Chatterley turns out to be the only real woman Mellors has ever had, the only one with whom he has enjoyed simultaneous orgasms. Mellors was not a successful lover until he met Connie; each sex has brought the other to flower.

In spite of Cipriano's talk of reciprocity, his manhood, perhaps because he is a primitive, seems in flower from the start; Kate can't do much for him. That may be why their relation, described as "a mindless communion of the blood," remains repellent to the reader. It is certainly inferior to the relation of Ramón and Teresa which involves, as Teresa explains to Kate, no " 'submission' " but a gentle interchange of souls: " 'Because a man like that is more gentle than a woman.' " Instead, " 'Cipriano is a soldier. . . . And you are a soldier among women, fighting all the time." [33] Like all modern women, Kate needs to be subdued.

Lawrence would want us to judge both these marriages inferior to the equality in difference, the star-equilibrium, of Tom and Lydia in *The Rainbow*, of Birkin and Ursula in *Women in Love*, of Mellors and Connie. Although Mellors behaves sexually like the Mexicans—his often-mentioned "tenderness" resembles Ramón's gentleness—Connie equals him intellectually, they exchange ideas as well as souls. Through the three versions of *Lady Chatterley's Lover*, Lawrence elevated the gamekeeper intellectually in order to achieve such equilibrium.

Characteristically, Lawrence offers only qualified approval of his organic Mexican society and its "blood" theology. We see this through Kate's continuing sense of the ridiculous, her sense, even as she becomes increasingly fascinated by the Quetzalcoatl revival, that it is pompous nonsense which might indeed solve all problems if one could only believe in it. The closer she comes to *unconscious* rebirth, the firmer is her *conscious* resolve to return to England and save Kate Forrester from the goddess Malintzi. Offended by her decision, Cipriano leaves her to rejoin Ramón. But she in the meantime has been moving through an internal process that brings her to recross the renovating waters of Lake Sayula in order to make partial submission to both men. The spectacular animal scenes at the end signify the process that brings about her partial rebirth.

The Plumed Serpent articulates completely the implications of all Lawrence's beast fables, in that the snake imagery symbolizes the archetypal identity Kate must recover through recognition of her archetypal opposite. Suddenly real animals appear—starting by a stroke of artistic genius with a real snake that, after all the snake *imagery,* springs a powerful surpise in the last paragraphs of the penultimate chapter, "Kate Is a Wife." Kate, having learned to be Cipriano's wife, says to herself, " 'I am like Teresa, really,' " when suddenly, like a warning of what being like Teresa involves, "before her she saw a long, dark soft rope, lying over a pale boulder. . . . It was a snake." As in the poem "Snake," the snake breaks upon her like a revelation, then retreats into its hole. But she feels no sexual revulsion as it eases "its dark length into the hole"; she no longer fights the phallic mystery. This snake is not called a god. The point is to portray, in contrast to the Quetzalcoatl symbolism, this snake's physical actuality and malevolence.

Kate must reconcile herself to the snake's malevolence, as she reconciled herself to the element of terror in Cipriano's impersonal love. Wondering "at all the unseen things in the hidden places of the earth," she comes to understand the snake's malevolence as an aspect of its "invisibility"—of those underground powers wielded by Cipriano when "with black, big, glittering eyes" he hypnotized Kate into acquiescence, or by the gentle Teresa when she rose "like a rearing, crested snake" to defend Ramón against an accusation, or by Kate herself when her love showed as the murderous ferocity that saved Ramón's life against assassins. Kate has come to understand these fiercely sexual underground powers as universal and self-justifying, as the authentically vital ground of our existence. She thinks the

snake must be reconciled to its low place in creation, because
"she felt a certain reconciliation between herself and it." [34] Kate
is ready for the final stage of her rebirth.

Even as she resolves to return to England, she sees—as a motive for staying—the snake's sexual powers in animals that are
above-ground and beneficent, beneficent because organically
connected with men. "Perched immobile in silhouette against
the lake, was a black-and-white cow, and a huge monolithic
black-and-white bull." It is in connection with the lake, which
now symbolizes the "cosmos," the great womb of nature and
history, that the whole silhouette, including white-clad men
and a waiting sailboat, makes a "monumental group of life," an
icon. Gods and civilizations arise—partly in Yeats but entirely
in Lawrence—from man's organic connection with nature.
Gods in this novel emerge from the lake and pass back into it
for renewal (the Christian icons are burnt and thrown into the
lake; the old pagan talismans are continually recovered from it).
It is through this organic connection that men achieve the
phase of identity that makes them gods. "Only in the heart of
the cosmos man can look for strength. . . . fulfilling his manhood": the snake " 'lies in the fire at the heart of the world.' "
Godhead is not elevation; it is the beyondness at the center. " 'I
shall look away to the heart of all the world,' " says Teresa,
explaining to Kate how she will present herself as a goddess,
" 'and try to be my sacred self.' " Ramón explains that even his
ordinary self " 'has a living Quetzalcoatl inside' " [35]—that our
identity derives from the god, the beyondness, within us.

The men maneuver the cow into the boat, then take elaborate measures to maneuver the mighty bull who dwarfs them.
The bull stands "spangled with black on its whiteness, like a
piece of the sky, immobile," but has "black snake markings."
The snake's "invisible" subterranean powers are manifest in the
bull who is lord of the two ways, sky and earth. The puny men
manage to maneuver the bull into the boat only because,
treated reverently, the bull cooperates; the reverence and coop-

eration contrast to the hideous Mexico City bullfight with which the novel opens. The ship crossing the waters, "with her massive sky-spangled cargo of life invisible," is a sacred ark veiling animals that are icons because visible manifestations of invisible powers. Kate is indoctrinated into the new religion when she understands that the object of worship is life and that life means sexuality. When peons give her a flash of recognition that is deference for her sexuality, she responds with a proud surge of power in limbs and breasts. When a newborn ass-foal takes its first steps with a little skip, she cries " 'Already it dances!' " The dance has a more specialized meaning than in Yeats; it is the unifying rhythm of sex. " 'How wonderful sex can be, when men keep it powerful and sacred, and it fills the world! like sunshine through and through one!' " She has arrived at the pagan belief in total fulfillment through organic connection with nature.

Nevertheless, " 'I'm not going to submit, even there. Why should one give in, to anything!' " Kate remains a modern Faustian who would rather forego happiness than sacrifice the sovereign self. Her partial submission comes not from the above climax of insight but from mere rejection of the alternative, mere desire for therapy. Through an ironical extension of the animal symbolism, Kate suddenly understands that the Faustian self toys with love like a cat with a mouse, turning love into *experience* in order to use it for self-aggrandizement. When she realizes that a lifetime of self-aggrandizement produces those hard, well-groomed middle-aged women, women like Mrs. Witt, whose company she would join in London, she decides: " 'My ego and my individuality are not worth *that* ghastly price. I'd better abandon some of my ego, and sink some of my individuality, rather than go like that.' " In the middle of her life's journey, Kate has to choose between spiritual death or rebirth and chooses *partial* rebirth: " 'I will make my submission; as far as I need, and no further.' "

Although certain feminists oversimplify and misunderstand

much of Lawrence, they are right to see him as the enemy. For he opposes two fundamental tenets of such feminists—that there is no inherent psychological difference between men and women, and that women ought to seek the same ego satisfactions as men. Lawrence does not approve of the enclosed ego in men or women. Kate recalls the words of a feminist writer: " 'Woman has suffered far more from the suppression of her ego than from sex suppression' "; then thinks with "pity" and "repulsion" of the modern grimalkins " 'who have cultivated their ego to the top of their bent!' "

She nevertheless protects her own ego in the final pages, where she makes submission to Ramón and Cipriano. Accusing them of not really wanting her, she thinks: "*What a fraud I am! I know all the time it is I who don't altogether want them. I want myself to myself. But I can fool them so they shan't find out.*" Yet the novel ends with Kate imploring Cipriano to bludgeon her into submission: " 'You won't let me go!' " [36]

Is such regression not, as Keith Sagar acutely asks, "renegade" by Lawrence's standards? "Is it not a reversal of Ursula's painful struggle towards selfhood and articulation?" [37] "The Princess," *The Plumed Serpent*, "The Woman Who Rode Away" move in one direction, the direction leading to oblivion, by which sophisticated moderns seek relief from the self-consciousness that produces sexual inadequacy. These are "sick" works, in which Lawrence writes out the very real sickness in himself and his generation; of the three, "The Woman Who Rode Away" is the masterpiece because the most imaginatively complete rendition of the regressive death-wish aborted in the other two. *St. Mawr*, instead, points toward the continuation of Ursula's direction from regression toward increasingly articulated selfhood, consciousness, humanity—the direction taken up in *Lady Chatterley's Lover*.

The Plumed Serpent is a glittering fabrication, very intelligent and carefully wrought. It is by Lawrence's own criteria a bad novel, because Lawrence does not really believe in his own fab-

rication; the personal relationships do not ring true, the affirma-
tions are a willed, abstract attempt to spin out of Lawrence's
genuine experience of right relationships a religion, culture, society that would make such relationships generally available. As
a novel of ideas, however, of sheer imaginative speculation, it is
fascinating and far more important than the critics, who are dis-
turbed by its occasional brutality and "fascism," will admit. *The
Plumed Serpent* is for our purposes important, because it clarifies Lawrence's thinking about the social requisites of identity-
making and the relation of animal and god to human identity.

The Plumed Serpent is the last of three novels that attempt social
solutions. Lawrence was finally repelled by the brutal, authori-
tarian nature of the societies he had projected. "The leader-
cum-follower relationship is a bore," he wrote after finishing
The Plumed Serpent. "And the new relationship will be some
sort of tenderness, sensitive, between men and men and men
and women." [38] Lawrence always negates his last step in order
to take the next one. In his next and final novel, *Lady Chatterley's Lover* (1928), he returns to the personal solution. *Tenderness*, the original title, is the quality that distinguishes Mellors as lover from Cipriano, and Connie from "the celluloid
women of today." The sign of humanity is tenderness, " 'the
touch of bodily awareness between human beings.' "

Connie, as she feels reborn into "another self" with which
she adores Mellors, fears to "lose herself, become effaced . . .
like a savage woman." But she does not like Kate have to sink
her individuality, only open it out to the female archetype. In
intercourse she becomes "ocean rolling. . . . she knew herself
touched, the consummation was upon her, and she was gone.
. . . she was not, and she was born: a woman." Now that she
has the capacity to touch this "unknown man. . . . it was the
sons of god with the daughters of men." [39] They achieve Ur-

sula's ideal by combining the archetypal and the human relation; they meet at an impersonal phase of identity, but are able
afterwards to pass back to their individual selves. Clifford's
friend Dukes likes to talk to women and therefore does not
desire them; Cipriano does not talk to Kate. But Mellors can
talk to and desire Connie after they have met as archetypes in
intercourse. They achieve an equilibrium. He takes the lead in
their exchange of ideas, she in their joint practical decisions.
When in "A Propos of *Lady Chatterley's Lover*" Lawrence calls
their kind of marriage "phallic," he means, with the old phallic
religions in mind, that their relation is archetypal in contrast to
the relation between "*personalities*" that "is excellent for friendship between the sexes, and fatal for marriage." Archetypal marriage opens out to cosmic rhythms, because the partners' identities open out to external male-female images: "the phallus is
only the great old symbol of godly vitality in a man." When
Mellors names their genitals John Thomas and Lady Jane, he is
naming their archetypal identities.

"We shall never free the phallic reality from the 'uplift'
taint," Lawrence writes, "till we give it its own phallic language,
and use the obscene words." [40] Mellors' nonidealistic love language, which never separates love from sex, is the thing in the
novel that has aroused the most moral hostility and has had the
most literary influence. With the cheapening of the old idealizing love tradition into popular sentiment, Lawrence, who took
love as seriously as Dante did, tried to re-establish its sacredness
through nonelevation. He makes love so inseparable from bodily and material necessities that, as Leavis points out, Henry's
desire for the farm in no way negates his love for March which
continues unabated after Banford says he will not get the farm.
In *Civilization and Its Discontents* (1930), Freud writes that
sexuality must suffer and complete sexual satisfaction be renounced as the price we pay for civilization. Freud settles for a
dissociation between tenderness and sex caused by the sublimation of sexual energy required by civilization. Lawrence thinks

that the right kind of civilization enriches sexuality, enhancing physical and spiritual satisfaction, and that the dissociation between tenderness and sex, the disease of a decadent civilization, is curable by a renewed culture of the feelings. This makes Lawrence a revisionist follower of the Medieval and Renaissance love tradition.

In his last novel, Lawrence takes yet another bold step forward; for he finally, after the highflown allusiveness of *The Rainbow* and *Women in Love*, tells us in explicit physical terms how the religion of love is practiced, and he does this without diminishing the sacredness of love. He manages to turn Mellors' refrain, " 'Tha's got the nicest woman's arse of anybody,' " into a love lyric. It is not living words like these, but "dead [conventionalized] words" that are "obscene." [41] Yeats, writing in 1933, could recognize Lawrence's achievement because it corresponded to the refined materialism of his own latest poetry; he understood the obscene language as a way of communicating outside the normal social channels. "*Lady Chatterley* is noble. . . . Those two lovers, the gamekeeper and his employer's wife, each separated from their class by their love, and by fate, are poignant in their loneliness, and the coarse language of the one, accepted by both, becomes a forlorn poetry uniting their solitudes, something ancient, humble and terrible." [42]

The lovers' fully human relationship contrasts to a social milieu of "tin people." In Ramón's society "the air seemed mysteriously alive, with a new Breath," [43] but here: " 'the steam of so much boredom, and discontent and anger out of all the people, just kills the vitality in the air.' " Mellors has a social program but is too isolated to work for it. His social ideas—" 'let's drop the whole industrial life, an' go back' "—are those of Ruskin and Morris, with the implications worked out as to what constitutes preindustrial identity and sexuality. If the men had satisfying work, they would be confident of their manliness, " 'then the women 'ud begin to be women.' " [44] Clifford's war wound, his paralysis from the waist down, symbolizes the defor-

mity of modern, head-centered industrialized men—the specialization of their faculties that leads to desexualization.

Mark Spilka considers Clifford's paralysis a moral condition,
agreeing with Connie that Clifford was "to blame" for his lack
of "simple, warm, physical contact." [45] Clifford is partly to
blame, since the moral condition, like the identity structure beneath it, depends on an inextricable combination of what Yeats
called chance and choice. The critics who condemn Lawrence's
callousness about Clifford's misfortune do not understand the
symbolic mode of Clifford's portrayal. Clifford's paralysis is symbolic in the overdetermined modern manner; the paralysis not
only caused, it also confirmed his sexual and emotional inadequacy. The paralysis was, Lawrence comments, "in the sense of
its happening, inevitable." [46] We are told enough about the
Chatterleys' brief sex life before the wound to realize that even if
Clifford had remained potent, Connie's womanhood would
have gone unfulfilled. For "the sex part did not mean much to
him." He regarded sex as "one of the curious obsolete, organic
processes which persisted in its own clumsiness." [47]

To understand the symbolism, we have only to compare Clifford's paralysis with the war wound in the story "The Blind
Man," written ten years earlier, where the wound has a quite
opposite because regressive effect. Maurice Pervin's blindness
restores "the almost incomprehensible peace of immediate contact in darkness." It improves his marriage; his wife Isabel has
become pregnant. Their life together is like the Chatterleys', except in quality. "She and he had been almost entirely alone
together since he was wounded. They talked and sang and read
together in a wonderful and unspeakable intimacy. . . . He did
not even regret the loss of his sight in these times of dark, palpable joy." They are visited by Isabel's old friend Bertie, who has a
hard-shelled, head-centered identity structure like Clifford's.
Bertie likes to talk to women but does not desire them, and has
turned his energies to achieving professional success. He is as
maimed as Maurice. In the confrontation between them, we see

two halves of a dissevered whole; but one can, we are to understand, evolve toward wholeness or communion, starting from
Maurice's half.

Since sight is the most intellectual sense, Bertie conceives
blindness as a void. " 'It always seems to me that when there is
no thought and no action, there is nothing.' " " 'There is something,' " says Maurice. " 'I couldn't tell you what it is.' " In a
dark barn, he introduces Bertie to the world of touch—knows
him through touch, then asks Bertie to touch his eyes and scar.
" 'We shall know each other now,' " he says ecstatically.
" 'We've become friends,' " he says afterwards to Isabel, "standing with his feet apart, like a strange colossus." He has achieved
complete self-realization, having extended the archetypal communion of sex to friendship. But Bertie is shattered: "his insane
reserve broken in. He was like a mollusc whose shell is broken." [48] The last sentence explains Clifford's characterization as
"one of the amazing crabs and lobsters" of the modern industrial world, "with shells of steel, like machines, and inner bodies of soft pulp."

As all Connie's faculties come alive, Clifford advances in
technical proficiency but regresses—in the wrong, dissociated
way—intellectually and emotionally. He spends his evenings at
the radio "with a blank entranced expression on his face, like a
person losing his mind." In the end Clifford, the tough busi-
nessman, finds his true sexual satisfaction in infantile volup-
tuousness, in the ministrations of the nurse Mrs. Bolton who
substitutes for the departed Connie.

> And when she sponged his great blond body, he would say the same:
> "Do kiss me!" and she would lightly kiss his body, anywhere, half in
> mockery. And he lay with a queer, blank face like a child, with a bit of
> the wonderment of a child. . . . And then he would put his hand into
> her bosom and feel her breasts, and kiss them in exaltation, the exalta-
> tion of perversity, of being a child when he was a man. [49]

It is because Clifford, no less than Connie, finds fulfillment
with a working-class partner that we need not pity him when

Connie leaves. Spurring Clifford on to success as Connie never did, Mrs. Bolton is the Magna Mater, the modern mother-wife who encourages sublimation.

The symbolic hyperbole alerts us to the emotional deprivation of what Yeats calls modern objective men; Clifford's development through antithesis illustrates Yeats's theory of the mask. The story of Connie and Mellors is at times artistically triumphant, at times merely discursive; but Clifford's story unfolds flawlessly as a procession of symbols from the original symbolic premise of his paralysis. The critics who complain about oversimplification in *Lady Chatterley's Lover* do not understand the book's modes; for simplification is what Lawrence worked for in revising the novel—he made Clifford always less and Mellors always more attractive. Like Shakespeare in the last plays, Lawrence, with the easy confidence of the master artist, swiftly recapitulates themes of his earlier work by diagraming characters and situations. The diagram of Clifford turns into tragicomic caricature because it must, like Dickens' later caricatures, bear the weight of an attack on the whole culture. (Clifford's motorized wheel chair, smashing its way through "blue encroaching hyacinths," is "sailing on the last voyage of our civilization!") [50] The symbolic satire of Clifford is the starkest rendering I know of the modern desexualization that leads to death in life.

Julian Moynahan, who has understood the book's modes, praises "the rich simplicity of its structural design," and shows how all England, past and present, is diagramed around three points—the feudal manor, Wragby Hall; the industrial village, Tevershall; and the wood, the remnant of Sherwood Forest, which has been despoiled by the wartime need for timber and the foul industrial air. The book also diagrams "two ways of knowing" [51]—that of the objective social world, Wragby-Tevershall, and that of the passional inner life, the wood. The book correspondingly divides, I would add, into two modes— the satiric, combining realism and symbolism; and the idyllic, turning sacramental. Connie, who moves between the two realms, enters the idyllic realm of the wood when, unknown to Mellors, she beholds him—alone, half-naked, washing—in "a visionary experience" that is Wordsworthian, except that she receives "the shock of vision in her womb." [52]

Their intercourses, as Frank Kermode has suggested, seem stages in a sacramental progress. Kermode sees "Connie's initiation into mystery [and rebirth] as having seven stages, like the seven stages in the [pagan] mystery-religion" that Lawrence, in his last "metaphysical" book *Apocalypse*, uncovers behind the Book of Revelation. [53] Mellors undergoes, I think, a parallel initiation and rebirth. Kermode does not describe the stages. There are nine intercourses; by combining the three unsuccessful intercourses into a single stage, we can count seven stages, but may prefer to keep the Dantesque nine.

The first two intercourses are failures; the activity, the orgasms are Mellors'. Connie gets no pleasure, but does learn to be passive instead of seeking her own pleasure. We should think of these intercourses as his failures, too; he, too, must learn how to love, for his previous sex life has been as rotten as Connie's. The gamekeeper of the final version is no full-blown primitive like Cipriano, but a sensitive, intelligent workingman, who having been exposed to the modern sickness, has chosen to regress, to seclude himself in the wood.

In the third intercourse, they achieve simultaneous orgasm because she feels the force of his desire and gives herself up to him. She experiences the flowing orgasm Kate has with Cipriano, and knows "another self . . . alive in her." It is with this other self that Connie recognizes, in her ride through Tevershall, the full depersonalizing horror of industrial England. The fourth intercourse is again a failure, because of his too hasty possession and her retreat into separateness. But when immediately afterwards, she meets him again with her other self, he is able to caress her, give her the necessary foreplay, and they achieve in their fifth intercourse a simultaneous orgasm which

is for her a "flood," revealing their archetypes: "the sons of god
with the daughters of men." Before the sixth intercourse, she
sees his phallus as an autonomous force, and hears their genitals
named John Thomas and Lady Jane. After their seventh intercourse, naked in the rain, they celebrate the "phallic marriage"
of John Thomas to Lady Jane by threading flowers in each
other's pubic hair (absurd if we do not read the scene sacramen-
tally). " 'I've never called him by any name: nor he me,' " Connie admits afterwards to her sister. " 'Unless we say Lady Jane
and John Thomas.' "

The terrible eighth intercourse is anal—"burning out the
shames, the deepest, oldest shames, in the most secret places,"
so that they may know each other completely, without reserve.
"What liars poets and everybody were!" Connie reflects afterwards. "They made one think one wanted sentiment." In
Lawrence's revision of the love tradition, there is no high or
low—the intensity of hell unfolds into the intensity of heaven.
Their ninth intercourse is accordingly paradisal. She has announced herself pregnant and says, in answer to his dismay
because he does not trust the future, " 'Be tender to [the child],
and that will be its future.' " So he is tender in intercourse to
her and the child; and she, "feeling the steam of tenderness
flowing in release from his bowels to hers, the bowels of com-
passion kindled between them," cries: " 'Oh, you love me! You
love me!' " Now she can use the word "love" that Mellors, like
Birkin, had banned as merely conventional. "As his seed sprang
in her, his soul sprang towards her too, in the creative act that is
far more than procreative" [54]—that is a leap, Lawrence had
written in the Hardy study, "into the unknown." [55] Connie and
Mellors complete Ursula and Birkin's story by conceiving a
child.

As in Dante, they arrive at a still higher spaceless stage
beyond even the ninth heavenly circle. "I love the chastity now
that it flows between us," Mellors writes after they have separated to secure their divorces. Such chastity differs from the cold

chastity of separated egos. Like Teresa and Ramón, unlike
March and Henry, they are together even in apartness. "I believe" only, Mellors writes, " in the little flame between us." He
repeats the Hardy study's triune pattern of Male-Female united
by Holy Ghost when he adds: "It's my Pentecost, the forked
flame between me and you." The Christian virtues have been
reconstituted in a new way. "The great words" that Connie says
"were cancelled for her generation," [56] "the higher emotions"
that Lawrence says are "strictly dead" [57]—all these have been
reconstituted because Lawrence begins again, in the Wordsworthian manner, from the biological roots of existence. When
Mellors writes that chastity "is the peace that comes of fuck-
ing," [58] he offers his equivalent to the Biblical "peace which
passeth understanding." The religion of love can go no farther.
Lawrence despised the religion of art; but a watered-down
amalgam of the two is the working religion of modern cultivated
people who are neither Communists nor Catholics, who do not
believe in any objective orthodoxy.

One can hardly consider such a book as this immoral. One
might consider the last sentence I have quoted bathetic. One
might object that Lawrence tries to derive from sexuality more
than it can possibly yield. The only answer is this—that
Lawrence, like Yeats with the artistic process, considers the
transformations of identity involved in successful sexuality
equivalent to the transformations of identity involved in religious conversion.

Chapter 9
THE RAINBOW:
THE WAY
THROUGH
HOPE

Although *Lady Chatterley's Lover* ranks below *Sons and Lovers* (1913), *The Rainbow* (1915) and *Women in Love* (1920) because it is smaller in scope—its modes of satire and idyll precluding the usual novelistic depth—it nevertheless ranks among Lawrence's four major novels because it so explicitly completes his thought. *The Rainbow* and *Women in Love* are the great novels because in them Lawrence not only expands his discovery in *Sons and Lovers* of the century's new subject matter—the unconscious and physical sexuality—but he evolves new techniques for articulating the underlife and for using it to give value to physical sexuality. Lawrence never advanced technically beyond these two novels. He was able in *The Rainbow* and *Women in Love* to articulate what in *Sons and Lovers* had been mere mystery, because he had come to understand the connection between sexuality and identity. Lawrence was unable to solve the problem of Paul Morel's unsatisfactory relations with the too spiritual Miriam and the too physical Clara until he had, in his own life, carried through successfully the relation with Frieda, and until he began like Yeats to understand his own perceptions by systematizing them, by inferring from them a world-view. Only so could he find the symbols necessary for articulating the underlife.

Lawrence formulated his system or "metaphysic" in two small books—*Study of Thomas Hardy* (1914), written while he was preparing the final draft of *The Rainbow*; and *The Crown* (1915), written while he was working on *Women in Love*. Together these two books make a partial equivalent to *A Vision* (the full equivalent would include also such later books as *Fantasia of the Unconscious* and *Apocalypse*). Lawrence had already, in *The Wedding Ring*, the penultimate draft of *The Rainbow*, projected his new sense of "carbon" identity described in the letter of 5 June 1914, when in July he announced his plan "to write a little book on Hardy's people." [1] He began *Study of Hardy* in September, soon after the penultimate draft came back from the publisher, and had almost finished it in late November when he began to rewrite his novel. Mark Kinkead-Weekes, in his illuminating essay on the drafts of *The Rainbow* and *Women in Love*, suggests that "the *Study* took Lawrence [far] beyond *The Wedding Ring*." [2]

What was accomplished in *Study of Hardy?* Lawrence saw how Hardy, by posing characters against portentous landscape, evolved an imagery for rendering the impersonal forces operating within and between people, for revealing archetypal identity. Lawrence advances beyond Hardy by diagraming the structure of Hardy's archetypes, by analyzing them as strung across the conflict of impersonal forces, across a series of corresponding antitheses that compose the structure of outer and inner worlds. These corresponding antitheses—Female-Male, Body-Spirit, Law-Love, Inertia-Motion, Dark-Light—are subsumed by God the Father on the Female side and God the Son on the Male side, with the Holy Ghost symbolizing the reconciliation necessary to a coherent identity. Lawrence solved Paul Morel's problems with his mother and his girl friends by discovering that sexual conflict was not only necessary but was reconcilable through a coherence of identity structure achievable through love. Marriage, the supreme aim, achieves for the couple and the race the reconciliation of opposites symbolized by the rainbow in the novel of that name. As in Yeats, the psychology of conflicting principles leads to characterizations of historical periods, since each culture "marries" a god opposite in principle to itself. "It is," Lawrence wrote a decade before Yeats published A Vision, "as if life were a double cycle, of men and women, facing opposite ways, travelling opposite ways, revolving upon each other." [3]

Lawrence connects Hardy's natural archetypes with cultural archetypes. He may have made the connection through his study, at the time he was rereading Hardy, of Greek tragedies. The Greek tragedies must have confirmed Lawrence's growing sense of archetypal identity, especially since he read along with them the commentators like Jane Harrison and Gilbert Murray who, following Frazer, made him aware that the personae of Greek tragedy started as seasons or natural forces that got embodied in the ritual songs and dances as animals and gods. Lawrence seems to conceive personae as carrying within them the rhythmic recollection of their ritual origins when he says, in the letter on "carbon" identity, that the characters of The Wedding Ring "fall into the form of some other rhythmic form." Greek sculpture shows even more markedly "the eternal stillness . . . under all life. . . . the great impersonal which never changes and out of which all change comes." [4]

"The marriage bed is the symbol of the solved antinomy," wrote Yeats, for whom marriage had no particular importance.[5] Lawrence instead works out in Hardy the theology of marriage that accounts for The Rainbow's Biblical quality as a family saga, in which marriages and begettings have providential significance—in which Tom Brangwen declares at Anna's wedding that " 'for a man to be a man, it takes a woman. . . . And for a woman to be a woman, it takes a man,' " so the only complete identity is a "married soul." [6] We see how far the theology goes when in *Hardy* Lawrence declares the sex act merely functional: the man seeks the female principle through the particular woman, and the woman seeks the male principle through the particular man. Since everything "is either male or female or both," we seek in all things our complement in order to find the final "unrealized complement" we call God. Such union also serves the creative evolution of the race:

> In love, a man, a woman, flows on to the very furthest edge of known feeling, being, and out beyond the furthest edge. . . . It is so arranged that the very act which carries us out into the unknown shall probably deposit seed for security to be left behind. But the act, called the sexual act, is not for the depositing of the seed. It is for leaping off into the unknown.

The sense of beyondness or strangeness is the sign in *The Rainbow* of a right sexual relation, a sign that the couple, and through the couple the race, are enlarging the range of consciousness, moving toward new modes of being.

With an acuity that throws light on both novelists, Lawrence interprets Hardy's *Tess* and *Jude* as Lawrencean novels *manqués—manqués* because Hardy stands morally with society against the individual while privately sympathizing with the individual. Lawrence's novels make overt Hardy's suppressed sympathy, in that the individual's need for self-realization is the standard of judgment. Lawrence explains the theme of his own novels when he declares that "The final aim of every living thing . . . is the full achievement of itself," and that Hardy's novels are about the struggle for identity: Hardy's "heroes and heroines . . . are struggling hard to come into being. . . . the first and chiefest factor is the struggle into love. . . . The *via media* to being, for man or woman, is love, and love alone." [7]

In interpreting Hardy's novels, Lawrence rewrites them in the style of *The Rainbow;* for he *analyzes* an underlife that Hardy merely suggests through the action as mysterious. *The Rainbow*'s technical innovation is the switch from presented action to analytical narration. Lawrence's description of his new novel, in early 1913, actually refers, as George H. Ford discovered, to an early draft of *The Lost Girl*. [8] But since the description suits *The Rainbow* so much better than *The Lost Girl*, one can only conclude, using Lawrencean psychology, that Lawrence was unconsciously describing the novel he *wanted* to write and had not realized in his first try at *The Sisters* (the single-novel original of *The Rainbow* and *Women in Love*), which seemed at the time a mere pot-boiler. "It's great," he wrote, "so new, so really a stratum deeper than I think anybody has ever gone, in a novel. . . . It is all analytical—quite unlike *Sons and Lovers*, not a bit visualised." A little later he wrote of *The Sisters:* "It is so different, so different from anything I have yet written, that I do nothing but wonder what it is like." [9]

Sons and Lovers is almost always visualized or presented. The unconscious is mainly suggested through the external action, but sometimes bubbles up into consciousness. "There was something between them [Paul and his mother] that neither dared mention." The line between conscious and unconscious is always maintained, even when at moments the mystery is dispelled—when Paul, for example, momentarily understands his Oedipal attachment to his mother: " 'I shall never meet the right woman while you live.' " Should Paul have such Freudian understanding, or is it there for the reader's benefit? Sometimes we are surprised to learn that material presented for the reader's benefit as though it were conscious is really unconscious, as when Paul reflects that Clara hardly exists for him as an individual: " 'She represents something, like a bubble of foam represents the sea. But what is *she?* It's not her I care for.' Then, startled by his own *unconscious* thoughts. . . ." [10] Such confusion—rising from a need to explain the underlife not sanctioned by the book's method—is one technical problem. Another is that penetration cannot go very deep or last long enough for precision, when suggestion is the only device for evoking unconsciousness.

In *The Rainbow*, Lawrence solves these problems by directly describing and analyzing a world where the unconscious is as manifest as the conscious. There is no mystery for us or the characters. The penetration goes deepest—deeper than realistic action could suggest with precision—in scenes like the one in which Ursula reverts through identification with the moon to the narcissistic female self-sufficiency that ruptures the unconscious connection between her and Skrebensky as they dance together. Suddenly "Ursula was aware of some influence looking in upon her," of a "great, white watching." The moon figures as the egoistic self-consciousness that separates.[11] When the music ceases, breaking the spell of unconscious connection, Ursula desires not Skrebensky but the moon—in other words, herself: "She wanted the moon to fill in to her, she wanted more, more communion with the moon, consummation. But Skrebensky put his arm round her, and led her away. He put a big, dark cloak round her." Skrebensky cannot consciously understand that the moon is his enemy; yet we are not told, as we would be in *Sons and Lovers*, what he *thinks* he is doing in shielding her from the moon. Nor are we told about Ursula's *conscious* thoughts when "her naked self was away there beating upon the moonlight," longing "for the coolness and entire liberty and brightness of the moon. . . . for the cold liberty to be herself, to do entirely as she liked." The dichotomy between conscious and unconscious has been resolved through metamorphosis; the characters are meeting at a phase of identity where unconsciousness is completely manifest, where what they *think* they are thinking and doing is no different from what they *are* thinking and doing. They are meeting as opposing principles, as natural elements of the scene—darkness and light, with her destructive light solidifying as white metal and salt.

When we finally get a few words of ordinary dialogue, the words derive their meaning entirely from the underlife:

> "Don't you like me to-night?" said his low voice, the voice of the *shadow* over her shoulder. She clenched her hands in the dewy *bril-*

liance of the moon . . . . A strange rage filled her, a rage to tear things asunder. Her hands felt destructive, like *metal blades* of destruction. "Let me alone," she said.

They resume dancing, but their "two wills" are no longer, as in the previous dance, "locked in one motion." He desires to overcome her; she remains "cold and unmoved as a pillar of *salt*." Her passivity is lethal: "She was bright as a piece of moonlight, *as bright as a steel blade*, he seemed to be clasping a *blade* that hurt him." Cornstacks (wheatstacks) glistening in moonlight recall the scene in which Ursula's parents sealed their union by stacking corn harmoniously through contrary movements. Now all is inharmonious. He feels himself contract into a dark bead, as she looms large, a kind of destructive moon goddess, perhaps also Cybele wielding her castrating blade, or a Maenad who tears men apart:

> She stood for some moments out in the overwhelming luminosity of the moon. She seemed a beam of gleaming power. She was afraid of what she was. Looking at him, at his shadowy, unreal, wavering presence a sudden lust seized her, to lay hold of him and tear him and make him into nothing. Her hands and wrists felt immeasurably hard and strong, like blades. He waited there beside her like a shadow which she wanted to dissipate, destroy as the moonlight destroys a darkness.

It is at the phase of "carbon" identity, where characters are in this instance reduced to natural elements, that they become archetypes. Ursula turns destructive because Skrebensky, with his "wavering presence," has not got sufficient strength of being to match her strength.

To net her moonlight in shadow, he kisses her. Through the medium of the kiss, the struggle goes on between his darkness, turned "allotropically" into warm soft iron, and her moonlight turned into salt and cold steel; each tries to achieve identity at the other's expense:

> But hard and fierce she had fastened upon him, cold as the moon and burning as a fierce salt. Till gradually his warm soft iron yielded, yielded, and she was there fierce, corrosive, seething with his destruc-

tion, seething like some cruel, corrosive salt around the last substance of his being, destroying him, destroying him in the kiss. . . . She had triumphed: he was not any more.

All this, while they dance, look at cornstacks, kiss—do loverlike things; yet we are not made aware of disparity between surface and depth, the view is from below. Lawrence requires not only narration (*The Rainbow* is one of the most *narrated* novels in English), but also an elaborate symbolism to render the underlife at such length and with such precisely articulated variety. It might be argued that Lawrence places too heavy a burden on his peculiar vocabulary, that it cannot do all the work of presentation. But his method—though it violates the objectivist standards of Flaubert and Joyce, and precariously skirts the plunge from overstatement into bathos—succeeds, because the symbols rendering the underlife follow so consistently from principles about the structure of identity set forth from the beginning. This rigorous theoretical consistency gives the book its own kind of objectivity.

When after the kiss Ursula returns "to herself," to her "daytime consciousness," we are returned to the world of surface and depth, the world of *Sons and Lovers* where surface masks depth. Ursula is ashamed of that other destructive self; it is not her, she is "good . . . loving." She plays the "adoring slave" to restore Skrebensky's male "shell"; but his "core" is dead—"she had broken him." [12] Lawrence is still concerned with the disparity between surface and depth; but the view in *The Rainbow* is from below, where reality is firmly located.

Surface and depth come together when in church the next day Ursula finds in the story of Noah the novel's central symbols—flood and rainbow—and realizes she has now encountered areas of experience not covered by the Biblical story's moralistic surface. She is repeating her mother's experience in the Gothic cathedral, where the gargoyles seemed to embody a knowledge not included in the absolute Christian scheme. Such repetitions with a difference make a pattern in *The Rainbow*.

Anna's and Ursula's repudiations do not discredit, they reinforce
the validity of the rainbow as a symbol of continuity and
change—the continuity of male-female union under the changing conditions of expanding consciousness and sharpening individuality.

The flood theme begins with the name of the Brangwen
farm—the Marsh, a breeding-place made fertile by corruption,
by the cycles of death and rebirth. Hence the rainbow theme
recurs after the flood at the Marsh that washes away Tom
Brangwen and the old order he represents. But we are made
aware at Tom's funeral that his son, Tom, is corrupt, probably
homosexual. The younger Tom is later called "marshy,"
suggesting an unfertile modern regression.

The pattern of Brangwen identity is established in the opening paragraphs, where we are told that whenever the uncounted
generations of traditional earthbound Brangwens lifted their
heads from the fields they looked up to "the church-tower at
Ilkeston in the empty sky." Brangwen identity is determined by
the conflict between rootedness and transcendence, a conflict
resolved by a third principle, that of an identity evolving
through the generations: "There was a look in the eyes of the
Brangwens as if they were expecting something unknown, about
which they were eager." The men are absorbed by organic connection with the female earth, by "blood-intimacy": "the pulse
of the blood of the teats of the cows beat into the pulse of the
hands of the men." But the women look toward the male tower
and aspire to a life of culture and spirit. The men, craving darkness, are "dark"; the women, craving light, are "light." [13]
Lawrence is generalizing from the cultural differences between
his sensuous coal-mining father, who came up black at evening
from underground work, and his blue-eyed refined middle-class
mother.

The opening of the mines around 1840 disrupts the age-old
balance between rootedness and transcendence. We are told
about the Brangwen couple of this period, the last of the tradi-

tional Brangwens, that she could rail at him, yet warm "his belly with pride and male triumph"—that they could play out with security the conflict necessary to a good marriage, because his male superiority was assured him by the tradition they both accepted. "They were two very separate beings, vitally connected, knowing nothing of each other, yet living in their separate ways from one root." [14] It is this combination of strangeness and connection, easily achieved in an era of Law when individuality and self-consciousness are rudimentary, that Birkin and Ursula try to recover in an era whose over-articulated individuality and self-consciousness produce isolation without the sexual magic of strangeness.

With Tom, who belongs to the first postindustrial Brangwen generation and is the first Grammar School–educated Brangwen, the balance already shifts toward transcendence, abstraction, idealization. He has to fabricate the strangeness necessary for love by choosing a foreign noblewoman who embodies an ideal already fabricated in his head. A sexual adventure with a girl whose escort was a foreigner of aristocratic demeanor led to dreams that associated sex with the beyondness of foreign aristocracy. His meeting with Lydia, an unknown woman on the road, is therefore a recognition: " 'That's her,' he said involuntarily."

Yet his courtship and marriage are mainly traditional. He feels with the expectancy of the Brangwens that "It was coming, he knew, his fate"; he waits "like a creature evolving to a new birth." In the book's most lyrical passage, Tom one evening is carried by a pollinating March wind to propose to Lydia. On the way he "did not think of anything, only knew that the wind was blowing." Looking at nightfall into Lydia's illuminated kitchen, he figures in the Brangwen pattern as dark; while she and her little girl by her first marriage figure as light. Mother and daughter, too, are transformed by the wind into agents of the life force, passively expectant: "Then a great burst of wind, the mother seemed to have drifted away, the child's eyes were black and dilated." When Tom enters, Lydia "did not know him, only she knew he was a man come for her." She accepts him "impersonally." [15] With that word Lawrence reverses the Western tradition of personal idealized love. The whole passage—with its moving portrayal of communications mightier than love talk, because stemming from a phase of identity in touch with external forces—should help us understand Birkin's perorations against "love."

Tom and Lydia's marriage is still traditional in that the husband's supremacy is not contested and there exists the strangeness necessary for good sex. But this deliberately sought strangeness is also a problem, because Lydia's tales of her feudal Polish childhood show she belongs to a world Tom cannot understand. Their differences would have developed into a clash of ideas if Tom were conscious of ideas as an issue. Instead their marriage stands midway between that of the next generation, where ideas will figure in marital conflict, and that of the traditional Brangwens who played out the conflict necessary to marriage within the same framework of received ideas.

Since it is natural that with Lydia's pregnancy Tom and Lydia's daughter Anna should feel rejected, Tom's solution is also natural. The night the new baby is born he takes the sobbing Anna to the cow barn where, attuned to the rhythm of the cows' breathing, they seal a union with each other through their pantheistic sense of the One Life. "He seemed to be sitting in a timeless stillness. What was he listening for? He seemed to be listening for some sound a long way off, from beyond life." Once again we see the pattern of rootedness and transcendence—the sound of the god rising from the sound of the animal.

The love between Tom and Anna, and the portrait of Anna as all light, motion, incandescence, must be the most beautiful account of father-daughter love and the most beautiful portrait of a child in the English novel. Lawrence's remarkable achievement is that he celebrates a child and love of a child without sentimentality. He avoids sentimentality because he pitches the child's life at the appropriate phase of identity; he treats her as a kind of energy. Sentimentality comes from treating as individual and rational emotions that are impersonal and generated by external forces.

When sexually exhilarating strangeness turns for Tom and Lydia into indifferent estrangement, Lydia—who like all the Brangwen women takes the initiative in important matters—accuses Tom of coming to her for sex perfunctorily: " 'I want you to know there is somebody there beside yourself.' " Conflict brings them alive to each other. " 'My love!' she said. And she put her arms round him as he stood before her, round his thighs." Her granddaughter Ursula will touch Birkin that way at the source of male power, and with the same effect: both women release the mystery of their men's manhood and consequently of their own womanhood. Lydia's

> hands on him seemed to reveal to him the mould of his own nakedness, he was passionately lovely to himself. . . . He looked down. Her face was shining, her eyes were full of light. . . . She was the awful unknown. . . . She was now the transfigured, she was wonderful, beyond him.

She insists, however, on "his active participation, not his submission." He resists: "It was torture to him, that he must give himself to her actively, participating in her," but then he "began to flow towards her." They have achieved what Birkin will call star-equilibrium.

What is accomplished in this scene? Tom does not know Lydia any more precisely as an individual; but he has had restored to him the sense of her otherness and can now through touch, the most concrete of the senses, believe in his connection with her otherness. Whenever "she touched him, he knew her instantly, that she was with him, near him, that she was the gateway and the way out, that she was beyond, and that he was travelling in her through the beyond." Tom's later vision of himself and his wife as "two little, upright figures walking across this plain, whilst the heavens shimmered and roared about them," [16] expresses the book's Biblical or Providential vision. Tom and Lydia have met at the phase of identity that makes them agents of evolution, with Anna, their inheritor, secure beneath the rainbow arch formed by their union in opposition. The rainbow symbolizes the evolutionary principle in marriage, transcendence within rootedness. It is a rounded, earth-returning arch uniting heaven and earth.[17] It represents a promise of renewal.

While creating problems, the admixture of self-consciousness makes Tom and Lydia's marriage a spiritual advance over the traditional Brangwen marriages. Their marriage has a more beneficial effect on Ursula than her parents' marriage, because Anna and Will were unable to surmount problems of self-consciousness and individuality greater than those of Tom and Lydia's generation. If Ursula and Birkin surmount their generation's still more formidable problems, this marriage will, we are to understand, make an advance over Tom and Lydia's.

For Tom it was the woman; for Anna it is the man—her cousin Will Brangwen, a lace designer from Nottingham—who brings the air of beyondness. But after marriage Will disappoints her by investing all his emotions in the marriage, sustaining no independent life beyond her. She therefore takes upon herself the evolutionary function by producing children with religious fervor. Will agrees that his work, civilization, "the whole monstrous superstructure of the world of to-day" leads nowhere, that the future is with Anna, the child and his "new, strange" faith in the future. She feels the same "satisfaction" in relinquishing "the adventure to the unknown. She was bearing her children." Yet they both feel transcendence in their rootedness. She is, as the chapter title has it, "Anna Victrix," because she alone "was a door and a threshold" to the future, "she herself" [18] and not the two of them together. The scene in which the pregnant Anna dances naked for her matriarchal deity signals a historical reversal; it is the obverse of the Biblical scene, which haunts Lawrence's imagination, of David dancing before the ark of his patriarchal God. Anna's dance—which Anna and Will understand, in the unconscious way characters in *The Rainbow* understand everything, as nullifying the male—establishes the female self-sufficiency Ursula inherits and has to overcome for success in love.

Anna and Will's marriage is the most sexually vibrant of the unions in *The Rainbow* and *Women in Love*, alternating continually between hate and love; the hate makes for passionate sex and the sex, because Will likes Anna to play the active role, leads back to hate. Anna and Will's section is the most internalized, and therefore the most *narrated*, of the three sections—perhaps because theirs was the first generation to retreat from society, to consider sexuality a purely private affair, whereas Ursula's generation already seeks a new way back to connection with the general life. Many readers are confused, because they don't know how to judge this marriage or whom to blame for the quarrels. Although less successful than Tom and Lydia's, Anna and Will's marriage can't be called *bad*; it has to be judged historically, since marriages grow progressively worse in *The Rainbow* and *Women in Love* as the times become less conducive to love.

Nor can blame be assigned where the conflict is between opposite identities. The dark-light symbolism is sharpest in this section. Will is "dark"—irrational, conservative, disposed to lose the self in oceanic feelings, religious and artistic; Anna is "light"—rational, boldly forward-looking, ego-centered. They could not make the necessary union out of conflict—"they were opposites not complements"—because the culture could no longer help them define their sexual roles. Instead of being sexually fruitful, their marital conflict has become ideological.

Anna respects neither Will's religious convictions, nor his

hobby of woodcarving, nor his breadwinning work as lace designer. She did not honor "what he represented," because "he
did not know himself what he represented"—the culture did not
tell him. Having destroyed Will's religious beliefs with her rationalist jeering, Anna "knew she had won. And an ashy desolation came over her." [19] For she does not want to win; she wants
him to hold up his end of the marital conflict. "Unless a
woman is held, by man, safe within the bounds of belief,"
Lawrence explains elsewhere, "she becomes inevitably a destructive force. . . . Unless a man believes in himself and his
gods, *genuinely* . . . his woman will destroy him." [20] If as
Birkin says there is only love to turn to in a world without God,
then woman, unhappily for herself, reigns supreme, since man
is beholden to her for his birth and fulfillment. Anna hates
Will, "because he depended on her so utterly," uses her, in the
book's recurrent metaphor, as ark in the flood. Lawrence takes
us to the heart of the late Victorian situation by showing how
the crisis of faith accounts for the rise of feminism and aestheticism. Will clings to religious *feeling* through a Ruskinian attachment to Gothic architecture and to church ritual and
music. When Anna attacks his woodcarving of Adam and Eve
as antifeminist because Adam is bigger than Eve, Will destroys
the panel and gives up woodcarving.

With male supremacy no longer taken for granted, every sexual relation becomes a contest for power; and we see with Anna
and Will the beginning of the sadomasochism that increasingly
characterizes every union except Ursula and Birkin's. In the
"Cathedral" chapter, we see how the Brangwen male attachment to the womblike earth appears as Will's attachment to the
womblike cathedral; while Anna sees beyond Christianity. With
her mockery of religion, Anna in this chapter deals the final
blow to Will's faith, reducing him to a mere attendant upon her
pregnancies.

Anna and Will's marriage is finally revivified in a way contrary to Tom and Lydia's, but which also creates a new

"strangeness." Tom, in his restlessness, secretly visited his brother's middle-class bookish mistress; Will picks up a working-class girl in Nottingham and tries to seduce her. He returns to Anna released from his "humble, good self." He seemed a cruel "stranger to her, seeking his own ends," and she, intrigued, felt herself "another woman, under the instance of a strange man." Their sex life revives through lust, without "tenderness" or "love," unashamed sensuous exploration "natural and unnatural"—the beginnings of what Lawrence in *Women in Love* calls "reduction." Such emotional disengagement restores Will's male confidence, releasing a new "purposive self" [21] that can at last attend to the outside life, to work. Will makes at this period big strides in his career.

In studying revisions of *The Rainbow*, Charles L. Ross has found that the last two chapters of the Will-Anna section, the chapters on the cathedral and their revived sex life, received the latest and most extensive revisions. The revisions emphasized the antagonism toward Will behind Anna's mockery of religion and Will's retort through their changed sex life. Having lost God, Will had to find a new absolute in sexuality. Lawrence carried back from the later Ursula-Skrebensky episodes the vocabulary of reduction, to show how through sadistic sexuality Will is able to regain his male dominance and thus function successfully in the world of work. [22] But Lawrence, we know from the context of *The Rainbow* and *Women in Love*, is not recommending Will's solution to the modern struggle between the sexes.

Will presents the most interesting example of Lawrence's steady concern with the relation between work and sex. Even Tom feels in the end that marriage rather than his farm work is all he has to show for his life. The value of work becomes a serious problem for the generations that have left the land. Gerald turns to Gudrun when work has ceased to satisfy. Ursula has to learn how to work and be a woman, but later Birkin feels it necessary for the sake of love that they resign their jobs. We

have seen how Clifford Chatterley makes progress as an industrialist while regressing sexually. Freud's criterion of psychological health, "Leiben und arbeiten," [23] the ability to love and
work, is also Lawrence's. But Lawrence is the more acute social
critic, for he understands that the energies and identity structure
required for modern work conflict with the energies and identity
structure required for love. Only in the organic society of *The
Plumed Serpent*, where the sexual act serves as model for values, is there no conflict between work and sex.

With Ursula, the first college-educated Brangwen and the first
Brangwen woman to hold a job, we arrive at the highest development of individuality and self-consciousness. Ursula, the first
Brangwen to consciously reject parents, is aware of a desire her
mother could hardly have articulated for the fulfillment of all
her faculties as an individual. Ursula fulfills the theme
Lawrence had projected in *The Sisters*: "woman becoming individual, self-responsible, taking her own initiative." [24] Yet in ac-
quiring from the Bible her ideal of manhood—"the Sons of
God who took to wife the daughters of men, these were such as
should take her to wife"—Ursula shows a desire to recover her
grandparents' kind of marriage. Ursula and Birkin will try to recover archetypal identity out of the most complex individuality
and the most unpropitious social circumstances.

Ursula begins her quest by mistaking young Anton Skrebensky, an officer in the Army Engineers, for one of these sons
of God. Skrebensky seems magical because he is the "stranger"
who brings her "a strong sense of the outer world," and because
in her attraction to him she is repeating her mother's attraction
to his titled father and Tom's love of a Polish noblewoman.
Ursula thinks that Skrebensky's aristocratic, military bearing
makes him a Lawrencean or existential aristocrat—that "his soul
stood alone," that he has "a nature like fate." She mistakes

rigidity—as Gudrun will later with Gerald—for strength of identity; whereas both men's rigidity disguises inner incoherence. The Bargeman episode alerts Ursula to the contrast between the Bargeman's easily flexible male confidence and Skrebensky's insecure conventionality, which brings out her destructiveness.

Skrebensky goes off to the Boer War, and Ursula, sexually unfulfilled, turns to education and career, to adventure in the "mysterious man's world . . . of daily work and duty." [25] Her work and female self-sufficiency affect her sex life; she is seduced by her admired teacher, Winifred Inger, a Cambridge B.A. (the passage excised from the Viking edition indicates consummation). [26] Ursula soon discovers, however, that Lesbianism is not for her. She introduces Winifred to her homosexual Uncle Tom; the two take to each other and marry.

The homosexuality of Tom and Winifred is analyzed as the product of an inorganic industrial society. The "real mistress" of Tom and the scientific Winifred "was the machine." Tom is mine manager in a dreary mining town, where the colliers, believing "they must alter themselves to fit the pits," have only the identity given them by their economic function. These workers, having lost identity and sexuality (the women get only what is left of the men after the pit has taken all that matters), are the walking dead. Having lost, through the breakdown of community and religion, their connection with the general life, these workers have lost the good of the body; just as Tom and Winifred have lost it through an analogous loss of connection, through the displacement of all life into their heads. Their heterosexual union will be as "marshy" and lizardlike, as regressive in the wrong way, as their homosexuality; for theirs is, we can infer from Lawrence's other work, the regressiveness of those who, like Clifford, allow the body to regress so the mind can progress.

In rejecting Tom and Winifred's "marshy, bitter-sweet corruption," Ursula, we are told, "grew up," presumably because she has recognized and overcome her own homosexuality. She revives, however, a misleading memory of Skrebensky as the way back to normal love: "as if, through him, in him, she might return to her own self." [27] She will have to live out the wrong kind of heterosexual love with Skrebensky before she can arrive at the right kind with Birkin.

In "The Man's World," Ursula learns as school teacher to put aside her real self and project a professional self in order to exert authority over her pupils. It may be because professional life requires false selves that Birkin and Ursula will resign their jobs, but Ursula's maturation at this stage requires increased control over empathy and sincerity. The point comes as a surprise in a chapter which otherwise is a triumph in turn-of-the-century realism—a style suitable to the subject matter, Ursula's development of a social self. She seems to have reconciled professionalism with sincerity when we see her teaching at the beginning of *Women in Love.*

On the one hand, Ursula rejects the suffragette movement, because she seeks a freedom more natural and complete than the vote could give her. On the other hand, she rejects marriage with the sensuously alive farmer Anthony Schofield, because the natural fulfillment he offers her would not give freedom either. He offers her rootedness without transcendence. "She was," she realizes, "a traveller." This is the key to Ursula's character. A Faustian heroine whose allegiance is to her own self-development, she moves through phases in which the other characters remain fixed. "In every phase she was so different," she reflects. "Yet she was always Ursula Brangwen." Here Lawrence takes his stand on the main issue of the identity question. He reconstitutes the romantic assertion that the self remains continuous in all its phases, by adding the idea that the self develops dialectically through sexual relations where the continuity of the self can be traced through the continuity of the dialectic.

So far Ursula has learned only what she is *not:* "she was full of rejection, of refusal. . . . That which she was, positively, was dark and unrevealed." Her sense of potentiality suggests an identity existing mainly in the darkness surrounding the small lighted area of her conscious self. She has inhabited this "lighted area" as though it were the whole world. "Yet all the time, within the darkness she had been aware of points of light, like the eyes of wild beasts, gleaming, penetrating, vanishing. And her soul had acknowledged in a great heave of terror only the outer darkness." She succumbs to the darkness, because she has had only *momentary*, ego-centered intuitions of it as "fenced out." The wild beasts are menacing when suppressed. Those who have "for a *moment* seen the darkness, saw it bristling with the tufts of the hyena and the wolf." But those who have "given up their vanity of the light," who have accepted the darkness within themselves, see the same beasts as fierce angels:

> saw the gleam in the eyes of the wolf and the hyena, that it was the flash of the sword of angels, flashing at the door to come in, that the angels in the darkness were lordly and terrible and not to be denied, like the flash of fangs.[28]

We find the same ambivalence in the stampeding horses of the last chapter. We have now two diagrams of identity: rootedness and transcendence, diagramed as dark earth and bright tower; and consciousness and unconsciousness, diagramed as concentric circles of light and darkness.

Having expanded her sense of identity to encompass the darkness, Ursula has only to articulate the philosophy of identity evolved from her biological studies to be ready to confront Skrebensky's quite opposite sense of identity—his sense of the conscious as something to be locked off from, protected against the unconscious. Ursula concludes from her study of unicellular organisms that the mystery of life is the mystery of identity. Life is distinguished from nonlife in appearing from the start as an organism whose purpose is "to be itself." We now know that the body's immune system functions according to this principle of cellular identity. In his book on cellular immunology called *Self and Not-Self,* Sir MacFarlane Burnet confirms Ursula's insight: "The need and the capacity to distinguish between what is acceptable as self and what must be rejected as alien is the evolutionary basis of immunology." [29] This self-realizing purpose, Ursula speculates is not mere "self-preservation" but "a consummation, a being infinite. Self was a oneness with the infinite." As in Yeats, "To be oneself was a supreme, gleaming triumph of infinity."

Skrebensky returns from South Africa at this point, when Ursula is prepared to recognize the antipathy that accounts for their physical attraction to each other. She discovers his rigidity: "He seemed made up of a set of habitual actions," and his fear of his unconscious: "His desires were so underground. . . . all must be kept so dark, the consciousness must admit nothing." The obscurity of his desires frightens and excites her. Yeats praised Lawrence for discovering the principle that physical love derives from spiritual hate—without realizing that Lawrence was not recommending such a relation.

Like Gerald, Skrebensky associates sensuality with oblivion. Both men have the heroic qualities that would seem to signal inner strength rather than weakness. Lawrence is attributing the falsification of the signal to cultural change; he is saying that the hero has become obsolete because incapable of development, that he appears in our time as the mechanical man—the industrialist or engineer. Ursula plays out with Skrebensky a sadomasochistic relation like that of Gudrun with Gerald. The difference is that Ursula has already passed Skrebensky in self-development; whereas Gudrun is locked in with Gerald at the same phase of identity. We have only glimpses of Gudrun in *The Rainbow,* but we are told that unlike Ursula she was "inalterable underneath." The sisters are in many ways alike; the main difference between them is Ursula's capacity for self-development.

Ursula and Skrebensky disagree ideologically along lines parallel to their antithetical identities. He believes in conventional abstractions like army, nation, Empire; she is antimilitary, anti-imperialist, judging only from the standpoint of the individual. " 'I'm against you, and all your old, dead things,' " she cries. "He felt cut off at the knees [castrated], a figure made worthless." Like her mother with her father, "she owned his body and enjoyed it with all the delight and carelessness of a possessor. But he had become gradually afraid of her body" [30] as destructive. Ursula destroys Skrebensky with words before she destroys him in intercourse. She belittles not only his intellectual powers, but also his sexual powers. A passage excised from the Viking edition reads:

> "Don't I satisfy you?" he asked of her, again going white to the throat.
> "No," she said. "You've never satisfied me since the first week in London. You never satisfy me now." [31]

It was in Rouen, where the Gothic cathedral put Ursula in touch with her father and her permanent self, that Skrebensky first understood the inevitable death of their relation and his own inner vacancy. Now he proposes marriage in order to possess her as a stay against "the horror of not-being"—always, as with Gerald's use of Gudrun and Clifford's of Connie—a wrong use of love. When she finally refuses, he weeps for his own inner desolation. Later she gives in, after she has failed her examinations for the B.A.; she takes the woman's way out. "So out of fear of herself Ursula was to marry Skrebensky" and sail for India. Unconsciously, however, she knows she will never sail. They both try to deceive themselves into believing that the hate that excites them sexually is love.

The African theme so conspicuous in *Women in Love* begins here with Skrebensky's account of the dark, fear-soaked sensuality he encountered in South Africa. Their sensuality is African, dissociated—with no lit clearing amid beast-filled forest darkness. It is through images confined to jungle beasts and darkness that Lawrence describes the movement toward their first intercourse, which takes place on a windy night recalling ironically the fertilizing wind that carried Tom to Lydia. Afterwards "her everyday self was just the same"; he had touched only her nighttime self. "It could not occur to her that anybody . . . should have anything at all to do" with the self beyond both of these, "her permanent self," the self Birkin will touch. Skrebensky in intercourse seems only the "dark, powerful vibration that encompassed her." [32] The price of sexual excitement is obliteration of their individuality.

Another time when they make love on the downs in a poetical intercourse that she, with her superior imagination, has stage-managed, she realizes he merely "served her. . . . it was as if the stars were lying with her. . . . It was not him." She is using him as an instrument for fathoming vicariously her own womb, for feeding the female self-sufficiency she displayed among the moonlit cornstacks, for continuing the pattern of their first meeting when she enjoyed the vision of herself in his eyes. Afterwards the gorgeous sunrise brings tears to her eyes— tears for the unsullied perfection of the glowing land. The beauty of the whole episode would make it difficult to judge this intercourse adversely, were it not that Skrebensky, echoing ironically Wordsworth's Westminster Bridge sonnet, thinks of the noisy smoking hell England will be in a few hours' time. The beauty suggests that the difference between what England ought to be and is parallels the difference between what the intercourse ought to be and is, and that the failure of industrial England has caused the failure of the intercourse. He has a vision of Ursula's permanent self and the rainbow promise for England and love toward which that self aspires: "Her face was wet with tears, very bright, like a transfiguration in the refulgent light." As in Rouen, he feels excluded by her permanent self; he is not the man with whom she can fulfill the promise.

Their final intercourse makes shatteringly clear their mutually destructive relation by crystallizing it as mythic, as a clash of "carbon" identities. Lawrence brings back the moon and the other images by which, in the dance and cornstacks scene, he established their "carbon" identities. She is moony, metallic, she speaks with the metallic voice of gulls and winged harpies; she fastens upon him a "fierce, beaked harpy's kiss" indicative of the vagina she will offer him in intercourse. Again he feels himself "fusing down to nothingness, like a bead"; again he is a shadow who leads her to "a dark hollow," but she insists on intercourse under full moonshine, her eyes fixed on the moon as if he were not there. Their intercourse is a fight, which she wins: "he gave way as if dead." Looking up he beholds another manifestation of her identity, this time of a temporary phase to be broken through: "Her face lay like an image in the moonlight, the eyes wide open, rigid. But out of the eyes, slowly, there rolled a tear, that glittered in the moonlight as it ran down her cheek." The moonlit weeping mask symbolizes her barren separateness. The contrast with the *inner* radiance and *warm* tears of the previous epiphany suggests that this latter self is at dead-end. She is more icon than person; and he flees "the horrible figure that lay stretched in the moonlight on the sands with the tears gathering and travelling on the motionless, eternal face," [33] as from a supernaturally destructive presence. Without a word spoken—exemplifying Lawrence's rendition of the underlife—they know it is over between them.

This wordless symbolical dramatization of unconscious states of being is a remarkable moment in *The Rainbow* and in the modern novel. The scene generates a pathos of nothingness and a projection of character through nonvital signs that were then new to the novel, though used a good deal since—notably by Beckett. This scene, the dance and cornstacks scene, and the great final scene with the horses stand out technically from the mainly *narrated* novel—pointing toward the more visualized, dramatic symbolical technique of *Women in Love*.

Discovering she is pregnant, Ursula recants, not knowing Skrebensky is to marry another woman. "Who was she to be wanting some fantastic fulfilment in her life?" She will humbly do her duty as Skrebensky's wife and mother of his children; she writes to tell him so. It is in this mood of false self-abnegation that she encounters the horses. They represent first of all the kicking up of her unconscious against such denial of her permanent self and its promise.

The horses offer another example of overdetermined modern symbolism in that, like Clifford's wound, they are really there and both confirm and cause a psychic state. One clue to their meaning is the earlier passage where Ursula feels "a yearning for something unknown. . . . And then, for personification, would come Skrebensky." [34] The horses signify that Skrebensky is the wrong personification; they represent the male principle that has still to be adequately manifested by a man who will prove to be a son of God.

In the beautiful passage of *Apocalypse* where Lawrence describes the horse as archetypal image—"Far back, far back in our dark soul the horse prances"—he reminds us that "The sons of God who came down and knew the daughters of men . . . had 'the members of horses.' " The horse represents the terror and mystery that links male potency to Godhead: "he links us, the first palpable and throbbing link with the ruddy-glowing Almighty of potence." [35] The horses' psychological meaning is explained in *Fantasia of the Unconscious:*

> A man has a persistent passionate fear-dream about horses. He suddenly finds himself among great, physical horses, which may suddenly go wild. Their great bodies surge madly round him, they rear above him, threatening to destroy him. At any minute he may be trampled down. . . . [Yet] the greatest desire of the living spontaneous soul is that this very male sensual nature, represented as a menace, shall be actually accomplished in life. [36]

Ursula learns from the horses awe of the male principle. She realizes that she had tried to create Skrebensky according to her own image, while annihilating him as a person. "It was not for her to create, but to recognize a man created by God" [37]—to recognize his otherness. The horses make her recognize her suppressed desire for the male principle she had feared and tried to conquer.

The best evidence for the horses' objective presence is that Ursula finally escapes by physical means. She climbs a tree and drops to the other side of a hedge through which she sees hooves cantering by; it is probably the physical exertion that brings on her miscarriage. Even with the horses there, however, the scene is hallucinatory since their significance is internally derived and since Lawrence refrains from saying until the end that Ursula *saw* them—she sees even then only flashing, possibly illusory fragments. One can't even be sure they are really menacing her. Lawrence establishes the horses as externalized internal presences. The landscape, too, is established as a psychic projection on to a real landscape, as a waving fluctuating country of psychic experience.

Ursula emerges suddenly from a menacing wood (a critical turning point like Dante's dark wood) onto a meadow. One recalls her earlier image of total psyche as a clearing in the forest (Keith Sagar connects the horses' flashing hooves with "the flash of eyes and fangs and swords of angels" in her forest image), and also Paul's question in *Sons and Lovers* whether Clara prefers the psychic movement from clearing into forest or from forest onto clearing.[38] The evidence here is that emergence from the wood is more frightening, because it represents the consciousness of unconsciousness. The horses on the meadow are eruptions into consciousness of unconscious forces: the horse "roams," says Lawrence in *Apocalypse*, "the dark underworld meadows of the soul." [39] The waving fluctuating fluidity of the rain-washed meadow dissolves distinctions between the two aspects of psyche. Ursula wants to retreat, to "beat her way back through all this fluctuation, back to stability." The horses represent the forces destructive of stability that she must encounter. But she panics *before* becoming aware of them; they confirm, though they seem to cause, her panic.

She becomes aware of them in the way she earlier became

aware of the moon, *before* she perceives them sensually—as a
psychic projection. "Suddenly she knew there was something
else. Some horses were looming in the rain, not near yet. But
they were going to be near." Her fear of the horses is always
apprehensive, always fear of what they *will* do; they are always
"beyond." She advances toward them, but "she did not want to
lift her face to them. She did not want to know they were
there." Without any tracing of sequence we are told that "the
horses had burst before her. . . . and drew on, beyond." This
is the pattern. The horses appear nearby blocking the way (the
way back to her old self); then they draw beyond, filling her
with apprehension of the way ahead. It would be impossible to
map movements that are disconnected miraculous manifestations.

As a solution to her fear, she evolves a purely imaginative
vision of them as apocalyptic horses: "she was aware of their red
nostrils flaming with long endurance, and of their haunches, so
rounded, so massive, pressing, pressing, pressing to burst the
grip upon their breasts, pressing for ever till they went mad,
running against the walls of time, and never bursting free."
Now they are destroyers, anarchic energies straining to shatter
all forms and boundaries; they are demonic in the salutary manner of Blake's tiger, Ursula's encounter with them parallels
Dante's salutary descent into hell.

The "crisis" comes when the way looks clear for her to pass
through a gate in the hedge "out to the high-road and the ordered world of man." But then, whether through her own fear
or because the horses block her, she loses heart. It is because
she finally eludes the horses through an act of will, by climbing
a tree, that she finally defeats them so that they seem "pathetic." After dropping to the other side of the hedge, she lies
like "a stone at rest on the bed of the stream, inalterable and
passive, sunk to the bottom of all change." She has regressed to
a state of pure being equivalent to inanimateness. As she staggers home afterwards, her nausea tells her she will find that

"bottom of all things" to which she sinks during the long illness around her miscarriage: "amid the ache of delirium, she had a dull firmness of being, a sense of permanency. . . . like the stone at the bottom of the river. . . . Her soul lay still and permanent, full of pain, but itself for ever."

This is the right kind of regression. For she has plumbed the depths, regressed through animal unconsciousness where her old self was destroyed by the form-shattering horses, to the rock-bottom permanent self from which she can—here Lawrence changes to an organic metaphor—like "acorns in February," with "shells burst and discarded," be reborn. "She was the naked, clear kernel thrusting forth the clear, powerful shoot, and the world was a by-gone winter, discarded, her mother and father and Anton, and college and all her friends, all cast off like a year that has gone by." [40] The whole episode, starting with the horses, is Lawrence's most detailed account of the rebirth of self that Birkin preaches and himself undergoes briefly after Hermione almost killed him. In her delirium Ursula claims a freedom of self-realization—freedom from family, society, tradition—that no earlier Brangwen could have conceived. The news, when she returns to consciousness, that she has lost Skrebensky and his child merely confirms the break with the past she has already accomplished psychologically. Now her fear of the future, expressed through the image of the horses, turns miraculously into confidence in the future, expressed through the image of the rainbow with which the book closes (this last chapter is called "The Rainbow").

The Rainbow is a profoundly optimistic novel, Lawrence's youthful hymn of praise for the unprecedented modern freedom of self-realization. Contrary to the writers who were already by 1915 devaluing the self and exposing its meagerness, Lawrence suggests the many-sided richness of the individual life and the limitless possibilities for self-development through the growth of sensuous and intellectual awareness. He expresses his essentially religious faith that men can—especially through sex, which is a kind of consciousness—become gods, attain an apex of perceptual power. Sex for Lawrence is a mode of knowing, knowing the mystery of the other person's identity and through it the potentiality of the race.

Since sex, identity and society come clustered in Lawrence's thought, Ursula's severance of sexual, family and social ties is presented as not selfish but prophetic of a coming liberation. Old forms of the self and old social forms are shattered in the same act, and this act produces new forms of self and society— because the act is intellectual: rebirth occurs through new concepts of self and society. The self dies, says Birkin, when we are " 'imprisoned within a limited, false set of concepts.' " [41]

Having discarded the husk of old ideas, Ursula conceives herself as "the kernel . . . free and naked and striving to take new root, to create a new knowledge of Eternity in the flux of Time"—a new world-view. Convalescing at her window, she can see the inexpressive colliers and their brittle wives as dead husks, showing "the swelling and the heaving contour of the new germination. In the still, silenced forms of the colliers she saw a sort of suspense, a waiting in pain for the new liberation." Like her ancestors she looks up at "the old church tower," rising now "in hideous obsoleteness above raw new houses." She is filled with nauseous despair, but then "saw a rainbow forming itself. . . . its pedestals luminous in the corruption of new houses on the low hill, its arch the top of heaven." She knows then that the faceless rigidity of the industrialized masses, the sign of their walking death, is the sign that society and personality must be reborn, "that the rainbow was arched in their blood and would quiver to life in their spirit. [42]

The church tower reminds us that Ursula has tried to maintain the Brangwen pattern of rootedness and transcendence only to discover that the roots are no longer communal, but must lodge for the time being in her own individuality. The rainbow reminds us that she has nevertheless maintained continuity, has increased the self-consciousness and freedom of the Brangwen identity in the face of an increasingly inimical industrialized world. *The Rainbow* remains nineteenth-century in its confidence in the inevitable evolution of consciousness and the inexhaustible fertility of the individual life, its endless capacity for change.

Chapter 10
WOMEN
IN LOVE:
THE WAY
THROUGH
DOOM

Not so *Women in Love*, which is mainly pessimistic, apocalyptic, "end-of-the-world" as Lawrence described it; he had thought of calling it *Dies Irae*. The war, he wrote in a letter of 1917, accounted for the difference between the two books. Although *The Rainbow* was rewritten during 1914–15, "the war" had not, Lawrence thought, "altered it, from its prewar statement. . . . I knew I was writing a destructive work, otherwise I couldn't have called it *The Rainbow*—in reference to the Flood." The book's "dark sensual . . . ecstasy," its "*consummation* in death," dissolves forms, bursts "the world-consciousness in every individual," in a way leading to rebirth. But the war yields "no Rainbow"; the death it brings is extinction. The still unpublished "sequel," *Women in Love*, written between 1913 and 1919, "actually does contain the results in one's soul of the war: it is purely destructive, not like *The Rainbow*, destructive-consummating." [1] Yet *Women in Love* contains almost no mention of the war nor any ostensible change from the prewar

328

setting of its earliest draft; its lack of temporal localization makes
it prophetic of a postwar world extending to our own time.

In calling *Women in Love* purely destructive, Lawrence ig-
nores the story of Ursula and Birkin which remains, like *The
Rainbow*, a story of development through the sensuality that is,
as Birkin puts it, " 'death to oneself—but . . . the coming into
being of another.' " [2] Ursula and Birkin are, however, exceptions; every other relation in the novel is destructive or at a
dead-end, offering no obvious hope of social regeneration. The
regenerative flood of *The Rainbow* has congealed into the snow,
the frozen cul-de-sac with which *Women in Love* closes;
Gerald's frozen corpse, representing the end of development, is
more typical than Birkin's final speculation over the next phase
of consciousness when it may be possible for a man to love
another man as well as a woman. Not until *Women in Love*
does Lawrence fully deal with the reconstitution of self; for it is
here that he first takes full measure of the twentieth-century
world in which the self is not only at dead-end, but engaged in
the process of taking itself apart—reducing itself, instead of
growing as in *The Rainbow* where the increasing problems of
the Brangwen generations come from their need to embrace
ever larger configurations of consciousness.

Women in Love traces the fortunes of two couples, who
through parallel incidents move in opposite directions—Ursula
and Birkin toward mutual fruition in love and marriage, Gudrun and Gerald toward mutual destruction. One might say that
Lawrence is distinguishing between the sexual attractions based
on love and hate, were it not that Ursula and Birkin contain
and transform the destructiveness that brings death to Gerald.
An idea that emerges toward *The Rainbow*'s end dominates
Women in Love—the idea that destructiveness can be necessary
and creative. Like Yeats, Lawrence came to believe that evil
must not be excluded.

He formulated this emerging idea in *The Crown* which, written in 1915 in response to the war, spells out the "metaphysic" of

Women in Love as the Hardy study spelled it out for *The Rainbow*. Lawrence carries over from *Hardy* the conflict between sensuality and spirit, called here Lion and Unicorn, but adds to it the conflict between the two streams of creation and dissolution; so that the processes of sexual union and identity-making now take place across a double dialectic:

> While we live, we are balanced between the flux of life and the flux of death. All the while our bodies are being composed and decomposed. But while every man *fully* lives, all the time the two streams keep fusing into the third reality, of real creation.[3]

Freud arrives at a similar distinction in *Beyond the Pleasure Principle* (1920), where he comes to see life as moving "with a vacillating rhythm" between expansive erotic instincts and reductive death instincts that want to return to original inanimateness. Now, writes Freud, "we describe the opposition as being, not between ego instincts and sexual instincts but between life instincts and death instincts."[4] To live fully, Lawrence says, to fuse the two streams, one has to change. "But once we fall into the state of egoism, we cannot change. The ego, the self-conscious ego remains fixed, a final envelope around us. . . . And as we can't be born, we can only rot."[5] This explains the difference between the two couples in *Women in Love*.

Birkin expounds the doctrine of the two streams in "Water-Party" where, inspired by the smell of a marsh, he unwittingly gives new meaning to the name of the Brangwen farm by describing the seething " 'river of darkness. . . . We always consider the silver river of life, rolling on . . . to heaven. . . . But the other is our real reality' " nowadays, when all our best achievements are born from " 'the black river of corruption.' " When Ursula asks whether she and Birkin are also " 'fleurs du mal' " since she doesn't feel so, he admits he doesn't " 'feel as if we were, *altogether*' " but can't as yet say why. The difference will prove to be their capacity to be reborn and thus turn dissolution (their destructive sexual habits—hers with Skrebensky, his with Hermione) into creation. To her protest, " 'You *want* us to be deathly,' " he answers, " 'I only want us to *know* what we are.' " [6]

This is partly the book's moral, that one has to know the worst about one's self, recognize one's own destructiveness. Gerald's father is deficient in such self-knowledge; so in a more sophisticated way is Hermione, who praises the unconsciousness she suppresses: her tranced manner indicates her suppressed murderousness. Gerald, though he does what he wants in sex and business, cuts off consciousness from unconsciousness. Although bold in action, Gerald is timid intellectually; he dares not allow his concepts to catch up with his desires and actions. He believes in doing as you like but preserving the *forms* of self, thought, society. *The Crown*, however, teaches:

> It is no use trying merely to modify present forms. The whole great form of our era will have to go. And nothing will really send it down but the new shoots of life springing up and slowly bursting the foundations. . . . We can but fight for the life that grows in us.

Make love not revolution, Lawrence is saying. For the transformation of identity involved in successful love will bypass the old society and prepare the new one. Gerald's ice-death corresponds to petrification of the old forms; while Ursula and Birkin, who seem selfish in withdrawing from society for the sake of love, are actually preparing the ground for a new society. *The Crown* also suggests another way to achieve a new identity and a new society—by giving one's self up to the corruption of the age, so that the ego dissolves by rotting. "The road of corruption leads back to one eternity. The activity of utter going apart has, in eternity, a result equivalent to the result of utter coming together." [7]

The shocking implication is that Gudrun may actually be doing well, or at least the best possible thing for her, in going on from the blondly heroic Gerald to the repulsive dwarf

Loerke; for with Loerke she will experience those final stages of reduction that Gerald balks at. With all his murderous desires, Gerald is still too fine or too conventional to break out of the closed shell of the Christian conception. Hence his death beneath a crucifix half-buried in snow. He is unwilling to follow Birkin in recognizing their homosexual attraction to each other; he cannot complete the strangling of Gudrun but goes on to kill himself instead; he probably cannot practice the perversions necessary to her increasing frigidity. Gudrun, instead, is intellectually bold; and with Loerke—a Jew, a Boehmian, a "troll" whose name recalls the mischievous Norse devil Loki, a practitioner one gathers of manifold perversions—she can follow the implications of her desires beyond the Christian conception.

Loerke, whose machinelike sculptures designed for factories seem based on Futurist principles, carries to a culmination Gerald's technocratism and Gudrun's inorganically miniature sculptures of animals. Loerke also carries to a culmination Gerald and Gudrun's sadomasochistic sexuality, which derives from a mechanistic world-view. Gudrun responds masochistically to Loerke's statuette of the girl on the rigid stallion as she responded to Gerald on the mare (Gerald made his mare submit to mechanical force, but the stallion is machinelike). Loerke and Gudrun come together in the frank denial of love—a denial different from Birkin's, which is for the purpose of union; their denial is for the purpose of coldly manipulating analyzed sensations one by one.

In turning to Loerke, Gudrun renounces the obvious humanistic evolutionary purpose, the expansion of human capacities.

> But there *were* no new worlds, there were no more *men*, there were only creatures, little, ultimate *creatures* like Loerke. The world was finished now, for her. There was only the inner, individual darkness, sensation within the ego, the obscene religious mystery of ultimate reduction. . . . Of the last series of subtleties, Gerald was not capable.

Starting with the Brangwen pattern of rootedness and transcendence, Ursula discovered that rootedness must reside within herself. Now Gudrun turns the impulse to transcendence inward, using it to take herself apart, to regress instead of evolving. With Loerke she has reached "the rock-bottom of all life." [8] This rock-bottom, which after the experience of the horses produced Ursula's rebirth, leaves Gudrun to disintegrate further where she lies. In *Women in Love*, Lawrence came to understand that even the wrong kind of regression has its uses. If you can't defy the age, he is saying in this novel, if you can't shatter its forms through miraculous rebirth, then immerse yourself in it thoroughly, drink its poisons to the last drop and share its self-destruction. "The human soul," he wrote later, "must suffer its own disintegration, *consciously*, if ever it is to survive." [9] Through her alliance with Loerke, Gudrun fulfills the evolutionary purpose in the contrary destructive way.

For the characters who do not evolve, Lawrence employs in *Women in Love* a new style of static characterization. Having alluded to this style in the "carbon"-identity letter, he describes it in the Hardy study, where he says that there is no "development of personal action" in Hardy's characters: "it is all explosive." Each character has "a real, vital, potential self," which "suddenly bursts the shell of manner and convention and commonplace opinion, and acts independently, absurdly, without mental knowledge or acquiescence." [10] In *Women in Love*, the static characters unfold a potentiality totally given at the outset, usually through symbols emerging from the realistic portrayal— as in Gudrun's first impression of Gerald:

> In his clear northern flesh and his fair hair was a glisten like sunshine refracted through crystals of ice. . . . His gleaming beauty, maleness, like a young, good-humoured, smiling wolf, did not blind her to the significant, sinister stillness in his bearing, the lurking danger of his unsubdued temper. "His totem is the wolf," she repeated to herself.

The recognition sends her into a swoon of masochistic excitement (sexual excitement always derives in Lawrence from recognition of the archetype). Gudrun sees clean through to Gerald's ice-death, where the images of arctic wolf and Norse god return. When a few pages after Gudrun's impression we hear about Gerald's deficiency of being, about the accidental murder of his brother that marks him psychologically as Cain, and about his latently homosexual attraction to Birkin, we have potentially the whole of Gerald—his repression, beneath a gleamingly pure surface, of criminality and love. The rest is a series of discontinuous explosive self-objectifications—such as the scenes in which Gerald's sadistic conquests of the mare and rabbit stir Gudrun's masochism; or the unexpected scene in which Gerald and Birkin derive erotic satisfaction from wrestling naked together; or the Dostoevskyan night scene in which Gerald, with the mud from his father's grave on his boots, steals like a criminal into the Brangwen house, finds Gudrun's room after close calls that are hair-raising only because he has cast himself in the role of criminal, and makes their first intercourse a kind of rape. Gerald learns nothing from these self-revelations, one does not lead to the other; they do not change his external character which remains frozen in the end as arctic machinelike purity.

Like Skrebensky, Gerald uses sex to fill his inner void. In an earlier chapter, "Industrial Magnate," we are shown how Gerald's feeling of nullity stems from the complete triumph of his will over his miners and himself: "The whole system was now so perfect that Gerald was hardly necessary any more." Now that he has through repression turned himself into a perfectly functioning machine, he stands up one evening "in terror, not knowing what he was," and discovers in a mirror his own nonexistence:

> He looked at his own face. . . . it was not real, it was a mask. He dared not touch it, for fear it should prove to be only a composition mask. His eyes were blue and keen as ever, and as firm in their look. Yet he was not sure that they were not blue false bubbles that would burst in a moment and leave clear annihilation. He could see the darkness in them, as if they were only bubbles of darkness. He was afraid that one day he would break down and be a purely meaningless bubble lapping round a darkness.

The water imagery suggests release into the stream of dissolution. The chapter closes with Gerald's reflection that women could no longer fill the void for him in the physical way, "that his *mind* needed acute stimulation, before he could be physically roused." [11] Now that he has thoroughly mechanized himself and his world, he needs the sadomasochistic *mental* stimulation he will get with Gudrun in the next chapter, "Rabbit."

Gudrun relates to Gerald and differs from Ursula through her deficiency of being and attraction to water. In "Water-Party," when the sisters disporting themselves like nymphs on the lake isle are hardly distinguishable from each other, Gudrun suddenly feels the difference between them as she beholds Ursula singing, so "sufficient unto herself," so "strong and unquestioned at the centre of her own universe. And Gudrun felt herself outside. Always this desolating, agonised feeling, that she was outside of life, an onlooker, whilst Ursula was a partaker, caused Gudrun to suffer from a sense of her own negation"— and to require constant connection with Ursula.

Gerald and Gudrun do not, like Paul Morel's parents, slowly change from love to hate through logical development of their differences in character. Love-hate draws them together from the start. The characterizations have thus a static quality that seems at times merely repetitive. Hermione, the most static of the major characters, seems always entranced. Her explosive self-objectification occurs early in the novel when, bursting the shell of manners and rationality, she crashes the paperweight on Birkin's skull. Her first appearance illustrates Lawrence's way of suggesting the underlife through surface signs and then, with depth analysis, explaining at the outset all we are ever to learn about her. "She was a woman of the new school, full of intellectuality, and heavy, nerve-worn with consciousness"; she has always to prove her superiority, because unconsciously "she always felt vulnerable," felt "a lack of robust self . . . a deficiency of being." She needs Birkin "to close up this deficiency." She mouths ideas about the value of sex and unconsciousness that sound like Birkin's, like Lawrence's; but they are distorted by a wrong identity structure that turns them into instruments of mental titillation and aggressiveness. More even than other twentieth-century novelists, Lawrence makes clear that strength of being is the modern criterion of judgment. But he does not make clear whether for Hermione and the others deficiency of being is the cause or result of repression and incapacity for development.

Gerald and Gudrun's original attraction to water ends with their attraction to the frozen water of the Alpine landscape. Ursula and Birkin seem also attracted to water; but there are divergences (when the sisters sketch by Willey Water, Ursula's eyes are on butterflies; Birkin recovers from Hermione's assault by rolling naked among flowers) that develop to the point where Ursula and Birkin finally flee the snow for the flowery earth of Italy. In "Diver," Gudrun has her second archetypal vision of Gerald, "a white figure. . . . launched in a white arc" into water.[12] The diver, says Lawrence in *Etruscan Places*, is a phallic symbol.[13] Significantly, Gudrun envies Gerald's male mastery over "the grey, uncreated water." She is overcome, in "Water-Party," by her archetypal vision of "his dim and luminous loins" as he climbs back into the boat after diving by night for his drowned sister. "He was not like a man to her, he was an incarnation, a great phase of life."

Gudrun and Gerald are attracted to the stream of dissolution, but not until "Water-Party" are the two streams, of creation and dissolution, sorted out. We see how the water that brings the two couples together also causes the death of Gerald's sister and the young man who tried to rescue her. The same water produces the conjunctions in which Birkin kisses Ursula and Gudrun slaps Gerald. To Gerald's " 'You have struck the first blow,' " she replies, " 'And I shall strike the last' "—thus predicting the final intensification of their static relation. After the two couples have been thus differentiated, Birkin delivers his discourse on the two streams; the announcement of the drowning follows. Gerald dives for the drowned bodies to depths "as cold as [the] hell" [14] he and Gudrun will share. She ends as frozen emotionally as he is physically; she cannot shed a tear for him, it is Ursula who weeps.

Ursula and Birkin have since their first meeting been quarrelling, as Gudrun and Gerald have not. The quarrel—whether their relation should be called "love," whether his notion of star-equilibrium gives him the upper hand, whether they are to meet in his way as archetypes or in her way as individuals—engages *all* their faculties; it is the salutary total conflict prescribed for love in the Hardy study. The ideological quarreling that destroys love in *The Rainbow* enriches it here, because Ursula and Birkin are evenly matched. Of the couples portrayed in both novels, Birkin is the first man who equals the Brangwen woman in strength of intellect and character. "It was a fight to the death between them—*or to new life.*" The last phrase, which I have italicized, establishes their difference from Gudrun and Gerald. Miraculously, Ursula and Birkin break through the deathly impasse by meeting at a new phase of identity.

But their first lovemaking, perhaps intercourse, takes place in "Water-Party" to the sound of the stream of dissolution—"the terrible crushing boom" of the water Birkin releases from the artificial lake to uncover the drowned bodies. Tired of " 'the death process,' " Birkin longs for a new kind of love, " 'like sleep, like being born again, *vulnerable* as a baby." Ursula, "reluctant to yield . . . her very identity," to meet at the phase of identity he desires, presses fierce kisses upon him. He succumbs, whimpering " 'Not this' " [15]—recognizing the old passionate oblivion that will overwhelm the other self, the vulnerable baby struggling to be born in him.

We are prepared for Gudrun's first blow against Gerald by a scene exemplifying the new method of *Women in Love*—

Gudrun's provocative dance before the bullocks and the aggressive behavior that drives them away. Her behavior is unmotivated; the bullocks are there to produce her self-revelation. Her dance continues Anna's antimale dance, but is more dramatic since the scene includes the male antagonist, symbolized by the bullocks who quickly turn into Gerald. In this scene, there is no distinction between conscious and unconscious; the unconscious has been completely projected—the world has been turned inside out or mythologized, so that external objects are symbols of psychic conditions and consciousness becomes a dramatic device that serves the myth or revelation of unconsciousness.

We have seen how in *The Rainbow* Lawrence mainly renounced the dramatic action of *Sons and Lovers*, in order to describe and analyze an underlife that could not be adequately manifested in action. In *Women in Love* he returns to dramatic action, but action organized around symbols that manifest the underlife. Thus we get a series of discontinuous set pieces (the sequence between them is accomplished through brief references), organized statically around such symbols as the mare, the rabbit, the African statue, the lake, the moon reflected in the lake, the snow; these tableaulike scenes exist mainly to reveal the characters' unconscious—though sometimes, as with the statue, they provide the occasion for a discourse by Birkin that later helps us understand not only his unconscious, but that of all the characters. The ritualized scenes of *The Rainbow* anticipate the method of *Women in Love*.

This method is adumbrated in technically the most remarkable scene of *Sons and Lovers*, the scene in which the Morels unwittingly re-enact the Oedipus myth. Paul assures his mother that he does not love Miriam, but prefers *her*. "In a whimpering voice, so unlike her own that he writhed in agony," she confesses: " 'I've never had a husband—not really.' " She kisses him fervently; then, hearing Morel, seems guiltily aware of what she is doing. "His mother looked so strange, Paul kissed her, trembling." Mrs. Morel looks and sounds strange because she is playing wife rather than mother to Paul. Morel staggers in drunk, and with his words to his wife—" 'At your mischief again?' "—turns the scene into a mythical re-enactment. The re-enactment remains, however, only potential: Paul and his father exchange blows that miss their mark, and to Paul's cry, " 'Don't sleep with him, mother,' " Mrs. Morel answers, " 'I'll sleep in my own bed.' " [16] The incompleteness maintains balance and distinction between the realistic action, in which the unconscious content is hidden, and the myth in which it is manifest. The characters seem for a moment to understand the scene's unconscious content, which then subsides into darkness.

In *Women in Love*, the unconscious content remains manifest as does the characters' unconscious understanding. Hermione really tries, as her sensuous consummation, to kill Birkin; and he, understanding from her action the destructive nature of their intellectualized love, rolls naked for cure among flowers. The manifestation has a permanent effect; it ends their affair. Gudrun fulfills the same destructive role more successfully, because she defeats Gerald from within—in the Tyrolean scene, where he as arctic wolf presses for the kill ("with his glistening stiff hair erect") but she gains "the whip hand over him" by making him at that moment fetch something from her handbag. The unconscious conflict is completely manifest, even though Gerald's psychological obtuseness keeps him from realizing how frightened she is. As hero, as wolf, Gerald lacks cunning. He is defeated by Gudrun's cunning and Loerke's— Loerke interrupts Gerald's strangling of Gudrun by turning it into a joke. From the Gerald who, after Gudrun's slap, follows her "white like a presence in his summer clothes. . . . a striding, mindless body," to the Gerald who now metamorphoses into the white wolf of Gudrun's first impression, there has been constant reconciling of the individual with an archetypal identity manifested through mindlessness—until Gerald becomes pure archetype in his white death amid the inside-out snow world of projected psyche: his, Gudrun's, and that of the whole abstract, modern North European culture.

Gerald, stiffening in the snow, has lost touch with the earth that renews Birkin. Birkin's flight to the flowers—because it is not, like the snow landscape, made plausible by realistic criteria—is ridiculous if we read only novelistically. *Women in Love* must be read as half novel, half myth. It is a novel, because most scenes can be explained realistically and because there remains some incompleteness in the manifestation of psyche—Hermione as Maenad curls her fingers around the bottom of the paperweight so it does not quite kill Birkin; Gerald does not physically turn into a wolf. But he does physically die his psychically motivated death in a landscape that is mythical because completely revelatory of individual and collective psyche.

There are in *Women in Love* two indirect statements that define its mythical element. One is Birkin's suggestion, when he hears how Gerald accidentally killed his brother, that Gerald is Cain since there are no accidents. The other occurs in "Moony," where Ursula illustrates Birkin's proposition by showing no surprise when she happens upon Birkin who has been abroad. Wondering whether she is wrong to spy on him, she reflects that there are no secrets since "we are all the same organisms" and "everything is known to all of us." There are no secrets and no accidents or coincidences in the world of projected psyche, of fairy tale and myth, where there is no distinction between desire and its materialization, between individual and collective mind. Ursula only "saw a shadow moving by the water," yet knew "it would be Birkin" for no reason except desire—desire to be delivered from her old identification with the moon. Sure enough, Birkin is casting stones at the reflection of the moon in the lake and cursing the Great Mother; Ursula feels "spilled out" [17]—she knows he is casting the stones at her. It is only at the archetypal phase of identity—where he in this case is shadow and she, moon and Great Mother—that desires materialize, mythical action takes place.

We have come a long way from *Sons and Lovers*, which in the realistic manner is organized around the frustration of desire by reality; psyche is consequently locked up in individualized characters, archetypes are only tentatively suggested. *The Rainbow*, without establishing consistently mythical action, does establish the consistent archetypalization of character with its contrast between "dark" sensuous men and "light" intellectual women. That contrast is muted here (except in "Moony"), probably because the culture has by now intellectualized everyone. The important contrast is between contemporary North European culture, which is all "light," all dissociated intellect, and the old African culture, represented by the statue, which was all "dark," all dissociated sensuality. In *Women in Love*, the distinctions are mainly among different kinds of light. Gerald's whiteness—signifying, like Ursula's mooniness, abstraction and separated ego—is a sign of his distance from the Brangwen male attachment to black earth. Ursula has to change her radiance from silver to golden.

Birkin presents complications, because his kind of intellect does not preclude sensuality. Nor is his sensuality portrayed as "dark," since it is the recovered sensuality of a man long separated from the land. Birkin is intended to show how modern men might recover sensuality and integrate it with mind. His sensuality is manifested in his loose-jointed, diabolic, libidinous dancing, which seems to Ursula "almost an obscenity, in a man who talked as a rule so very seriously." Lawrence is trying to show in Birkin the union of Dionysus with Apollo. His sensuous or Dionysian side appears in Ursula's first archetypal vision of him in "ruddy, copper-coloured light . . . the face of a man. . . . gleaming like fire." [18] She is aroused sexually, experiencing a fear Skrebensky never stirred in her—a fear adumbrated by her encounter with the horses. In the first archetypal visions of their lovers, Ursula and Gudrun see right through to the end of the relation.

My way of discussing these characters suggests that arche-typalization requires characterization by symbols that are static because they encapsulate the character's whole life. It might be argued that even Ursula and Birkin's capacity for change is symbolized statically. Ursula's golden radiance signifies potenti-ality. The flexibility Birkin demonstrates in the dance enables him to win the wrestling match against the stronger but inflexi-ble Gerald. Gerald, whose identity depends on "one form of ex-istence, one knowledge, one activity," recognizes Birkin's "odd mobility and changeableness" as the key to a salvation denied him.

Rather than argue the dynamic into the static, however, it is easier to treat Ursula and Birkin as the only characters in *Women in Love* for whom the symbols change and who un-dergo the change of ideas that for Lawrence constitutes rebirth. Ursula precedes Birkin in development, because of her rebirth at the end of *The Rainbow* and because of the innate sensuality and humor demonstrated by her deflation of Birkin's theorizing on sensuality. " 'But we are sensual enough, without making ourselves so, aren't we?' she asked, turning to him with a certain golden laughter flickering under her greenish eyes, like a challenge." [19] The challenge is the genuine sensuality of her eyes as they respond to the physical attractiveness she finds in him despite the sex in the head he condemns in others. If Birkin is Lawrence, then Lawrence laughs at himself a good deal through Ursula.

We watch Birkin repudiate his avant-garde London friends and then the seductive charms of the past at Hermione's country house, Breadalby. In "Totem," he places all these peo-ple culturally and historically through the African wood carving that represents the pseudo-primitivist taste and life style of the London Bohemians (the men stand naked around the statue). The statue, says Birkin, is anything but primitive; it expresses a late cultural phase, corresponding to our own, in which sensation has got dissociated from other aspects of the self: the Africans absorbed mentality into sensation; we, despite our modern craze for sensation, have mentalized it. Either way the dissociation produces the sadomasochistic sexuality expressed by the carved African woman and by Pussum, [20] who is masochistic with Gerald and sadistic with Halliday. The modern taste for so-called primitive art is connected throughout *Women in Love* with sadomasochistic sexuality.

Ursula and Birkin advance their relation through the battle of ideas fought out in "Mino." He, to overcome the mentalized sexuality of the ego, insists that they meet at an impersonal phase of identity, beyond a personal emotion like love. She protests that he wants submission, but he insists he is asking her to submit not to him but to a principle before which he makes equal submission: " 'I deliver *myself* over to the unknown, in coming to you, I am without reserves or defences' "—he is, as Lawrence says of Cipriano, "vulnerable." Birkin wants not a loss of selfhoods, not a " 'mingling . . . but an equilibrium, a pure balance of two single beings:—as the stars balance each other.' " The concept of star-equilibrium is designed to reconcile individual with archetype. Ursula shows she does not understand the archetypal relation when she compares the male cat's amatory domination of the female cat to Gerald's mechanical violation of his mare's instincts. Birkin shows he does not understand the individual relation when he uses the two cats to illustrate star-equilibrium, as though human love were only archetypal.

Birkin begins to acknowledge Ursula's individuality by asking about herself and her family. As she talks, the "baffled light" in her eyes is individual and tender. But "a strange flash of yellow light coming from her eyes" recalls the female cat's "great green fires." The fusion of individual and archetype is complete when Ursula shows her full potentiality for creativity and destructiveness in "strange golden-lighted eyes, very tender, but with a curious devilish look lurking underneath." Each displays the demonic component of the archetype that inspires the other with awe. The chapter ends charmingly with Birkin's temporary submission to the individual element: " 'Yes,—my love, yes,—my love. Let love be enough then. I love you then—I love you.' " [21]

When in the climactic chapter "Excurse," they finally meet at the phase of identity Birkin has been projecting, the phase is archetypal. They get there, however, through the individualizing development of "Moony." This chapter opens with Ursula "hard and indifferent, isolated in herself"—with her mooniness of *The Rainbow*. As in *The Rainbow*, the moon breaks upon her suddenly, like a supernatural watching presence, an emblem of self-consciousness. Here, however, she wants to escape self-consciousness: "She was glad to pass into the shade out of the moon." Critics agree that Birkin, in stoning the reflection of the moon upon the water, is stoning an image of Ursula's identity. Most critics think he is attacking her possessiveness, her Great Mother aspect; Colin Clarke argues persuasively that he is attacking her separated ego. Actually the attack is on both, because on her female self-sufficiency. Birkin stones the reflection of the moon three times. Twice the shattered reflection re-forms—the first time with harder outline than the second, when the regathering reflection is compared to a rose winning home its scattered petals. Birkin returns vehemently to the attack until the third time, when we are left with "a ragged rose, a distorted, frayed moon . . . shaking upon the water." I agree with Colin Clarke that the fluidly "ragged rose" is a model of the fluid, indefinitely outlined self Ursula must achieve, of an individuality open to connection. [22] Lawrence does not, after all, go on to describe the re-forming; Birkin makes no further move toward stoning; and Ursula, ostensibly to prevent further assault on her (she feels "spilled out"), takes this moment to announce herself. Ursula and Birkin seem to understand that the purpose of the stoning has been achieved.

One of the most brilliantly written passages in the book, the description of the complexly organic comings and goings of the reflection becomes a model of identity-making, which shows the necessary function of dissolution and Ursula's decreasing resistance to dissolution. The symbolism fulfills modern requirements in that the meaning is physically and psychologically substantiated—as a study of ripples and of an interplay between Ursula and Birkin (so intimate it seems vicarious intercourse) through the external image of Ursula's self. The book's mythical method works perfectly; for we are unaware of any line between the internal and external action.

Ursula and Birkin show that they understand the stoning by renewing immediately afterward their old argument over whether to meet as archetypes or individuals. " 'Give me,' " he says, " 'that golden light which is you' ": change, in other words, from the silver light of separation to the golden light of connection. Nevertheless, he admits again that he loves her. But when they fall to lovemaking, he realizes he no longer desires the old oblivious passion, but "only gentle communion." He refuses to satisfy her desire for intercourse.

Realizing the next day that he has changed direction, that he does not want to develop further along the line of sensual experience, he recalls another of Halliday's African wood carvings—this one portrays a woman of "astonishing cultured elegance" with "diminished, beetle face," "astounding long elegant body" and unexpectedly "protuberant buttocks." The woman derives from a cultural tradition of "purely sensual, purely unspiritual knowledge." Since the African culture specialized in sensation as modern North European culture specializes in mental experience, the "organic hold" in both cultures is broken—leading to an egocentric identity and a reductive sexuality abstracted from all values. After this "death-break" the postorganic culture regresses, in its coldly experimental exploration of sensations, beyond genital sexuality, "far beyond any phallic knowledge"—substituting the excremental flow of dissolution for the creative sexual flow. Given the traditional association of beetles with excrement, the African woman's "beetle face" and "protuberant buttocks" suggest anal intercourse as the most obvious expression of reductive sexuality.[23] In rejecting "this awful African process," this absorption of mind into sense, Birkin is also rejecting the modern European way of fulfilling the postorganic disintegration of self through the opposite absorption of sense into mind, through "the vast abstraction of ice and snow." Just as the "ragged rose . . . shaking on the water" is the positive model of an identity structure to be achieved, so the African statue is the negative model of an identity structure to be rejected.

There is another, a "paradisal" way, Birkin reflects: "a lovely state of free proud singleness, which accepted the obligation of the permanent connection with others." [24] This statement sums up Lawrence's ideas about the relation between identity and sexuality. Far from opposing individuality, Lawrence is salvaging it from modern conditions. In the essay ". . . Love Was Once a Little Boy" (*Phoenix II*), he attacks the modern individualism that isolates the self in the ego and sexuality in the genitals. Our sexuality is inherent in our identity. Genuine individuality lives in inescapably sexual archetypal connection, like a deep pool that is replenished steadily by unseen springs.

Our identity is not fixed but manifests itself through different phases, coming to flower when the sexual archetype is revealed in the individual form. This is the flowering that takes place in "Excurse" where, as the title suggests, Ursula and Birkin take an excursion beyond ordinary self to meet *out there*—where Birkin always said they should meet—in manifestations of being that are epiphanic because each comes to flower in the other's perception. The unpublished Prologue to *Women in Love* explains the psychological origin of Birkin's doctrine of love. His sexual

problem, deriving from self-consciousness, has been "the incapacity to love, the incapacity to desire any woman, positively.
. . . never to be able to love spontaneously, never to be moved
by a power greater than oneself, but always to be within one's
own control." The only escape from self-consciousness would
be possession from outside: "an impersonal, imperative love
should take hold of him." [25]
Their rebirth begins on the way to the inn. He feels newly
"conscious all over, all his body awake"; she binds her days
together when the sight of the Gothic cathedral her father loved
has an effect opposite to the sight with Skrebensky of Rouen Cathedral: it makes her present happiness seem "the dream-world
of one's childhood." At the inn, each fulfills the other's
dream—he as one of those sons of God she desired in *The Rainbow*, she as a radiant flower, the potential self he intuited from
the start: "Her face was now one dazzle of released, golden
light." His godhead becomes more real as his body becomes
more really other, when she apprehends it through touch:

> Unconsciously, with her sensitive finger-tips, she was tracing the
> back of his thighs, following some mysterious life-flow there. She had
> discovered something, something more than wonderful, more wonder-
> ful than life itself. It was the strange mystery of his life-motion, there, at
> the back of his thighs, down the flanks. It was a strange reality of his
> being, the very stuff of being, there in the straight downflow of the
> thighs. It was here she discovered him one of the sons of God . . . not
> a man, something other, something more.

G. Wilson Knight follows J. Middleton Murry in suggesting
that Ursula is exploring the anal zone and thus doing for Birkin
what he has apparently already done for her: "He had taken her
at the roots of her darkness and shame." [26] Knight connects
such passages with the anal intercourse that deepens the relation
of Connie and Mellors, and with the group of three poems
about the Lawrences—"New Heaven and Earth," "Elysium,"
"Manifesto"—in which the man escapes the prisonhouse of self
and discovers a new identity when he discovers the woman's

otherness through mutual touching of what Knight interprets as the anal zone.[27] At times the reference probably is localized; but more often the area touched is the whole lower back, as at the inn. The key to these passages is the anatomy of *Psychoanalysis and the Unconscious*, where the primitive consciousness that drinks in the universe is located beneath the navel, in the solar plexus, and the primitive consciousness of separation or singleness is located in the lumbar ganglion, the lower back. Identity at this phase is polarized between the minds of lower front and lower back, but the polarity can only be established through the circuit between two individuals. Thus love brings identity to fruition, but is itself complete only at the right phase of identity.

We see why Lawrence's love psychology is an identity psychology and vice versa; for identity is, in Lawrence and Erik Erikson, as somatic as sexuality: Lawrence even anticipates Erikson in founding identity on the polarity between ingestion and excretion. In *Psychoanalysis and the Unconscious*, Lawrence is telling us that the whole body is erotic. This total eroticism, communicated through touch, explains the puzzling contradictions by which Lawrence appears to condemn the anal eroticism represented by the African statue and yet to see its usefulness in the lovemaking of Ursula and Birkin, Connie and Mellors, Anna and Will. In the same way, he condemns the homosexuality of Tom and Winifred, yet suggests that Birkin and Gerald ought to have expressed theirs—perhaps even physically, as a passage excised from the Viking edition may imply. To Gerald's objection that " 'Nature doesn't provide the basis' " for love between men, Birkin insists, " 'she does.' " [28] In the Prologue to *Women in Love*, Lawrence traces Birkin's sexual problem to his latent homosexuality—he is attracted by the bodies of men and the souls of women because he cannot reconcile sexual desire with love. His homosexuality is a pathological symptom of the Oedipal dissociation that connects him with Paul Morel. In the published novel, however, body and soul are

both comprised in Birkin's relations with Ursula and with
Gerald. Lawrence has changed the friendship with Gerald from
a corrupting "alternative" to a relation "coordinate" with heterosexuality.[29] We see this in "Gladiatorial," where Birkin wrestles
with Gerald out of anger with Ursula for having rejected his
marriage proposal, but the erotic relief of the wrestling returns
his thoughts to Ursula. The homosexual relation has proved
fruitful for the heterosexual relation. Lawrence seems to approve of homosexuality and anal intercourse as supplements to,
but not substitutes for, heterosexual genital intercourse. Ursula
finally exults over the variousness of her sex life with Birkin:
"Why not be bestial, and go the whole round of experience?
. . . She was free, when she knew everything, and no dark
shameful things were denied her."

Ursula's touching of Birkin's loins brings them both, through
perfect gratification, to "the most intolerable accession into
being . . . outflooding from the source of the deepest life-force
. . . at the back and base of the loins"—which is also the
source of identity. She rises from the experience "an essential
new being . . . her complete self." "He stood before her, glim-
mering, so awfully real, that her heart almost stopped beating.
He stood there in his strange, *whole* body, that had its mar-
vellous *fountains*, like the bodies of the sons of God." Such
rhetoric is justified by the statement in the Foreword, a statement that explains all Lawrence's work starting with *The Rainbow:* "Let us hesitate no longer to announce that the sensual
passions and mysteries are equally sacred with the spiritual mysteries and passions."[30]

The "meeting" accomplished here is confirmed by the successful genital intercourse that follows in the organic setting of
Sherwood Forest. Driving away from the inn, Birkin feels like
the statue of an Egyptian Pharaoh,

> seated in immemorial potency. . . . He knew what it was to have the
> strange and magical current of force in his back and loins, and down his
> legs, force so perfect that it stayed him immobile, and left his face

subtly, mindlessly smiling. He knew what it was to be awake and potent
in that other basic mind, the deepest physical mind.

This passage, often criticized as extravagant, follows logically
the developing symbolism by which the evolution of Birkin's
identity is projected. In its smiling mindlessness the Egyptian
statue contrasts with the unsmiling mindlessness of the African
statues, as the expression of a flourishing phase when culture
and self are organic—when "physical mind" does not exclude
growth into mental consciousness. We are told that Birkin had
also a Greek consciousness, that he had not the "slumbering
head" of an Egyptian statue. We see him evolve, the way Western culture did, into wholeness. These symbols, perhaps because they shift, have not the accumulating emotional power of
the sustained exteriorization of Gudrun and Gerald's psyches in
the arctic landscape; but they contribute by contrast to the
meaning of the arctic landscape.

Birkin rounds out the book's moral by reading Gerald's frozen
death in a cul-de-sac as a sign that nature "could dispense with
man," as she dispensed with the dinosaurs, "should he too fail
creatively to change and develop." Nature could replace man
"with a finer created being." It is this faith in evolution—in the
next cultural or even biological phase—that consoles Birkin
rather than the rebirth he and Ursula have achieved. Their
solution is offered as sheer miracle and no social cure. Ursula's
radiance, Birkin's intellectual adventurousness signal intuitions
of new selves and worlds and the evolving concepts that make
new selves and worlds. Lawrence seems to be telling us that
rebirth, like art, can and cannot be willfully achieved, that there
is in both the same individual chanciness, the same rarity of
achievement. Hence the book closes with Birkin's restless antici-
pation of a future when love of a man will be compatible with
love of a woman. " 'He should have loved me,' " [31] he says
mournfully over Gerald's corpse—meaning that Gerald would
have freed himself for love, had he broken through his culturally restricted identity to discover his real desire.

What accounts for the success of Ursula and Birkin in the reconstitution of self? And how can those of us who heed Lawrence's message to burst out of our old identities save ourselves—since a new identity can hardly be willed? Ursula and Birkin *start* with the radiance and flexibility that enable them to outgrow the egos that finally imprison Gudrun and Gerald in the frozen hell of self-consciousness and clock-time.[32] We can perhaps find the beginnings of an answer in the sisters' conversation after Ursula and Birkin have decided to abandon the Alpine snow for Italy. It is a sign of the snow's connection in their minds with modern Western culture that Gudrun interprets this decision as a spiritual parting of the ways for the sisters, as Ursula's decision to drop out of modern society. " 'The only thing to do with the world, is to see it through,' " she argues. Ursula replies: " 'One can see it through in one's soul, long enough before it sees itself through in actuality. And then, when one has seen one's soul, one is something else.' " We can, in other words, forestall disintegration by living it through imaginatively, by absorbing it into consciousness and curing it through understanding. This process, which resembles that of psychoanalysis and art, changes our identity, perhaps because the transformation of unconsciousness into consciousness involves a return to the matrix from which our individuality emerges so that we remake our individuality. When Gudrun finds "in Loerke the rock-bottom of all life," [33] we recall that Ursula, after her encounter with the horses, found the stonelike "bottom of all things." [34] The difference is that Ursula experienced psychically what Gudrun will live through in actuality, and was thus able to save herself. Imagination is the saving power. Art, love—as imaginative, personal, self-creating activities: as religions—are means of rebirth into new identities.

Gudrun carries the argument a step further, by insisting that " 'you can't suddenly fly off to a new planet, because you think you can see to the end of this [one].' " Ursula then announces climactically: " 'One has a sort of other self, that belongs to a new planet, not to this. You've got to hop off.' " [35] To break through the impasse of having seen to the end of this civilization and our present selves, we have got, by a tremendous imaginative leap, to transcend the present world-view and see the identity structure that goes with it as only one of many possible modes of being. Ursula and Birkin's rebirth brings the future to life—now. *Women in Love* might be read as a comparison among: the obsolete identity structures of Gerald's humanitarian father, of the heroic Gerald, of the pseudo-Lawrencean Hermione; the forward-looking identity structures of Ursula and Birkin; the quite different forward-looking identity structures of the London Bohemians and of Gudrun and Loerke, who will bring the new age to birth by living out the disintegration of this one—by living out, as Yeats wrote of the late-nineteenth-century Decadents, "the autumn of the body."

"The arts," Yeats wrote, "lie dreaming of things to come." [36] One may prefer other writers for other reasons. But Yeats and Lawrence, more than other English-speaking twentieth-century writers, even those who succeed them, have liberated us from the present and shown us at least their vision of things to come. Eliot and Joyce move in this direction with their mythical analogues, but do not portray *transformations* of identity (though Joyce may be doing this in *Finnegans Wake*, a book I cannot yet claim to understand fully). Eliot's speakers, in the later, Christian writings, settle for what they are and rely for the rest on grace; while in *Ulysses*, the main characters' mythical identities enter the readers' consciousness but not apparently the characters' consciousnesses so as to transform them. The fact that younger writers from Beckett to Pynchon are still toying with the husks of our dead selves, are still deploring our deficiencies of being, shows that our sense of self has still not taken the positive shape augured by Yeats and Lawrence and leaves us wondering whether any positive shape will emerge.

The twentieth-century writers I have discussed, however, as well as the ones I have alluded to, are all saying, whether negatively, partially, or through complete vision, much the same things about what the self ought and ought not to be. Out of what they are saying we could formulate the secular working religion of modern self-conscious people—a religion that recognizes the spiritual problem of our time as a problem of identity and that seems always, whether its solutions come through art or love or even through the return, with a special modern purpose, to received religions, to regard salvation as self-realization.

NOTES

INTRODUCTION

1. *The Identity Society*, rev. ed. (Harper and Row, Harper Colophon, 1975), p. 5.
2. "The Narcissist Society," *The New York Review of Books* (September 30, 1976), p. 5.
3. *Childhood and Society*, 2nd ed. rev. (New York: Norton, 1963), p. 279.
4. "The Narcissist Society," p. 10.
5. For Hegel, in *The Phenomenology of the Spirit* (1807), the self is alienated from itself in the necessary evolution of self-consciousness. But for Marx, in *Economic and Philosophical Manuscripts* (1844), the self is alienated from its humanity when it becomes a specialized economic function the value of which is alienated into monetary value. "The worker feels *himself* only when he is not working; when he is working he does not feel *himself*" (*Early Writings*, tr. Rodney Livingstone and Gregor Benton, New York: Random House, Vintage, 1975, p. 326, my italics).
6. *Thus Spoke Zarathustra* (1892), translated with a preface by Walter Kaufmann (New York: Viking Press, 1966), p. 138.
7. In William James, the sense of identity derives from the somatic "warmth and intimacy" that suffuses the thoughts we call ours because we connect them with our body-ego ("The Consciousness of Self," *The Principles of Psychology*, 2 vols., New York: Henry Holt, 1923, I, 331–36).
8. *Loss of the Self in Modern Literature and Art* (New York: Random House, Vintage, 1964), p. 28. Lionel Trilling connects the rise of the idea of the individual with the rise of the idea of society as an entity that could be judged by the individual and so changed (*Sincerity and Authenticity*, Cambridge: Harvard University Press, 1972, pp. 19–25. For the twentieth-century situation, however, see *Identity and Anxiety: Survival of the Person in Mass Society*, eds. M. R. Stein, A. J. Vidich, D. M. White (New York: Free Press, London: Collier-Macmillan, 1960).

355

9. *Identity: Youth and Crisis* (New York: Norton, 1968), pp. 41–42, 133.
10. *The Standard Edition of the Complete Psychological Works of Sigmund Freud*, translated under the editorship of James Strachey, 24 vols. (London: Hogarth Press and Institute of Psycho-analysis, 1953–74), XVIII, 19.
11. *Identity: Youth and Crisis*, pp. 91, 159.
12. *Complete Psychological Works*, XIV, 85.
13. *Identity: Youth and Crisis*, p. 186.
14. *Complete Psychological Works*, XIX, 23, 27, 36, 38.
15. *Identity: Youth and Crisis*, pp. 50, 46; *Childhood and Society*, pp. 277–78.
16. *Race and Culture* (Glencoe, Ill.: Free Press, 1950), p. 249.
17. *The Presentation of Self in Everyday Life* (Garden City, N.Y.: Doubleday, Anchor, 1959), pp. 121–22, 81, 48, 56–57. See James, *Principles of Psychology*, I, 294. For discussions of sincerity, see Trilling, *Sincerity and Authenticity*, and David Perkins, *Wordsworth and the Poetry of Sincerity* (Cambridge: Harvard University Press, 1964). See also Morse Peckham, *Beyond the Tragic Vision: The Quest for Identity in the Nineteenth Century* (New York: Braziller, 1962).
18. *Being and Nothingness: An Essay on Phenomenological Ontology*, translated with an introduction by Hazel E. Barnes (New York: Philosophical Library, 1956), p. 59, in Ch. 2 called "Bad Faith" or insincerity.
19. For an analysis of romantic role-playing, see George H. Mead, *Movements of Thought in the Nineteenth Century*, ed. M. H. Moore (Chicago: University of Chicago Press, 1944).
20. See *Science and the Modern World* (New York: Macmillan, 1931), p. 110.
21. *Thus Spoke Zarathustra*, pp. 59–60.
22. In *Dimensions of Mind*, ed. Sidney Hook (New York: Collier, 1961), pp. 165–67, 171, 148–49. For a physiological approach to identity and culture, see Charles N. Fair, *The Dying Self* (Garden City, N.Y.: Doubleday, Anchor, 1970).
23. "Discoveries," *Essays and Introductions* (New York: Macmillan, 1961), p. 292.
24. *The Marriage of Heaven and Hell*, plate 4, *The Complete Writings of William Blake*, ed. Geoffrey Keynes (London: Oxford University Press, 1966), p. 149.
25. *Thus Spoke Zarathustra*, p. 34.
26. *Notes from Underground*, tr. Andrew R. MacAndrew (New York: New American Library, 1961), pp. 202, 113, 96, 120, 118, 200, 199.
27. *Identity: Youth and Crisis*, pp. 174–76.
28. *Notes from Underground*, p. 203.
29. *The Good Soldier* (New York: Random House, Vintage, 1951), pp. 108–9.
30. *The Notebooks of Malte Laurids Brigge*, tr. M. D. Herter Norton (New York: Putnam, Capricorn, 1958), pp. 15–17, 35, 145.
31. *The Double: A Psychoanalytic Study*, translated and edited with an introduction by Harry Tucker, Jr. (Chapel Hill: University of North Carolina Press, 1971), p. 72. See Ralph Tymms, *Doubles in Literary Psychology* (Cambridge: Bowes and Bowes, 1949); Robert Rogers, *A Psychoanalytic Study of the Double in Literature* (Detroit: Wayne State University Press, 1970); and Dr. D. W. Abse, "Delusional Identity and the Double," *Psychiatry* 39:2 (May 1976), 163–75. See also Masao Myoshi, *The Divided Self: A Perspective on the Literature of the Victorians* (New York: New York University Press; London: University of London Press, 1969).
32. *Notebooks of Malte Laurids Brigge*, pp. 164, 169, 194–96.
33. *Identity: Youth and Crisis*, pp. 218, 220.
34. *I and Thou*, 2nd ed. with added postscript, tr. Ronald Gregor Smith (New York: Scribner's, 1958).

I. THE ROMANTIC SELF

Chapter 1. WORDSWORTH: THE SELF AS PROCESS

1. *Oxford English Dictionary*, Unabridged.
2. David Hume, *A Treatise of Human Nature*, ed. L. A. Selby-Bigge (Oxford: Clarendon Press, 1965), Book I, Part IV, Section II, p. 201.
3. *Treatise* I, IV, VI, pp. 251–52, and p. 254 where Hume cites Lord Shaftesbury's reasonings on "the identity of plants and animals."
4. *Treatise* I, IV, VI, pp. 260–62.
5. *Treatise* I, IV, VII, pp. 267–70, 265.
6. *Treatise* I, IV, VI, pp. 257, 259.
7. For example, *Treatise* II, II, IV, p. 354.
8. To George and Georgiana Keats, 14 February–3 May, 1819, *The Letters of John Keats*, ed. Hyder E. Rollins, 2 vols. (Cambridge: Harvard University Press, 1958), II, 102–4. Rollins thinks this passage may have been written when Keats was reading John Locke's *Essay Concerning Human Understanding*, especially Book II, Ch. XXVII, "Of Identity and Diversity."
9. While there is no conclusive documentation, there is abundant circumstantial evidence that Wordsworth early in his career read Hartley's *Observations on Man* and Locke's *Essay*. But whether Wordsworth imbibed Locke through Hartley, or both through Godwin and Coleridge, he would have been conditioned by Locke's sensationalist psychology as part of what Basil Willey calls the " 'reality-standards' of his time" ("On Wordsworth and the Locke Tradition," *The Seventeenth Century Background*, London: Chatto and Windus, 1962, p. 304).
10. *An Essay Concerning Human Understanding*, collated and annotated by A. C. Fraser, 2 vols. (Oxford: Clarendon Press, 1894), Book II, Ch. XXI, Par. 24, I, 327.
11. "For thinkers of the seventeenth century, to whom all ideas of development were entirely foreign, the place which is now filled by the conception of evolution was occupied by the idea of composition, with the implied distinction between the simple and the complex. . . . The whole temporal process containing nothing but different combinations of the same simples, out of which nothing genuinely new could emerge, the historical point of view from which we trace development in time, and seek to comprehend the new determinations which arise in its course, was without significance" (James Gibson, *Locke's Theory of Knowledge and its Historical Relations*, Cambridge: Cambridge University Press, 1917, p. 47).
12. Ed. E. de Selincourt, 2nd ed. revised by H. Darbishire (Oxford: Clarendon Press, 1959). Other poems will be quoted from *The Poetical Works of William Wordsworth*, ed. E. de Selincourt and H. Darbishire, 5 vols. (Oxford: Clarendon Press, 1940–49).
13. *Essay*, Book II, Ch. XI, Par. 17, I, 212.
14. The strongest case for the Locke-Hartley influence is Arthur Beatty's in *William Wordsworth: His Doctrine and Art in Their Historical Relations*, 2nd ed. (Madison: University of Wisconsin Press, 1927). Beatty, however, sees Wordsworth only as following, and not also as answering or transcendentalizing, Locke and Hartley.
15. *The Prose Works of William Wordsworth*, ed. W. J. B. Owen and J. W. Smyser (Oxford: Clarendon Press, 1974), pp. 52–53.
16. Leavis, *Revaluation* (London: Chatto and Windus, 1936), Ch. V; Davie, *Articulate*

Energy: An Inquiry into the Syntax of English Poetry (London: Routledge and Kegan Paul, 1955), pp. 106–16. Colin Clarke, instead, finds the blurring precisely philosophical (*Romantic Paradox*, London: Routledge and Kegan Paul, 1962).

17. *Essay*, Book II, Ch. XXVII, Par. 16; Ch. XXXIII, I, 458.
18. *Observations on Man*, in Two Parts, 6th ed. corrected and revised (London: Tegg, 1834), Prop. XIV, Cor. VIII, p. 52.
19. To Robert Southey, [7 August 1803], *Collected Letters of Samuel Taylor Coleridge*, ed. E. L. Griggs, 6 vols. (Oxford: Clarendon Press, 1956–71), II, 961.
20. *Beyond the Pleasure Principle* (1920), *The Standard Edition of the Complete Psychological Works of Sigmund Freud*, translated under the editorship of James Strachey, 24 vols. (London: Hogarth Press and Institute of Psycho-analysis, 1953–74), XVIII, 25.
21. *Essay*, Book II, Ch. XVII, Par. 16, I, 280; Ch. XXVII, Par. 14, I, 455.
22. *Proust's Binoculars* (New York: Random House, 1963), pp. 42–43. See also Christopher Salvesen, *The Landscape of Memory: A Study of Wordsworth's Poetry* (Lincoln: University of Nebraska Press, 1965); and M. H. Abrams's comparison of Wordsworth and Proust in *Natural Supernaturalism* (New York: Norton, 1973), pp. 80–83.
23. See *Excursion* IV.1264–66, written at about the same time:

> —So build we up the Being that we are;
> Thus deeply drinking-in the soul of things,
> We shall be wise perforce.

24. *The Unmediated Vision* (New Haven: Yale University Press, 1954), pp. 33–34.
25. See Geoffrey Hartman's subtle analysis of Wordsworth's sense of place throughout *Wordsworth's Poetry 1787–1814* (New Haven and London: Yale University Press, 1964).
26. *Proust* (New York: Grove Press; London: Evergreen, 1931), p. 46.
27. "The primary IMAGINATION," says Coleridge, is " a repetition in the finite mind of the eternal act of creation" (*Biographia Literaria*, ed. J. Shawcross, Oxford: Oxford University Press, 1965, Ch. XIII, p. 202).

II. LOSS OF SELF

Chapter 2. ARNOLD: WANING ENERGY

1. Verse will be quoted from *The Poems of Matthew Arnold*, ed. Kenneth Allott (London: Longmans, 1965).
2. December 14, 1852, *The Letters of Matthew Arnold to Arthur Hugh Clough*, ed. H. F. Lowry (London and New York: Oxford University Press, 1932), p. 126.
3. *Victorian England: Portrait of an Age*, 2nd ed. (New York: Oxford University Press, 1964), see p. 14.
4. See, for example, U. C. Knoepflmacher, "Dover Revisited: The Wordsworthian Matrix in the Poetry of Matthew Arnold," *Victorian Poetry* 1:1 (January 1963), 17–26.

5. *Imaginative Reason: The Poetry of Matthew Arnold* (New Haven and London: Yale University Press, 1966), p. 183.

6. The transposition has puzzled readers who seek a direct rather than a reverse parallel between the scholar-gipsy and the Tyrians. Culler tries to explain the reversal by citing Kinglake's *Eothen* (1844), which Arnold *may* have read, where we find "the same picture" of the Greeks as "a debased, modern civilization, whose sailors timidly hug the shore, which Arnold exploits here." But Arnold's poem gives no such picture of the Greeks; nor are they characterized by "low cunning" (*Imaginative Reason*, p. 190). Both Greeks and Tyrians are attractive. The Greeks hug the shore as inheritors of civilization; the Tyrians put out to sea only after they realize they must flee civilization.

7. *Poems*, p. 142n.

8. February 12, 1853. As a sign that Arnold is leveling the injunction half against himself, this letter begins: "I am past thirty, and three parts iced over" (*Letters to Clough*, pp. 128, 130).

9. For a brief account, see M. H. Abrams, *Natural Supernaturalism* (New York: Norton, 1973), pp. 217–37.

10. *The Disappearance of God* (New York: Schocken, 1965), p. 260.

11. For the 1849 volume, Arnold prefixed to verses untitled in the 1844 manuscript the name of a fourth-century monk—called Stagyre in 1849, Stagirius in 1877—probably to give the verses an air of objectivity. He had learned from Saint-Marc Girardin's *Cours de littérature dramatique* (1843) that Stagirius's malaise resembled modern romantic malaise. The 1855 title, "Desire," made clearer the modern application, especially since the title derived from the passage in George Sand's *Lélia* which Arnold translates in his essay on her (*The Complete Prose Works of Matthew Arnold*, 10 vols., ed. R. H. Super, Ann Arbor: University of Michigan Press, 1960–74), VIII, 221.

12. Sir Alexander Burnes, *Travels into Bokhara*, 1834, I, 307–9; quoted in *Poems*, pp. 75–76.

13. To Henry Savage [?Autumn 1913], *The Collected Letters of D. H. Lawrence*, ed. Harry T. Moore, 2 vols. (New York: Viking Press, 1962), I, 241. Frank Kermode traces the aesthetic of expressionless faces in "The Dancer," *Romantic Image* (New York: Random House, Vintage, 1964).

14. Tr. Michael Bullock, in Herbert Read, *The True Voice of Feeling* (London: Faber and Faber, 1953), pp. 337, 335. See Kenneth Allott, "Matthew Arnold's Reading-Lists in Three Early Diaries," *Victorian Studies* 2:3 (March 1959), 263–64.

15. "Luca della Robbia," *The Renaissance* (New York: Random House, Modern Library, n.d.), p. 54; see also "The Poetry of Michelangelo," "The School of Giorgione," "Winckelmann."

16. *Matthew Arnold* (Cleveland and New York: World, Meridian, 1968), pp. 93–94.

17. In a letter to Clough—written September 23, 1849, from Thun, where he may have been seeing "Marguerite" for the last time—Arnold alludes to John 3: "Except a man be born again, he cannot see the Kingdom of God," and then quotes his own still unpublished lines: "The children of the second birth / Whom the world could not tame." This crucial letter summarizes Arnold's identity crisis and suggests its solution in his "snuffing after a moral atmosphere" and his need to leave Switzerland for England. By classing the activist Clough with the reclusive Obermann as "children of the second birth," Arnold suggests a way of synthesizing these opposite stances (*Letters to Clough*, pp. 109–11).

18. See *Poems*, pp. 239–40.
19. C. B. Tinker and H. F. Lowry, *The Poetry of Matthew Arnold: A Commentary* (London and New York: Oxford University Press, 1940), p. 291.
20. See Arnold's *Literature and Dogma* and the opening paragraph in his "Study of Poetry." For Yeats, instead, poems are like bibles literally true; see p. 194.
21. The influence on Arnold of the *Bhagavad Gita* exemplifies the way in which Indian religious philosophy, with its doctrine that the self is God, that Atman or individual soul is identical with Brahman or universal soul, intrigues psychologically oriented modern writers—Eliot, Yeats, Lawrence among others. S. Nagarajan, however—in "Arnold and the *Bhagavad Gita*: A Reinterpretation of *Empedocles on Etna*," *Comparative Literature* 12:4 (1960), 335–47—errs in interpreting *Empedocles* solely in terms of the *Bhagavad Gita*.
22. "Arnold's '*Empedocles on Etna*,' " *Victorian Studies* 1:4 (June 1958), 311–36.
23. *Commentary*, p. 292 (my italics). I have edited this passage slightly to make the meaning clearer.
24. *Matthew Arnold*, p. 140.
25. From Arnold's characterization of his own age as a modern period, in "On the Modern Element in Literature," where he goes on to describe Lucretius, the poet-philosopher of the Roman modern period, in terms applicable to Empedocles as the poet-philosopher of the Greek modern period. "The predominance of thought, of reflection, in modern epochs . . . has produced a state of feeling unknown to less enlightened but perhaps healthier epochs—the feeling of depression, the feeling of *ennui*" (*Complete Prose Works*, I, 20, 32).

Chapter 3. ELIOT: THE WALKING DEAD

1. W. D. Paden's phrase to describe Tennyson's strategy in certain early poems (*Tennyson in Egypt*, Lawrence: University of Kansas Publications, 1942, pp. 53, 74).
2. Verse will be quoted from *The Complete Poems and Plays of T. S. Eliot* (London: Faber and Faber, 1970).
3. Explained in "Hamlet and His Problems," *Selected Essays*, new ed. (New York: Harcourt, Brace, 1950), pp. 124–25.
4. Review of *Ulysses* in *The Dial* 75: 5 (November 1923), p. 483. See *The Waste Land: A Facsimile and Transcript of the Original Drafts Including the Annotations of Ezra Pound*, edited with an Introduction by Valerie Eliot (New York: Harcourt Brace Jovanovich, 1971); the Introduction gives biographical background.
5. *Modern Poetry and the Tradition* (New York: Oxford University Press, 1965), p. 145.
6. Eliot knew Colin Still's interpretation of *The Tempest* as a Mystery ritual of initiation (*Shakespeare's Mystery Play*, London: Cecil Palmer, 1921).
7. *Facsimile*, p. 47.
8. *The Use of Poetry and the Use of Criticism* (Cambridge: Harvard University Press, 1933), p. 119.
9. For a sampling of critical opinions, see *T. S. Eliot, The Waste Land: A Casebook*, eds. C. B. Cox and A. P. Hinchliffe (London: Macmillan, 1969; Nashville: Aurora, 1970). For more recent opinions, see *Eliot in His Time: Essays on the Occasion of the Fiftieth Anniversary of The Waste Land*, ed. A. Walton Litz (Princeton: Princeton University Press, 1973).
10. This poem may derive from Bergson's theory of the way perceptions lead to memo-

ries detached from personality and then to detached motor habits. "All these clearly defined elements," Bergson wrote, "appear more distinct from me, the more distinct they are from each other" (quoted in Lyndall Gordon, *Eliot's Early Years*, Oxford and New York: Oxford University Press, 1977, p. 40).

11. *Knowledge and Experience in the Philosophy of F. H. Bradley* (London: Faber and Faber, 1964), p. 19.
12. *Appearance and Reality*, 2nd edition, 5th impression (London: Macmillan, 1908), p. 346. This is the edition in Eliot's library, annotated by him and dated, in his hand, June 1913.
13. *Appearance and Reality*, p. 79.
14. *Appearance and Reality*, pp. 92–93.
15. Reprinted as Appendix in *Knowledge and Experience*, pp. 203–4.
16. Such idealistic solipsism is, according to Lawrence, the real meaning of Freud's incest motive (*Psychoanalysis and the Unconscious and Fantasia of the Unconscious*, New York: Viking Press, 1965, pp. 7–11).
17. *Appearance and Reality*, p. 85.
18. *Knowledge and Experience*, pp. 146, 162–63.
19. Quoted in E. Martin Browne, *The Making of T. S. Eliot's Plays* (Cambridge: Cambridge University Press, 1969), p. 285.

Chapter 4. BECKETT: ZERO IDENTITY

1. *Happy Days* (New York: Grove Press, 1961), p. 7.
2. *Waiting for Godot* (New York: Grove Press, 1954), p. 44.
3. *Happy Days*, pp. 43–44, 21. I shall omit stage directions unless necessary for meaning.
4. *Godot*, pp. 42, 55.
5. *Endgame* (New York: Grove Press, 1958), p. 11.
6. *Happy Days*, p. 34.
7. *Endgame*, pp. 11, 71, 77.
8. *Godot*, pp. 7, 60.
9. *Happy Days*, pp. 22, 21.
10. Günther Anders, "Being Without Time: On Beckett's Play *Waiting for Godot*," in *Samuel Beckett: A Collection of Critical Essays*, ed. Martin Esslin (Englewood Cliffs, N.J.: Prentice-Hall, 1965), p. 141.
11. *Godot*, p. 60.
12. *Endgame*, pp. 13, 32, 42.
13. *Godot*, p. 59.
14. *Proust* (New York: Grove Press, 1931), p. 19.
15. *Krapp's Last Tape and Other Dramatic Pieces* (New York: Grove Press, 1960), p. 28.
16. "Samuel Beckett, or 'Presence' in the Theatre," in *Beckett: Critical Essays*," ed. Esslin.
17. *Godot*, p. 59.
18. *Endgame*, pp. 78, 53, 33.
19. *Krapp's Last Tape and Other Dramatic Pieces*, p. 74.
20. *Endgame*, pp. 13, 77.
21. *Godot*, p. 39.
22. *Happy Days*, p. 64.

23. "Failure of an Attempt at De-Mythologization," in *Beckett: Critical Essays*, ed. Esslin, p. 105.
24. *Endgame*, pp. 46, 62.
25. *Proust*, p. 8.
26. *Endgame*, p. 74.
27. *Godot*, p. 52.
28. *Happy Days*, pp. 40, 51–52.
29. Introduction to *Beckett: Critical Essays*, pp. 2, 4.
30. *Endgame*, pp. 44, 36.
31. *Krapp's Last Tape and Other Dramatic Pieces*, pp. 20–22, 15. See Vivian Mercier, *Beckett/Beckett* (New York: Oxford University Press, 1977), pp. 6–7.
32. *Krapp's Last Tape and Other Dramatic Pieces*, pp. 24, 16, 28, 25.
33. Quoted in *Beckett/Beckett*, p. 8. See Wolfgang Iser, "The Pattern of Negativity in Beckett's Prose," *Georgia Review* 29:3 (Fall 1975), 719. Two contradictory remarks from *Proust* apply to *Krapp's Last Tape:* "The aspirations of yesterday were valid for yesterday's ego, not for to-day's" (p. 3). "There is no escape from yesterday because yesterday has deformed us, or been deformed by us" (p. 2).
34. *Krapp's Last Tape and Other Dramatic Pieces*, pp. 112, 116, 118.
35. *Krapp's Last Tape and Other Dramatic Pieces*, pp. 119–21. The fictions of Henry and Hamm are about the old cycle, whether to let it die; but Hamm's is also about the new cycle, whether to let it be born. Beckett, according to Ruby Cohn, "is rumored to have remarked that in *Godot*, the audience wonders whether Godot will ever come, and in *Endgame* they wonder whether Clov will ever leave" (*Samuel Beckett: The Comic Gamut*, New Brunswick, N.J.: Rutgers University Press, 1962, p. 241). In both cases the audience is left wondering whether the cycle will be completed. Beckett's preoccupation with cycles recalls Vico, about whom he wrote in the essay "Dante... Bruno. Vico.. Joyce," contributed to *Our Exagmination Round His Factification for Incamination of Work in Progress* (London: Faber and Faber, 1972). Beckett observes that Dante's Purgatory "is conical and consequently implies culmination," whereas "Mr. Joyce's is spherical and excludes culmination" because of "the absolute absence of the Absolute" (pp. 21–22). See Ch. 7, p. 235, where I make a similar comparison between the systems of Dante and Yeats.
36. Introduction to *Beckett: Critical Essays*, p. 7.
37. *Play and Two Short Pieces for Radio* (London: Faber and Faber, 1964), p. 9.
38. *Play*, pp. 15–18, 21–22.
39. *Godot*, p. 41.
40. *Endgame*, p. 46.
41. *Godot*, pp. 40–41.
42. *A Discourse on Method*, tr. John Veitch (London: Dent; New York: Dutton, 1937), p. 27.
43. *Murphy* (New York: Grove Press, 1957), p. 109.
44. *Samuel Beckett: A Critical Study* (New York: Grove Press, 1961); see p. 17 and chapter, "The Cartesian Centaur." Lawrence, who tried to undo Descartes' work by re-animalizing both body and mind, calls the Cartesian centaur the "god in the machine." He argues that the Cartesian split mechanizes body and mind: "in the end pure idealism is identical with pure materialism. . . . The ideal is but the god in the machine—the little, fixed machine-principle which works the human psyche automatically" (*Psychoanalysis and the Unconscious*, p. 12).
45. *Godot*, p. 41.
46. *The Novels of Samuel Beckett* (London: Chatto and Windus, 1964), p. 149.

47. *Proust*, pp. 8, 18–19.
48. *Proust*, pp. 46–47, 49.
49. *Endgame*, p. 83.
50. *Beckett: Critical Essays*, ed. Esslin, p. 115.
51. *Knowledge and Experience*, p. 154.
52. *Three Novels: Molloy, Malone Dies, The Unnamable* (New York: Grove Press, 1965), p. 386.
53. *Three Novels*, pp. 327, 333, 370 (my italics), 372, 393.
54. *Beckett: Comic Gamut*, pp. 237, 325 n. 9.
55. *Three Novels*, p. 386.
56. *Thus Spoke Zarathustra*, translated with a preface by Walter Kaufmann (New York: Viking Press, 1966), Prologue: 5, pp. 17–18.

III. RECONSTITUTION OF SELF: YEATS

Chapter 5. EXTERIORITY OF SELF

1. Reprinted in *Explorations*, selected by Mrs. W. B. Yeats (London: Macmillan, 1962), pp. 392–94.
2. Reprinted in *The Variorum Edition of the Plays*, eds. Russell K. and Catharine C. Alspach (New York and London: Macmillan, 1966), p. 761.
3. Reprinted in *Mythologies* (New York: Macmillan, 1959), p. 334.
4. *Explorations*, p. 394.
5. *A Vision*, a reissue with the author's final revisions (New York: Macmillan, 1956), pp. 13, 72, 144, 272–73, 214.
6. *Explorations*, p. 397.
7. *The Collected Plays of W. B. Yeats*, new edition (New York: Macmillan, 1962), p. 267. Plays will be quoted from this edition.
8. *Per Amica Silentia Lunae*, *Mythologies*, p. 329.
9. See *Plays*, pp. 261–62.
10. Nondramatic verse will be quoted from *The Collected Poems of W. B. Yeats* (New York: Macmillan, 1955).
11. *Plays*, p. 267.
12. "The Autumn of the Body," *Essays and Introductions* (New York: Macmillan, 1961), p. 191.
13. "Introduction to *The Resurrection*," *Explorations*, p. 398.
14. *Plays*, pp. 272, 259.
15. *Autobiography* (New York: Macmillan, Collier, 1971), p. 194.
16. "Introduction to *The Resurrection*," *Explorations*, pp. 398, 397.
17. *Mythologies*, p. 341.
18. "Introduction to *The Resurrection*," *Explorations*, p. 397.
19. Richard Ellmann warns us that *belief* is not the word for Yeats's convictions, that Yeats wondered "whether the word *belief* belonged to our age at all." He quotes the young Yeats: " 'The whole doctrine of the reincarnation of the soul is hypothetic; it is the most plausible of the explanations of the world,' " but admits that "Yeats came to present the theme of reincarnation with a vehemence that increased with

age and with the general strengthening of his mature verse." I would omit "never more than" in Ellmann's statement that reincarnation "was never more for him than the 'most plausible of the explanations of the world,' " for Yeats's *emotional* attitude was one of belief not skepticism. The hypothesis of reincarnation grew upon him with increasing conviction because it worked, it explained his sense of identity. (*The Identity of Yeats*, New York: Oxford University Press, 1970, pp. xviii, 48).

20. *Mythologies*, pp. 341, 333–34.
21. *Essays*, tr. H. T. Lowe-Porter (New York: Random House, Vintage, 1957), pp. 317, 312–13, 319–20.
22. *Mythologies*, pp. 336–37.
23. *Morals*, IV. Quoted in F. A. C. Wilson, *W. B. Yeats and Tradition* (London: Gollancz, 1958), pp. 244–45.
24. *Mythologies*, p. 335.
25. *Explorations*, p. 397.
26. *Mythologies*, p. 331.
27. "A General Introduction for my Work," *Essays and Introductions*, p. 509.
28. See Yeats's commentary on Spectre and Emanation in *The Works of William Blake*, eds. E. J. Ellis and W. B. Yeats, 3 vols. (London: Quaritch, 1893), I, 275–77.
29. *Essays and Introductions*, p. 509.
30. Keats was reaching toward a similar concept of transformed identity when he wrote that "A Man's life of any worth is a continual allegory—and very few eyes can see the Mystery of his life—a life like the scriptures, figurative." Byron "cuts a figure," but "is not figurative" because still recognizable in his poems; whereas Shakespeare "led a life of Allegory," transformed himself entirely in his plays (To George and Georgiana Keats, 14 February–3 May 1819, *The Letters of John Keats*, ed. Hyder E. Rollins, 2 vols., Cambridge: Harvard University Press, 1958, II, 67). Keats had not the concepts to understand that poets like Wordsworth and Byron might turn the materials of their life into phantasmagoria.
31. *Mythologies*, p. 331.
32. *Essays and Introductions*, pp. 522–23.
33. *Per Amica, Mythologies*, pp. 333–34.
34. "The Decay of Lying," *The Artist as Critic: Critical Writings of Oscar Wilde*, ed. Richard Ellmann (New York: Random House, Vintage, 1970), p. 297.
35. *Mythologies*, p. 340.
36. *Essays and Introductions*, p. 511.
37. *Mythologies*, p. 343.
38. "A General Introduction for My Work," *Essays and Introductions*, p. 525. These followers of Browning "employ an intricate psychology, action in character, not as in the ballads character in action."
39. *Mythologies*, pp. 344–46.
40. *The Integration of the Personality*, tr. Stanley Dell (New York: Farrar and Rinehart, 1939), pp. 222, 213, 222–23.
41. *Mythologies*, pp. 344–47. I have reprinted Yeats's modernization of Coleridge's spelling and punctuation to show how Yeatsian the lines seem.
42. *Mythologies*, pp. 349–50.
43. Reprinted in *Explorations*, p. 54.
44. *Mythologies*, pp. 359–60.
45. *Mythologies*, pp. 359, 351–53, 364, 356.

Chapter 6. THE SELF AS A WORK OF ART

1. "If I Were Four-and-Twenty," reprinted in *Explorations*, p. 263.
2. *The Secret Rose* (London: Lawrence and Bullen, 1897), p. vii. "I was soon to write many poems," says Yeats in *The Autobiography*, "where an always personal emotion was woven into a general pattern of myth and symbol" (pp. 101–2); and he criticizes Spenser for not having "that visionary air which can alone make allegory real" ("Edmund Spenser," *Essays and Introductions*, p. 369).
3. *Irish Fairy and Folk Tales* (New York: Random House, Modern Library, n.d.), p. xvi.
4. The three phases also correspond, without contradiction, to Vico's cycles, as Thomas Whitaker suggests (*Swan and Shadow: Yeats's Dialogue with History*, Chapel Hill: University of North Carolina Press, 1964), and to phases in the romantic Quest, as Harold Bloom suggests (*Yeats*, New York: Oxford University Press, 1970).
5. "William Blake and the Imagination," *Essays and Introductions*, p. 111.
6. *Mythologies*, p. 314.
7. *Mythologies*, pp. 268, 275–76, 278–79.
8. *Mythologies*, p. 303.
9. *Mythologies*, pp. 286, 284–85, 289.
10. *A Vision: An Explanation of Life Founded Upon the Writings of Giraldus and Upon Certain Doctrines Attributed to Kusta Ben Luka* (London: Laurie, 1925), pp. xvii–xviii, xxi.
11. *Vision* (1925), pp. xi–xii. Yeats wanted to avoid the mistake he thought Blake had made by expounding his system in prophetic poems that were therefore largely unintelligible. Yeats reserved prose and certain plays for working out ideas, distilling their quintessence in his short poems. He never, as Ellmann points out, uses in the poems the "special terms" of his system, "unless they have accepted as well as eccentrically personal meanings" (*Identity of Yeats*, p. xi). "The chief difference," Yeats wrote in his commentary on Blake, "between the metaphors of poetry and the symbols of mysticism is that the latter are woven together into a complete system" (*Works of Blake*, eds. Ellis and Yeats, I, 238).
12. "If I were Four-and-Twenty," *Explorations*, p. 269.
13. *Vision* (1925), p. 9.
14. *On the Boiler*, *Wheels and Butterflies*, reprinted in *Explorations*, pp. 430, 345.
15. Quoted in Richard Ellmann, *Eminent Domain: Yeats Among Wilde, Joyce, Pound, Eliot and Auden* (New York: Oxford University Press, 1967), pp. 12–13.
16. "At Stratford-on-Avon," *Essays and Introductions*, p. 107.
17. *Autobiography*, p. 312.
18. *Autobiography* p. 221.
19. "Magic," *Essays and Introductions*, p. 36.
20. Introduction to his edition of *The Oxford Book of Modern Verse: 1892–1935* (New York: Oxford University Press, 1936), p. xxx.
21. "The Autumn of the Body," *Essays and Introductions*, p. 192; see *Vision*, p. 291.
22. Yeats, *Autobiography*, pp. 338–39, 252. See Nietzsche, *Beyond Good and Evil*, Par. 40, tr. Helen Zimmern, in *The Philosophy of Nietzsche* (New York: Random House, Modern Library, n.d.), p. 425. For a discussion of Nietzsche's *unmasking* psychology, see Karl Jaspers, *Nietzsche*, tr. C. F. Wallraff and F. J. Schmitz (Tucson: University of Arizona Press, 1965), pp. 131–39.

23. *Autobiography*, pp. 202, 221–22, 228, 222, 209–10 (the next to last sentence is versified in "Two Songs from a Play").
24. *Autobiography*, pp. 231, 102, 182–83 (my italics).
25. *Essays and Introductions*, p. 226.
26. *Autobiography*, p. 166.
27. *Vision*, pp. 209, 52.
28. "Introduction to *The Words upon the Window-pane*," *Explorations*, pp. 368–69.
29. *Autobiography*, p. 60.
30. "The Moods," *Essays and Introductions*, p. 195.
31. *Vision*, pp. 136, 234, 233 n. 1.
32. "William Blake and his Illustrations to *The Divine Comedy*," *Essays and Introductions*, p. 139.
33. *Vision*, p. 72.
34. August 5 [1936], *Letters on Poetry from W. B. Yeats to Dorothy Wellesley* (London: Oxford University Press, 1964), p. 86.
35. *Vision*, p. 268.
36. To Lady Gregory, [?September 26, 1902], *The Letters of W. B. Yeats*, ed. Allan Wade (London: Rupert Hart-Davis, 1954), p. 379. Denis Donoghue dates this letter between December 27, 1902 and January 3, 1903 (*William Butler Yeats*, New York: Viking Press, 1971, p. 52 n. 29).
37. *Letters to Dorothy Wellesley*, p. 86.
38. *Vision*, pp. 84, 158, 160–61. The Lake of Udan-Adan is the condition of formlessness in Blake; see S. Foster Damon, *A Blake Dictionary* (New York: E. P. Dutton, 1971), p. 416.
39. *Vision*, pp. 131, 134, 214.
40. *Autobiography*, p. 326.
41. Yeats alludes comically through these names to Blake's poems "Long John Brown & Little Mary Bell," in which Mary is wrong to refuse illicit intercourse, and "William Bond," in which William's fiancée wins his love by sanctioning his infidelity; to Villiers de l'Isle Adam's *Axel*, in which the lovers are wrong to choose death rather than physical consummation of their love; and to the child's rhyme "Huddon, Duddon and Daniel O'Leary," which introduced him, as he suggests in the poem prefatory to "Stories of Michael Robartes and His Friends," to the triangle (*Vision*, p. 32).
42. *Vision*, pp. 83, 94.
43. James Joyce, *Ulysses* (New York: Random House, Modern Library, 1961), p. 213.
44. *Vision*, p. 237.
45. "The Personal and the Collective (or Transpersonal) Unconscious," *Two Essays on Analytical Psychology*, tr. R. F. C. Hull (New York: Meridian, 1956), p. 76.
46. *Vision*, pp. 227, 223, 226.
47. *Plays*, p. 434.
48. *Vision*, pp. 230–35.
49. *Vision*, pp. 68, 105, 81, 52, 124, 172.
50. Denis Donoghue suggests that Yeats's dialectic combines "structuralism," the concern with unchanging structures, and "historicism," the concern with change conditioned by time and place (*Yeats*, pp. 6–7).
51. *Vision*, pp. 206, 143, 85, 148.
52. *Vision*, pp. 177–82.
53. *The Decline of the West*, 2 vols. (in German 1918, 1922); tr. C. F. Atkinson, 1926, 1928 (New York: Knopf, 1946), I, 281. The debt Yeats acknowledges for his art his-

tory is to "that most philosophical of archaeologists Josef Strzygowski [1862–1941]" (*Vision*, p. 257, also pp. 281–82).
54. *Vision*, pp. 281, 136, 279, 268.
55. It is because we have learned that the role remains, though new gods fill it, that "A modern man, *The Golden Bough* . . . in his head," can repeat the Creed, "believe it even, without a thought of the historic Christ . . . ; I repeat it and think of 'the Self' in the Upanishads" ("A General Introduction for My Work," *Essays and Introductions*, p. 514).
56. This visual image may derive from the mosaic in the Church of San Vitale, Ravenna, of the staring, expressionless, rigidly front-facing figure of Empress Theodora, who with both hands holds to her right side the chalice used in the Mass to receive Christ's blood which would correspond to Dionysus's heart.
57. *Vision*, pp. 270, 268.
58. *Vision*, pp. 273, 276, 289–92, 294, 296–97.
59. *Vision*, pp. 297, 299–300.
60. *Vision* (1925), pp. 211–15.

Chapter 7. THE SELF AS GOD

1. *Essays and Introductions*, pp. 241, 243.
2. August 5 [1936], *Letters to Dorothy Wellesley*, p. 86.
3. *Autobiography*, p. 235.
4. Yeats Ms. 13, 576: "Notebook begun April 7, 1921," National Library, Dublin.
5. Quoted in Richard Ellmann, *Yeats: The Man and the Masks* (New York: E. P. Dutton, 1948), p. 216. See also A. Norman Jeffares, *A Commentary on the Collected Poems of W. B. Yeats* (Stanford: Stanford University Press, 1968), pp. 299–300.
6. W. B. Yeats: *The Later Poetry* (Berkeley and Los Angeles: University of California Press, 1964), p. 97.
7. To Olivia Shakespear, September 24, [1926], *Letters*, p. 719.
8. *Plays*, p. 267.
9. Quoted in Parkinson, *Yeats: Later Poetry*, p. 105 (my italics).
10. Frank Kermode traces the aesthetic behind these lines in his chapters "The Dancer" and "The Tree" in *Romantic Image* (New York: Random House, Vintage, 1964).
11. Proust makes the same point when he says that the novelist, through his transparent characters, "sets free within us all the joys and sorrows in the world" (*Swann's Way*, tr. C. K. Scott Moncrieff, New York: Random House, Modern Library, 1956, p. 119).
12. See Thomas Whitaker's clarification of the poem's somewhat obscure historical meaning (*Swan and Shadow: Yeats's Dialogue with History*, pp. 235–45).
13. *The King of the Great Clock Tower*, *Plays*, p. 402.
14. *Vision*, p. 271. See Helen Vendler's poetically suggestive reading of these two plays in *Yeats's VISION and the Later Plays* (Cambridge: Harvard University Press; London: Oxford University Press, 1963), pp. 139–58. I disagree, however, with her definition of the conflict as between poet and Muse or image, because the Queen cannot be both Muse and image and because it is the combination of man and Queen that makes the image or art work (the song-dance). Similarly, Vendler considers that *A Vision* is about art, with the system a metaphor for the artistic process; while I consider that Yeats uses an analogy with art to explain identity and history.
15. To Edith Shackleton Heald, January 1 [1939], *Letters*, p. 922.

16. "Then they began to sing," says Yeats in Dorothy Wellesley's account of his prose
    draft, "and they did not sing like men and women, but like linnets that had been
    stood on a perch and taught by a singing master" (*Letters to Dorothy Wellesley*,
    p. 193). "Taught"—like "singing school" in "Sailing to Byzantium"—suggests that
    the singing was supernatural.
17. *Plays*, p. 444.
18. *Vision*, p. 232. Definitely purgatorial, the experience is specifically locatable in
    Yeats's purgatory though not locatable on any one terrace of Dante's. Helen
    Vendler may be right, however, in finding some similarity of imagery with Dante's
    Brunetto Latini passage, *Inferno* XV (*Yeats's VISION and Later Plays*,
    pp. 248–49).
19. This new concept of identity derives from Blake: "Aristotle says Characters are ei-
    ther Good or Bad; now Goodness or Badness has nothing to do with Character:
    . . . a Good Apple tree or a Bad is an Apple tree still; a Horse is not more a Lion
    for being a Bad Horse: that is its Character: its Goodness or Badness is another con-
    sideration" ("On Homer's Poetry," *The Complete Writings of William Blake*, ed.
    Geoffrey Keynes, London: Oxford University Press, 1966, p. 778). Thus in Blake's
    poem "The Tyger," the Tiger's identity includes that of the Lamb. Keats wrote
    similarly: "Minds would leave each other in contrary directions, traverse each other
    in Numberless points, and [at] last greet each other at the Journey's end" (To J. H.
    Reynolds, February 19, 1818, *Letters*, I, 232). See p. 362, n. 35.
20. *Yeats and Tradition*, p. 163.
21. October 9, 20 [1938], *Letters*, pp. 916–17.
22. See *Per Amica*, *Mythologies*, p. 333. Proust makes an analogous distinction. The
    "real" person is "opaque" because all that we sense about him or that he senses
    about himself has not been brought to consciousness: "it is only in one small sec-
    tion of the complete idea we have of him [and "he has of himself"] that we are [and
    "he is"] capable of feeling any emotion." The novelist substitutes "for those opaque
    sections, impenetrable by the human spirit, their equivalent in immaterial sections,
    things, that is, which the spirit can assimilate to itself," and so renders transparent
    all the character's actions and feelings "since it is in ourselves that they are happen-
    ing" (*Swann's Way*, pp. 118–19). Pater's "crystal" man exemplifies transparent
    identity in life ("Diaphaneitè," *Miscellaneous Studies*, New York and London:
    Macmillan, 1896, p. 220).
23. "*King Lear* or *Endgame*," *Shakespeare Our Contemporary*, tr. Boleslaw Taborski
    (Garden City, N.Y.: Doubleday, Anchor, 1966): "The tragic situation becomes gro-
    tesque when both alternatives of the choice imposed are absurd" or undesirable
    (p. 135). See also Martin Esslin's *The Theatre of the Absurd* (Garden City, N.Y.:
    Doubleday, Anchor, 1961); and, for a discussion of tragicomedy, my essay "*The
    Tempest* and Tragicomic Vision," *The Modern Spirit* (New York: Oxford University
    Press, 1970).
24. *Plays*, p. 426.
25. *Vision*, p. 25.
26. *Autobiography*, p. 326; in *The Secret Rose* (1897), *Mythologies*, p. 184; "The Uni-
    corn from the Stars," *Plays*, p. 245; letter to Sturge Moore, quoted in John Un-
    terecker, *A Reader's Guide to William Butler Yeats* (New York: Noonday Press,
    1959), p. 253.
27. *Essays and Introductions*, p. 448.
28. *Yeats and Tradition*, p. 100.
29. "*Louis Lambert*," *Essays and Introductions*, pp. 439, 446.

30. "*The Holy Mountain,*" *Essays and Introductions,* p. 448. Yeats wrote an introduction to Bhagwan Shree Patanjali's *Aphorisms of Yoga,* tr. Shree Purohit Swami (London: Faber and Faber, 1938).
31. "*Gitanjali,*" *Essays and Introductions,* p. 393.
32. *Essays and Introductions,* pp. 405, 406 n. 1, 408 n. 1.
33. *Essays and Introductions,* pp. 421–22, 425.
34. "The Philosophy of Shelley's Poetry," *Essays and Introductions,* p. 65.
35. To Olivia Shakespear, February 21 [1933], *Letters,* p. 805.
36. "*The Holy Mountain,*" "*Prometheus Unbound,*" *Essays and Introductions,* pp. 463, 424.
37. "An Indian Monk," *Essays and Introductions,* p. 436. Writing as though he had in mind the bearing of this passage on sexual morality, Yeats tells Olivia Shakespear, March 9 [1933]: "Joyce and D. H. Lawrence have however almost restored to us the Eastern simplicity. Neither perfectly, for D. H. Lawrence romanticises his material, with such words as 'essential fire,' 'darkness' etc, and Joyce never escapes from his Catholic sense of sin." He holds up Swedenborg's intercourse of angels as a model (*Letters,* p. 807).
38. "Crazy Jane Talks with the Bishop."
39. *Essays and Introductions,* pp. 467–68, 471.
40. *Essays and Introductions,* pp. 439, 442.
41. H. de Balzac, *Louis Lambert* in *Séraphita and Other Stories,* tr. Clara Bell and R. S. Scott (Philadelphia: Gebbie, 1899), p. 207.
42. "The Mandukya Upanishad," "*The Holy Mountain,*" *Essays and Introductions,* pp. 481, 461, 477.
43. *Essays and Introductions,* pp. 476–77, 482–83, 479–80.
44. *Essays and Introductions,* pp. 509–10.
45. "Blake . . . Illustrations to *The Divine Comedy,*" *Essays and Introductions,* p. 139.
46. To Lady Elizabeth Pelham, January 4, 1939, *Letters,* p. 922.

IV. RECONSTITUTION OF SELF: LAWRENCE

Chapter 8. IDENTITY AND SEXUALITY

1. *Women in Love* (New York: Random House, Modern Library, 1949), p. 358. This is the most complete text so far.
2. *Phoenix: The Posthumous Papers of D. H. Lawrence,* ed. Edward D. McDonald (New York: Viking Press, 1936), pp. 519–20 (my italics).
3. *Phoenix,* p. 520.
4. *Phoenix,* pp. 521, 523, 525.
5. *Phoenix,* pp. 419, 415, 417.
6. *Phoenix,* pp. 527–28.
7. *Lady Chatterley's Lover* (New York: Grove Press, 1962), p. 146.
8. *Phoenix,* p. 531.
9. To Sara Hutchinson, 14 June [1802], *The Early Letters of William and Dorothy Wordsworth,* ed. E. de Selincourt (Oxford: Clarendon Press, 1935), p. 306.
10. *Phoenix,* p. 533.

11. "Discoveries," *Essays and Introductions* (New York: Macmillan, 1961), p. 292.
12. *Phoenix*, pp. 535–37.
13. "John Galsworthy," *Phoenix*, p. 541.
14. *The Collected Letters of D. H. Lawrence*, ed. Harry T. Moore, 2 vols. (New York: Viking Press, 1962), I, 281–82.
15. "Baby Tortoise," "Lui et Elle," "Tortoise Gallantry," "Lui et Elle." Poems will be quoted from *The Complete Poems of D. H. Lawrence*, ed. Vivian de Sola Pinto and Warren Roberts (New York: Viking Press, 1971).
16. *St. Mawr and The Man Who Died* (New York: Random House, Vintage, 1953), p. 178.
17. *St. Mawr*, p. 54.
18. Hence Lawrence's attack on Wordsworth's *Peter Bell* in ". . . Love Was Once a Little Boy," *Phoenix II: Uncollected, Unpublished, and Other Prose Works by D. H. Lawrence*, eds. Warren Roberts and Harry T. Moore (New York: Viking Press, 1970), pp. 447–49.
19. Yeats, "At Stratford-on-Avon," *Essays and Introductions*, p. 107.
20. *Phoenix II*, pp. 469–70.
21. *Psychoanalysis and the Unconscious and Fantasia of the Unconscious* (New York: Viking Press, 1965), pp. 13, 15. Hume says similarly that if you cannot draw the notion of the self from a "mind . . . reduc'd even below the life of an oyster, . . . the addition of other perceptions can never give you that notion" (A *Treatise of Human Nature*, ed. L. A. Selby-Bigge, Oxford: Clarendon Press, 1965, Appendix, p. 634).
22. *Four Short Novels* (New York: Viking Press, 1968), pp. 116, 120, 163, 125–26.
23. *Four Short Novels*, pp. 156–57, 161, 160, 163, 170.
24. "Herman Melville's *Typee* and *Omoo*," *Studies in Classic American Literature* (Garden City, N.Y.: Doubleday, Anchor, 1953), pp. 149–50.
25. *D. H. Lawrence: Novelist* (London: Chatto and Windus, 1955), p. 225.
26. *St. Mawr*, pp. 26 and throughout, 95, 15, 19–20,16, 18, 49–50.
27. *St. Mawr*, pp. 66–71; see *Women in Love*, p. 289.
28. *St. Mawr*, pp. 139, 137, 139, 85, 147, 152–54.
29. *The Plumed Serpent* (New York: Random House, Vintage, 1955), pp. 250, 277, 355.
30. *Plumed Serpent*, pp. 114–16, 231, 260, 341–42.
31. *Plumed Serpent*, pp. 426–27, 451, 448, 462–64.
32. *Lady Chatterley's Lover*, pp. 281, 261.
33. *Plumed Serpent*, pp. 464, 476.
34. *Plumed Serpent*, pp. 465–66, 71, 475, 466.
35. *Plumed Serpent*, pp. 473–74, 214–15, 475, 468.
36. *Plumed Serpent*, pp. 473–74, 477–78, 481–82, 486–87.
37. *The Art of D. H. Lawrence* (Cambridge: Cambridge University Press, 1966), p. 166.
38. To Witter Bynner, 13 March 1928, *Letters*, II, 1045.
39. *Lady Chatterley's Lover*, pp. 167, 348, 185, 229–30.
40. *Phoenix II*, pp. 505–8, 514.
41. *Lady Chatterley's Lover*, pp. 296, 138.
42. To Olivia Shakespear, May 22 [1933], *The Letters of W. B. Yeats*, ed. Allan Wade (London: Rupert Hart-Davis, 1954), p. 810.
43. *Plumed Serpent*, p. 472.
44. *Lady Chatterley's Lover*, pp. 136, 280–81.

45. *The Love Ethic of D. H. Lawrence* (Bloomington and London: Indiana University Press, 1971), p. 195.
46. "A Propos of *Lady Chatterley's Lover*," *Phoenix II*, p. 514.
47. *Lady Chatterley's Lover*, p. 46.
48. *The Complete Short Stories*, 3 vols. (New York: Viking Press, 1967), II, 347, 360, 364–65.
49. *Lady Chatterley's Lover*, pp. 156, 362.
50. *Lady Chatterley's Lover*, p. 241. See first two versions (London: Heinemann, 1972).
51. *The Deed of Life: The Novels and Tales of D. H. Lawrence* (Princeton: Princeton University Press, 1966), pp. 145–46.
52. *Lady Chatterley's Lover*, p. 107.
53. *D. H. Lawrence* (New York: Viking Press, 1973), p. 140.
54. *Lady Chatterley's Lover*, pp. 164, 174–75, 182–85, 226–27, 228–30, 269–70, 282–83, 289–90, 304, 312–13, 347–48.
55. *Phoenix*, p. 441.
56. *Lady Chatterley's Lover*, pp. 373–74, 102.
57. "A Propos of *Lady Chatterley's Lover*," *Phoenix II*, p. 493.
58. *Lady Chatterley's Lover*, p. 374.

Chapter 9. THE RAINBOW: THE WAY THROUGH HOPE

1. To Edward Marsh, 15 July 1914, *Letters*, I, 287.
2. "The Marble and the Statue: The Exploratory Imagination of D. H. Lawrence," in *Imagined Worlds*, eds. Maynard Mack and Ian Gregor (London: Methuen, 1968), p. 375. The letters to Edward Garnett of 9 and 16 May 1914 propose the new title *The Rainbow* for the penultimate draft (*Letters*, I, 276).
3. *Phoenix*, p. 449.
4. To Garnett; to Henry Savage [?Autumn 1913], *Letters*, I, 282, 241. See Charles L. Ross, "D. H. Lawrence's Use of Greek Tragedy: Euripides and Ritual," *D. H. Lawrence Review* 10:1 (Spring 1977).
5. *A Vision*, a reissue with the author's final revisions (New York: Macmillan, 1956), p. 52.
6. *The Rainbow* (New York: Viking Press, 1968), pp. 134–35; (Harmondsworth: Penguin, 1975), pp. 137–39. For *The Rainbow*, I am also quoting the British Penguin edition as the most complete text so far.
7. *Phoenix*, pp. 446, 441, 403, 410.
8. *Double Measure: A Study of the Novels and Stories of D. H. Lawrence* (New York: Norton, 1969), pp. 41–42n.
9. To Edward Garnett, 11 March, 6 October, 1913, *Letters*, I, 193, 230.
10. *Sons and Lovers* (New York: Viking Press, 1970), pp. 368, 351, 358 (my italics).
11. *Rainbow*, Viking: p. 317; Penguin: pp. 318–19. "She [the moon] is the fierce centre of retraction, of frictional withdrawal into separateness" (*Fantasia of the Unconscious*, p. 192).
12. *Rainbow*, Viking: pp. 317–18 (my italics), 316, 318–21; Penguin: pp. 319–20, 318, 320–23.
13. Instead, H. M. Daleski—reasoning from the Hardy study's dark-light, female-male correspondence and its statement that each sex contains female and male elements—suggests that "the disposition of the Brangwen men is essentially female. In consequence the Brangwen women are not fulfilled; their yearnings for the outside

world are only vicariously satisfied" (*The Forked Flame: A Study of D. H. Lawrence*, Evanston: Northwestern University Press, 1965, p. 81).

14. *Rainbow*, Viking: pp. 350, 1–2, 7–8; Penguin: pp. 351, 7–8, 13.
15. *Rainbow*, Viking: pp. 24, 27, 34–35, 37–40; Penguin: pp. 29, 32, 39, 42–45.
16. *Rainbow*, Viking: pp. 75, 89–90, 92, 131; Penguin: pp. 80, 94–96, 135.
17. In *Sons and Lovers*, Paul expresses his preference for the rounded Norman arch, as opposed to Miriam's for the pointed, all-transcendentalizing Gothic arch (p. 177).
18. *Rainbow*, Viking: pp. 190, 192–93; Penguin: pp. 193, 195–96.
19. *Rainbow*, Viking: pp. 166–67, 169; Penguin: pp. 169, 171–72.
20. "Nathaniel Hawthorne and *The Scarlet Letter*," *Studies in Classic American Literature*, pp. 102–3.
21. *Rainbow*, Viking: pp. 183, 231–33, 235; Penguin: pp. 186, 234–36, 238.
22. "The Revisions of the Second Generation in *The Rainbow*," *Review of English Studies*, New Series 27:107 (August 1976), 278–91.
23. Quoted in Erik H. Erikson, *Childhood and Society*, 2nd ed. rev. and enlarged (New York: Norton, 1963), p. 265.
24. To Edward Garnett, 22 April 1914, *Letters*, I, 273.
25. *Rainbow*, Viking: pp. 275, 288, 290, 333; Penguin: pp. 276, 290, 292, 334.
26. *Rainbow*, Viking, p. 339; the excised four lines, between Winifred's " 'I shall carry you into the water,' " and "After a while the rain," appear in Penguin, p. 340.
27. *Rainbow*, Viking: pp. 349, 346, 350, 355; Penguin: pp. 350, 347, 351, 356.
28. *Rainbow*, Viking, Penguin: pp. 417, 437, 433–38 (my italics).
29. *Self and Not-Self: Cellular Immunology, Book One* (Carlton: Melbourne University Press; London: Cambridge University Press, 1969), p. vii.
30. *Rainbow*, Viking, Penguin: pp. 443, 441–43, 432, 462, 460.
31. *Rainbow*, Viking, Penguin: p. 462. The excised passage appears in Penguin between "he hung round others" and "She lifted her shoulders."
32. *Rainbow*, Viking: pp. 457, 475, 452, 451; Penguin: pp. 458, 476, 452, 451.
33. *Rainbow*, Viking: pp. 464–65, 479, 478–80; Penguin: pp. 465–66, 480, 479–81.
34. *Rainbow*, Viking: pp. 484, 477; Penguin, pp. 485, 478.
35. *Apocalypse* (New York: Viking Press, 1973), pp. 97–98.
36. *Fantasia of the Unconscious*, p. 199.
37. *Rainbow*, Viking: p. 493; Penguin, p. 494.
38. Sagar, "The Third Generation," in *Twentieth Century Interpretations of The Rainbow*, ed. Mark Kinkead-Weekes (Englewood Cliffs, N.J.: Prentice-Hall, 1971), p. 69. See *Sons and Lovers*, p. 239.
39. *Apocalypse*, p. 97.
40. *Rainbow*, Viking: pp. 486–90, 492; Penguin: pp. 487–91, 493.
41. *Women in Love*, p. 45.
42. *Rainbow*, Viking: pp. 492–95; Penguin: pp. 493–96.

Chapter 10. WOMEN IN LOVE: THE WAY THROUGH DOOM

1. To Waldo Frank, 27 July 1917, *Letters*, I, 519.
2. *Women in Love* (New York: Random House, Modern Library, 1949), p. 47. This is the most complete text so far.
3. *Phoenix II*, p. 396 (my italics).
4. *The Standard Edition of the Complete Psychological Works of Sigmund Freud*,

translated under the editorship of James Strachey, 24 vols. (London: Hogarth Press and Institute of Psycho-analysis, 1953–74), XVIII, 41, 53.

5. *Phoenix II*, p. 396.
6. *Women in Love*, pp. 195–97.
7. *Phoenix II*, pp. 364 ("Note to *The Crown*"), 388.
8. *Women in Love*, pp. 515–16, 486.
9. In the essay on Poe, where he says that in concentrating on disintegration Poe performed a necessary task, "because old things need to die and disintegrate, because the old white psyche has to be gradually broken down before anything else can come to pass." But Poe was more scientist than artist, because "in true art there is always the double rhythm of creating and destroying" (*Studies in Classic American Literature*, p. 74).
10. *Phoenix*, p. 410.
11. *Women in Love*, pp. 15–16, 264–65.
12. *Women in Love*, pp. 188, 17–18, 50.
13. *Etruscan Places* (New York: Viking Press, 1968); see pp. 89–90.
14. *Women in Love*, pp. 51, 206, 194, 209.
15. *Women in Love*, pp. 162, 210–11 (my italics), 213.
16. *Sons and Lovers*, pp. 213–15. There is a similarly potential re-enactment of Euripides' *The Bacchae* in "Tickets Please," *Complete Short Stories*, II.
17. *Women in Love*, pp. 471, 474, 195, 280, 282.
18. *Women in Love*, pp. 192, 38.
19. *Women in Love*, pp. 236, 265, 49.
20. The Modern Library text is based on the original American edition (1920), which was not subject to the threat of a libel suit that forced Lawrence to change Pussum to Minette and the African to West Pacific statues in most places in the English editions after 1921.
21. *Women in Love*, pp. 166, 168, 174, 169, 174–75.
22. *Women in Love*, pp. 278, 280, 283. See Colin Clarke's " 'Living Disintegration': A Scene from *Women in Love* Reinterpreted," in *D. H. Lawrence, The Rainbow and Women in Love: A Casebook*, ed. Colin Clarke (London: Macmillan, 1969), pp. 219–34; also Clarke's *River of Dissolution: D. H. Lawrence and English Romanticism* (London: Routledge and Kegan Paul, 1969).
23. *Women in Love*, pp. 284, 288–89. See George H. Ford's convincing argument along this line in *Double Measure*, pp. 188–97; also the "Critical Exchange" among Ford, Kermode, Clarke and Spilka on Lawrence's evaluation of anal intercourse and the disintegrative function generally (*Novel* 5:1, Fall 1971, 54–70).
24. *Women in Love*, pp. 289–90.
25. "Prologue to *Women in Love*," with Introductory Note by George H. Ford, *Rainbow and Women in Love: Casebook*, ed. Clarke, p. 52. Originally published in *Texas Quarterly* 6:1 (Spring 1963).
26. *Women in Love*, pp. 356–58, 348.
27. See "Lawrence, Joyce and Powys," *Essays in Criticism* 11:4 (October 1961), of which pp. 403–9 are reprinted in *The Rainbow and Women in Love: Casebook*, ed. Clarke, pp. 135–41.
28. *Women in Love*, p. 403. The excision occurs on p. 345 of the Viking edition (New York, 1966), between " 'if you like' " and " 'I know,' said Gerald." Even in the letter most favorable to homosexuality, however, Lawrence insists that heterosexuality is the more demanding because the more *polar* relation: "I believe a man projects

his own image on another man, like on a mirror. But from a woman he wants himself re-born, re-constructed" (To Henry Savage, 2 December 1913, *Letters*, I, 251). He criticizes Whitman's homosexuality as self-annihilating because it is a merging with one's likeness (*Studies in Classic American Literature*, pp. 180–82).

29. George H. Ford, Introductory Note to "Prologue to *Women in Love*," *Rainbow and Women in Love: Casebook*, ed. Clarke, p. 41.
30. *Women in Love*, pp. 470, 359 (my italics), ix.
31. *Women in Love*, pp. 363–64, 545–46.
32. *Women in Love*, see pp. 529–33. Confronted with Ursula's streaming tears for Gerald's death, the tearless Gudrun is so frozen in self-consciousness that she can only think, as she hides her face on Ursula's shoulder, " 'Ha, ha! this is the right behaviour' " (p. 542).
33. *Women in Love*, pp. 499, 486.
34. *Rainbow*, Viking: p. 490; Penguin: p. 491.
35. *Women in Love*, p. 499.
36. "The Autumn of the Body," *Essays and Introductions*, p. 191.

Index

375